Along Interstate 75

9th Edition

by Dave Hunter

The ***Local Knowledge*** Driving Guide for interstate travelers between Detroit and the Florida Border

Along Interstate-75 is updated annually and available from:

bookstores in the USA and Canada. The book order number is 1-896-819-125,

from **internet** booksellers such as **amazon.com** or **chapters.ca**

from selected **American Automobile Association** (AAA) and **Canadian Automobile Association** Ontario (CAA) travel offices,

or by phoning us at 905-274-4356.

Mile Oak Publishing Inc.
Suite 81, 20 Mineola Road East,
Mississauga, ON Canada L5G 4N9

e.mail: mile_oak@compuserve.com
Phone: 905-274-4356
Fax: 905-274-8656

This book is dedicated to . . .

my father, Reg Hunter - who, in the 1950s discovered a new respect for life while teaching me how to drive and, who helped me develop a love of maps and an uncanny sense of direction as we traveled together through the winding backroads of post-war Britain . . .

and to **my mother, Olive Hunter** - who gave me her love of art and crafts, and the gift of patience essential for producing a highly detailed work such as this.

Much love to both of you.

Research Assistance: David Archer, Kathy Hunter, Greg Mark
Editorial Associates: Joan Gingras, Kathy Hunter.
Cover: design by Margrie Wallace; photograph by Akis Sofroniou; textures by Geoffrey Fairbank

Cataloging in Publication Data

Hunter, Dave, 1941 -
Along Interstate-75, Local knowledge for the I-75 between Detroit & the Florida Border
9th annual edition
ISBN 1-896819-12-5
1. Interstate-75 - Guidebooks. 2. United States - Guidebooks
3. Automobile Travel - United States - Guidebooks
I. Title II. Series

Artwork courtesy of Softkey Clipmaster Pro and Corel Corporation's Gallery, Gallery 2, Mega Gallery and IMSI USA including: Image Club Graphics Inc., One Mile Up Inc., Techpool Studios Inc. and Totem Graphics Inc.

A Word About the Production of this Book . . .

A highly detailed book such as *"Along Interstate-75"* could not be written without the aid of powerful computers and graphics/publishing software. For those interested in such matters, we use Corel Draw 9 for all our maps and then transfer these to QuarkXPress publishing software. Many of the small pieces of art throughout the book are either drawn or adapted by myself, or are courtesy of Corel's wonderful gallery collections of clipart - Gallery, Gallery 2 and Mega Gallery. Several pieces are also courtesy of Softkey's ClipMaster Pro collection.

All of this comes together on a computer using MS Windows 98. The entire process is driven by one person — myself — who within five weeks, takes all of your ideas, letters and our field notes — and melds them into a brand new edition of *"Along Interstate-75"* — ready for the forthcoming season.

The resulting computer files are then, through the electronic pre-press magic of Toronto's ***PC Imaging Inc.***, turned into large sheets of printer's film (each containing 16 pages) from which our printer, ***Gerrie-Young Lithography,*** produces the shiny finished book now in your hands.

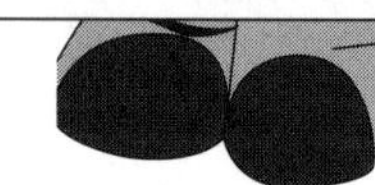

Printed in Canada by Gerrie-Young Lithography, Mississauga, Ontario

Contents at a Glance . . .

Quick Start Hints . . . . see page 5

Plus, **Local Knowledge** . . .

many **$avings hints, "Insider Tips"** & **Special Reports,** to help you <u>save money</u> and <u>enjoy your trip</u>.

Contents

Page

Hello and Welcome to the 9th Annual Edition of Along I-75

Hello to all my I-75 friends,

Do you mind if I brag . . . just a little? This edition is the 9th annual edition of *Along Interstate-75*, published by my wife Kathy and myself, to help those of us who are constantly traveling up and down I-75, to and from Florida. We are a tiny company - known in the trade as a *Small Press*; unlike most large publishing houses, we receive no government grants or funding, and yet *Along I-75* continues to pick up many awards and recognitions.

As soon as the 2000 edition hit the bookstands in October, 1999, we knew it was going to be a "gold medal" edition. First, the *Chicago Tribune* honored it as their travel book *"Pick of the Week."* And then the prestigious U.S. *Library Journal* magazine gave us an excellent review and recommended the book to all public libraries on or near the Interstate. Believe me, many try to get a review in LJ, only a small percentage of small press book succeed. Then *Publishers Weekly*, the North American "bible" to the publishing trade ran a feature article in which it highlighted our companion website - **www.i75online.com** - as the type of website which all travel publishers should provide to continually update and support their readers.

By April, we were getting quite used to all these accolades when we received word that *ForeWord Magazine*, the Number One publication for the Small Press world short-listed us as a finalist for their annual *"Travel Book of the Year"* award.

Last year, a major publishing house decided to bring out its version of an I-75 book - *I-75 and the 401*. Three major North American newspapers ran comparative reviews between *Along Interstate-75* and the "competitor;" in each case, we won hands down . . . and newspaper travel editors do not hand out critical praise, lightly!

But the best and most valuable of the awards and recognitions are those I receive daily from you, my readers. Your letters, faxes, phone calls and e.mails telling me how much you enjoy the book and how helpful it is . . . are worth a thousand "industry" accolades. They lift me up on the "down" days and keep me forging ahead with a smile on my face, knowing I'm giving you what you want. Please keep them coming - I try and personally answer each and every one of them.

In particular, many of you contacted me to thank me for indexing all of Georgia's exits with the new exit numbers, in last year's book. This information had been publically available for the past three years and yet as far as we know, we were the ONLY travel book which had the forethought to make this change (our "competition" missed it completely). There are other major changes like this planned in the next few years (Tennessee is changing most of its phone area codes this October) and another state will shortly change its exit numbers. I will continue to do my best to bring you the best and most recent information in *Along Interstate-75*.

"INTY"

Have a great trip . . . and remember, getting there is half the fun!.

Dave

Quick Start Hints - Getting the most from this book

Along Interstate-75 is quite different from other travel books. A few moments reviewing these notes will greatly enhance your use of it, both as a planning guide and as a source of information and entertainment during your I-75 drive. So let's take a few minutes before you hit the road.

By now, you will have noticed that the book is divided into colored sections. The orange and blue pages are 25 mile-per-page strip maps - we'll come back to those in a minute.

The white pages in the center of the book contain the unfolding story of the country around you - milepost by milepost - as you proceed on your journey. Everything is here - things you see along the way, roadside history, money saving tips, notes about the countryside and local knowledge about the best places to eat and stay. This section is the "heart" of the book; you'll probably be using these pages for most of your journey.

The yellow section will help you get the best bargain rates at motels. Who accepts pets . . . and much more.

The pink section contains useful information and phone numbers - here you'll find local radio stations with your favorite type of music, campgrounds for RVers and even information to help you should the weather become nasty.

The light green section gives you all the radio stations (and personalities) for the best traffic reports in urban areas. Rush hour information and bypass route maps are also included.

The white section at the end contains "housekeeping" items: additional resources, index to abbreviations, daily log sheet and other bits and pieces.

And now back to the maps: They are quite unique and very easy to use. As you can see from this diagram, they are printed in the direction you travel; things drawn on the right side of the map pass you on the right side of your car, and vice-versa.

They include all the usual things - exit services, landmarks, etc., but there are other items which may not be as apparent at first - 24 hour superstores, pharmacies, vets & animal clinics, "dry" counties, radar traps, rest area information and hours, color coded road speeds . . . even when "local knowledge" such as which is the best lane to use so you don't interfere with other traffic.

WATER
75
Exit 25
Rice Rd
City
Water Tower
75
197
Actual mileposts beside the road relate to the milepost scale on your map
Simply read "up" the page as the book sits in your lap — the road outside your car appears exactly as drawn on the map.

I think you'll agree they are like no other maps you've ever seen. Study them before you go - they'll ensure you have a fun yet safe journey.

Interstate-75 between Detroit and the Florida Border

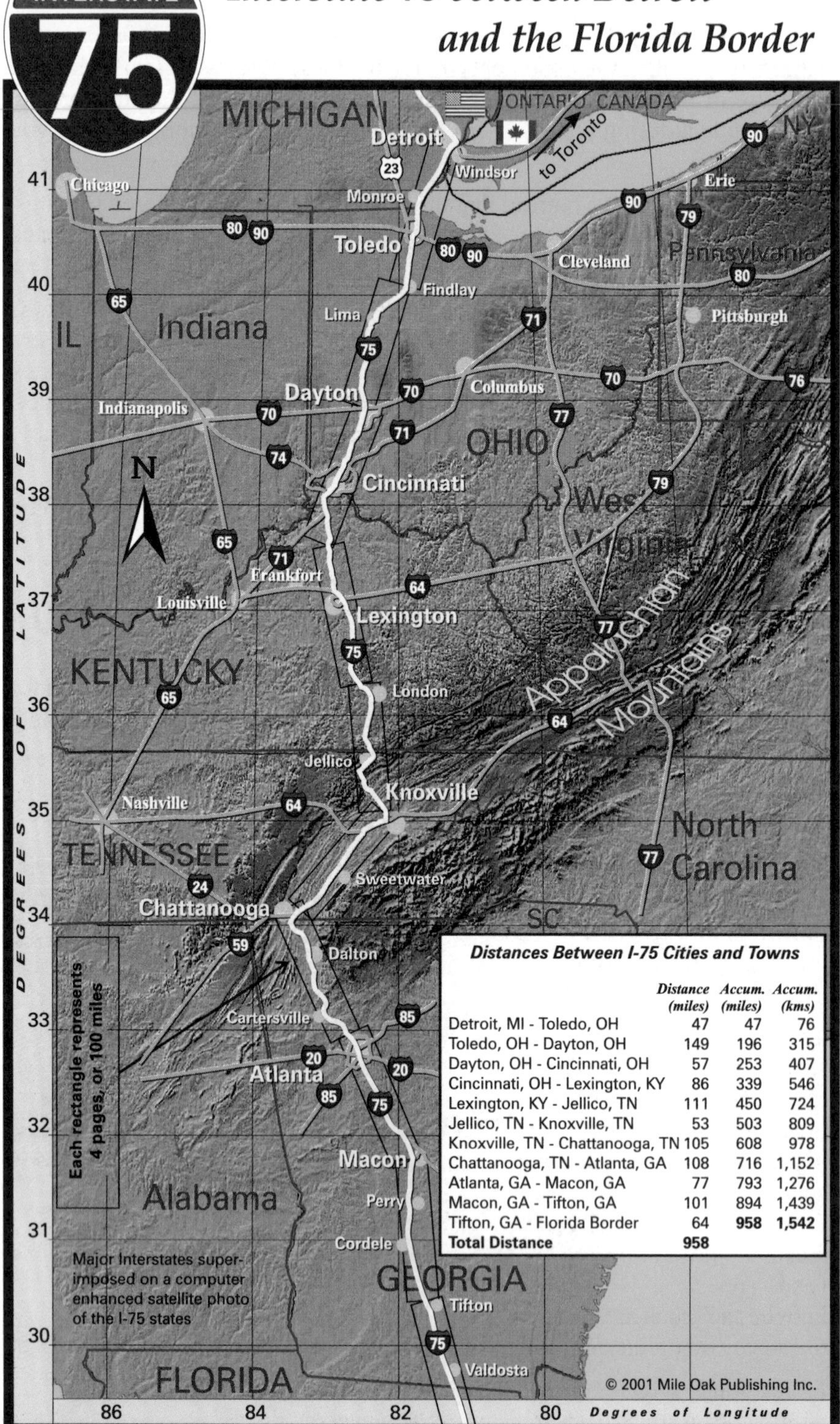

Distances Between I-75 Cities and Towns

	Distance (miles)	Accum. (miles)	Accum. (kms)
Detroit, MI - Toledo, OH	47	47	76
Toledo, OH - Dayton, OH	149	196	315
Dayton, OH - Cincinnati, OH	57	253	407
Cincinnati, OH - Lexington, KY	86	339	546
Lexington, KY - Jellico, TN	111	450	724
Jellico, TN - Knoxville, TN	53	503	809
Knoxville, TN - Chattanooga, TN	105	608	978
Chattanooga, TN - Atlanta, GA	108	716	1,152
Atlanta, GA - Macon, GA	77	793	1,276
Macon, GA - Tifton, GA	101	894	1,439
Tifton, GA - Florida Border	64	**958**	**1,542**
Total Distance	**958**		

Southbound Route

From Detroit to the Florida Border

Insider Tip for Southbound Travelers
Avoiding "Drive South" Sunburn

Did you know that you can get a sunburn and dangerous overload of cancer causing ultraviolet (UV) light while driving south, especially if you are not used to being outdoors for long periods of time? Three days of driving into the sun - the average run from Michigan to Florida on I-75 - can create a very high exposure to UV light on the face and arms, even on cloudy days.

The thick glass and plastic laminate of car windshields helps filter UV light so that only about 15% of UVA* and virtually no UVB* reach the car's interior, but the extra long hours of constant exposure and UV light coming through the thinner, non-laminated side windows can mean that you are receiving too much higher UV radiation than under normal circumstances.

To protect yourself from these harmful rays, wear long sleeves and use a sunscreen with protection factor of at least SPF15 on your face - and of course, keep your side windows rolled up.

Note: UVA ages the skin and can cause skin cancer; UVB causes burning.

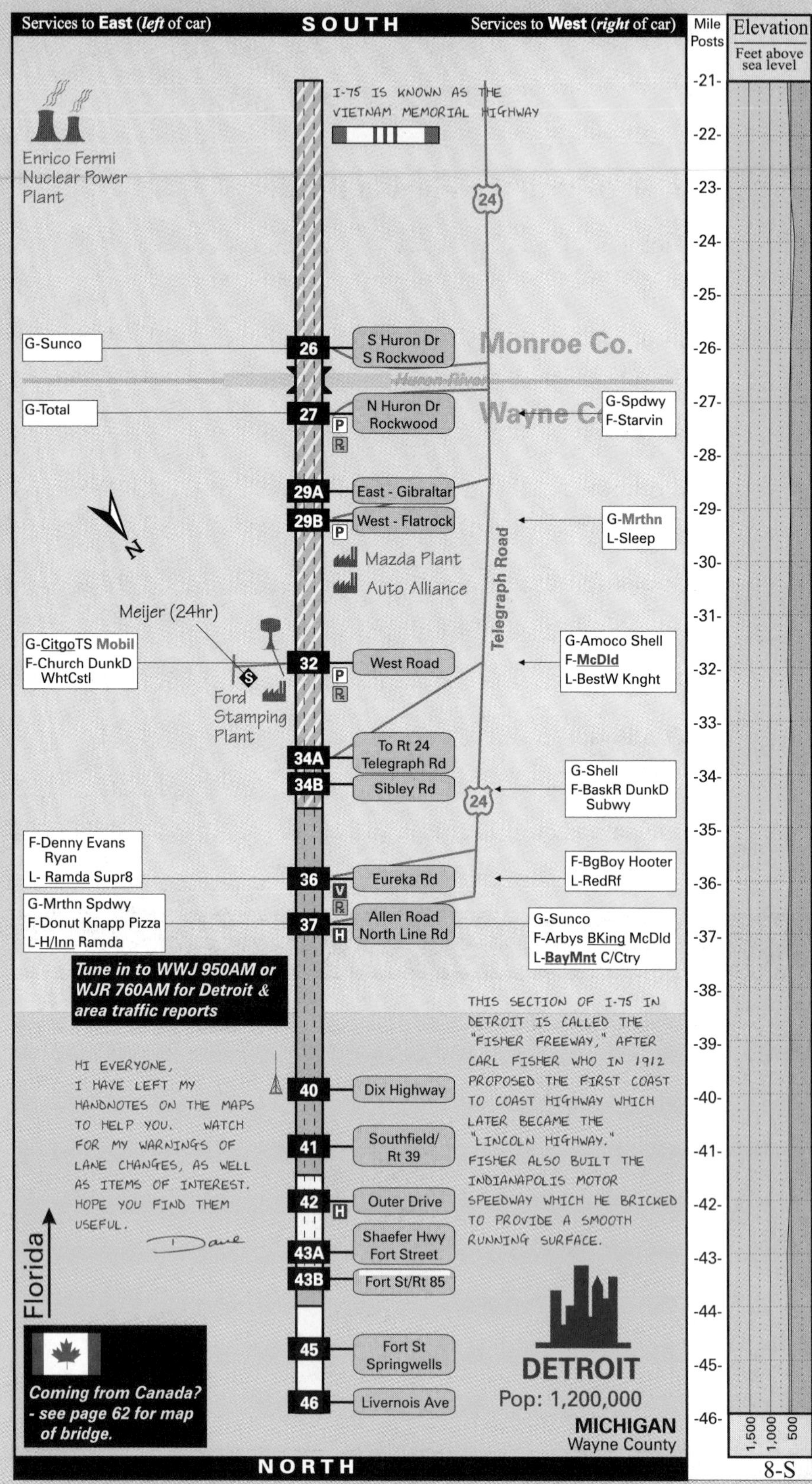
Services to East (left of car)
SOUTH
Services to West (right of car)
Mile Posts
Elevation
Feet above sea level
I-75 IS KNOWN AS THE VIETNAM MEMORIAL HIGHWAY
Enrico Fermi Nuclear Power Plant
24
G-Sunco
26
S Huron Dr
S Rockwood
Monroe Co.
Huron River
G-Total
27
N Huron Dr
Rockwood
Wayne Co.
G-Spdwy
F-Starvin
29A
East - Gibraltar
29B
West - Flatrock
G-Mrthn
L-Sleep
N
Mazda Plant
Auto Alliance
Telegraph Road
Meijer (24hr)
G-CitgoTS Mobil
F-Church DunkD WhtCstl
32
West Road
G-Amoco Shell
F-McDld
L-BestW Knght
Ford Stamping Plant
34A
To Rt 24
Telegraph Rd
34B
Sibley Rd
G-Shell
F-BaskR DunkD Subwy
F-Denny Evans Ryan
L- Ramda Supr8
36
Eureka Rd
F-BgBoy Hooter
L-RedRf
G-Mrthn Spdwy
F-Donut Knapp Pizza
L-H/Inn Ramda
37
Allen Road
North Line Rd
G-Sunco
F-Arbys BKing McDld
L-BayMnt C/Ctry
Tune in to WWJ 950AM or WJR 760AM for Detroit & area traffic reports
THIS SECTION OF I-75 IN DETROIT IS CALLED THE "FISHER FREEWAY," AFTER CARL FISHER WHO IN 1912 PROPOSED THE FIRST COAST TO COAST HIGHWAY WHICH LATER BECAME THE "LINCOLN HIGHWAY." FISHER ALSO BUILT THE INDIANAPOLIS MOTOR SPEEDWAY WHICH HE BRICKED TO PROVIDE A SMOOTH RUNNING SURFACE.
HI EVERYONE, I HAVE LEFT MY HANDNOTES ON THE MAPS TO HELP YOU. WATCH FOR MY WARNINGS OF LANE CHANGES, AS WELL AS ITEMS OF INTEREST. HOPE YOU FIND THEM USEFUL.
Dave
40
Dix Highway
41
Southfield/
Rt 39
42
Outer Drive
43A
Shaefer Hwy
Fort Street
43B
Fort St/Rt 85
Florida
45
Fort St
Springwells
46
Livernois Ave
Coming from Canada? - see page 62 for map of bridge.
DETROIT
Pop: 1,200,000
MICHIGAN
Wayne County
NORTH
-21- -22- -23- -24- -25- -26- -27- -28- -29- -30- -31- -32- -33- -34- -35- -36- -37- -38- -39- -40- -41- -42- -43- -44- -45- -46-
1,500
1,000
500

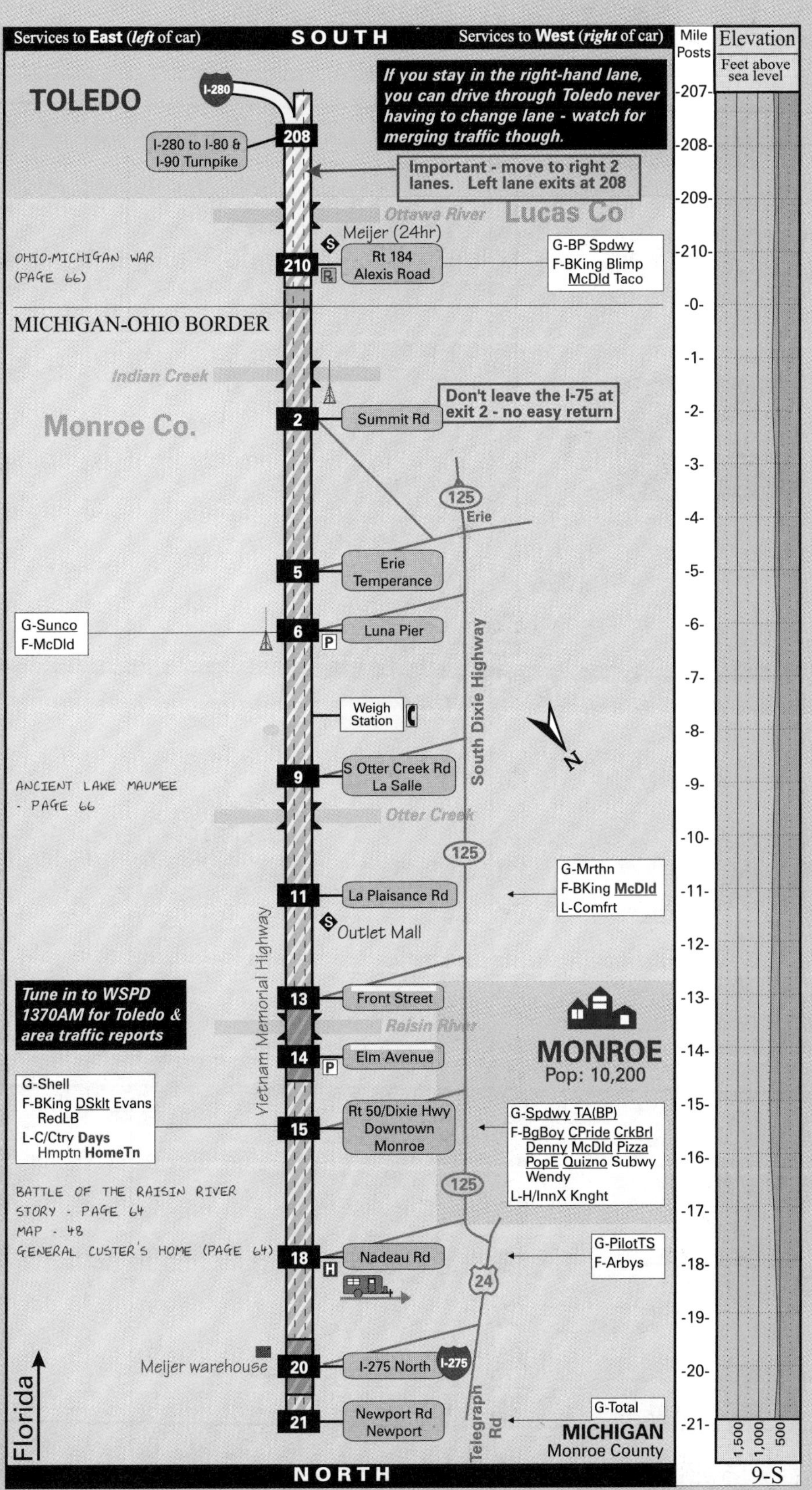
Services to East (left of car)
SOUTH
Services to West (right of car)
TOLEDO
I-280
If you stay in the right-hand lane, you can drive through Toledo never having to change lane - watch for merging traffic though.
208
I-280 to I-80 & I-90 Turnpike
Important - move to right 2 lanes. Left lane exits at 208
Ottawa River
Lucas Co
Meijer (24hr)
OHIO-MICHIGAN WAR (PAGE 66)
210
Rt 184 Alexis Road
G-BP Spdwy
F-BKing Blimp McDld Taco
MICHIGAN-OHIO BORDER
Indian Creek
Don't leave the I-75 at exit 2 - no easy return
2
Summit Rd
Monroe Co.
125
Erie
5
Erie Temperance
G-Sunco
F-McDld
6
Luna Pier
Weigh Station
South Dixie Highway
N
ANCIENT LAKE MAUMEE - PAGE 66
9
S Otter Creek Rd La Salle
Otter Creek
125
G-Mrthn
F-BKing McDld
L-Comfrt
11
La Plaisance Rd
Outlet Mall
Vietnam Memorial Highway
Tune in to WSPD 1370AM for Toledo & area traffic reports
13
Front Street
Raisin River
14
Elm Avenue
MONROE
Pop: 10,200
G-Shell
F-BKing DSklt Evans RedLB
L-C/Ctry Days Hmptn HomeTn
15
Rt 50/Dixie Hwy Downtown Monroe
G-Spdwy TA(BP)
F-BgBoy CPride CrkBrl Denny McDld Pizza PopE Quizno Subwy Wendy
L-H/InnX Knght
125
BATTLE OF THE RAISIN RIVER STORY - PAGE 64
MAP - 48
GENERAL CUSTER'S HOME (PAGE 64)
18
Nadeau Rd
G-PilotTS
F-Arbys
24
Meijer warehouse
20
I-275 North
I-275
G-Total
21
Newport Rd Newport
Telegraph Rd
MICHIGAN
Monroe County
Florida
NORTH
Mile Posts
-207- -208- -209- -210- -0- -1- -2- -3- -4- -5- -6- -7- -8- -9- -10- -11- -12- -13- -14- -15- -16- -17- -18- -19- -20- -21-
Elevation
Feet above sea level
1,500 1,000 500

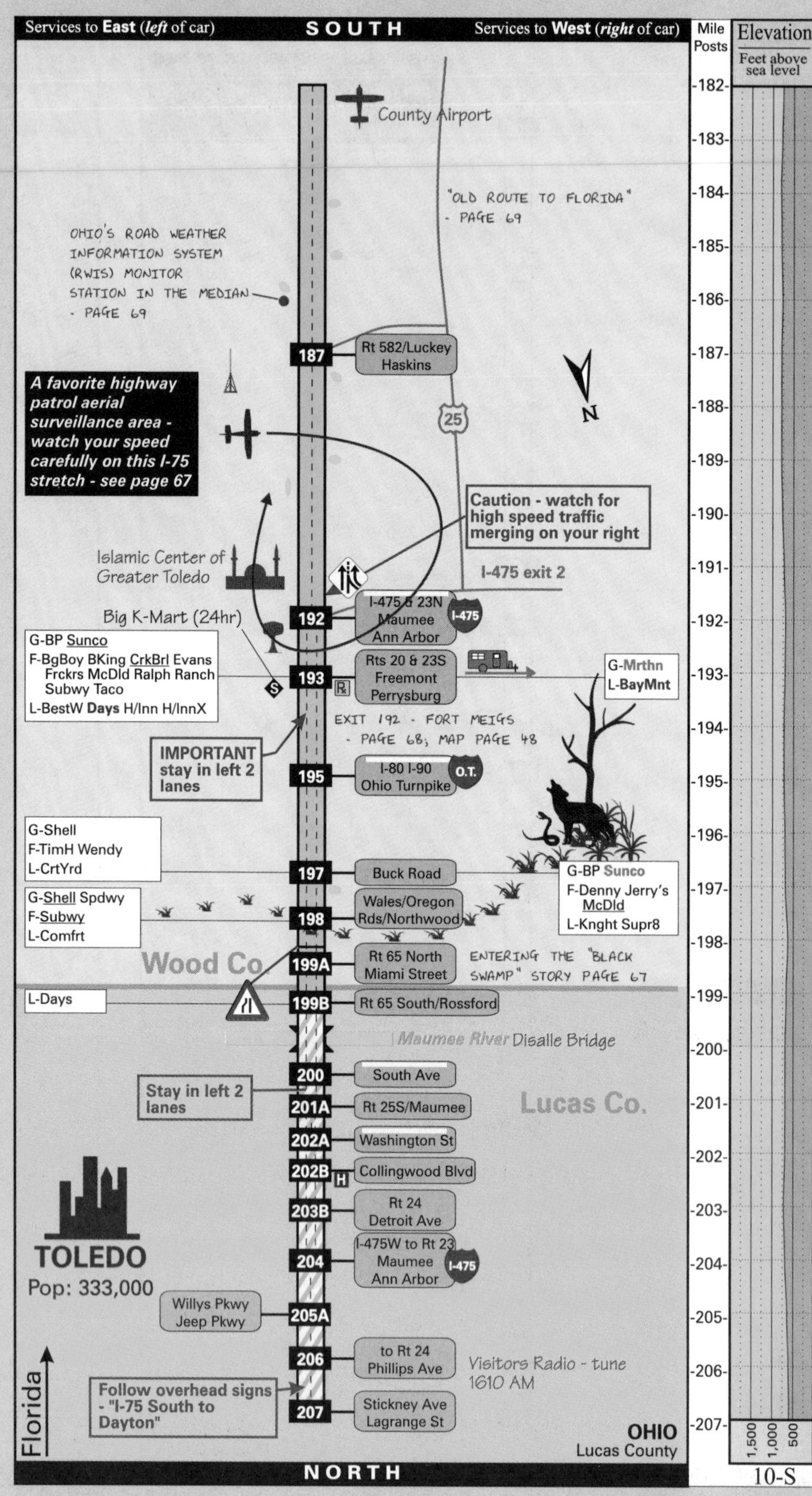

Services to East (left of car)
SOUTH
Services to West (right of car)
Mile Posts
Elevation
Feet above sea level
County Airport
"OLD ROUTE TO FLORIDA" - PAGE 69
OHIO'S ROAD WEATHER INFORMATION SYSTEM (RWIS) MONITOR STATION IN THE MEDIAN - PAGE 69
187
Rt 582/Luckey Haskins
A favorite highway patrol aerial surveillance area - watch your speed carefully on this I-75 stretch - see page 67
25
N
Caution - watch for high speed traffic merging on your right
Islamic Center of Greater Toledo
I-475 exit 2
Big K-Mart (24hr)
192
I-475 & 23N Maumee Ann Arbor
I-475
G-BP Sunco
F-BgBoy BKing CrkBrl Evans Frckrs McDld Ralph Ranch Subwy Taco
L-BestW Days H/Inn H/InnX
193
Rts 20 & 23S Freemont Perrysburg
G-Mrthn
L-BayMnt
EXIT 192 - FORT MEIGS - PAGE 68; MAP PAGE 48
IMPORTANT stay in left 2 lanes
195
I-80 I-90 Ohio Turnpike
O.T.
G-Shell
F-TimH Wendy
L-CrtYrd
197
Buck Road
G-BP Sunco
F-Denny Jerry's McDld
L-Knght Supr8
G-Shell Spdwy
F-Subwy
L-Comfrt
198
Wales/Oregon Rds/Northwood
Wood Co.
199A
Rt 65 North Miami Street
ENTERING THE "BLACK SWAMP" STORY PAGE 67
L-Days
199B
Rt 65 South/Rossford
Maumee River Disalle Bridge
200
South Ave
Stay in left 2 lanes
201A
Rt 25S/Maumee
Lucas Co.
202A
Washington St
202B
Collingwood Blvd
203B
Rt 24 Detroit Ave
TOLEDO
Pop: 333,000
204
I-475W to Rt 23 Maumee Ann Arbor
I-475
Willys Pkwy Jeep Pkwy
205A
206
to Rt 24 Phillips Ave
Visitors Radio - tune 1610 AM
Follow overhead signs - "I-75 South to Dayton"
207
Stickney Ave Lagrange St
Florida
OHIO
Lucas County
NORTH
-182- -183- -184- -185- -186- -187- -188- -189- -190- -191- -192- -193- -194- -195- -196- -197- -198- -199- -200- -201- -202- -203- -204- -205- -206- -207-
1,500 1,000 500

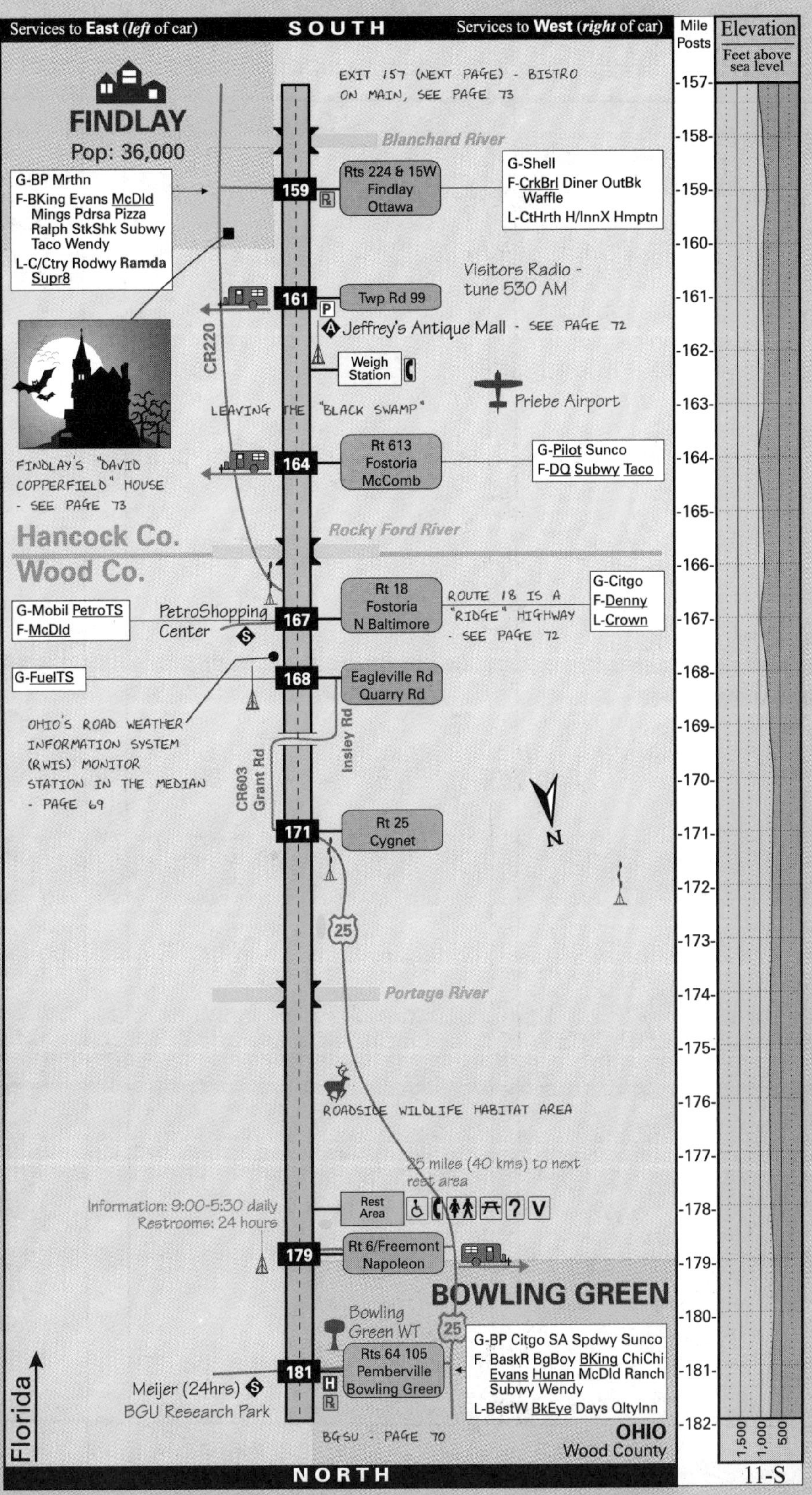

Services to East (left of car)
SOUTH
Services to West (right of car)
Mile Posts
Elevation
Feet above sea level
EXIT 157 (NEXT PAGE) - BISTRO ON MAIN, SEE PAGE 73
FINDLAY
Pop: 36,000
Blanchard River
G-BP Mrthn
F-BKing Evans McDld Mings Pdrsa Pizza Ralph StkShk Subwy Taco Wendy
L-C/Ctry Rodwy Ramda Supr8
159
Rts 224 & 15W Findlay Ottawa
G-Shell
F-CrkBrl Diner OutBk Waffle
L-CtHrth H/InnX Hmptn
Visitors Radio - tune 530 AM
161
Twp Rd 99
Jeffrey's Antique Mall - SEE PAGE 72
CR220
Weigh Station
Priebe Airport
LEAVING THE "BLACK SWAMP"
164
Rt 613 Fostoria McComb
G-Pilot Sunco
F-DQ Subwy Taco
FINDLAY'S "DAVID COPPERFIELD" HOUSE - SEE PAGE 73
Hancock Co.
Wood Co.
Rocky Ford River
Rt 18 Fostoria N Baltimore
ROUTE 18 IS A "RIDGE" HIGHWAY - SEE PAGE 72
G-Citgo
F-Denny
L-Crown
G-Mobil PetroTS
F-McDld
PetroShopping Center
167
G-FuelTS
168
Eagleville Rd Quarry Rd
OHIO'S ROAD WEATHER INFORMATION SYSTEM (RWIS) MONITOR STATION IN THE MEDIAN - PAGE 69
Insley Rd
CR603 Grant Rd
171
Rt 25 Cygnet
N
25
Portage River
ROADSIDE WILDLIFE HABITAT AREA
25 miles (40 kms) to next rest area
Information: 9:00-5:30 daily
Restrooms: 24 hours
Rest Area
179
Rt 6/Freemont Napoleon
BOWLING GREEN
Bowling Green WT
25
G-BP Citgo SA Spdwy Sunco
F- BaskR BgBoy BKing ChiChi Evans Hunan McDld Ranch Subwy Wendy
L-BestW BkEye Days QltyInn
181
Rts 64 105 Pemberville Bowling Green
Meijer (24hrs)
BGU Research Park
BGSU - PAGE 70
OHIO
Wood County
Florida
NORTH
-157- -158- -159- -160- -161- -162- -163- -164- -165- -166- -167- -168- -169- -170- -171- -172- -173- -174- -175- -176- -177- -178- -179- -180- -181- -182-
1,500 1,000 500

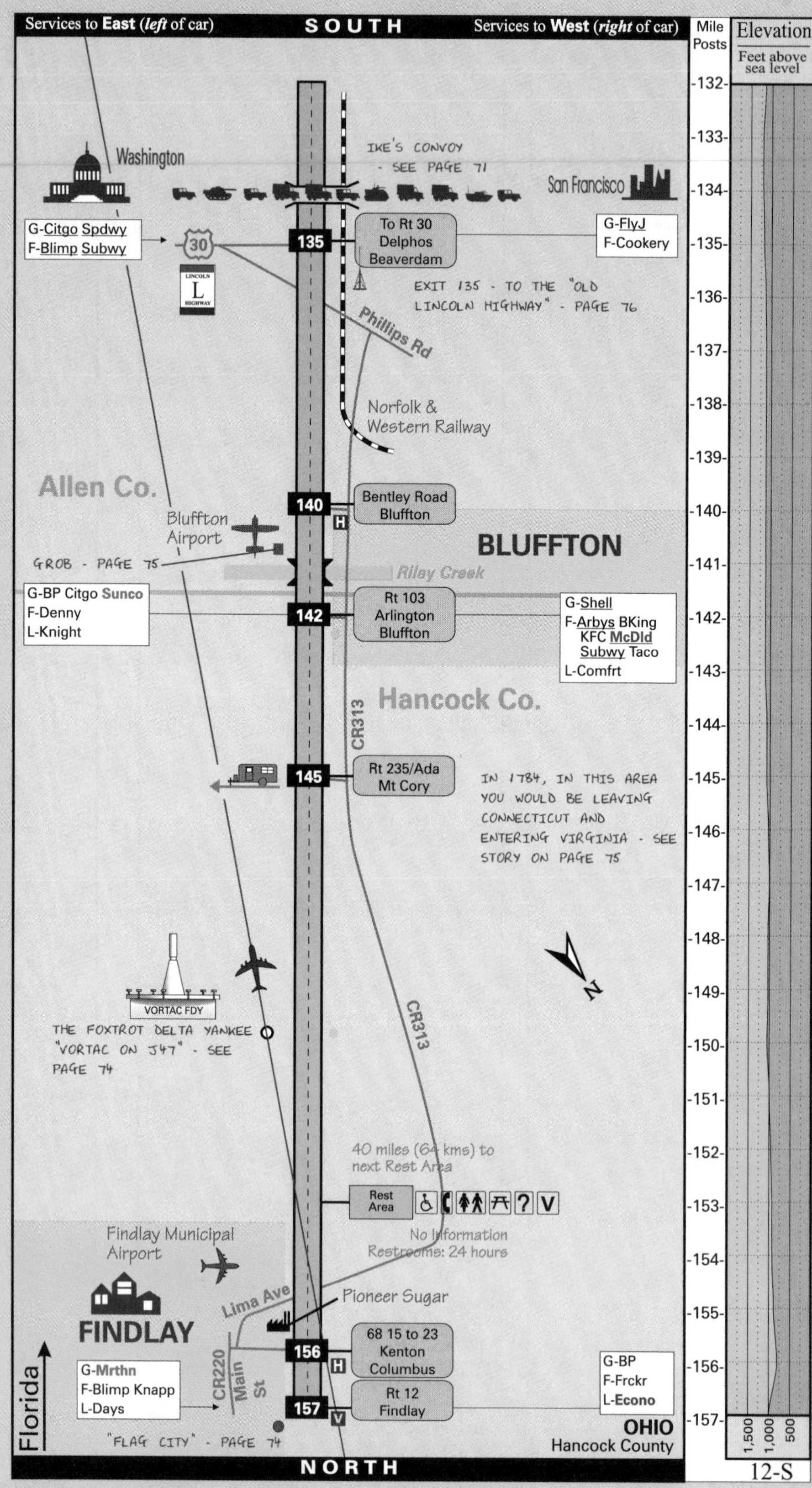
Services to East (left of car)
SOUTH
Services to West (right of car)
Mile Posts
Elevation
Feet above sea level
Washington
IKE'S CONVOY - SEE PAGE 71
San Francisco
G-Citgo Spdwy
F-Blimp Subwy
30
LINCOLN L HIGHWAY
135
To Rt 30
Delphos
Beaverdam
G-FlyJ
F-Cookery
EXIT 135 - TO THE "OLD LINCOLN HIGHWAY" - PAGE 76
Phillips Rd
Norfolk & Western Railway
Allen Co.
140
Bentley Road
Bluffton
H
Bluffton Airport
BLUFFTON
GROB - PAGE 75
Riley Creek
G-BP Citgo Sunco
F-Denny
L-Knight
142
Rt 103
Arlington
Bluffton
G-Shell
F-Arbys BKing
KFC McDld
Subwy Taco
L-Comfrt
CR313
Hancock Co.
145
Rt 235/Ada
Mt Cory
IN 1784, IN THIS AREA YOU WOULD BE LEAVING CONNECTICUT AND ENTERING VIRGINIA - SEE STORY ON PAGE 75
N
VORTAC FDY
THE FOXTROT DELTA YANKEE "VORTAC ON J47" - SEE PAGE 74
CR313
40 miles (64 kms) to next Rest Area
Rest Area
?
V
No Information
Restrooms: 24 hours
Findlay Municipal Airport
Lima Ave
Pioneer Sugar
FINDLAY
CR220
Main St
156
H
68 15 to 23
Kenton
Columbus
157
V
Rt 12
Findlay
G-Mrthn
F-Blimp Knapp
L-Days
G-BP
F-Frckr
L-Econo
Florida
"FLAG CITY" - PAGE 74
OHIO
Hancock County
NORTH
-132-
-133-
-134-
-135-
-136-
-137-
-138-
-139-
-140-
-141-
-142-
-143-
-144-
-145-
-146-
-147-
-148-
-149-
-150-
-151-
-152-
-153-
-154-
-155-
-156-
-157-
1,500
1,000
500

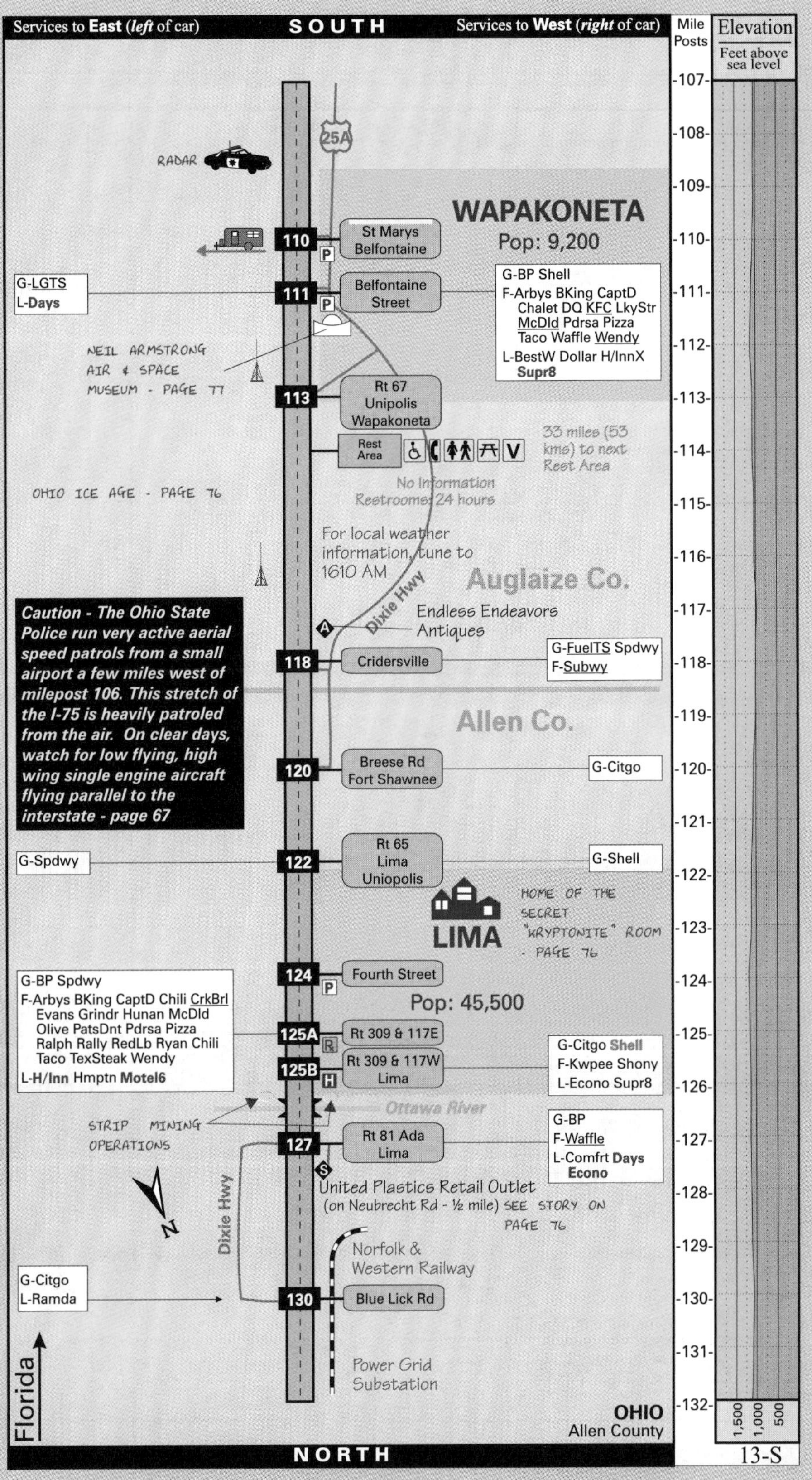

Services to East (left of car)
SOUTH
Services to West (right of car)
Mile Posts
Elevation
Feet above sea level
25A
RADAR
WAPAKONETA
Pop: 9,200
110
St Marys Belfontaine
G-LGTS
L-Days
111
Belfontaine Street
G-BP Shell
F-Arbys BKing CaptD Chalet DQ KFC LkyStr McDld Pdrsa Pizza Taco Waffle Wendy
L-BestW Dollar H/InnX Supr8
NEIL ARMSTRONG AIR & SPACE MUSEUM - PAGE 77
113
Rt 67 Unipolis Wapakoneta
Rest Area
33 miles (53 kms) to next Rest Area
No Information
Restrooms: 24 hours
OHIO ICE AGE - PAGE 76
For local weather information, tune to 1610 AM
Dixie Hwy
Auglaize Co.
Endless Endeavors Antiques
Caution - The Ohio State Police run very active aerial speed patrols from a small airport a few miles west of milepost 106. This stretch of the I-75 is heavily patroled from the air. On clear days, watch for low flying, high wing single engine aircraft flying parallel to the interstate - page 67
118
Cridersville
G-FuelTS Spdwy
F-Subwy
Allen Co.
120
Breese Rd Fort Shawnee
G-Citgo
G-Spdwy
122
Rt 65 Lima Uniopolis
G-Shell
LIMA
HOME OF THE SECRET "KRYPTONITE" ROOM - PAGE 76
124
Fourth Street
Pop: 45,500
G-BP Spdwy
F-Arbys BKing CaptD Chili CrkBrl Evans Grindr Hunan McDld Olive PatsDnt Pdrsa Pizza Ralph Rally RedLb Ryan Chili Taco TexSteak Wendy
L-H/Inn Hmptn Motel6
125A
Rt 309 & 117E
125B
Rt 309 & 117W Lima
G-Citgo Shell
F-Kwpee Shony
L-Econo Supr8
Ottawa River
STRIP MINING OPERATIONS
127
Rt 81 Ada Lima
G-BP
F-Waffle
L-Comfrt Days Econo
United Plastics Retail Outlet
(on Neubrecht Rd - ½ mile) SEE STORY ON PAGE 76
N
Dixie Hwy
Norfolk & Western Railway
G-Citgo
L-Ramda
130
Blue Lick Rd
Power Grid Substation
Florida
OHIO
Allen County
NORTH
-107-
-108-
-109-
-110-
-111-
-112-
-113-
-114-
-115-
-116-
-117-
-118-
-119-
-120-
-121-
-122-
-123-
-124-
-125-
-126-
-127-
-128-
-129-
-130-
-131-
-132-
1,500
1,000
500

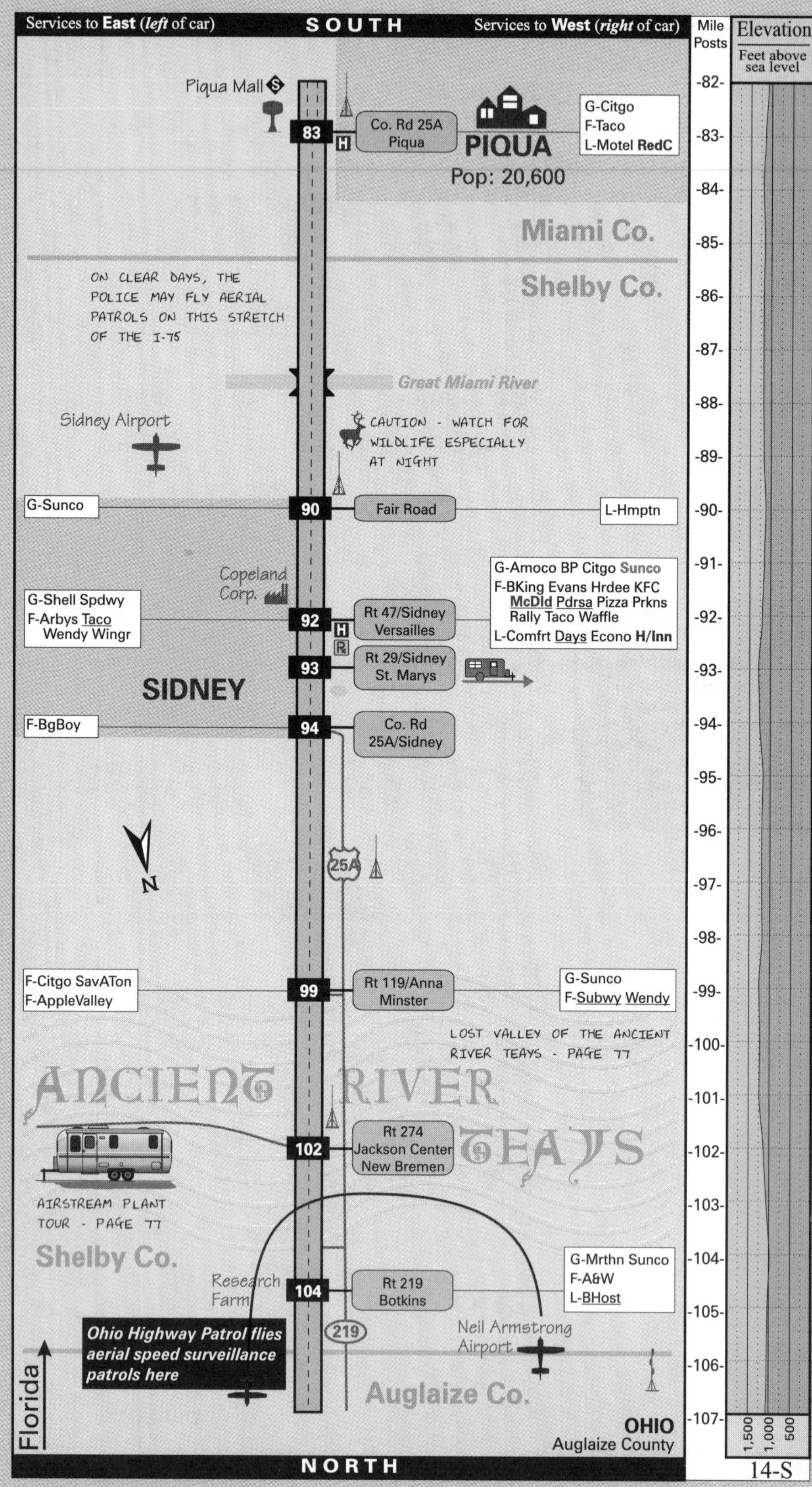

Services to East (left of car)
SOUTH
Services to West (right of car)
Mile Posts
Elevation
Feet above sea level
Piqua Mall
83
Co. Rd 25A Piqua
PIQUA
Pop: 20,600
G-Citgo
F-Taco
L-Motel RedC
Miami Co.
Shelby Co.
ON CLEAR DAYS, THE POLICE MAY FLY AERIAL PATROLS ON THIS STRETCH OF THE I-75
Great Miami River
Sidney Airport
CAUTION - WATCH FOR WILDLIFE ESPECIALLY AT NIGHT
G-Sunco
90
Fair Road
L-Hmptn
Copeland Corp.
G-Shell Spdwy
F-Arbys Taco
Wendy Wingr
92
Rt 47/Sidney Versailles
G-Amoco BP Citgo Sunco
F-BKing Evans Hrdee KFC
McDld Pdrsa Pizza Prkns
Rally Taco Waffle
L-Comfrt Days Econo H/Inn
93
Rt 29/Sidney St. Marys
SIDNEY
F-BgBoy
94
Co. Rd 25A/Sidney
25A
N
F-Citgo SavATon
F-AppleValley
99
Rt 119/Anna Minster
G-Sunco
F-Subwy Wendy
LOST VALLEY OF THE ANCIENT RIVER TEAYS - PAGE 77
ANCIENT RIVER TEAYS
102
Rt 274 Jackson Center New Bremen
AIRSTREAM PLANT TOUR - PAGE 77
Shelby Co.
Research Farm
104
Rt 219 Botkins
G-Mrthn Sunco
F-A&W
L-BHost
Ohio Highway Patrol flies aerial speed surveillance patrols here
219
Neil Armstrong Airport
Florida
Auglaize Co.
OHIO
Auglaize County
NORTH
-82-
-83-
-84-
-85-
-86-
-87-
-88-
-89-
-90-
-91-
-92-
-93-
-94-
-95-
-96-
-97-
-98-
-99-
-100-
-101-
-102-
-103-
-104-
-105-
-106-
-107-
1,500
1,000
500

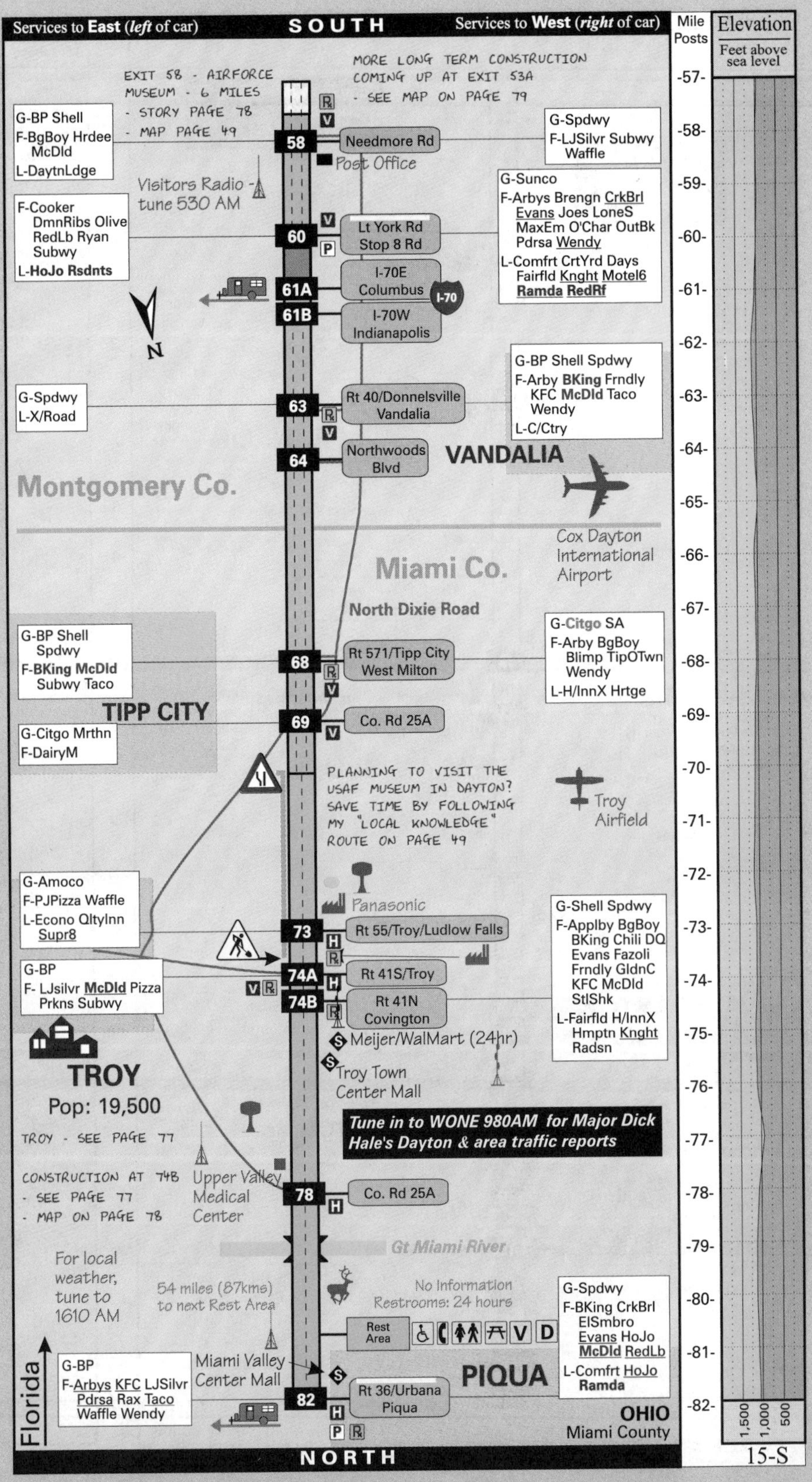

Services to East (left of car)
SOUTH
Services to West (right of car)
Mile Posts
Elevation
Feet above sea level
EXIT 58 - AIRFORCE MUSEUM - 6 MILES
- STORY PAGE 78
- MAP PAGE 49
MORE LONG TERM CONSTRUCTION COMING UP AT EXIT 53A
- SEE MAP ON PAGE 79
G-BP Shell
F-BgBoy Hrdee McDld
L-DaytnLdge
58
Needmore Rd
G-Spdwy
F-LJSilvr Subwy Waffle
Post Office
Visitors Radio - tune 530 AM
G-Sunco
F-Arbys Brengn CrkBrl Evans Joes LoneS MaxEm O'Char OutBk Pdrsa Wendy
L-Comfrt CrtYrd Days Fairfld Knght Motel6 Ramda RedRf
F-Cooker DmnRibs Olive RedLb Ryan Subwy
L-HoJo Rsdnts
60
Lt York Rd
Stop 8 Rd
61A
I-70E Columbus
I-70
61B
I-70W Indianapolis
N
G-BP Shell Spdwy
F-Arby BKing Frndly KFC McDld Taco Wendy
L-C/Ctry
G-Spdwy
L-X/Road
63
Rt 40/Donnelsville Vandalia
64
Northwoods Blvd
VANDALIA
Montgomery Co.
Cox Dayton International Airport
Miami Co.
North Dixie Road
G-Citgo SA
F-Arby BgBoy Blimp TipOTwn Wendy
L-H/InnX Hrtge
G-BP Shell Spdwy
F-BKing McDld Subwy Taco
68
Rt 571/Tipp City West Milton
TIPP CITY
69
Co. Rd 25A
G-Citgo Mrthn
F-DairyM
PLANNING TO VISIT THE USAF MUSEUM IN DAYTON? SAVE TIME BY FOLLOWING MY "LOCAL KNOWLEDGE" ROUTE ON PAGE 49
Troy Airfield
G-Amoco
F-PJPizza Waffle
L-Econo QltyInn Supr8
Panasonic
73
Rt 55/Troy/Ludlow Falls
G-Shell Spdwy
F-Applby BgBoy BKing Chili DQ Evans Fazoli Frndly GldnC KFC McDld StlShk
L-Fairfld H/InnX Hmptn Knght Radsn
G-BP
F- LJsilvr McDld Pizza Prkns Subwy
74A
Rt 41S/Troy
74B
Rt 41N Covington
Meijer/WalMart (24hr)
Troy Town Center Mall
TROY
Pop: 19,500
TROY - SEE PAGE 77
Tune in to WONE 980AM for Major Dick Hale's Dayton & area traffic reports
CONSTRUCTION AT 74B
- SEE PAGE 77
- MAP ON PAGE 78
Upper Valley Medical Center
78
Co. Rd 25A
Gt Miami River
For local weather, tune to 1610 AM
54 miles (87kms) to next Rest Area
No Information
Restrooms: 24 hours
Rest Area
V
D
G-Spdwy
F-BKing CrkBrl ElSmbro Evans HoJo McDld RedLb
L-Comfrt HoJo Ramda
Florida
G-BP
F-Arbys KFC LJSilvr Pdrsa Rax Taco Waffle Wendy
Miami Valley Center Mall
PIQUA
82
Rt 36/Urbana Piqua
OHIO
Miami County
NORTH
-57- -58- -59- -60- -61- -62- -63- -64- -65- -66- -67- -68- -69- -70- -71- -72- -73- -74- -75- -76- -77- -78- -79- -80- -81- -82-
1,500 1,000 500

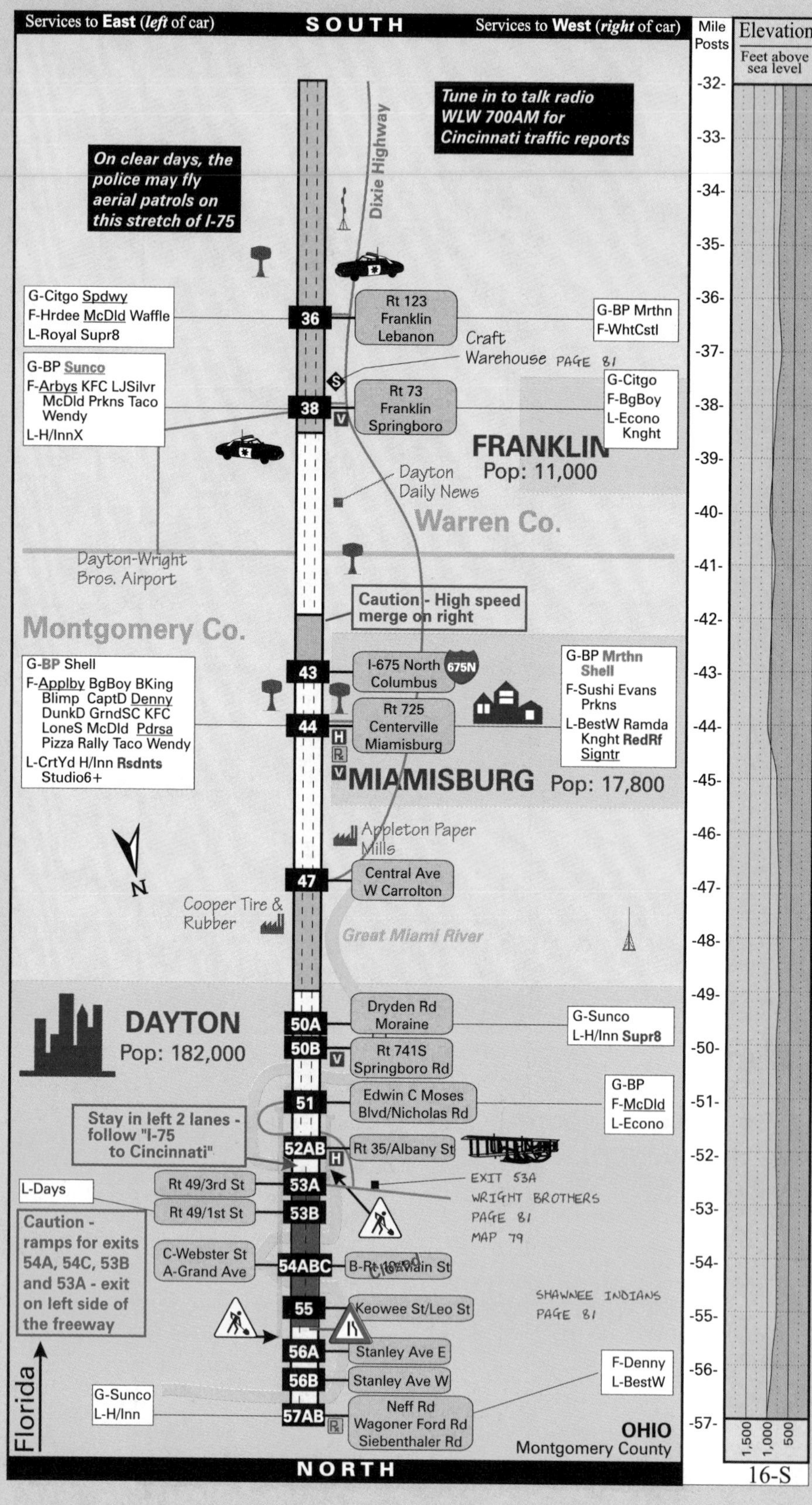

Services to East (left of car)
SOUTH
Services to West (right of car)
Mile Posts
Elevation
Feet above sea level
Tune in to talk radio WLW 700AM for Cincinnati traffic reports
On clear days, the police may fly aerial patrols on this stretch of I-75
Dixie Highway
G-Citgo Spdwy
F-Hrdee McDld Waffle
L-Royal Supr8
36
Rt 123 Franklin Lebanon
G-BP Mrthn
F-WhtCstl
Craft Warehouse PAGE 81
G-BP Sunco
F-Arbys KFC LJSilvr McDld Prkns Taco Wendy
L-H/InnX
38
Rt 73 Franklin Springboro
G-Citgo
F-BgBoy
L-Econo Knght
FRANKLIN Pop: 11,000
Dayton Daily News
Warren Co.
Dayton-Wright Bros. Airport
Caution - High speed merge on right
Montgomery Co.
G-BP Shell
F-Applby BgBoy BKing Blimp CaptD Denny DunkD GrndSC KFC LoneS McDld Pdrsa Pizza Rally Taco Wendy
L-CrtYd H/Inn Rsdnts Studio6+
43
I-675 North Columbus
675N
44
Rt 725 Centerville Miamisburg
G-BP Mrthn Shell
F-Sushi Evans Prkns
L-BestW Ramda Knght RedRf Signtr
MIAMISBURG Pop: 17,800
Appleton Paper Mills
N
47
Central Ave W Carrolton
Cooper Tire & Rubber
Great Miami River
DAYTON
Pop: 182,000
50A
Dryden Rd Moraine
G-Sunco
L-H/Inn Supr8
50B
Rt 741S Springboro Rd
51
Edwin C Moses Blvd/Nicholas Rd
G-BP
F-McDld
L-Econo
Stay in left 2 lanes - follow "I-75 to Cincinnati"
52AB
Rt 35/Albany St
EXIT 53A WRIGHT BROTHERS PAGE 81 MAP 79
L-Days
Rt 49/3rd St
53A
Rt 49/1st St
53B
Caution - ramps for exits 54A, 54C, 53B and 53A - exit on left side of the freeway
C-Webster St
A-Grand Ave
54ABC
B-Rt 4/Main St
Closed
SHAWNEE INDIANS PAGE 81
55
Keowee St/Leo St
56A
Stanley Ave E
56B
Stanley Ave W
F-Denny
L-BestW
G-Sunco
L-H/Inn
57AB
Neff Rd Wagoner Ford Rd Siebenthaler Rd
OHIO
Montgomery County
Florida
NORTH
-32- -33- -34- -35- -36- -37- -38- -39- -40- -41- -42- -43- -44- -45- -46- -47- -48- -49- -50- -51- -52- -53- -54- -55- -56- -57-
1,500 1,000 500

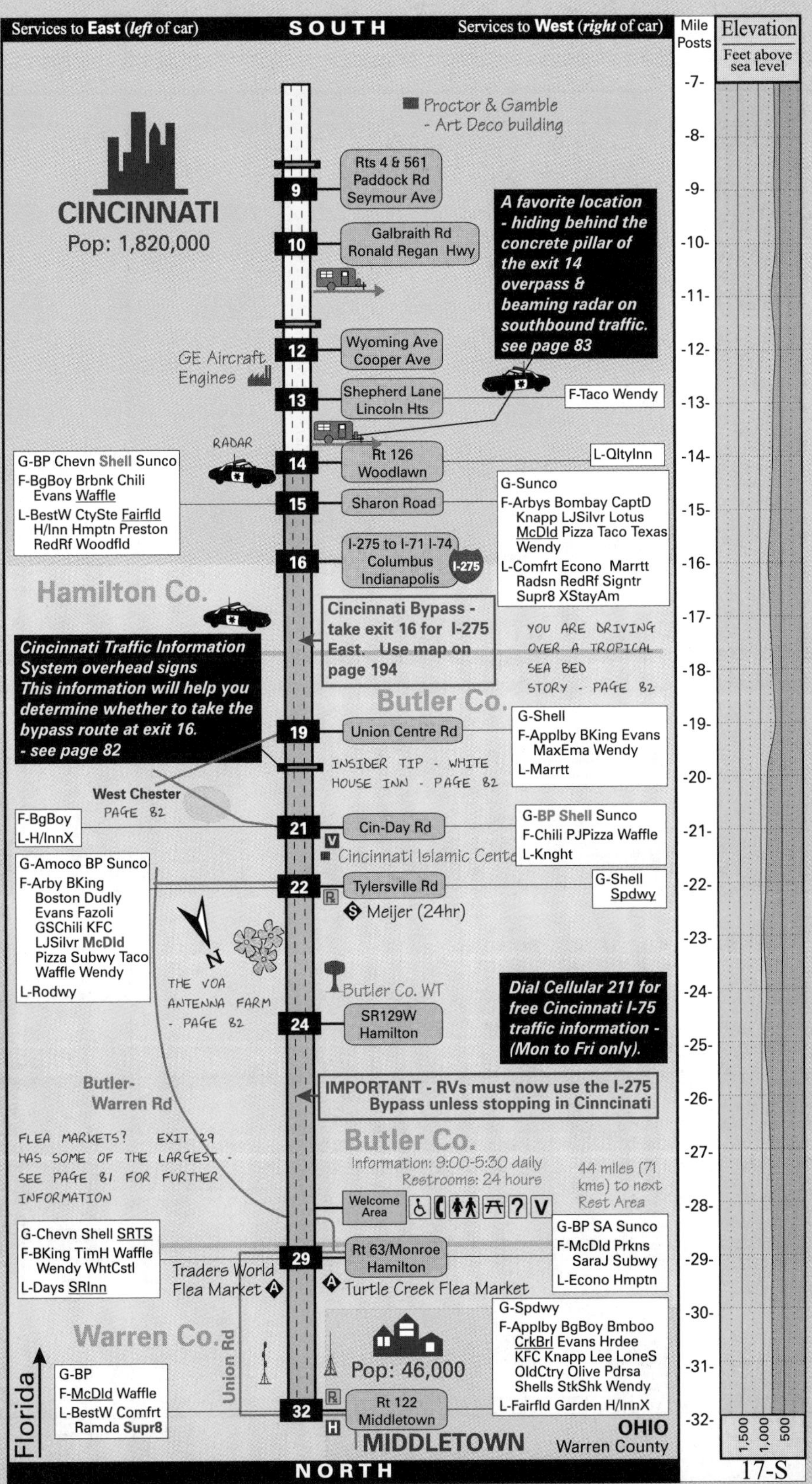

Services to East (left of car)
SOUTH
Services to West (right of car)
Mile Posts
Elevation
Feet above sea level
CINCINNATI
Pop: 1,820,000
Proctor & Gamble - Art Deco building
9 Rts 4 & 561 Paddock Rd Seymour Ave
10 Galbraith Rd Ronald Regan Hwy
A favorite location - hiding behind the concrete pillar of the exit 14 overpass & beaming radar on southbound traffic. see page 83
GE Aircraft Engines
12 Wyoming Ave Cooper Ave
13 Shepherd Lane Lincoln Hts
F-Taco Wendy
RADAR
14 Rt 126 Woodlawn
L-QltyInn
G-BP Chevn Shell Sunco
F-BgBoy Brbnk Chili Evans Waffle
L-BestW CtySte Fairfld H/Inn Hmptn Preston RedRf Woodfld
15 Sharon Road
G-Sunco
F-Arbys Bombay CaptD Knapp LJSilvr Lotus McDld Pizza Taco Texas Wendy
L-Comfrt Econo Marrtt Radsn RedRf Signtr Supr8 XStayAm
16 I-275 to I-71 I-74 Columbus Indianapolis
I-275
Hamilton Co.
Cincinnati Bypass - take exit 16 for I-275 East. Use map on page 194
YOU ARE DRIVING OVER A TROPICAL SEA BED STORY - PAGE 82
Cincinnati Traffic Information System overhead signs This information will help you determine whether to take the bypass route at exit 16. - see page 82
Butler Co.
19 Union Centre Rd
G-Shell
F-Applby BKing Evans MaxEma Wendy
L-Marrtt
INSIDER TIP - WHITE HOUSE INN - PAGE 82
West Chester PAGE 82
F-BgBoy
L-H/InnX
21 Cin-Day Rd
G-BP Shell Sunco
F-Chili PJPizza Waffle
L-Knght
Cincinnati Islamic Cente
G-Amoco BP Sunco
F-Arby BKing Boston Dudly Evans Fazoli GSChili KFC LJSilvr McDld Pizza Subwy Taco Waffle Wendy
L-Rodwy
22 Tylersville Rd
G-Shell Spdwy
Meijer (24hr)
N
THE VOA ANTENNA FARM - PAGE 82
Butler Co. WT
24 SR129W Hamilton
Dial Cellular 211 for free Cincinnati I-75 traffic information - (Mon to Fri only).
Butler-Warren Rd
IMPORTANT - RVs must now use the I-275 Bypass unless stopping in Cinncinati
FLEA MARKETS? EXIT 29 HAS SOME OF THE LARGEST - SEE PAGE 81 FOR FURTHER INFORMATION
Butler Co.
Information: 9:00-5:30 daily
Restrooms: 24 hours
44 miles (71 kms) to next Rest Area
Welcome Area
G-Chevn Shell SRTS
F-BKing TimH Waffle Wendy WhtCstl
L-Days SRInn
29 Rt 63/Monroe Hamilton
G-BP SA Sunco
F-McDld Prkns SaraJ Subwy
L-Econo Hmptn
Traders World Flea Market
Turtle Creek Flea Market
G-Spdwy
F-Applby BgBoy Bmboo CrkBrl Evans Hrdee KFC Knapp Lee LoneS OldCtry Olive Pdrsa Shells StkShk Wendy
L-Fairfld Garden H/InnX
Warren Co.
Union Rd
Pop: 46,000
Florida
G-BP
F-McDld Waffle
L-BestW Comfrt Ramda Supr8
32 Rt 122 Middletown
MIDDLETOWN
OHIO Warren County
NORTH
-7- -8- -9- -10- -11- -12- -13- -14- -15- -16- -17- -18- -19- -20- -21- -22- -23- -24- -25- -26- -27- -28- -29- -30- -31- -32-
1,500 1,000 500

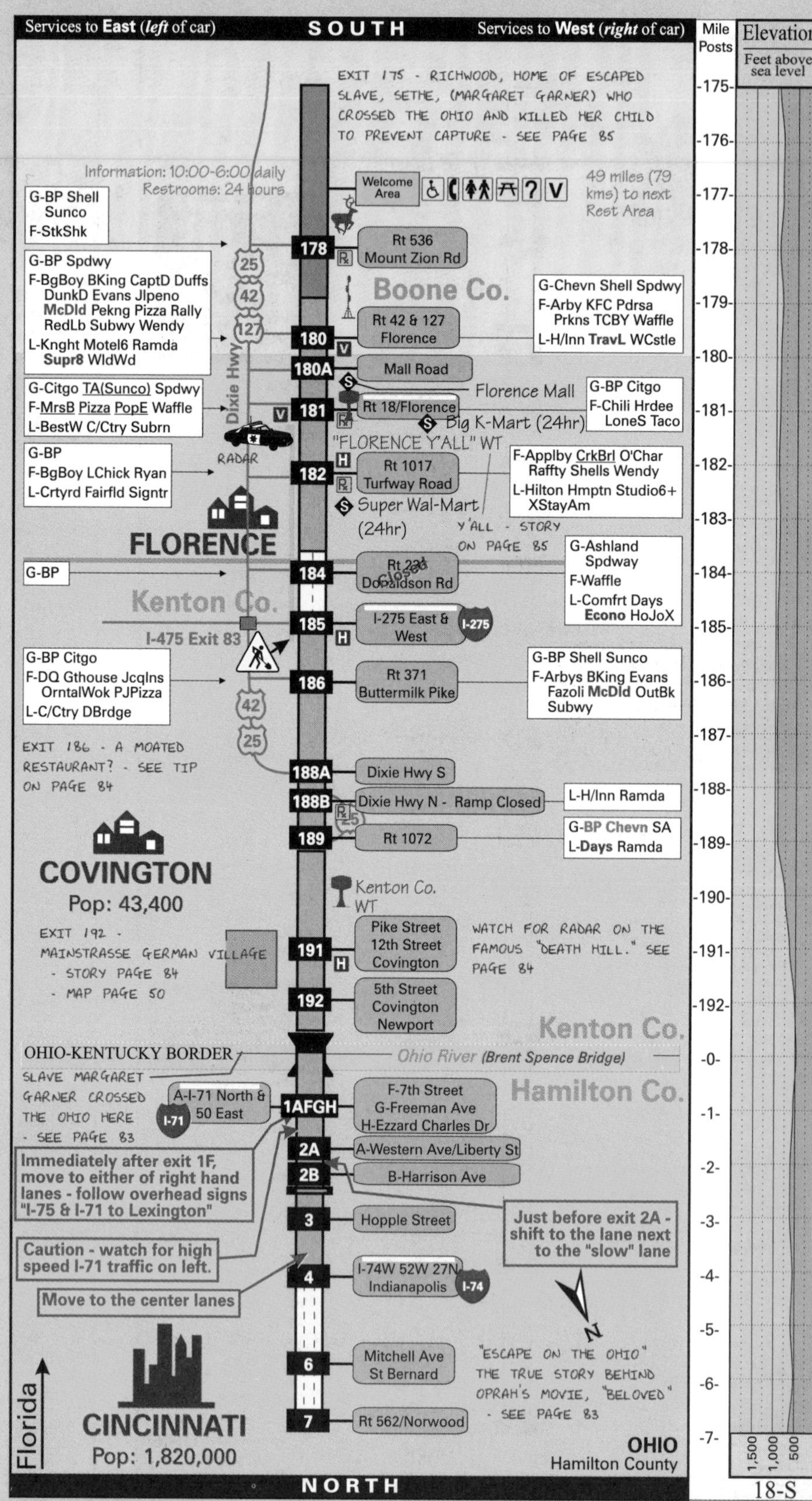

Services to East (left of car)
SOUTH
Services to West (right of car)
Mile Posts
Elevation
Feet above sea level
EXIT 175 - RICHWOOD, HOME OF ESCAPED SLAVE, SETHE, (MARGARET GARNER) WHO CROSSED THE OHIO AND KILLED HER CHILD TO PREVENT CAPTURE - SEE PAGE 85
Information: 10:00-6:00 daily
Restrooms: 24 hours
Welcome Area
49 miles (79 kms) to next Rest Area
G-BP Shell Sunco
F-StkShk
178
Rt 536 Mount Zion Rd
G-BP Spdwy
F-BgBoy BKing CaptD Duffs DunkD Evans Jlpeno McDld Pekng Pizza Rally RedLb Subwy Wendy
L-Knght Motel6 Ramda Supr8 WldWd
Boone Co.
G-Chevn Shell Spdwy
F-Arby KFC Pdrsa Prkns TCBY Waffle
L-H/Inn TravL WCstle
180
Rt 42 & 127 Florence
180A
Mall Road
Florence Mall
Dixie Hwy
G-Citgo TA(Sunco) Spdwy
F-MrsB Pizza PopE Waffle
L-BestW C/Ctry Subrn
181
Rt 18/Florence
G-BP Citgo
F-Chili Hrdee LoneS Taco
Big K-Mart (24hr)
"FLORENCE Y'ALL" WT
RADAR
G-BP
F-BgBoy LChick Ryan
L-Crtyrd Fairfld Signtr
182
Rt 1017 Turfway Road
F-Applby CrkBrl O'Char Raffty Shells Wendy
L-Hilton Hmptn Studio6+ XStayAm
Super Wal-Mart (24hr)
Y'ALL - STORY ON PAGE 85
FLORENCE
G-BP
184
Rt 236 Donaldson Rd
Closed
G-Ashland Spdway
F-Waffle
L-Comfrt Days Econo HoJoX
Kenton Co.
185
I-275 East & West
I-275
I-475 Exit 83
G-BP Citgo
F-DQ Gthouse JcqIns OrntalWok PJPizza
L-C/Ctry DBrdge
186
Rt 371 Buttermilk Pike
G-BP Shell Sunco
F-Arbys BKing Evans Fazoli McDld OutBk Subwy
EXIT 186 - A MOATED RESTAURANT? - SEE TIP ON PAGE 84
188A
Dixie Hwy S
188B
Dixie Hwy N - Ramp Closed
L-H/Inn Ramda
189
Rt 1072
G-BP Chevn SA
L-Days Ramda
COVINGTON
Pop: 43,400
Kenton Co. WT
EXIT 192 - MAINSTRASSE GERMAN VILLAGE - STORY PAGE 84 - MAP PAGE 50
191
Pike Street 12th Street Covington
WATCH FOR RADAR ON THE FAMOUS "DEATH HILL." SEE PAGE 84
192
5th Street Covington Newport
Kenton Co.
OHIO-KENTUCKY BORDER
Ohio River (Brent Spence Bridge)
SLAVE MARGARET GARNER CROSSED THE OHIO HERE - SEE PAGE 83
Hamilton Co.
A-I-71 North & 50 East
I-71
1AFGH
F-7th Street G-Freeman Ave H-Ezzard Charles Dr
Immediately after exit 1F, move to either of right hand lanes - follow overhead signs "I-75 & I-71 to Lexington"
2A
A-Western Ave/Liberty St
2B
B-Harrison Ave
3
Hopple Street
Just before exit 2A - shift to the lane next to the "slow" lane
Caution - watch for high speed I-71 traffic on left.
4
I-74W 52W 27N Indianapolis
I-74
Move to the center lanes
N
6
Mitchell Ave St Bernard
"ESCAPE ON THE OHIO" THE TRUE STORY BEHIND OPRAH'S MOVIE, "BELOVED" - SEE PAGE 83
7
Rt 562/Norwood
Florida
CINCINNATI
Pop: 1,820,000
OHIO
Hamilton County
NORTH
-175- -176- -177- -178- -179- -180- -181- -182- -183- -184- -185- -186- -187- -188- -189- -190- -191- -192- -0- -1- -2- -3- -4- -5- -6- -7-
1,500 1,000 500

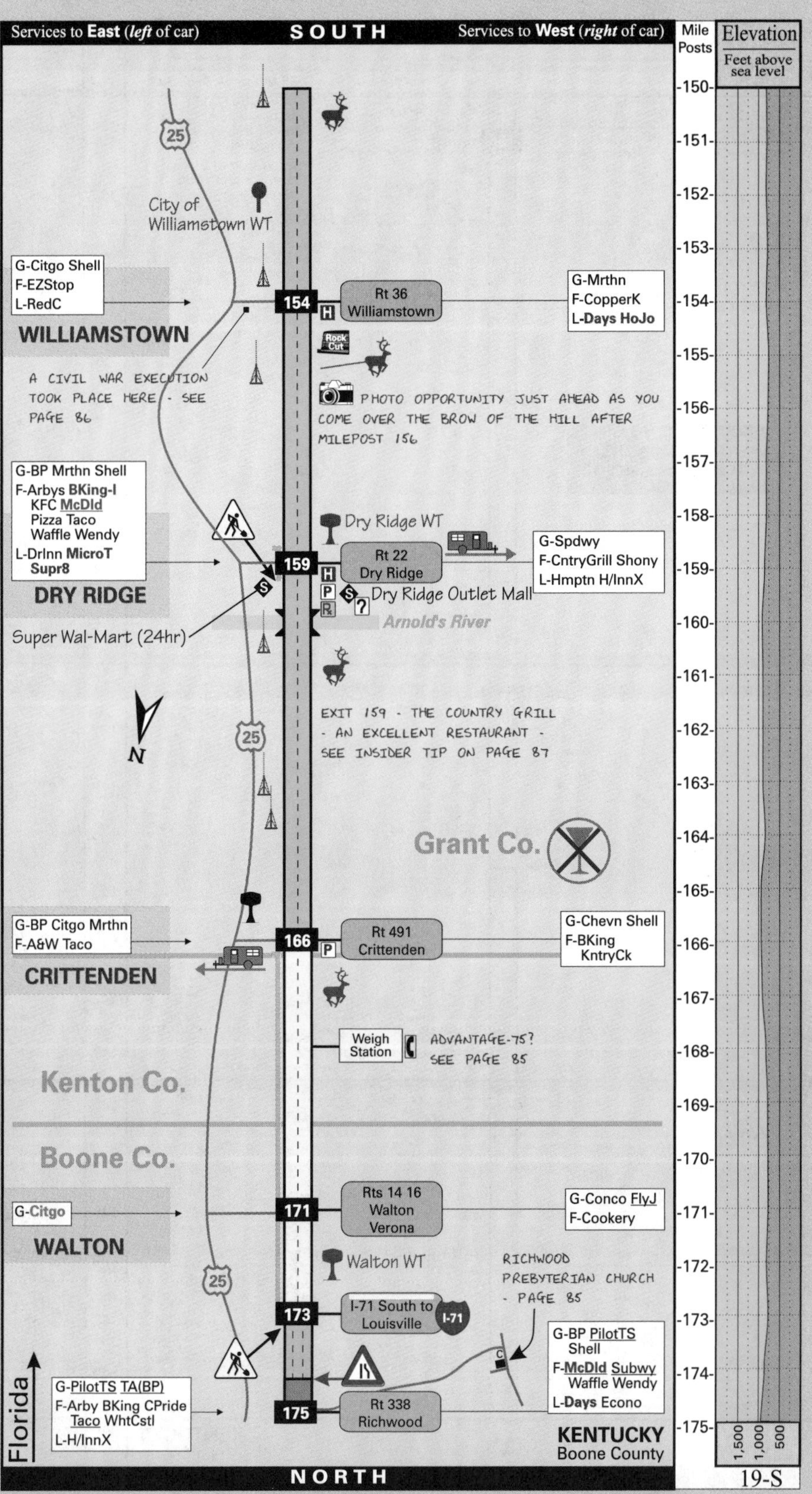

Services to East (left of car)
SOUTH
Services to West (right of car)
Mile Posts
Elevation
Feet above sea level
City of Williamstown WT
G-Citgo Shell
F-EZStop
L-RedC
WILLIAMSTOWN
154
Rt 36 Williamstown
G-Mrthn
F-CopperK
L-Days HoJo
Rock Cut
A CIVIL WAR EXECUTION TOOK PLACE HERE - SEE PAGE 86
PHOTO OPPORTUNITY JUST AHEAD AS YOU COME OVER THE BROW OF THE HILL AFTER MILEPOST 156
G-BP Mrthn Shell
F-Arbys BKing-I KFC McDld Pizza Taco Waffle Wendy
L-DrInn MicroT Supr8
DRY RIDGE
Dry Ridge WT
159
Rt 22 Dry Ridge
G-Spdwy
F-CntryGrill Shony
L-Hmptn H/InnX
Dry Ridge Outlet Mall
Arnold's River
Super Wal-Mart (24hr)
N
EXIT 159 - THE COUNTRY GRILL - AN EXCELLENT RESTAURANT - SEE INSIDER TIP ON PAGE 87
Grant Co.
G-BP Citgo Mrthn
F-A&W Taco
CRITTENDEN
166
Rt 491 Crittenden
G-Chevn Shell
F-BKing KntryCk
Weigh Station
ADVANTAGE-75? SEE PAGE 85
Kenton Co.
Boone Co.
G-Citgo
WALTON
171
Rts 14 16 Walton Verona
G-Conco FlyJ
F-Cookery
Walton WT
RICHWOOD PREBYTERIAN CHURCH - PAGE 85
173
I-71 South to Louisville
I-71
G-BP PilotTS Shell
F-McDld Subwy Waffle Wendy
L-Days Econo
G-PilotTS TA(BP)
F-Arby BKing CPride Taco WhtCstl
L-H/InnX
175
Rt 338 Richwood
KENTUCKY
Boone County
Florida
NORTH
25
-150- -151- -152- -153- -154- -155- -156- -157- -158- -159- -160- -161- -162- -163- -164- -165- -166- -167- -168- -169- -170- -171- -172- -173- -174- -175-
1,500 1,000 500

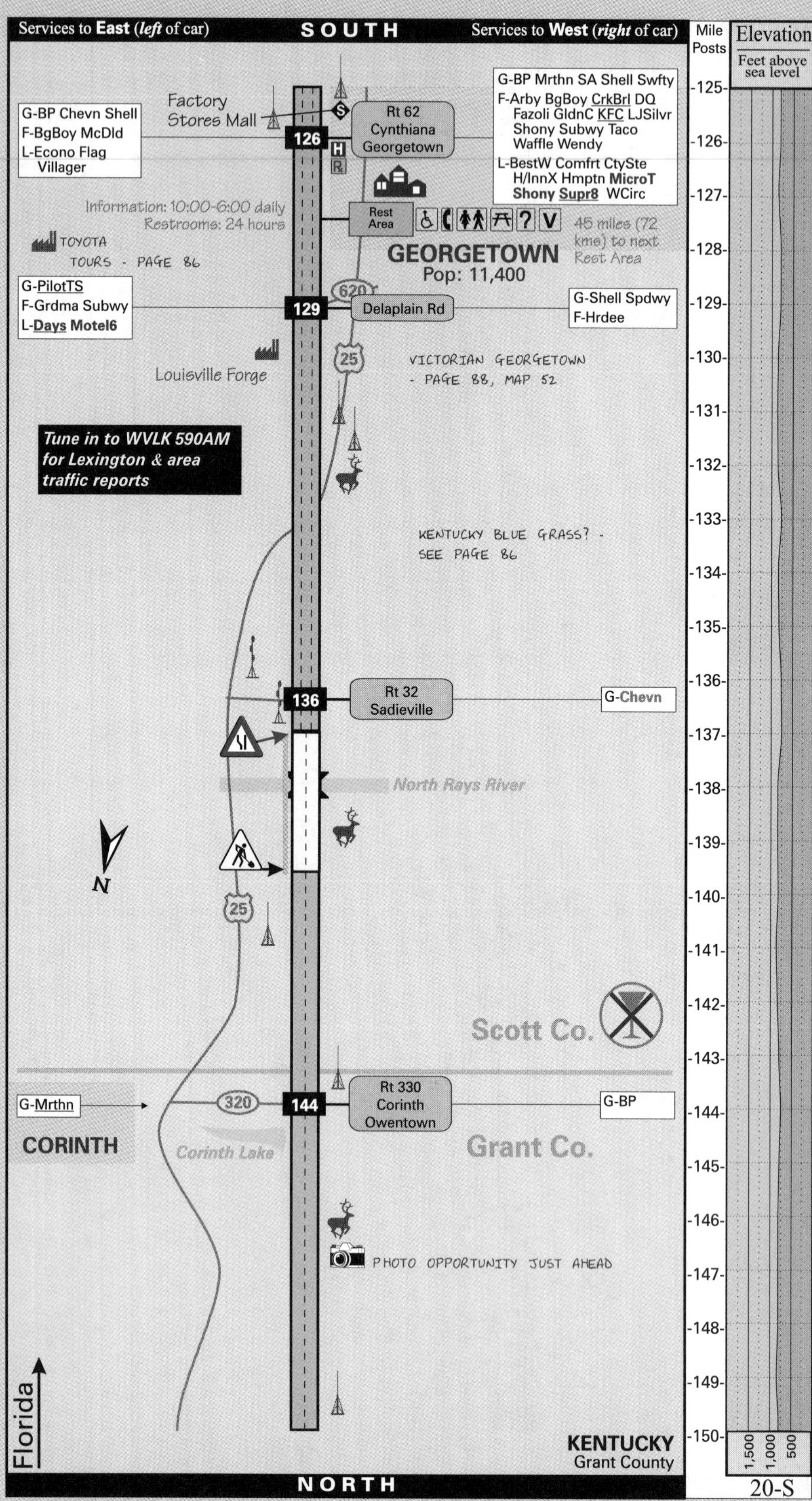

Services to East (left of car)
SOUTH
Services to West (right of car)
Mile Posts
Elevation
Feet above sea level
G-BP Chevn Shell
F-BgBoy McDld
L-Econo Flag Villager
Factory Stores Mall
126
Rt 62
Cynthiana
Georgetown
G-BP Mrthn SA Shell Swfty
F-Arby BgBoy CrkBrl DQ Fazoli GldnC KFC LJSilvr Shony Subwy Taco Waffle Wendy
L-BestW Comfrt CtySte H/InnX Hmptn MicroT Shony Supr8 WCirc
Information: 10:00-6:00 daily
Restrooms: 24 hours
Rest Area
45 miles (72 kms) to next Rest Area
TOYOTA TOURS - PAGE 86
GEORGETOWN
Pop: 11,400
G-PilotTS
F-Grdma Subwy
L-Days Motel6
620
129
Delaplain Rd
G-Shell Spdwy
F-Hrdee
25
Louisville Forge
VICTORIAN GEORGETOWN - PAGE 88, MAP 52
Tune in to WVLK 590AM for Lexington & area traffic reports
KENTUCKY BLUE GRASS? - SEE PAGE 86
136
Rt 32
Sadieville
G-Chevn
North Rays River
N
25
Scott Co.
G-Mrthn
320
144
Rt 330
Corinth
Owentown
G-BP
CORINTH
Corinth Lake
Grant Co.
PHOTO OPPORTUNITY JUST AHEAD
Florida
KENTUCKY
Grant County
NORTH
-125- -126- -127- -128- -129- -130- -131- -132- -133- -134- -135- -136- -137- -138- -139- -140- -141- -142- -143- -144- -145- -146- -147- -148- -149- -150-
1,500 1,000 500

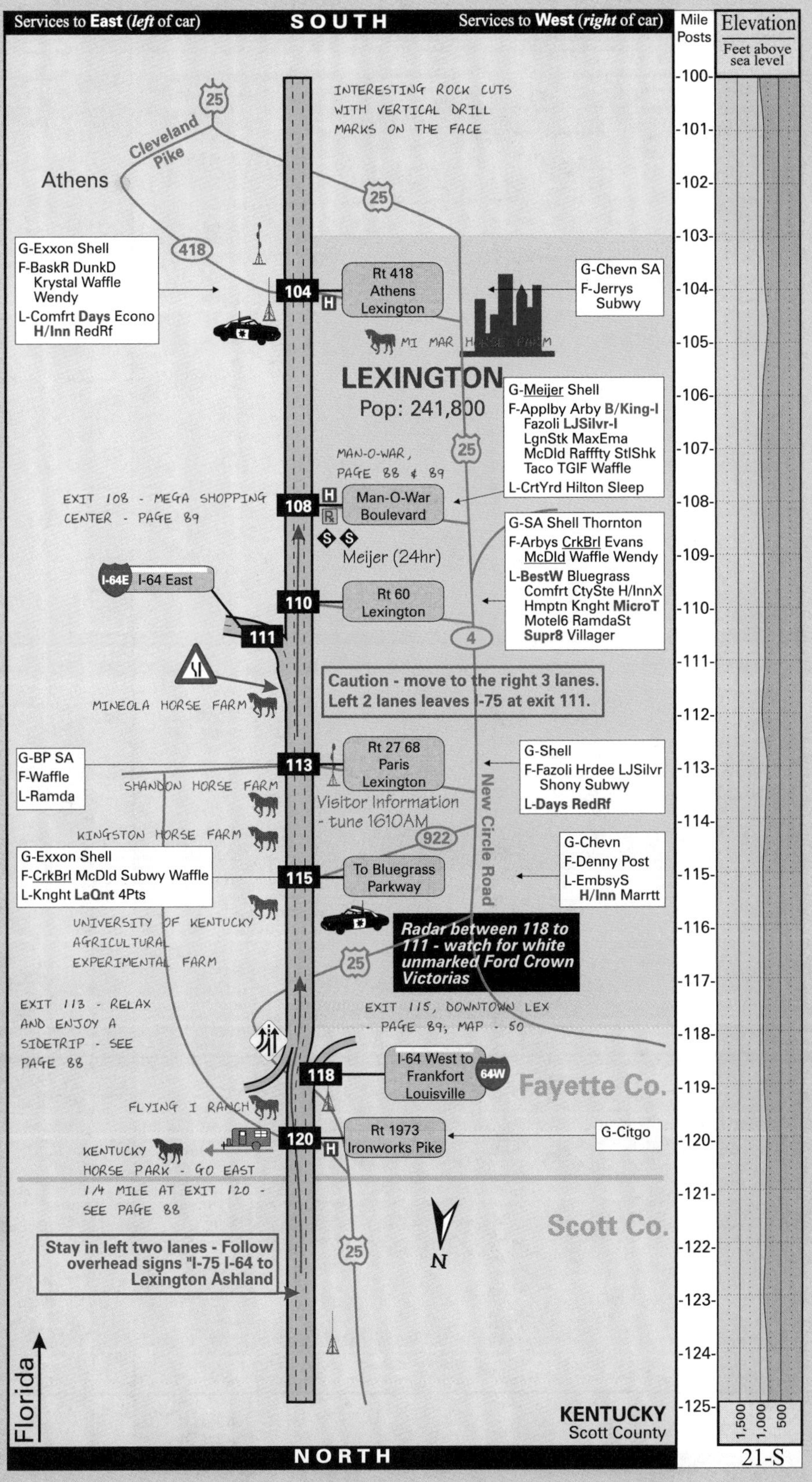

Services to East (left of car)
SOUTH
Services to West (right of car)
Mile Posts
Elevation
Feet above sea level
INTERESTING ROCK CUTS WITH VERTICAL DRILL MARKS ON THE FACE
25
Cleveland Pike
Athens
25
418
G-Exxon Shell
F-BaskR DunkD Krystal Waffle Wendy
L-Comfrt Days Econo H/Inn RedRf
104
Rt 418 Athens Lexington
G-Chevn SA
F-Jerrys Subwy
MI MAR HORSE FARM
LEXINGTON
Pop: 241,800
G-Meijer Shell
F-Applby Arby B/King-I Fazoli LJSilvr-I LgnStk MaxEma McDld Rafffty StlShk Taco TGIF Waffle
L-CrtYrd Hilton Sleep
MAN-O-WAR, PAGE 88 & 89
25
EXIT 108 - MEGA SHOPPING CENTER - PAGE 89
108
Man-O-War Boulevard
Meijer (24hr)
G-SA Shell Thornton
F-Arbys CrkBrl Evans McDld Waffle Wendy
L-BestW Bluegrass Comfrt CtySte H/InnX Hmptn Knght MicroT Motel6 RamdaSt Supr8 Villager
I-64E I-64 East
110
Rt 60 Lexington
4
111
Caution - move to the right 3 lanes. Left 2 lanes leaves I-75 at exit 111.
MINEOLA HORSE FARM
G-BP SA
F-Waffle
L-Ramda
113
Rt 27 68 Paris Lexington
G-Shell
F-Fazoli Hrdee LJSilvr Shony Subwy
L-Days RedRf
SHANDON HORSE FARM
Visitor Information - tune 1610AM
New Circle Road
KINGSTON HORSE FARM
922
G-Exxon Shell
F-CrkBrl McDld Subwy Waffle
L-Knght LaQnt 4Pts
115
To Bluegrass Parkway
G-Chevn
F-Denny Post
L-EmbsyS H/Inn Marrtt
UNIVERSITY OF KENTUCKY AGRICULTURAL EXPERIMENTAL FARM
Radar between 118 to 111 - watch for white unmarked Ford Crown Victorias
25
EXIT 113 - RELAX AND ENJOY A SIDETRIP - SEE PAGE 88
EXIT 115, DOWNTOWN LEX - PAGE 89, MAP - 50
118
I-64 West to Frankfort Louisville
64W
Fayette Co.
FLYING I RANCH
120
Rt 1973 Ironworks Pike
G-Citgo
KENTUCKY HORSE PARK - GO EAST 1/4 MILE AT EXIT 120 - SEE PAGE 88
Scott Co.
N
25
Stay in left two lanes - Follow overhead signs "I-75 I-64 to Lexington Ashland
Florida
KENTUCKY
Scott County
NORTH
-100- -101- -102- -103- -104- -105- -106- -107- -108- -109- -110- -111- -112- -113- -114- -115- -116- -117- -118- -119- -120- -121- -122- -123- -124- -125-
1,500 1,000 500

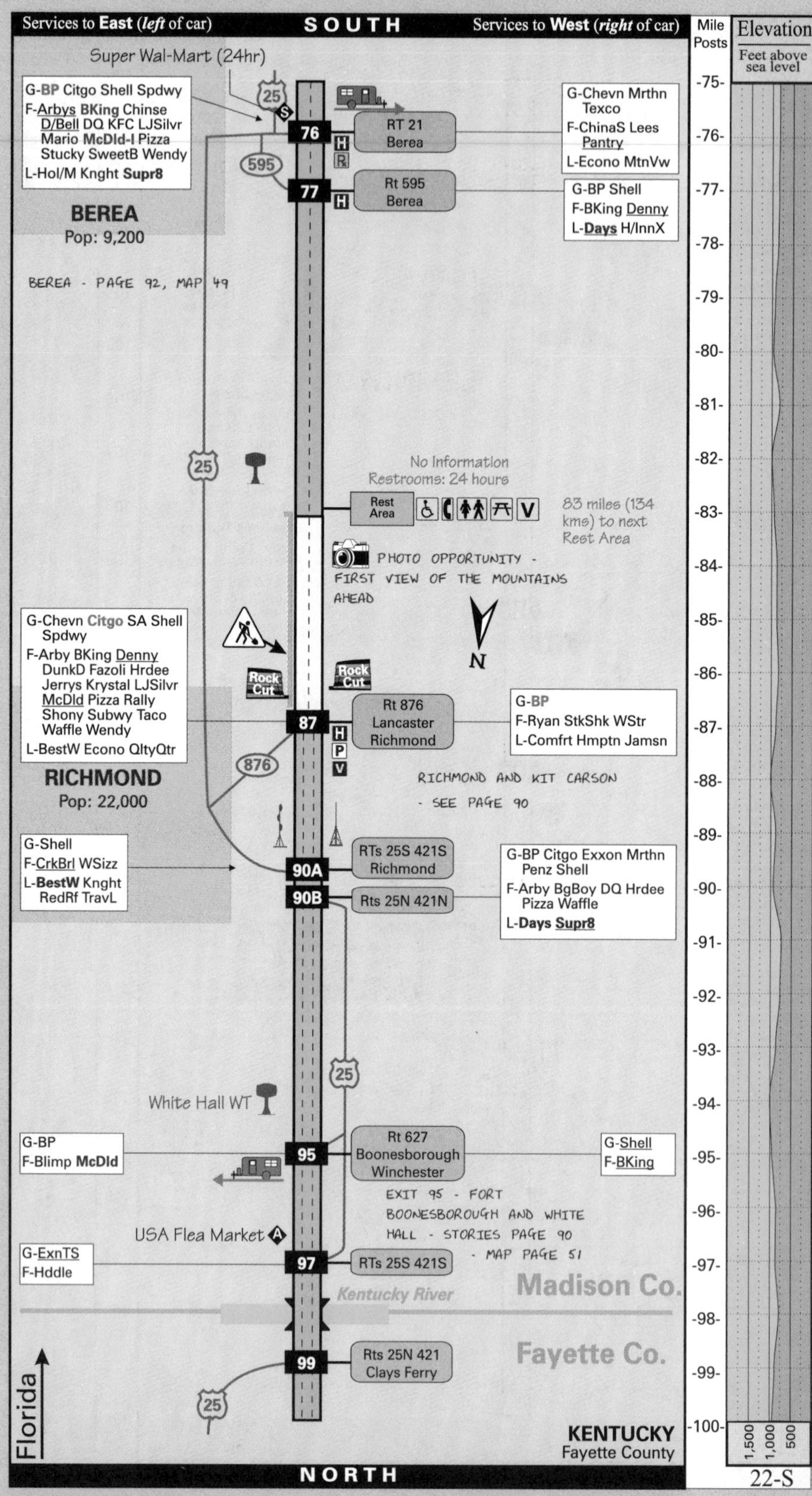

Services to East (left of car)
SOUTH
Services to West (right of car)
Mile Posts
Elevation
Feet above sea level
Super Wal-Mart (24hr)
G-BP Citgo Shell Spdwy
F-Arbys BKing Chinse D/Bell DQ KFC LJSilvr Mario McDld-I Pizza Stucky SweetB Wendy
L-Hol/M Knght Supr8
76
RT 21 Berea
G-Chevn Mrthn Texco
F-ChinaS Lees Pantry
L-Econo MtnVw
595
77
Rt 595 Berea
G-BP Shell
F-BKing Denny
L-Days H/InnX
BEREA
Pop: 9,200
BEREA - PAGE 92, MAP 49
25
No Information
Restrooms: 24 hours
Rest Area
83 miles (134 kms) to next Rest Area
PHOTO OPPORTUNITY - FIRST VIEW OF THE MOUNTAINS AHEAD
N
G-Chevn Citgo SA Shell Spdwy
F-Arby BKing Denny DunkD Fazoli Hrdee Jerrys Krystal LJSilvr McDld Pizza Rally Shony Subwy Taco Waffle Wendy
L-BestW Econo QltyQtr
Rock Cut
Rock Cut
87
Rt 876 Lancaster Richmond
G-BP
F-Ryan StkShk WStr
L-Comfrt Hmptn Jamsn
876
RICHMOND
Pop: 22,000
RICHMOND AND KIT CARSON - SEE PAGE 90
G-Shell
F-CrkBrl WSizz
L-BestW Knght RedRf TravL
90A
RTs 25S 421S Richmond
90B
Rts 25N 421N
G-BP Citgo Exxon Mrthn Penz Shell
F-Arby BgBoy DQ Hrdee Pizza Waffle
L-Days Supr8
25
White Hall WT
G-BP
F-Blimp McDld
95
Rt 627 Boonesborough Winchester
G-Shell
F-BKing
EXIT 95 - FORT BOONESBOROUGH AND WHITE HALL - STORIES PAGE 90 - MAP PAGE 51
USA Flea Market
G-ExnTS
F-Hddle
97
RTs 25S 421S
Kentucky River
Madison Co.
Fayette Co.
99
Rts 25N 421 Clays Ferry
25
Florida
KENTUCKY
Fayette County
NORTH
-75- -76- -77- -78- -79- -80- -81- -82- -83- -84- -85- -86- -87- -88- -89- -90- -91- -92- -93- -94- -95- -96- -97- -98- -99- -100-
1,500 1,000 500

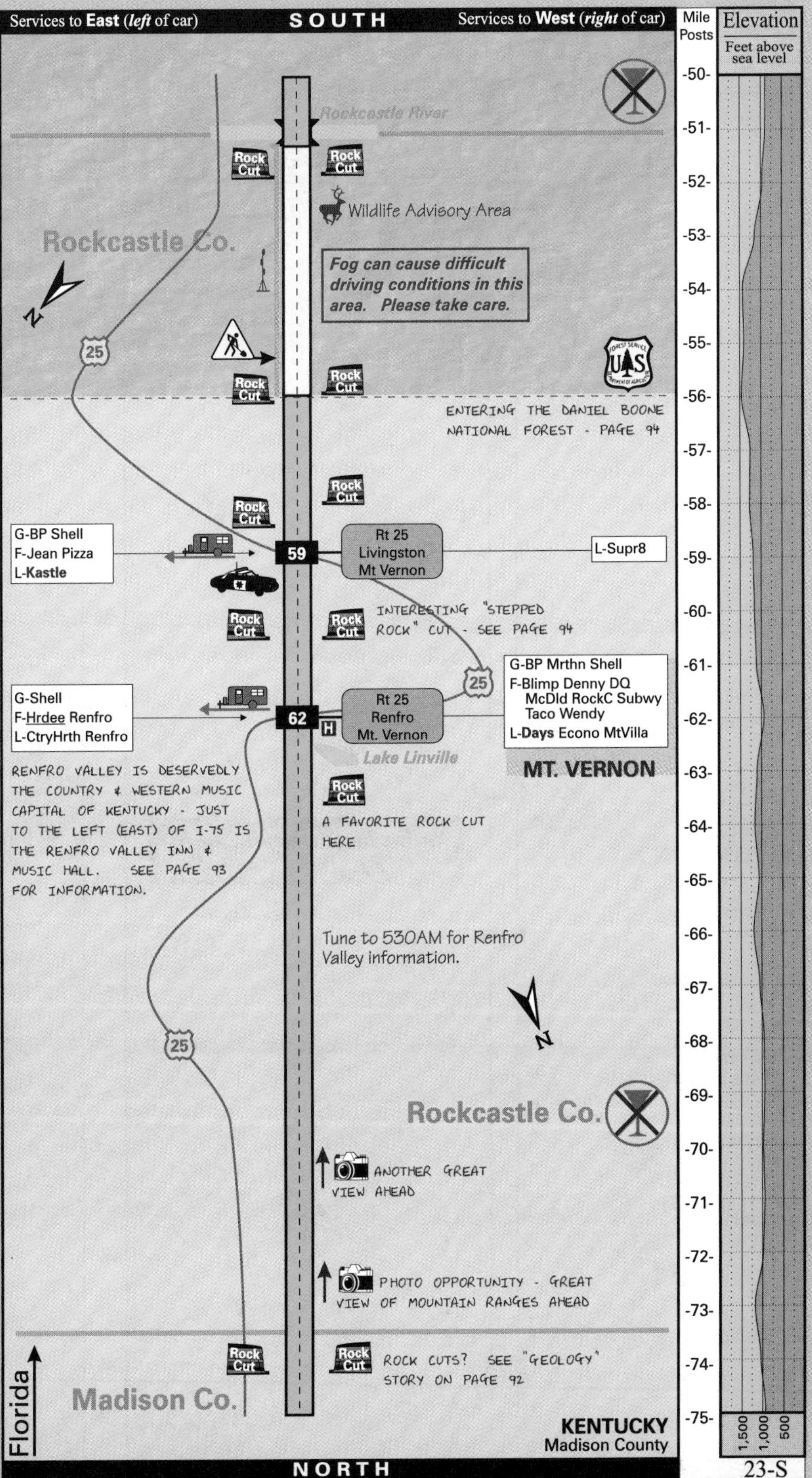

Services to East (left of car)
SOUTH
Services to West (right of car)
Mile Posts
Elevation
Feet above sea level
Rockcastle River
Rock Cut
Wildlife Advisory Area
Rockcastle Co.
Fog can cause difficult driving conditions in this area. Please take care.
25
N
ENTERING THE DANIEL BOONE NATIONAL FOREST - PAGE 94
G-BP Shell
F-Jean Pizza
L-Kastle
59
Rt 25 Livingston Mt Vernon
L-Supr8
INTERESTING "STEPPED ROCK" CUT - SEE PAGE 94
G-BP Mrthn Shell
F-Blimp Denny DQ McDld RockC Subwy Taco Wendy
L-Days Econo MtVilla
G-Shell
F-Hrdee Renfro
L-CtryHrth Renfro
62
Rt 25 Renfro Mt. Vernon
Lake Linville
MT. VERNON
RENFRO VALLEY IS DESERVEDLY THE COUNTRY & WESTERN MUSIC CAPITAL OF KENTUCKY - JUST TO THE LEFT (EAST) OF I-75 IS THE RENFRO VALLEY INN & MUSIC HALL. SEE PAGE 93 FOR INFORMATION.
A FAVORITE ROCK CUT HERE
Tune to 530AM for Renfro Valley information.
Rockcastle Co.
ANOTHER GREAT VIEW AHEAD
PHOTO OPPORTUNITY - GREAT VIEW OF MOUNTAIN RANGES AHEAD
ROCK CUTS? SEE "GEOLOGY" STORY ON PAGE 92
Madison Co.
Florida
KENTUCKY
Madison County
NORTH
-50- -51- -52- -53- -54- -55- -56- -57- -58- -59- -60- -61- -62- -63- -64- -65- -66- -67- -68- -69- -70- -71- -72- -73- -74- -75-
1,500 1,000 500

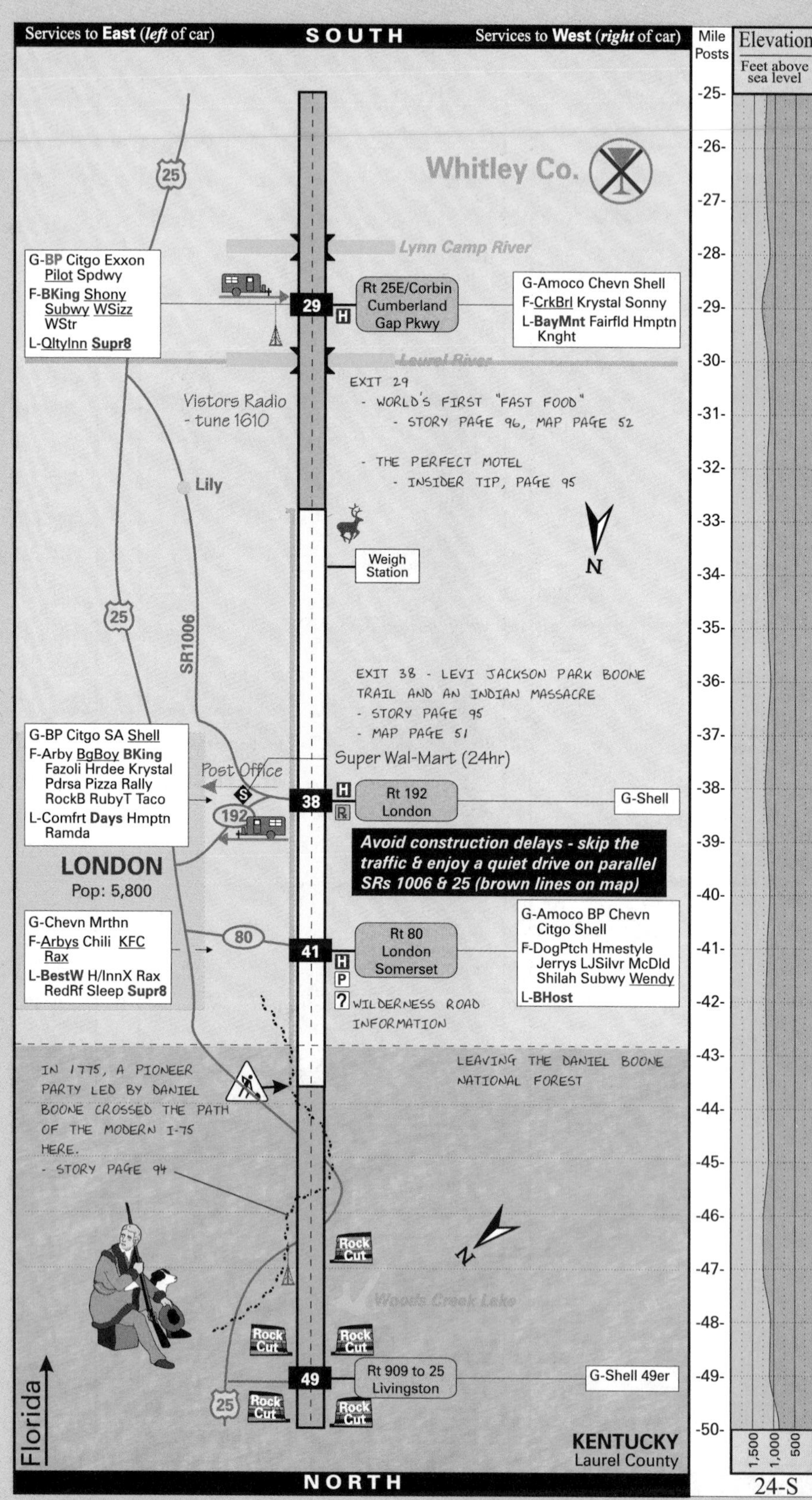

Services to East (left of car)
SOUTH
Services to West (right of car)
Mile Posts
Elevation
Feet above sea level
Whitley Co.
Lynn Camp River
G-BP Citgo Exxon Pilot Spdwy
F-BKing Shony Subwy WSizz WStr
L-QltyInn Supr8
29
Rt 25E/Corbin Cumberland Gap Pkwy
G-Amoco Chevn Shell
F-CrkBrl Krystal Sonny
L-BayMnt Fairfld Hmptn Knght
Laurel River
EXIT 29
- WORLD'S FIRST "FAST FOOD"
- STORY PAGE 96, MAP PAGE 52
- THE PERFECT MOTEL
- INSIDER TIP, PAGE 95
Vistors Radio - tune 1610
Lily
Weigh Station
N
25
SR1006
EXIT 38 - LEVI JACKSON PARK BOONE TRAIL AND AN INDIAN MASSACRE
- STORY PAGE 95
- MAP PAGE 51
G-BP Citgo SA Shell
F-Arby BgBoy BKing Fazoli Hrdee Krystal Pdrsa Pizza Rally RockB RubyT Taco
L-Comfrt Days Hmptn Ramda
Post Office
Super Wal-Mart (24hr)
192
38
Rt 192 London
G-Shell
Avoid construction delays - skip the traffic & enjoy a quiet drive on parallel SRs 1006 & 25 (brown lines on map)
LONDON
Pop: 5,800
G-Chevn Mrthn
F-Arbys Chili KFC Rax
L-BestW H/InnX Rax RedRf Sleep Supr8
80
41
Rt 80 London Somerset
G-Amoco BP Chevn Citgo Shell
F-DogPtch Hmestyle Jerrys LJSilvr McDld Shilah Subwy Wendy
L-BHost
WILDERNESS ROAD INFORMATION
LEAVING THE DANIEL BOONE NATIONAL FOREST
IN 1775, A PIONEER PARTY LED BY DANIEL BOONE CROSSED THE PATH OF THE MODERN I-75 HERE.
- STORY PAGE 94
Rock Cut
Woods Creek Lake
49
Rt 909 to 25 Livingston
G-Shell 49er
Florida
KENTUCKY
Laurel County
NORTH
-25- -26- -27- -28- -29- -30- -31- -32- -33- -34- -35- -36- -37- -38- -39- -40- -41- -42- -43- -44- -45- -46- -47- -48- -49- -50-
1,500 1,000 500

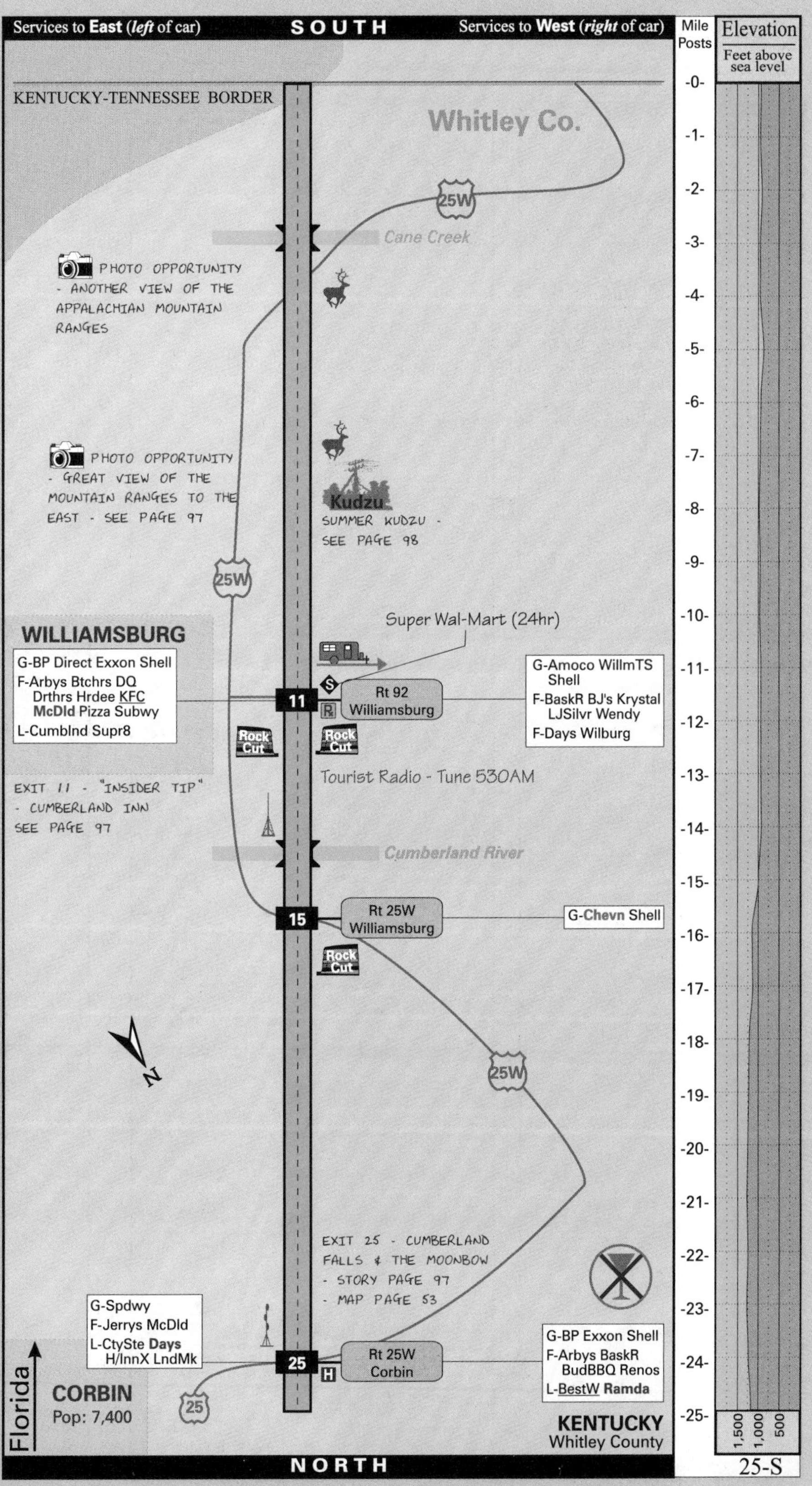

Services to East (left of car)
SOUTH
Services to West (right of car)
Mile Posts
Elevation
Feet above sea level
KENTUCKY-TENNESSEE BORDER
Whitley Co.
25W
Cane Creek
PHOTO OPPORTUNITY - ANOTHER VIEW OF THE APPALACHIAN MOUNTAIN RANGES
PHOTO OPPORTUNITY - GREAT VIEW OF THE MOUNTAIN RANGES TO THE EAST - SEE PAGE 97
Kudzu
SUMMER KUDZU - SEE PAGE 98
25W
Super Wal-Mart (24hr)
WILLIAMSBURG
G-BP Direct Exxon Shell
F-Arbys Btchrs DQ Drthrs Hrdee KFC McDld Pizza Subwy
L-Cumblnd Supr8
11
Rt 92 Williamsburg
G-Amoco WillmTS Shell
F-BaskR BJ's Krystal LJSilvr Wendy
F-Days Wilburg
Rock Cut
Rock Cut
Tourist Radio - Tune 530AM
EXIT 11 - "INSIDER TIP" - CUMBERLAND INN SEE PAGE 97
Cumberland River
15
Rt 25W Williamsburg
G-Chevn Shell
Rock Cut
N
25W
EXIT 25 - CUMBERLAND FALLS & THE MOONBOW - STORY PAGE 97 - MAP PAGE 53
G-Spdwy
F-Jerrys McDld
L-CtySte Days H/InnX LndMk
25
Rt 25W Corbin
G-BP Exxon Shell
F-Arbys BaskR BudBBQ Renos
L-BestW Ramda
Florida
CORBIN
Pop: 7,400
25
KENTUCKY
Whitley County
NORTH
-0-
-1-
-2-
-3-
-4-
-5-
-6-
-7-
-8-
-9-
-10-
-11-
-12-
-13-
-14-
-15-
-16-
-17-
-18-
-19-
-20-
-21-
-22-
-23-
-24-
-25-
1,500
1,000
500

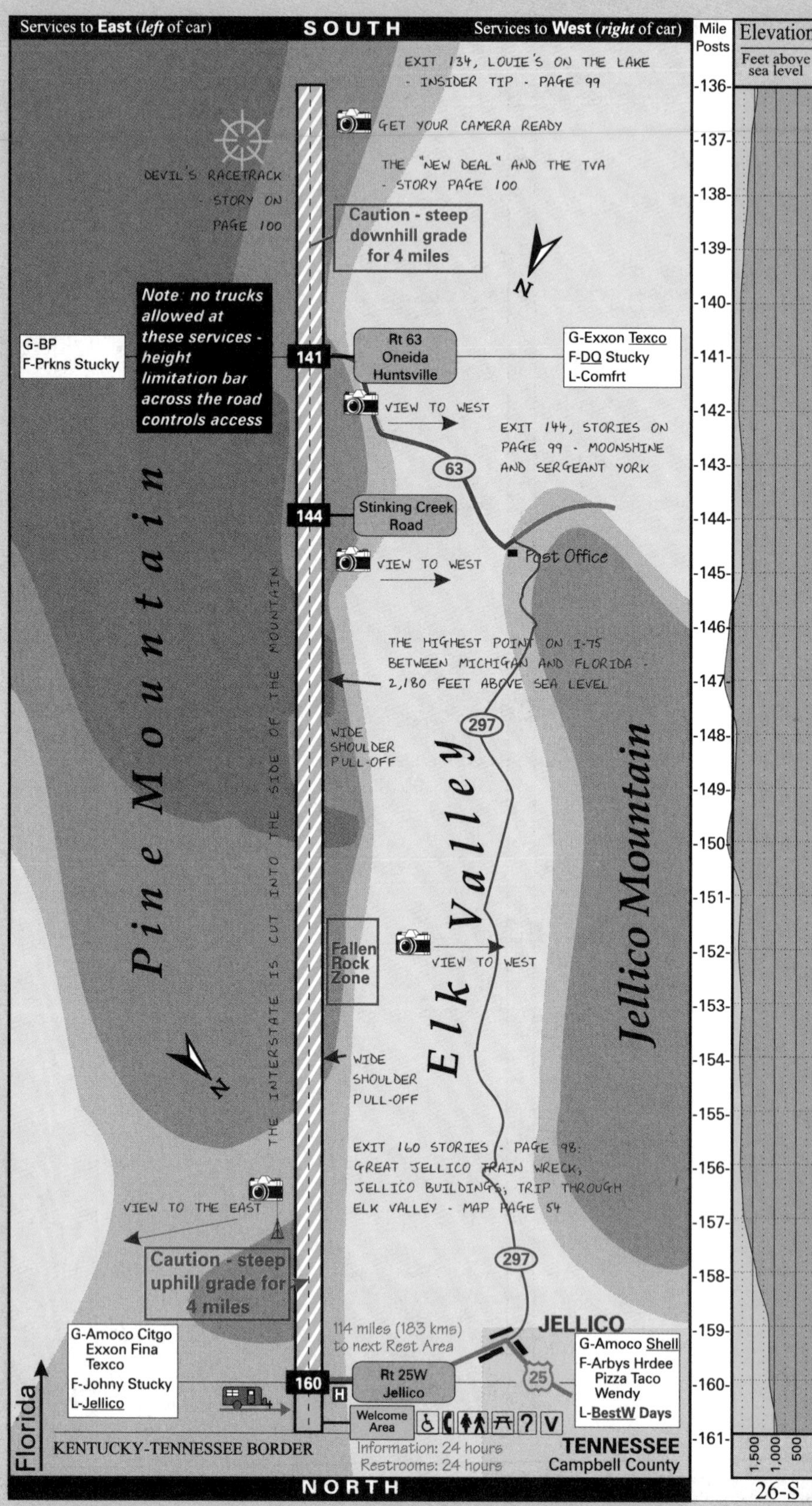

Services to East (left of car)
SOUTH
Services to West (right of car)
Mile Posts
Elevation
Feet above sea level
EXIT 134, LOUIE'S ON THE LAKE - INSIDER TIP - PAGE 99
GET YOUR CAMERA READY
THE "NEW DEAL" AND THE TVA - STORY PAGE 100
DEVIL'S RACETRACK - STORY ON PAGE 100
Caution - steep downhill grade for 4 miles
N
Note: no trucks allowed at these services - height limitation bar across the road controls access
G-BP
F-Prkns Stucky
141
Rt 63 Oneida Huntsville
G-Exxon Texco
F-DQ Stucky
L-Comfrt
VIEW TO WEST
EXIT 144, STORIES ON PAGE 99 - MOONSHINE AND SERGEANT YORK
63
144
Stinking Creek Road
VIEW TO WEST
Post Office
Pine Mountain
THE INTERSTATE IS CUT INTO THE SIDE OF THE MOUNTAIN
THE HIGHEST POINT ON I-75 BETWEEN MICHIGAN AND FLORIDA - 2,180 FEET ABOVE SEA LEVEL
297
WIDE SHOULDER PULL-OFF
Elk Valley
Jellico Mountain
Fallen Rock Zone
VIEW TO WEST
N
WIDE SHOULDER PULL-OFF
EXIT 160 STORIES - PAGE 98: GREAT JELLICO TRAIN WRECK; JELLICO BUILDINGS; TRIP THROUGH ELK VALLEY - MAP PAGE 54
VIEW TO THE EAST
297
Caution - steep uphill grade for 4 miles
JELLICO
114 miles (183 kms) to next Rest Area
G-Amoco Citgo Exxon Fina Texco
F-Johny Stucky
L-Jellico
160
Rt 25W Jellico
25
G-Amoco Shell
F-Arbys Hrdee Pizza Taco Wendy
L-BestW Days
Florida
H
Welcome Area
KENTUCKY-TENNESSEE BORDER
Information: 24 hours
Restrooms: 24 hours
TENNESSEE
Campbell County
NORTH
-136-
-137-
-138-
-139-
-140-
-141-
-142-
-143-
-144-
-145-
-146-
-147-
-148-
-149-
-150-
-151-
-152-
-153-
-154-
-155-
-156-
-157-
-158-
-159-
-160-
-161-
1,500
1,000
500

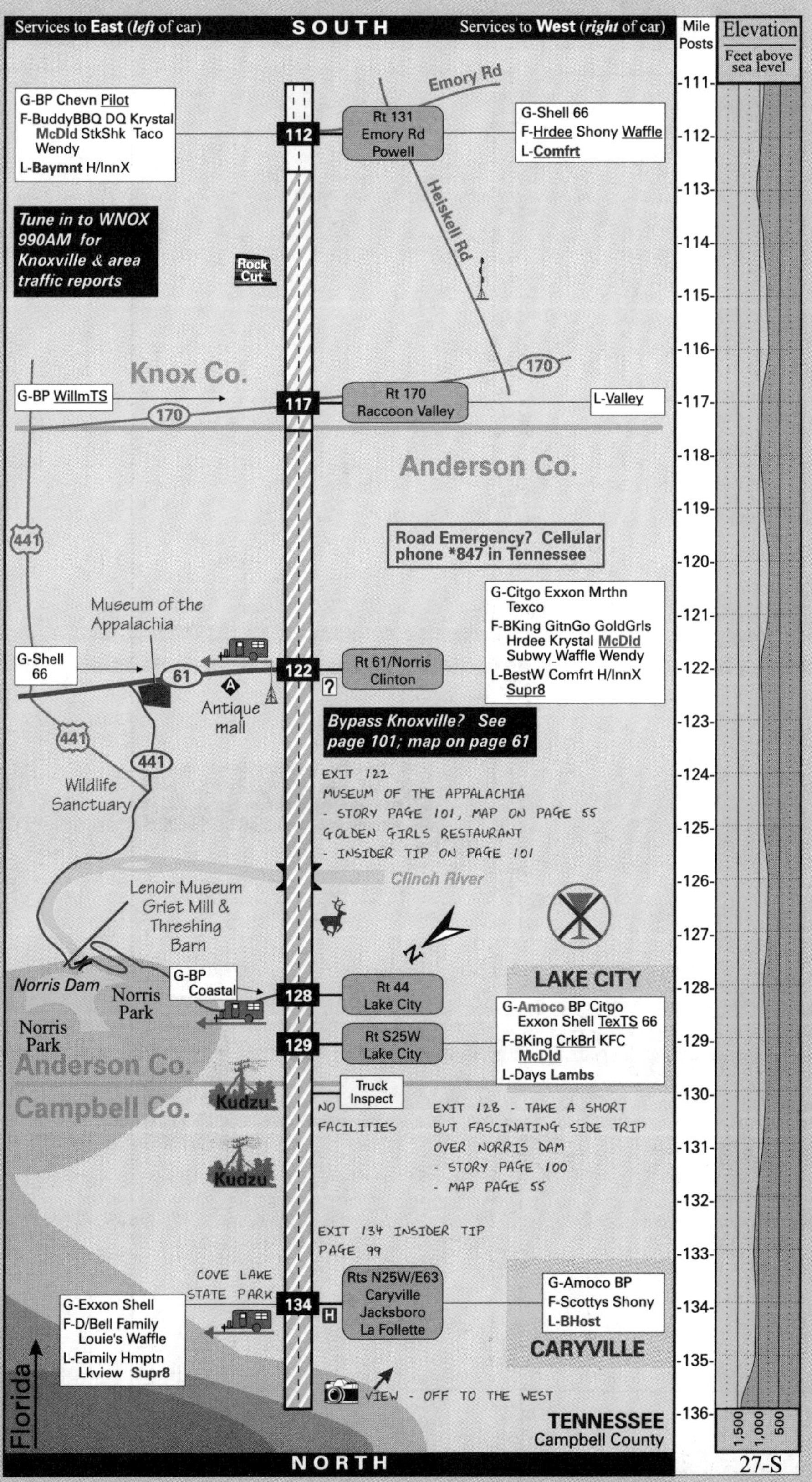

Services to East (left of car)
SOUTH
Services to West (right of car)
Mile Posts
Elevation
Feet above sea level
G-BP Chevn Pilot
F-BuddyBBQ DQ Krystal McDld StkShk Taco Wendy
L-Baymnt H/InnX
112
Rt 131 Emory Rd Powell
Emory Rd
G-Shell 66
F-Hrdee Shony Waffle
L-Comfrt
Heiskell Rd
Tune in to WNOX 990AM for Knoxville & area traffic reports
Rock Cut
Knox Co.
G-BP WillmTS
170
117
Rt 170 Raccoon Valley
170
L-Valley
Anderson Co.
441
Road Emergency? Cellular phone *847 in Tennessee
Museum of the Appalachia
G-Shell 66
61
Antique mall
122
Rt 61/Norris Clinton
G-Citgo Exxon Mrthn Texco
F-BKing GitnGo GoldGrls Hrdee Krystal McDld Subwy Waffle Wendy
L-BestW Comfrt H/InnX Supr8
Bypass Knoxville? See page 101; map on page 61
441
441
Wildlife Sanctuary
EXIT 122
MUSEUM OF THE APPALACHIA
- STORY PAGE 101, MAP ON PAGE 55
GOLDEN GIRLS RESTAURANT
- INSIDER TIP ON PAGE 101
Clinch River
Lenoir Museum Grist Mill & Threshing Barn
N
Norris Dam
G-BP Coastal
Norris Park
128
Rt 44 Lake City
LAKE CITY
G-Amoco BP Citgo Exxon Shell TexTS 66
F-BKing CrkBrl KFC McDld
L-Days Lambs
Norris Park
129
Rt S25W Lake City
Anderson Co.
Campbell Co.
Kudzu
Truck Inspect
NO FACILITIES
EXIT 128 - TAKE A SHORT BUT FASCINATING SIDE TRIP OVER NORRIS DAM
- STORY PAGE 100
- MAP PAGE 55
Kudzu
EXIT 134 INSIDER TIP PAGE 99
COVE LAKE STATE PARK
G-Exxon Shell
F-D/Bell Family Louie's Waffle
L-Family Hmptn Lkview Supr8
134
H
Rts N25W/E63 Caryville Jacksboro La Follette
G-Amoco BP
F-Scottys Shony
L-BHost
CARYVILLE
VIEW - OFF TO THE WEST
Florida
TENNESSEE
Campbell County
NORTH
-111- -112- -113- -114- -115- -116- -117- -118- -119- -120- -121- -122- -123- -124- -125- -126- -127- -128- -129- -130- -131- -132- -133- -134- -135- -136-
1,500 1,000 500

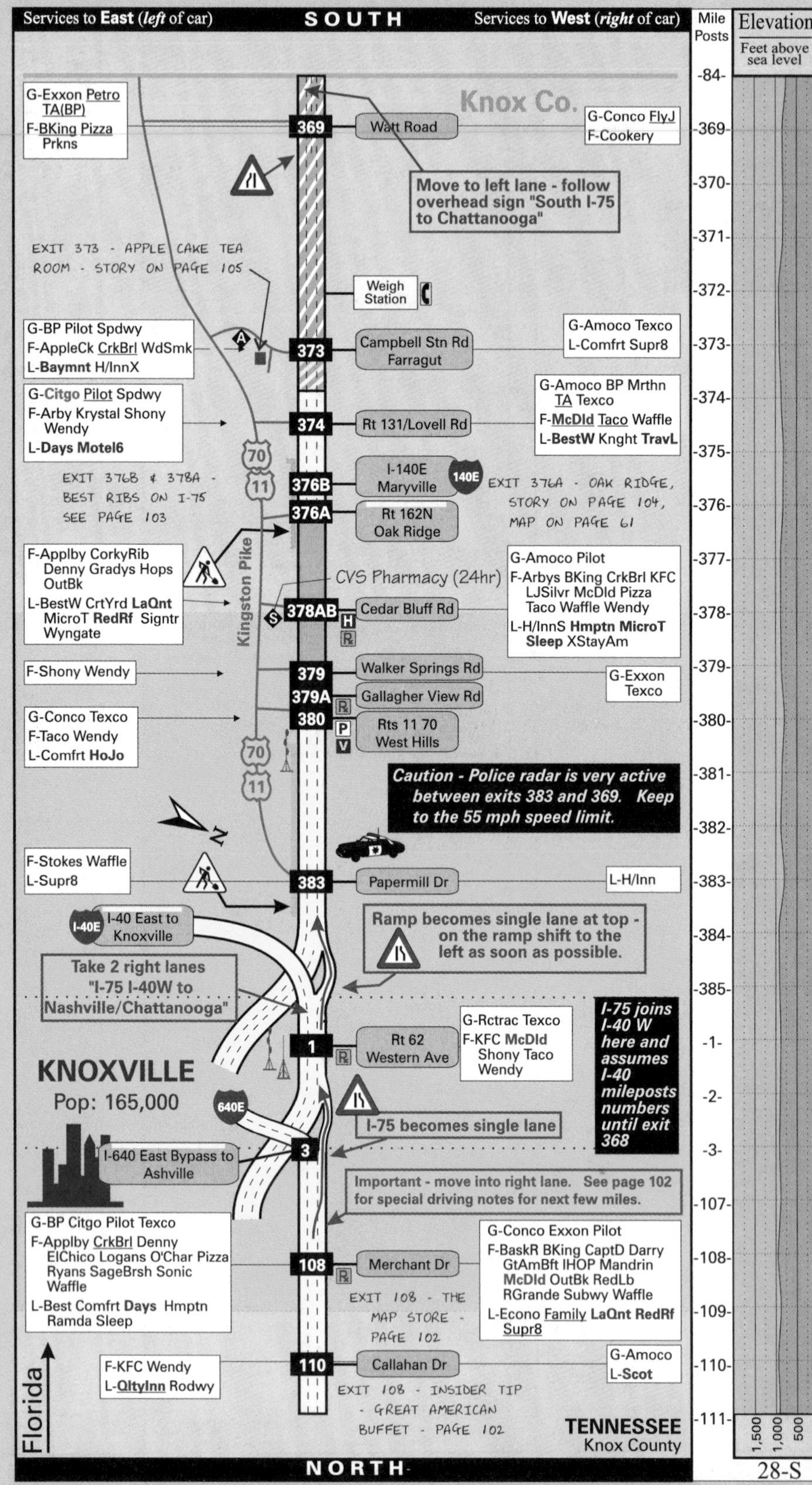
Services to East (left of car)
SOUTH
Services to West (right of car)
Mile Posts
Elevation
Feet above sea level
Knox Co.
G-Exxon Petro TA(BP)
F-BKing Pizza Prkns
369
Watt Road
G-Conco FlyJ
F-Cookery
Move to left lane - follow overhead sign "South I-75 to Chattanooga"
EXIT 373 - APPLE CAKE TEA ROOM - STORY ON PAGE 105
Weigh Station
G-BP Pilot Spdwy
F-AppleCk CrkBrl WdSmk
L-Baymnt H/InnX
373
Campbell Stn Rd Farragut
G-Amoco Texco
L-Comfrt Supr8
G-Citgo Pilot Spdwy
F-Arby Krystal Shony Wendy
L-Days Motel6
374
Rt 131/Lovell Rd
G-Amoco BP Mrthn TA Texco
F-McDld Taco Waffle
L-BestW Knght TravL
EXIT 376B & 378A - BEST RIBS ON I-75 SEE PAGE 103
376B
I-140E Maryville
140E
EXIT 376A - OAK RIDGE, STORY ON PAGE 104, MAP ON PAGE 61
376A
Rt 162N Oak Ridge
Kingston Pike
F-Applby CorkyRib Denny Gradys Hops OutBk
L-BestW CrtYrd LaQnt MicroT RedRf Signtr Wyngate
CVS Pharmacy (24hr)
G-Amoco Pilot
F-Arbys BKing CrkBrl KFC LJSilvr McDld Pizza Taco Waffle Wendy
L-H/InnS Hmptn MicroT Sleep XStayAm
378AB
Cedar Bluff Rd
F-Shony Wendy
379
Walker Springs Rd
G-Exxon Texco
379A
Gallagher View Rd
G-Conco Texco
F-Taco Wendy
L-Comfrt HoJo
380
Rts 11 70 West Hills
70
11
Caution - Police radar is very active between exits 383 and 369. Keep to the 55 mph speed limit.
N
F-Stokes Waffle
L-Supr8
383
Papermill Dr
L-H/Inn
I-40E
I-40 East to Knoxville
Ramp becomes single lane at top - on the ramp shift to the left as soon as possible.
Take 2 right lanes "I-75 I-40W to Nashville/Chattanooga"
G-Rctrac Texco
F-KFC McDld Shony Taco Wendy
1
Rt 62 Western Ave
I-75 joins I-40 W here and assumes I-40 mileposts numbers until exit 368
KNOXVILLE
Pop: 165,000
640E
I-75 becomes single lane
3
I-640 East Bypass to Ashville
Important - move into right lane. See page 102 for special driving notes for next few miles.
G-BP Citgo Pilot Texco
F-Applby CrkBrl Denny ElChico Logans O'Char Pizza Ryans SageBrsh Sonic Waffle
L-Best Comfrt Days Hmptn Ramda Sleep
108
Merchant Dr
G-Conco Exxon Pilot
F-BaskR BKing CaptD Darry GtAmBft IHOP Mandrin McDld OutBk RedLb RGrande Subwy Waffle
L-Econo Family LaQnt RedRf Supr8
EXIT 108 - THE MAP STORE - PAGE 102
F-KFC Wendy
L-QltyInn Rodwy
110
Callahan Dr
G-Amoco
L-Scot
EXIT 108 - INSIDER TIP - GREAT AMERICAN BUFFET - PAGE 102
Florida
TENNESSEE
Knox County
NORTH
-84-
-369-
-370-
-371-
-372-
-373-
-374-
-375-
-376-
-377-
-378-
-379-
-380-
-381-
-382-
-383-
-384-
-385-
-1-
-2-
-3-
-107-
-108-
-109-
-110-
-111-
1,500
1,000
500

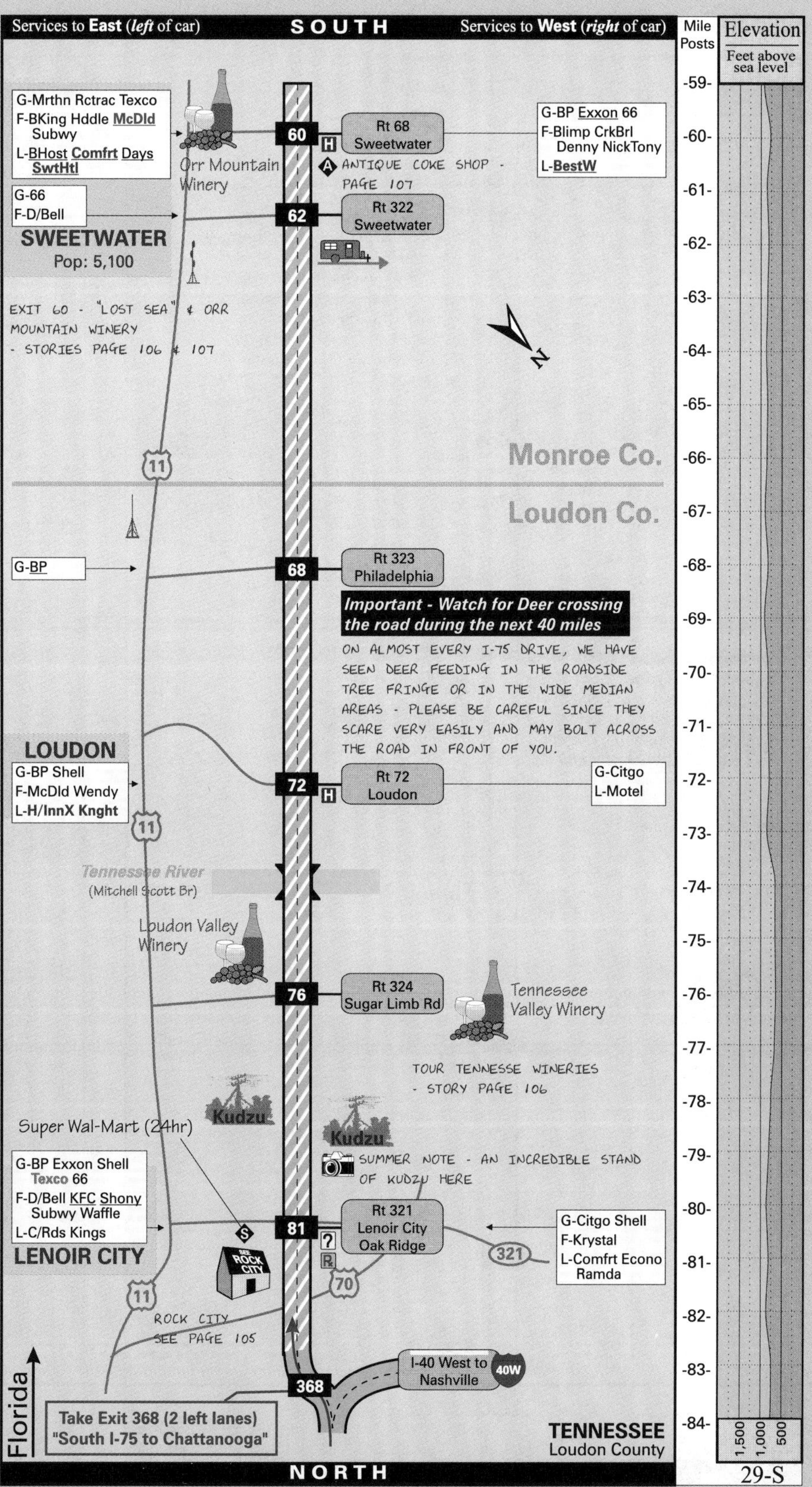

Services to East (left of car)
SOUTH
Services to West (right of car)
Mile Posts
Elevation
Feet above sea level
G-Mrthn Rctrac Texco
F-BKing Hddle McDld Subwy
L-BHost Comfrt Days SwtHtl
Orr Mountain Winery
60
Rt 68 Sweetwater
G-BP Exxon 66
F-Blimp CrkBrl Denny NickTony
L-BestW
ANTIQUE COKE SHOP - PAGE 107
G-66
F-D/Bell
62
Rt 322 Sweetwater
SWEETWATER
Pop: 5,100
EXIT 60 - "LOST SEA" & ORR MOUNTAIN WINERY - STORIES PAGE 106 & 107
N
Monroe Co.
Loudon Co.
G-BP
68
Rt 323 Philadelphia
Important - Watch for Deer crossing the road during the next 40 miles
ON ALMOST EVERY I-75 DRIVE, WE HAVE SEEN DEER FEEDING IN THE ROADSIDE TREE FRINGE OR IN THE WIDE MEDIAN AREAS - PLEASE BE CAREFUL SINCE THEY SCARE VERY EASILY AND MAY BOLT ACROSS THE ROAD IN FRONT OF YOU.
LOUDON
G-BP Shell
F-McDld Wendy
L-H/InnX Knght
72
Rt 72 Loudon
G-Citgo
L-Motel
11
Tennessee River
(Mitchell Scott Br)
Loudon Valley Winery
76
Rt 324 Sugar Limb Rd
Tennessee Valley Winery
TOUR TENNESSE WINERIES - STORY PAGE 106
Kudzu
Kudzu
Super Wal-Mart (24hr)
SUMMER NOTE - AN INCREDIBLE STAND OF KUDZU HERE
G-BP Exxon Shell Texco 66
F-D/Bell KFC Shony Subwy Waffle
L-C/Rds Kings
LENOIR CITY
81
Rt 321 Lenoir City Oak Ridge
G-Citgo Shell
F-Krystal
L-Comfrt Econo Ramda
321
70
SEE ROCK CITY
ROCK CITY SEE PAGE 105
I-40 West to Nashville
40W
368
Florida
Take Exit 368 (2 left lanes) "South I-75 to Chattanooga"
TENNESSEE
Loudon County
NORTH
-59- -60- -61- -62- -63- -64- -65- -66- -67- -68- -69- -70- -71- -72- -73- -74- -75- -76- -77- -78- -79- -80- -81- -82- -83- -84-
1,500 1,000 500

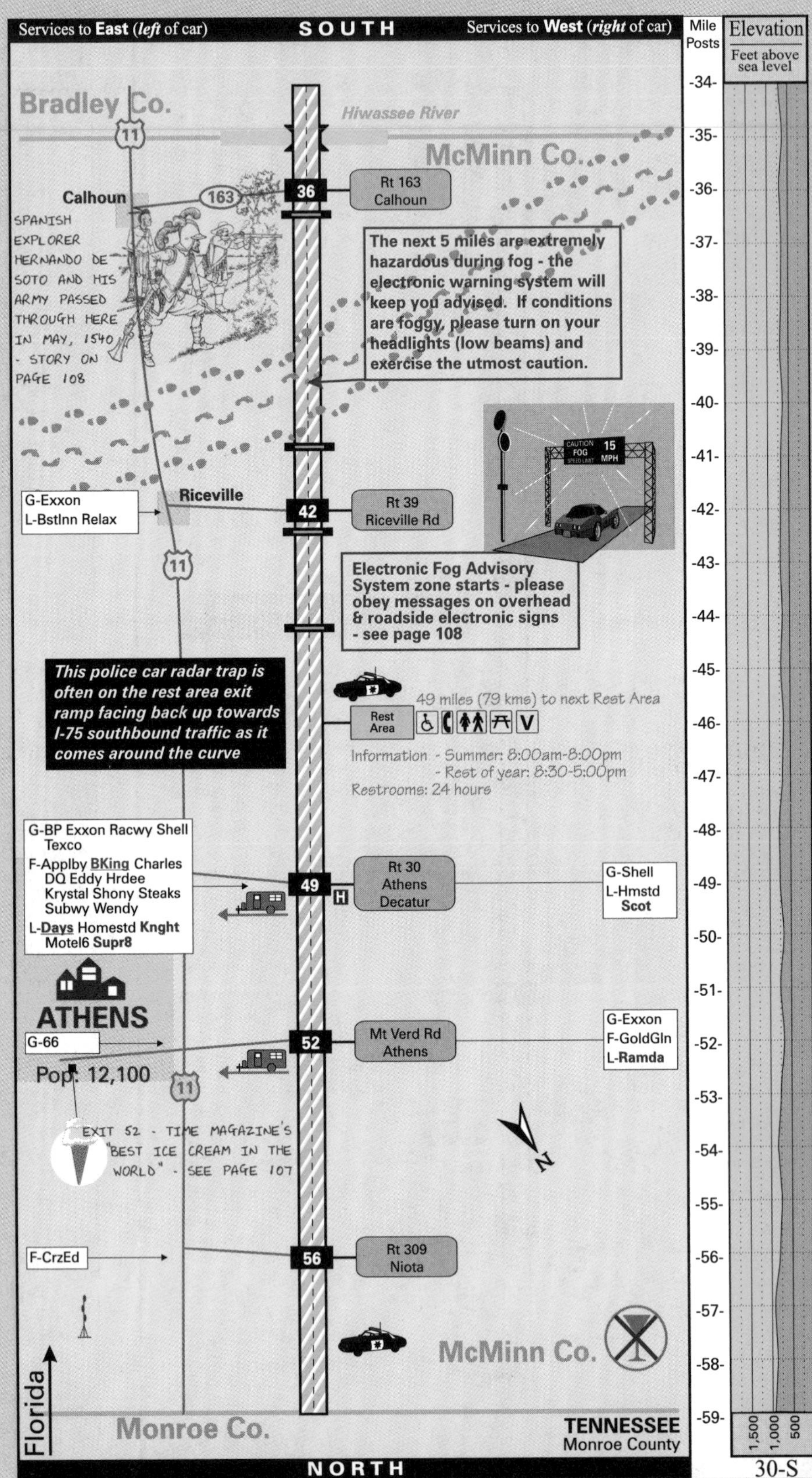

Services to East (left of car)
SOUTH
Services to West (right of car)
Mile Posts
Elevation
Feet above sea level
Bradley Co.
Hiwassee River
McMinn Co.
11
Calhoun
163
36
Rt 163 Calhoun
SPANISH EXPLORER HERNANDO DE SOTO AND HIS ARMY PASSED THROUGH HERE IN MAY, 1540 - STORY ON PAGE 108
The next 5 miles are extremely hazardous during fog - the electronic warning system will keep you advised. If conditions are foggy, please turn on your headlights (low beams) and exercise the utmost caution.
CAUTION FOG SPEED LIMIT 15 MPH
G-Exxon
L-BstInn Relax
Riceville
42
Rt 39 Riceville Rd
11
Electronic Fog Advisory System zone starts - please obey messages on overhead & roadside electronic signs - see page 108
This police car radar trap is often on the rest area exit ramp facing back up towards I-75 southbound traffic as it comes around the curve
Rest Area
49 miles (79 kms) to next Rest Area
V
Information - Summer: 8:00am-8:00pm
- Rest of year: 8:30-5:00pm
Restrooms: 24 hours
G-BP Exxon Racwy Shell Texco
F-Applby BKing Charles DQ Eddy Hrdee Krystal Shony Steaks Subwy Wendy
L-Days Homestd Knght Motel6 Supr8
49
H
Rt 30 Athens Decatur
G-Shell
L-Hmstd Scot
ATHENS
G-66
Pop. 12,100
52
Mt Verd Rd Athens
G-Exxon
F-GoldGln
L-Ramda
11
EXIT 52 - TIME MAGAZINE'S "BEST ICE CREAM IN THE WORLD" - SEE PAGE 107
N
F-CrzEd
56
Rt 309 Niota
McMinn Co.
Florida
Monroe Co.
TENNESSEE
Monroe County
NORTH
-34-
-35-
-36-
-37-
-38-
-39-
-40-
-41-
-42-
-43-
-44-
-45-
-46-
-47-
-48-
-49-
-50-
-51-
-52-
-53-
-54-
-55-
-56-
-57-
-58-
-59-
1,500
1,000
500

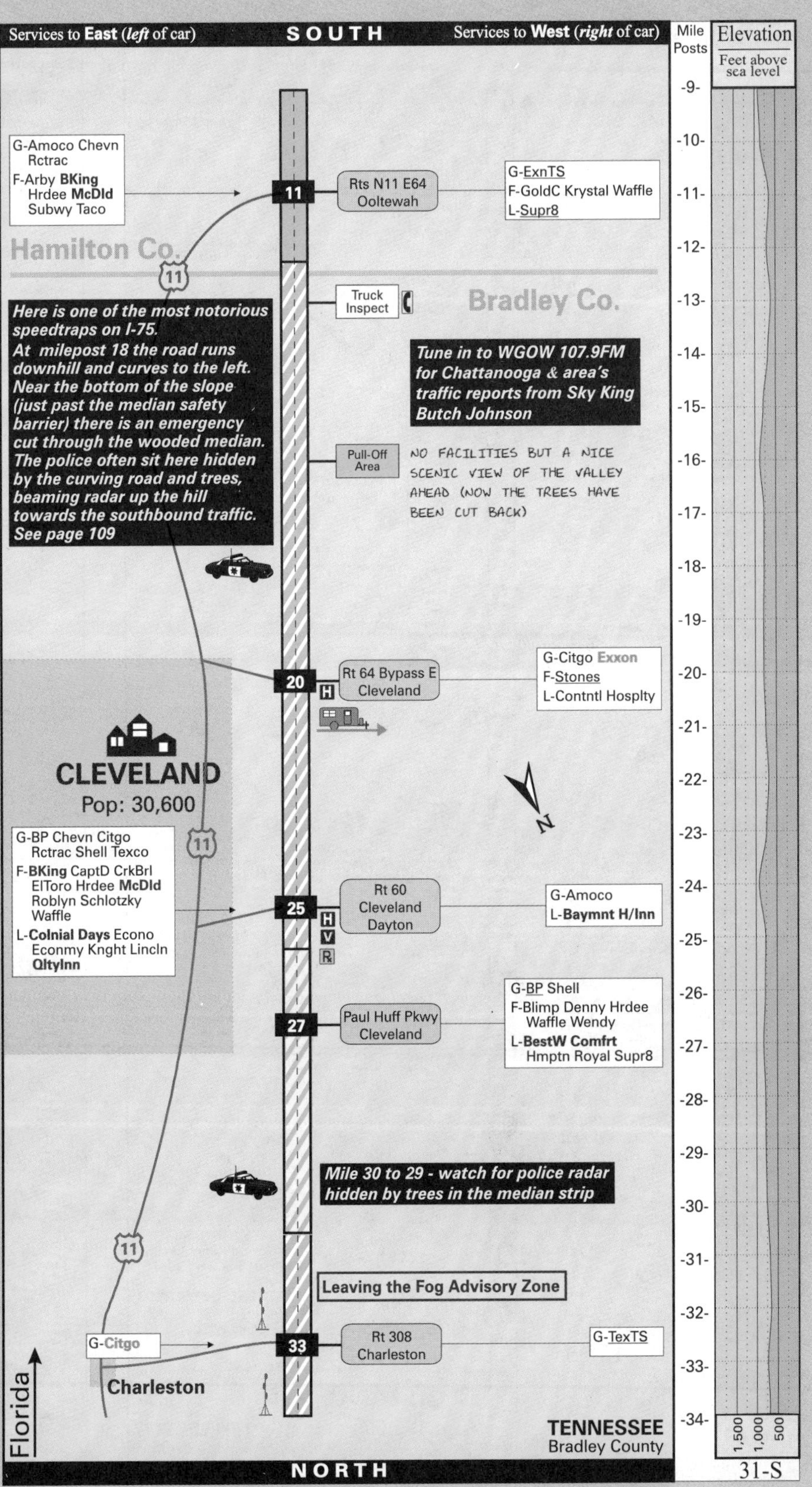

Services to East (left of car)
SOUTH
Services to West (right of car)
Mile Posts
Elevation
Feet above sea level
G-Amoco Chevn Rctrac
F-Arby BKing Hrdee McDld Subwy Taco
11
Rts N11 E64 Ooltewah
G-ExnTS
F-GoldC Krystal Waffle
L-Supr8
Hamilton Co.
11
Truck Inspect
Bradley Co.
Here is one of the most notorious speedtraps on I-75.
At milepost 18 the road runs downhill and curves to the left. Near the bottom of the slope (just past the median safety barrier) there is an emergency cut through the wooded median. The police often sit here hidden by the curving road and trees, beaming radar up the hill towards the southbound traffic.
See page 109
Tune in to WGOW 107.9FM for Chattanooga & area's traffic reports from Sky King Butch Johnson
Pull-Off Area
NO FACILITIES BUT A NICE SCENIC VIEW OF THE VALLEY AHEAD (NOW THE TREES HAVE BEEN CUT BACK)
20
Rt 64 Bypass E Cleveland
H
G-Citgo Exxon
F-Stones
L-Contntl Hosplty
CLEVELAND
Pop: 30,600
N
G-BP Chevn Citgo Rctrac Shell Texco
F-BKing CaptD CrkBrl ElToro Hrdee McDld Roblyn Schlotzky Waffle
L-Colnial Days Econo Econmy Knght Lincln QltyInn
11
25
H
V
R
Rt 60 Cleveland Dayton
G-Amoco
L-Baymnt H/Inn
27
Paul Huff Pkwy Cleveland
G-BP Shell
F-Blimp Denny Hrdee Waffle Wendy
L-BestW Comfrt Hmptn Royal Supr8
Mile 30 to 29 - watch for police radar hidden by trees in the median strip
11
Leaving the Fog Advisory Zone
G-Citgo
33
Rt 308 Charleston
G-TexTS
Charleston
Florida
TENNESSEE
Bradley County
NORTH
-9-
-10-
-11-
-12-
-13-
-14-
-15-
-16-
-17-
-18-
-19-
-20-
-21-
-22-
-23-
-24-
-25-
-26-
-27-
-28-
-29-
-30-
-31-
-32-
-33-
-34-
1,500
1,000
500

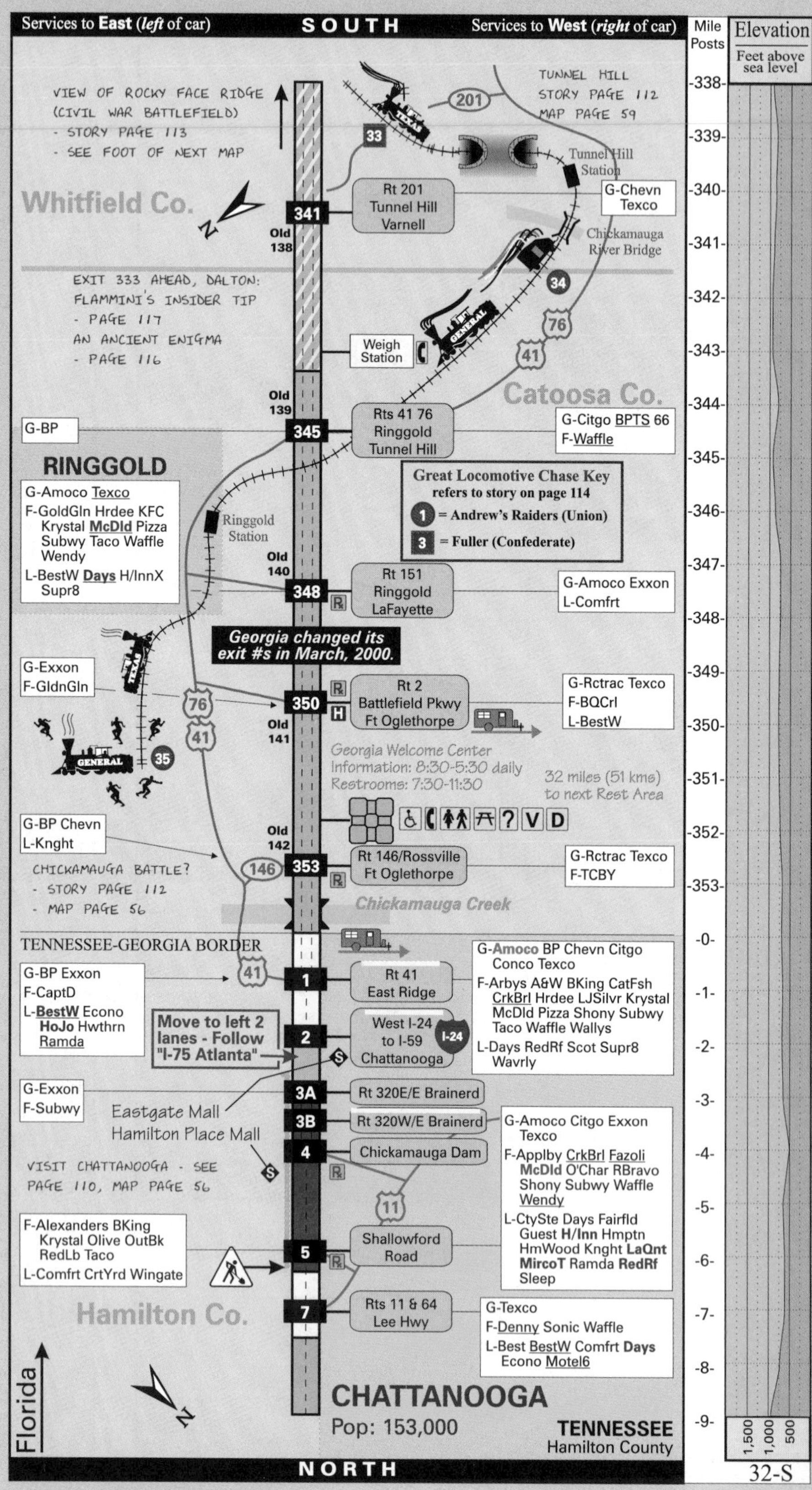

Services to East (left of car)
SOUTH
Services to West (right of car)
Mile Posts
Elevation
Feet above sea level
VIEW OF ROCKY FACE RIDGE (CIVIL WAR BATTLEFIELD)
- STORY PAGE 113
- SEE FOOT OF NEXT MAP
TUNNEL HILL
STORY PAGE 112
MAP PAGE 59
201
33
Tunnel Hill Station
Whitfield Co.
341
Rt 201
Tunnel Hill
Varnell
G-Chevn
Texco
Old 138
Chickamauga River Bridge
34
EXIT 333 AHEAD, DALTON:
FLAMMINI'S INSIDER TIP
- PAGE 117
AN ANCIENT ENIGMA
- PAGE 116
76
Weigh Station
41
Catoosa Co.
Old 139
G-BP
345
Rts 41 76
Ringgold
Tunnel Hill
G-Citgo BPTS 66
F-Waffle
RINGGOLD
G-Amoco Texco
F-GoldGln Hrdee KFC Krystal McDld Pizza Subwy Taco Waffle Wendy
L-BestW Days H/InnX Supr8
Ringgold Station
Great Locomotive Chase Key
refers to story on page 114
1 = Andrew's Raiders (Union)
3 = Fuller (Confederate)
Old 140
348
Rt 151
Ringgold
LaFayette
G-Amoco Exxon
L-Comfrt
Georgia changed its exit #s in March, 2000.
G-Exxon
F-GldnGln
76
41
350
Rt 2
Battlefield Pkwy
Ft Oglethorpe
G-Rctrac Texco
F-BQCrl
L-BestW
Old 141
35
Georgia Welcome Center
Information: 8:30-5:30 daily
Restrooms: 7:30-11:30
32 miles (51 kms) to next Rest Area
? V D
G-BP Chevn
L-Knght
Old 142
146
353
Rt 146/Rossville
Ft Oglethorpe
G-Rctrac Texco
F-TCBY
CHICKAMAUGA BATTLE?
- STORY PAGE 112
- MAP PAGE 56
Chickamauga Creek
TENNESSEE-GEORGIA BORDER
G-BP Exxon
F-CaptD
L-BestW Econo HoJo Hwthrn Ramda
41
1
Rt 41
East Ridge
G-Amoco BP Chevn Citgo Conco Texco
F-Arbys A&W BKing CatFsh CrkBrl Hrdee LJSilvr Krystal McDld Pizza Shony Subwy Taco Waffle Wallys
L-Days RedRf Scot Supr8 Wavrly
Move to left 2 lanes - Follow "I-75 Atlanta"
2
West I-24 to I-59 Chattanooga
I-24
G-Exxon
F-Subwy
3A
Rt 320E/E Brainerd
Eastgate Mall
Hamilton Place Mall
3B
Rt 320W/E Brainerd
G-Amoco Citgo Exxon Texco
F-Applby CrkBrl Fazoli McDld O'Char RBravo Shony Subwy Waffle Wendy
L-CtySte Days Fairfld Guest H/Inn Hmptn HmWood Knght LaQnt MircoT Ramda RedRf Sleep
4
Chickamauga Dam
VISIT CHATTANOOGA - SEE PAGE 110, MAP PAGE 56
11
F-Alexanders BKing Krystal Olive OutBk RedLb Taco
L-Comfrt CrtYrd Wingate
5
Shallowford Road
Hamilton Co.
7
Rts 11 & 64
Lee Hwy
G-Texco
F-Denny Sonic Waffle
L-Best BestW Comfrt Days Econo Motel6
Florida
CHATTANOOGA
Pop: 153,000
TENNESSEE
Hamilton County
NORTH
-338- -339- -340- -341- -342- -343- -344- -345- -346- -347- -348- -349- -350- -351- -352- -353-
-0- -1- -2- -3- -4- -5- -6- -7- -8- -9-
1,500 1,000 500

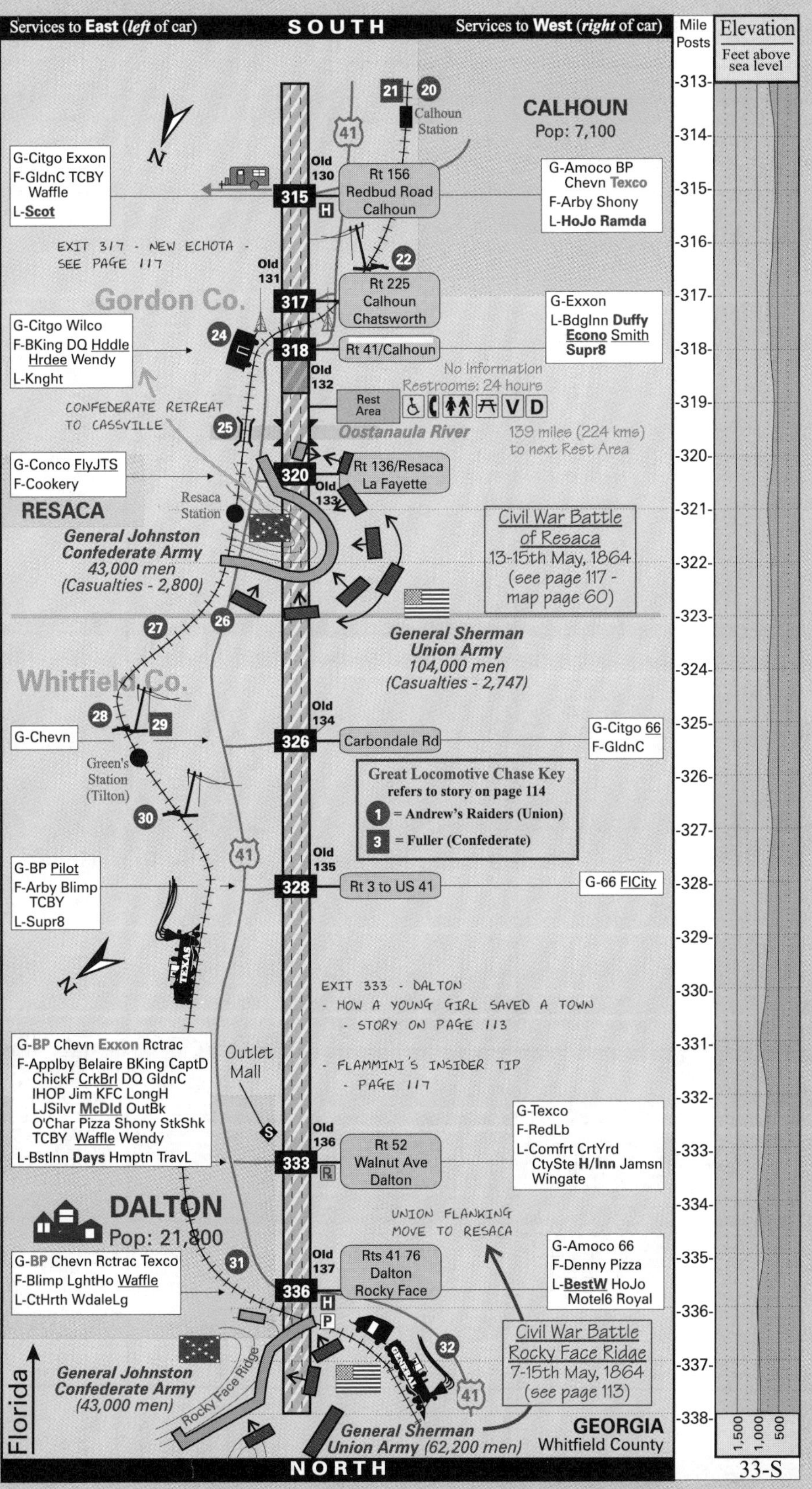
Services to East (left of car)
SOUTH
Services to West (right of car)
Mile Posts
Elevation
Feet above sea level
CALHOUN
Pop: 7,100
Calhoun Station
G-Citgo Exxon
F-GldnC TCBY Waffle
L-Scot
Old 130
315
Rt 156 Redbud Road Calhoun
G-Amoco BP Chevn Texco
F-Arby Shony
L-HoJo Ramda
EXIT 317 - NEW ECHOTA - SEE PAGE 117
Old 131
Gordon Co.
317
Rt 225 Calhoun Chatsworth
G-Exxon
L-BdgInn Duffy Econo Smith Supr8
G-Citgo Wilco
F-BKing DQ Hddle Hrdee Wendy
L-Knght
318
Rt 41/Calhoun
Old 132
No Information
Restrooms: 24 hours
Rest Area
CONFEDERATE RETREAT TO CASSVILLE
Oostanaula River
139 miles (224 kms) to next Rest Area
G-Conco FlyJTS
F-Cookery
320
Rt 136/Resaca La Fayette
Old 133
RESACA
Resaca Station
Civil War Battle of Resaca
13-15th May, 1864
(see page 117 - map page 60)
General Johnston Confederate Army
43,000 men
(Casualties - 2,800)
General Sherman Union Army
104,000 men
(Casualties - 2,747)
Whitfield Co.
Old 134
G-Chevn
326
Carbondale Rd
G-Citgo 66
F-GldnC
Green's Station (Tilton)
Great Locomotive Chase Key
refers to story on page 114
1 = Andrew's Raiders (Union)
3 = Fuller (Confederate)
Old 135
G-BP Pilot
F-Arby Blimp TCBY
L-Supr8
328
Rt 3 to US 41
G-66 FlCity
TEXAS
EXIT 333 - DALTON
- HOW A YOUNG GIRL SAVED A TOWN
- STORY ON PAGE 113
- FLAMMINI'S INSIDER TIP
- PAGE 117
G-BP Chevn Exxon Rctrac
F-Applby Belaire BKing CaptD ChickF CrkBrl DQ GldnC IHOP Jim KFC LongH LJSilvr McDld OutBk O'Char Pizza Shony StkShk TCBY Waffle Wendy
L-BstInn Days Hmptn TravL
Outlet Mall
Old 136
333
Rt 52 Walnut Ave Dalton
G-Texco
F-RedLb
L-Comfrt CrtYrd CtySte H/Inn Jamsn Wingate
DALTON
Pop: 21,800
UNION FLANKING MOVE TO RESACA
G-BP Chevn Rctrac Texco
F-Blimp LghtHo Waffle
L-CtHrth WdaleLg
Old 137
336
Rts 41 76 Dalton Rocky Face
G-Amoco 66
F-Denny Pizza
L-BestW HoJo Motel6 Royal
Civil War Battle Rocky Face Ridge
7-15th May, 1864
(see page 113)
GENERAL
Rocky Face Ridge
General Johnston Confederate Army
(43,000 men)
General Sherman Union Army (62,200 men)
GEORGIA
Whitfield County
Florida
NORTH
-313- -314- -315- -316- -317- -318- -319- -320- -321- -322- -323- -324- -325- -326- -327- -328- -329- -330- -331- -332- -333- -334- -335- -336- -337- -338-
1,500 1,000 500

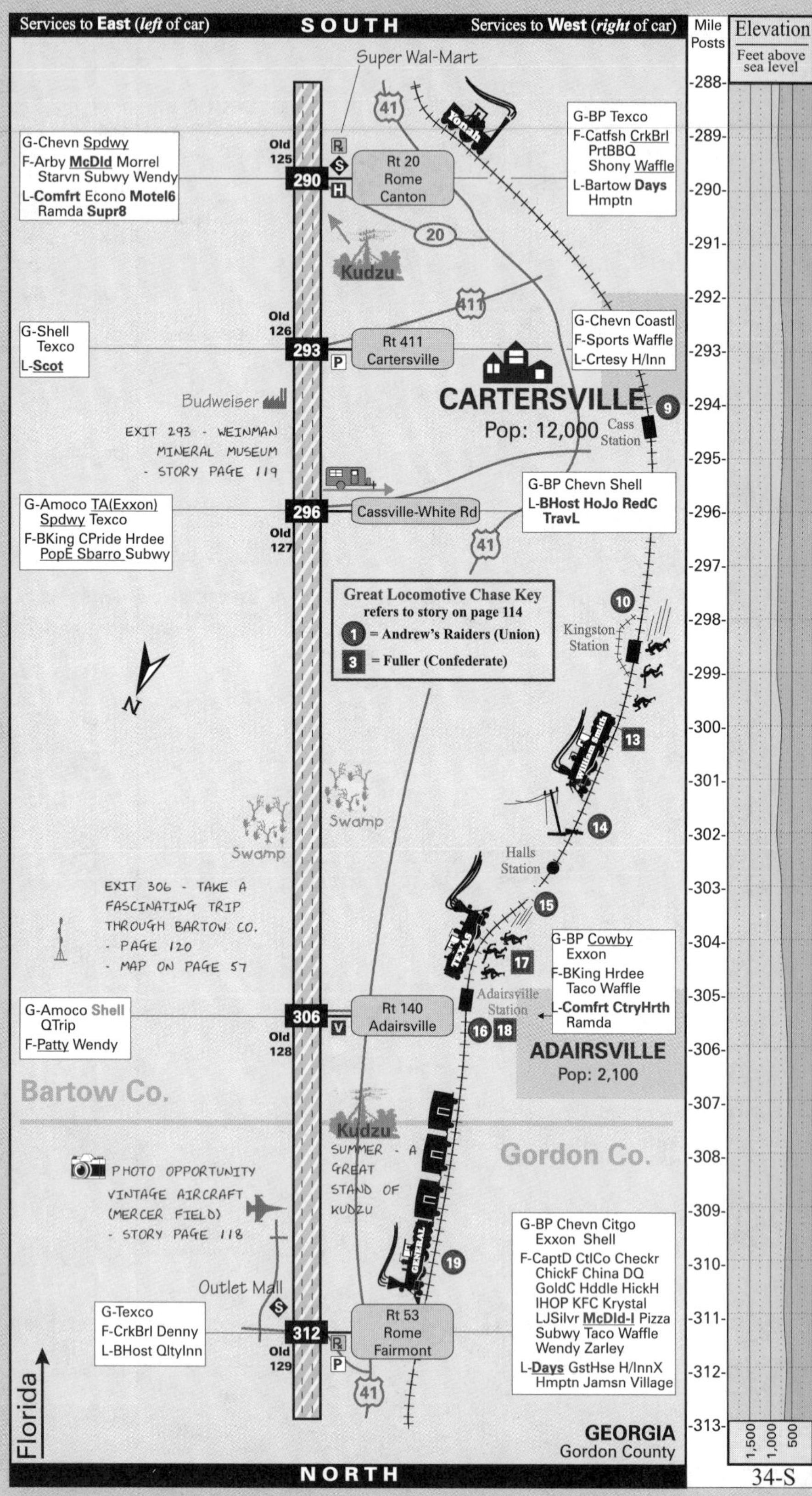

Services to East (left of car)
SOUTH
Services to West (right of car)
Mile Posts
Elevation
Feet above sea level
Super Wal-Mart
G-Chevn Spdwy
F-Arby McDld Morrel Starvn Subwy Wendy
L-Comfrt Econo Motel6 Ramda Supr8
Old 125
290
Rt 20 Rome Canton
G-BP Texco
F-Catfsh CrkBrl PrtBBQ Shony Waffle
L-Bartow Days Hmptn
Yonah
20
41
Kudzu
411
Old 126
G-Shell Texco
L-Scot
293
Rt 411 Cartersville
G-Chevn Coastl
F-Sports Waffle
L-Crtesy H/Inn
CARTERSVILLE
Pop: 12,000
Cass Station
Budweiser
EXIT 293 - WEINMAN MINERAL MUSEUM - STORY PAGE 119
G-Amoco TA(Exxon) Spdwy Texco
F-BKing CPride Hrdee PopE Sbarro Subwy
296
Old 127
Cassville-White Rd
G-BP Chevn Shell
L-BHost HoJo RedC TravL
Great Locomotive Chase Key
refers to story on page 114
= Andrew's Raiders (Union)
= Fuller (Confederate)
N
Kingston Station
William Smith
Swamp
Swamp
Halls Station
EXIT 306 - TAKE A FASCINATING TRIP THROUGH BARTOW CO. - PAGE 120 - MAP ON PAGE 57
Texas
G-BP Cowby Exxon
F-BKing Hrdee Taco Waffle
L-Comfrt CtryHrth Ramda
Adairsville Station
G-Amoco Shell QTrip
F-Patty Wendy
306
Old 128
Rt 140 Adairsville
ADAIRSVILLE
Pop: 2,100
Bartow Co.
Gordon Co.
Kudzu
SUMMER - A GREAT STAND OF KUDZU
PHOTO OPPORTUNITY VINTAGE AIRCRAFT (MERCER FIELD) - STORY PAGE 118
General
G-BP Chevn Citgo Exxon Shell
F-CaptD CtlCo Checkr ChickF China DQ GoldC Hddle HickH IHOP KFC Krystal LJSilvr McDld-I Pizza Subwy Taco Waffle Wendy Zarley
L-Days GstHse H/InnX Hmptn Jamsn Village
Outlet Mall
G-Texco
F-CrkBrl Denny
L-BHost QltyInn
312
Old 129
Rt 53 Rome Fairmont
Florida
GEORGIA
Gordon County
NORTH

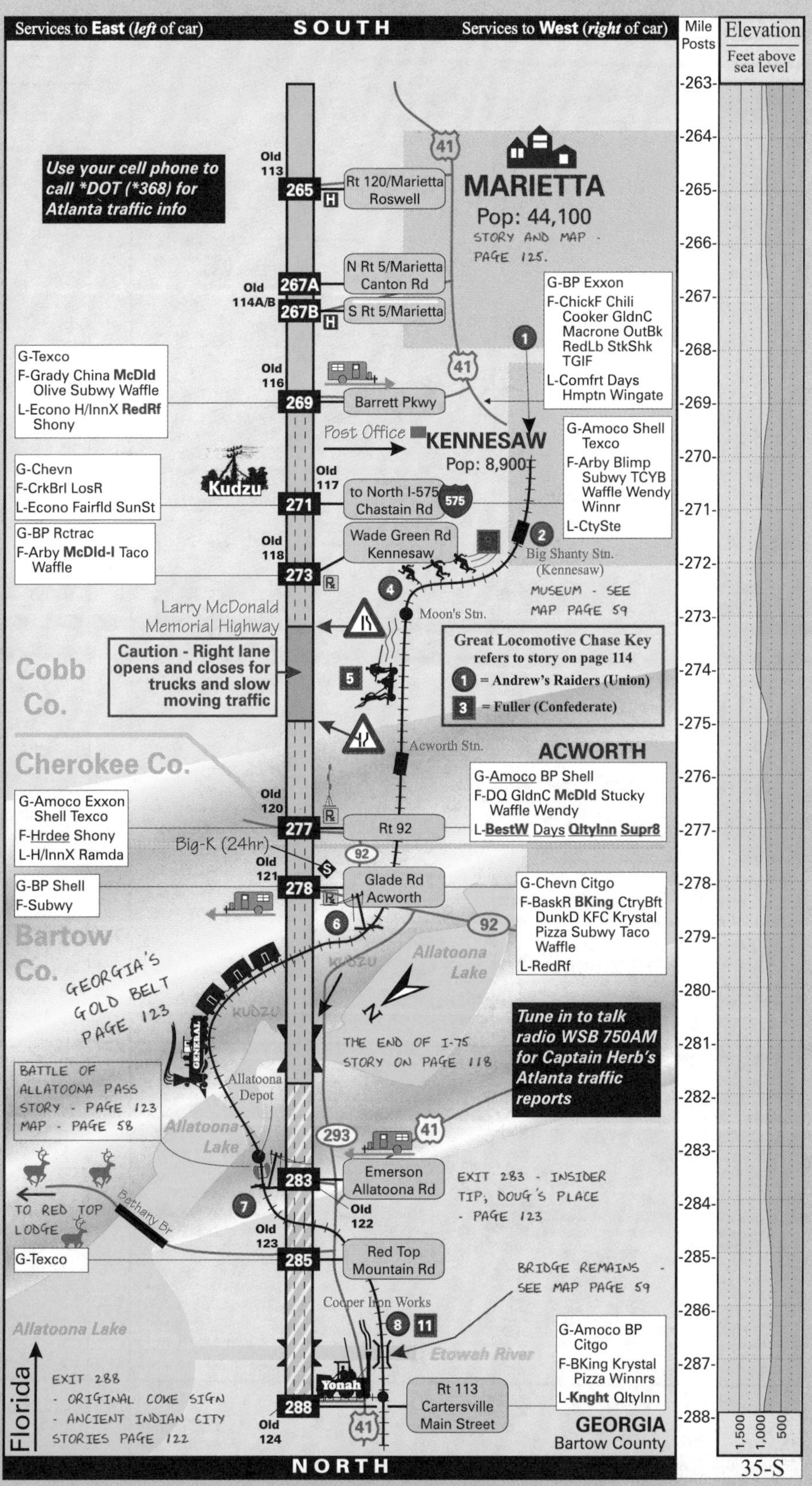

Services to East (left of car)
SOUTH
Services to West (right of car)
Mile Posts
Elevation
Feet above sea level
Use your cell phone to call *DOT (*368) for Atlanta traffic info
Old 113
265
Rt 120/Marietta Roswell
MARIETTA
Pop: 44,100
STORY AND MAP - PAGE 125.
Old 114A/B
267A
N Rt 5/Marietta Canton Rd
267B
S Rt 5/Marietta
G-BP Exxon
F-ChickF Chili Cooker GldnC Macrone OutBk RedLb StkShk TGIF
L-Comfrt Days Hmptn Wingate
G-Texco
F-Grady China McDld Olive Subwy Waffle
L-Econo H/InnX RedRf Shony
Old 116
269
Barrett Pkwy
Post Office
KENNESAW
Pop: 8,900
G-Amoco Shell Texco
F-Arby Blimp Subwy TCYB Waffle Wendy Winnr
L-CtySte
G-Chevn
F-CrkBrl LosR
L-Econo Fairfld SunSt
Kudzu
Old 117
271
to North I-575 Chastain Rd
575
G-BP Rctrac
F-Arby McDld-I Taco Waffle
Old 118
273
Wade Green Rd Kennesaw
Big Shanty Stn. (Kennesaw)
MUSEUM - SEE MAP PAGE 59
Larry McDonald Memorial Highway
Moon's Stn.
Caution - Right lane opens and closes for trucks and slow moving traffic
Great Locomotive Chase Key
refers to story on page 114
1 = Andrew's Raiders (Union)
3 = Fuller (Confederate)
Cobb Co.
Acworth Stn.
ACWORTH
Cherokee Co.
G-Amoco Exxon Shell Texco
F-Hrdee Shony
L-H/InnX Ramda
Old 120
277
Rt 92
G-Amoco BP Shell
F-DQ GldnC McDld Stucky Waffle Wendy
L-BestW Days QltyInn Supr8
Big-K (24hr)
Old 121
278
Glade Rd Acworth
G-BP Shell
F-Subwy
G-Chevn Citgo
F-BaskR BKing CtryBft DunkD KFC Krystal Pizza Subwy Taco Waffle
L-RedRf
Bartow Co.
GEORGIA'S GOLD BELT PAGE 123
Allatoona Lake
KUDZU
THE END OF I-75 STORY ON PAGE 118
Tune in to talk radio WSB 750AM for Captain Herb's Atlanta traffic reports
BATTLE OF ALLATOONA PASS STORY - PAGE 123 MAP - PAGE 58
Allatoona Depot
293
283
Emerson Allatoona Rd
Old 122
EXIT 283 - INSIDER TIP; DOUG'S PLACE - PAGE 123
TO RED TOP LODGE
Bethany Br
Old 123
285
Red Top Mountain Rd
G-Texco
BRIDGE REMAINS - SEE MAP PAGE 59
Cooper Iron Works
Allatoona Lake
Etowah River
G-Amoco BP Citgo
F-BKing Krystal Pizza Winnrs
L-Knght QltyInn
Florida
EXIT 288
- ORIGINAL COKE SIGN
- ANCIENT INDIAN CITY
STORIES PAGE 122
Yonah
288
Old 124
Rt 113 Cartersville Main Street
GEORGIA
Bartow County
NORTH
-263- -264- -265- -266- -267- -268- -269- -270- -271- -272- -273- -274- -275- -276- -277- -278- -279- -280- -281- -282- -283- -284- -285- -286- -287- -288-
1,500 1,000 500

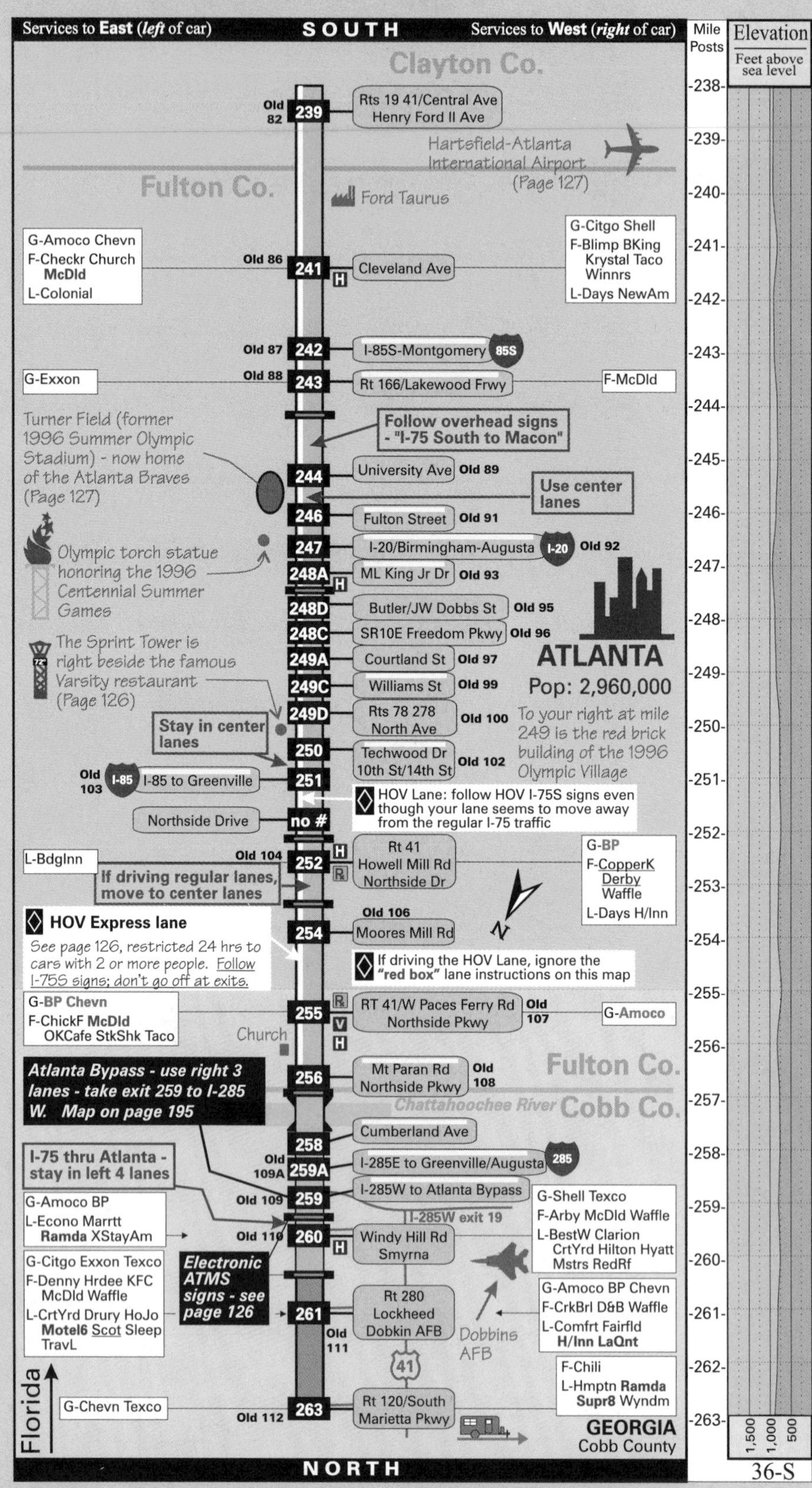

Services to East (left of car)
SOUTH
Services to West (right of car)
Mile Posts
Elevation
Feet above sea level
Clayton Co.
Old 82
239
Rts 19 41/Central Ave
Henry Ford II Ave
Hartsfield-Atlanta International Airport (Page 127)
Fulton Co.
Ford Taurus
G-Amoco Chevn
F-Checkr Church McDld
L-Colonial
Old 86
241
H
Cleveland Ave
G-Citgo Shell
F-Blimp BKing Krystal Taco Winnrs
L-Days NewAm
Old 87
242
I-85S-Montgomery
85S
G-Exxon
Old 88
243
Rt 166/Lakewood Frwy
F-McDld
Turner Field (former 1996 Summer Olympic Stadium) - now home of the Atlanta Braves (Page 127)
Follow overhead signs - "I-75 South to Macon"
244
University Ave
Old 89
Use center lanes
246
Fulton Street
Old 91
Olympic torch statue honoring the 1996 Centennial Summer Games
247
I-20/Birmingham-Augusta
I-20
Old 92
248A
H
ML King Jr Dr
Old 93
248D
Butler/JW Dobbs St
Old 95
248C
SR10E Freedom Pkwy
Old 96
The Sprint Tower is right beside the famous Varsity restaurant (Page 126)
249A
Courtland St
Old 97
ATLANTA
Pop: 2,960,000
249C
Williams St
Old 99
249D
Rts 78 278
North Ave
Old 100
To your right at mile 249 is the red brick building of the 1996 Olympic Village
Stay in center lanes
250
Techwood Dr
10th St/14th St
Old 102
Old 103
I-85
I-85 to Greenville
251
HOV Lane: follow HOV I-75S signs even though your lane seems to move away from the regular I-75 traffic
Northside Drive
no #
L-BdgInn
Old 104
252
H
R
Rt 41
Howell Mill Rd
Northside Dr
G-BP
F-CopperK Derby Waffle
L-Days H/Inn
If driving regular lanes, move to center lanes
HOV Express lane
See page 126, restricted 24 hrs to cars with 2 or more people. Follow I-75S signs; don't go off at exits.
Old 106
254
Moores Mill Rd
N
If driving the HOV Lane, ignore the "red box" lane instructions on this map
G-BP Chevn
F-ChickF McDld OKCafe StkShk Taco
255
R
V
H
RT 41/W Paces Ferry Rd
Northside Pkwy
Old 107
G-Amoco
Church
Atlanta Bypass - use right 3 lanes - take exit 259 to I-285 W. Map on page 195
256
Mt Paran Rd
Northside Pkwy
Old 108
Fulton Co.
Chattahoochee River
Cobb Co.
258
Cumberland Ave
I-75 thru Atlanta - stay in left 4 lanes
Old 109A
259A
I-285E to Greenville/Augusta
285
Old 109
259
I-285W to Atlanta Bypass
I-285W exit 19
G-Amoco BP
L-Econo Marrtt Ramda XStayAm
G-Shell Texco
F-Arby McDld Waffle
L-BestW Clarion CrtYrd Hilton Hyatt Mstrs RedRf
Old 110
260
H
Windy Hill Rd
Smyrna
G-Citgo Exxon Texco
F-Denny Hrdee KFC McDld Waffle
L-CrtYrd Drury HoJo Motel6 Scot Sleep TravL
Electronic ATMS signs - see page 126
261
Old 111
Rt 280
Lockheed
Dobkin AFB
Dobbins AFB
G-Amoco BP Chevn
F-CrkBrl D&B Waffle
L-Comfrt Fairfld H/Inn LaQnt
41
F-Chili
L-Hmptn Ramda Supr8 Wyndm
Florida
G-Chevn Texco
Old 112
263
Rt 120/South
Marietta Pkwy
GEORGIA
Cobb County
NORTH
-238- -239- -240- -241- -242- -243- -244- -245- -246- -247- -248- -249- -250- -251- -252- -253- -254- -255- -256- -257- -258- -259- -260- -261- -262- -263-
1,500
1,000
500
36-S

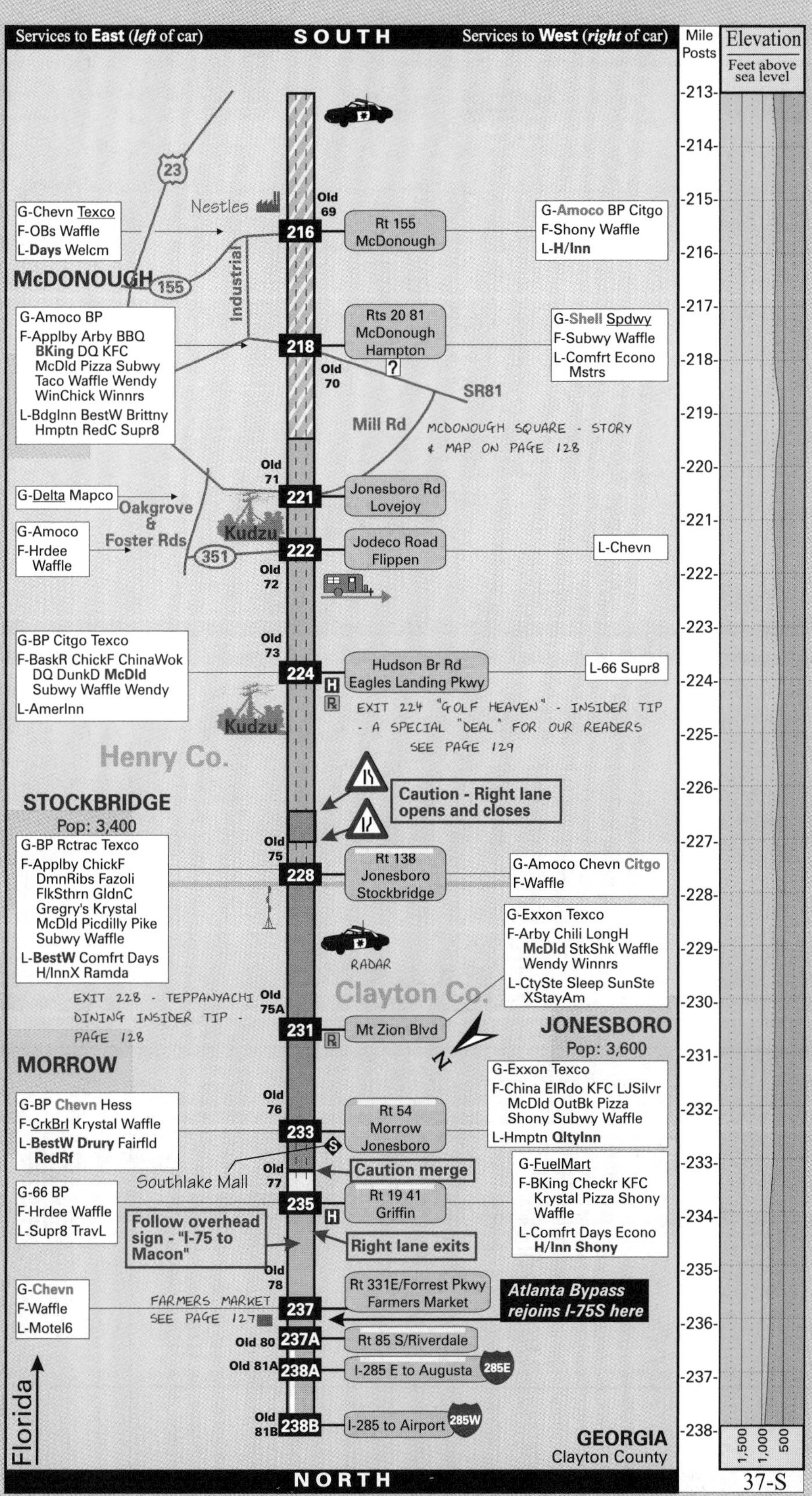

Services to East (left of car)
SOUTH
Services to West (right of car)
Mile Posts
Elevation
Feet above sea level
23
Nestles
Old 69
216
Rt 155 McDonough
G-Chevn Texco
F-OBs Waffle
L-Days Welcm
G-Amoco BP Citgo
F-Shony Waffle
L-H/Inn
McDONOUGH
155
Industrial
G-Amoco BP
F-Applby Arby BBQ
BKing DQ KFC
McDld Pizza Subwy
Taco Waffle Wendy
WinChick Winnrs
L-BdgInn BestW Brittny
Hmptn RedC Supr8
218
Rts 20 81 McDonough Hampton
Old 70
G-Shell Spdwy
F-Subwy Waffle
L-Comfrt Econo
Mstrs
SR81
Mill Rd
MCDONOUGH SQUARE - STORY & MAP ON PAGE 128
Old 71
221
G-Delta Mapco
Oakgrove & Foster Rds
Jonesboro Rd Lovejoy
Kudzu
G-Amoco
F-Hrdee
Waffle
351
222
Jodeco Road Flippen
L-Chevn
Old 72
G-BP Citgo Texco
F-BaskR ChickF ChinaWok
DQ DunkD McDld
Subwy Waffle Wendy
L-AmerInn
Old 73
224
Hudson Br Rd Eagles Landing Pkwy
L-66 Supr8
EXIT 224 "GOLF HEAVEN" - INSIDER TIP - A SPECIAL "DEAL" FOR OUR READERS SEE PAGE 129
Kudzu
Henry Co.
STOCKBRIDGE
Pop: 3,400
Caution - Right lane opens and closes
G-BP Rctrac Texco
F-Applby ChickF
DmnRibs Fazoli
FlkSthrn GldnC
Gregry's Krystal
McDld Picdilly Pike
Subwy Waffle
L-BestW Comfrt Days
H/InnX Ramda
Old 75
228
Rt 138 Jonesboro Stockbridge
G-Amoco Chevn Citgo
F-Waffle
G-Exxon Texco
F-Arby Chili LongH
McDld StkShk Waffle
Wendy Winnrs
L-CtySte Sleep SunSte
XStayAm
RADAR
Clayton Co.
EXIT 228 - TEPPANYACHI DINING INSIDER TIP - PAGE 128
Old 75A
231
Mt Zion Blvd
JONESBORO
Pop: 3,600
N
MORROW
G-Exxon Texco
F-China ElRdo KFC LJSilvr
McDld OutBk Pizza
Shony Subwy Waffle
L-Hmptn QltyInn
G-BP Chevn Hess
F-CrkBrl Krystal Waffle
L-BestW Drury Fairfld
RedRf
Old 76
233
Rt 54 Morrow Jonesboro
Southlake Mall
Old 77
Caution merge
G-FuelMart
F-BKing Checkr KFC
Krystal Pizza Shony
Waffle
L-Comfrt Days Econo
H/Inn Shony
G-66 BP
F-Hrdee Waffle
L-Supr8 TravL
235
Rt 19 41 Griffin
Follow overhead sign - "I-75 to Macon"
Right lane exits
Old 78
G-Chevn
F-Waffle
L-Motel6
FARMERS MARKET SEE PAGE 127
237
Rt 331E/Forrest Pkwy Farmers Market
Atlanta Bypass rejoins I-75S here
Old 80
237A
Rt 85 S/Riverdale
Old 81A
238A
I-285 E to Augusta
285E
Old 81B
238B
I-285 to Airport
285W
Florida
GEORGIA
Clayton County
NORTH
-213-
-214-
-215-
-216-
-217-
-218-
-219-
-220-
-221-
-222-
-223-
-224-
-225-
-226-
-227-
-228-
-229-
-230-
-231-
-232-
-233-
-234-
-235-
-236-
-237-
-238-
1,500
1,000
500

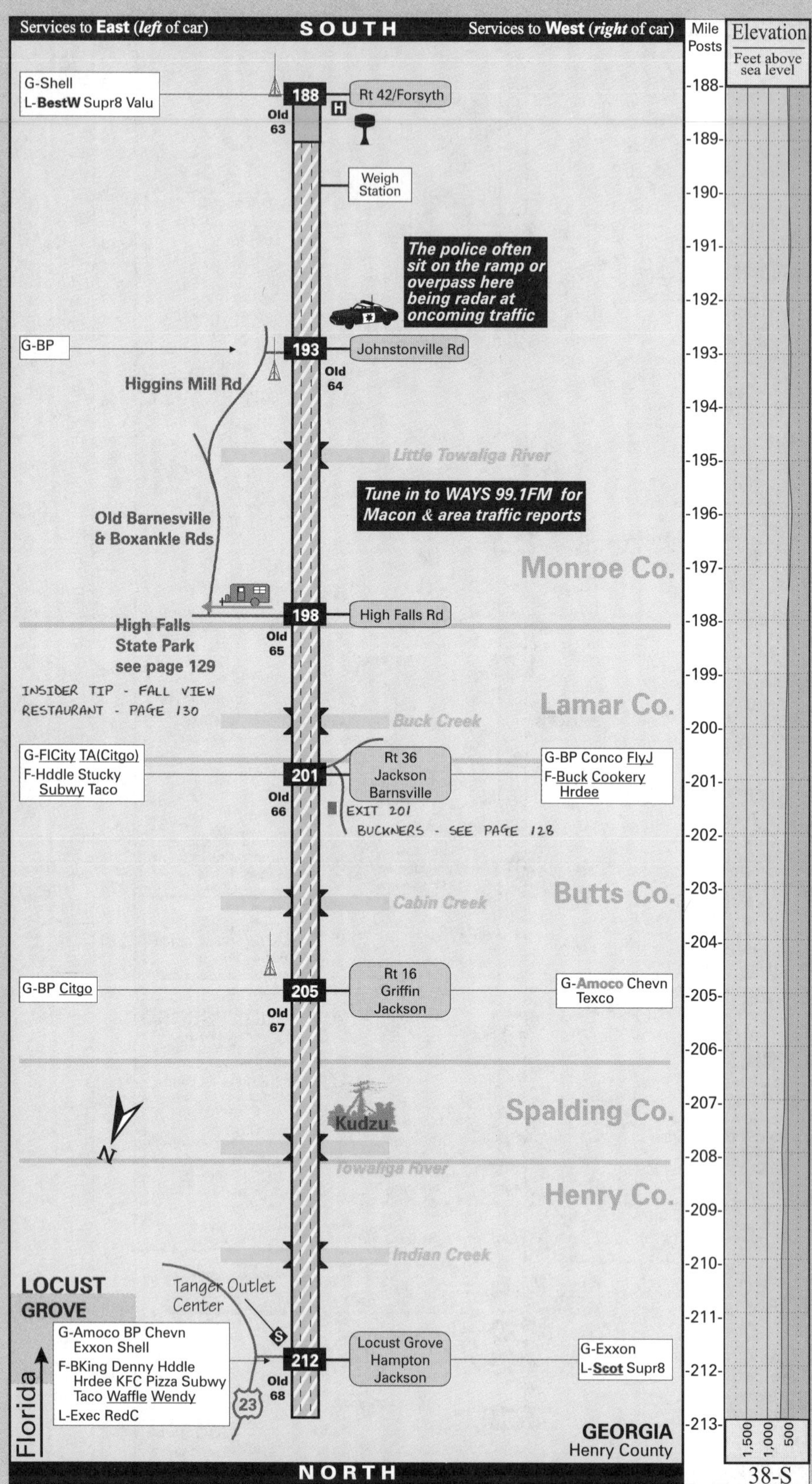

Services to East (left of car)
SOUTH
Services to West (right of car)
Mile Posts
Elevation
Feet above sea level
G-Shell
L-BestW Supr8 Valu
188
Old 63
Rt 42/Forsyth
Weigh Station
The police often sit on the ramp or overpass here being radar at oncoming traffic
G-BP
193
Johnstonville Rd
Old 64
Higgins Mill Rd
Little Towaliga River
Tune in to WAYS 99.1FM for Macon & area traffic reports
Old Barnesville & Boxankle Rds
Monroe Co.
198
High Falls Rd
High Falls State Park see page 129
Old 65
INSIDER TIP - FALL VIEW RESTAURANT - PAGE 130
Lamar Co.
Buck Creek
G-FlCity TA(Citgo)
F-Hddle Stucky Subwy Taco
201
Rt 36 Jackson Barnsville
G-BP Conco FlyJ
F-Buck Cookery Hrdee
Old 66
EXIT 201 BUCKNERS - SEE PAGE 128
Butts Co.
Cabin Creek
G-BP Citgo
205
Rt 16 Griffin Jackson
G-Amoco Chevn Texco
Old 67
Kudzu
Spalding Co.
N
Towaliga River
Henry Co.
Indian Creek
LOCUST GROVE
Tanger Outlet Center
G-Amoco BP Chevn Exxon Shell
F-BKing Denny Hddle Hrdee KFC Pizza Subwy Taco Waffle Wendy
L-Exec RedC
212
Locust Grove Hampton Jackson
G-Exxon
L-Scot Supr8
Old 68
23
Florida
GEORGIA
Henry County
NORTH
-188- -189- -190- -191- -192- -193- -194- -195- -196- -197- -198- -199- -200- -201- -202- -203- -204- -205- -206- -207- -208- -209- -210- -211- -212- -213-
1,500 1,000 500

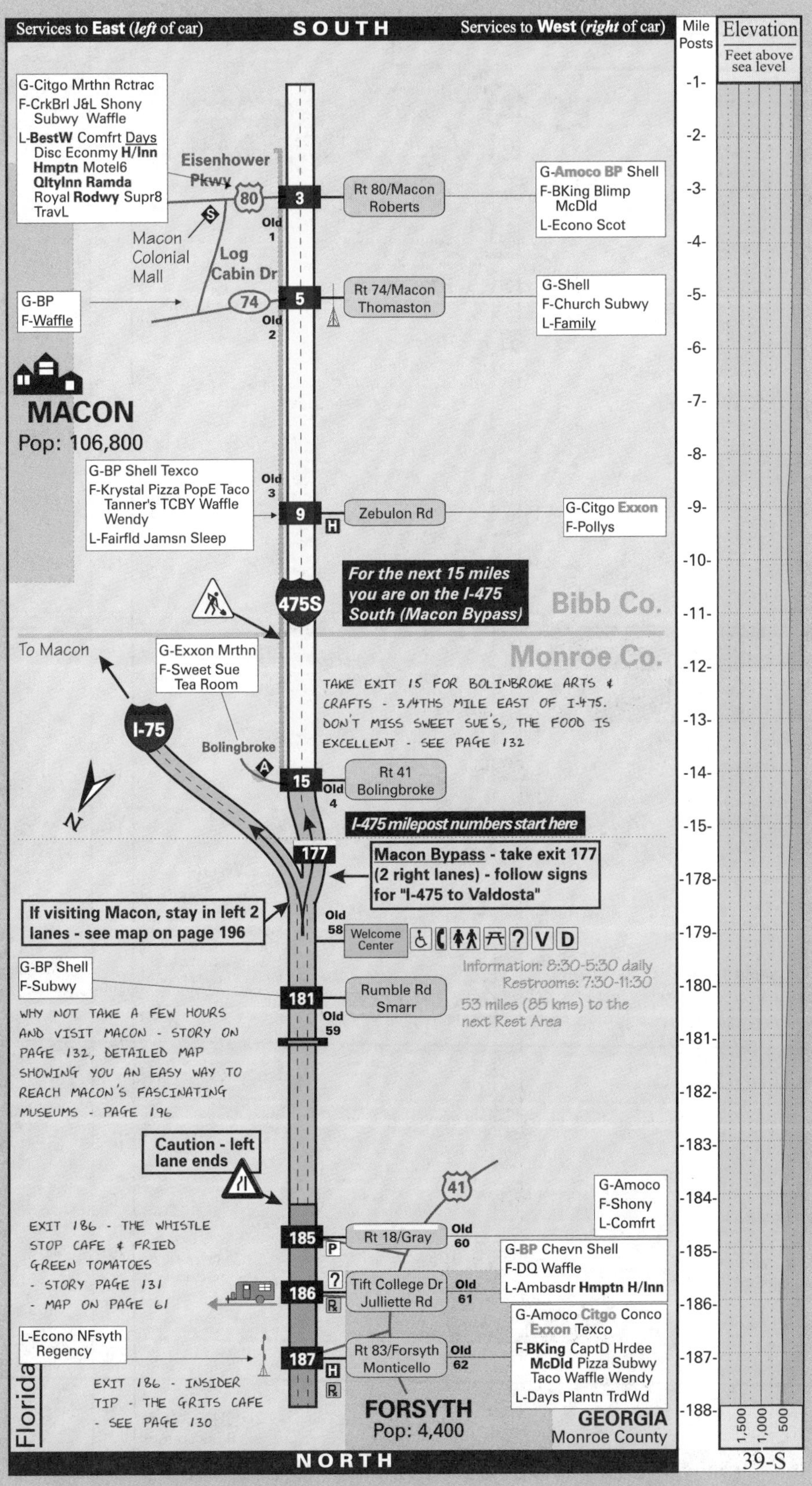

Services to East (left of car)
SOUTH
Services to West (right of car)
Mile Posts
Elevation
Feet above sea level
G-Citgo Mrthn Rctrac
F-CrkBrl J&L Shony Subwy Waffle
L-BestW Comfrt Days Disc Econmy H/Inn Hmptn Motel6 QltyInn Ramda Royal Rodwy Supr8 TravL
Eisenhower Pkwy
80
3
Rt 80/Macon Roberts
G-Amoco BP Shell
F-BKing Blimp McDld
L-Econo Scot
Old 1
Macon Colonial Mall
Log Cabin Dr
G-BP
F-Waffle
74
5
Rt 74/Macon Thomaston
G-Shell
F-Church Subwy
L-Family
Old 2
MACON
Pop: 106,800
G-BP Shell Texco
F-Krystal Pizza PopE Taco Tanner's TCBY Waffle Wendy
L-Fairfld Jamsn Sleep
Old 3
9
Zebulon Rd
G-Citgo Exxon
F-Pollys
For the next 15 miles you are on the I-475 South (Macon Bypass)
475S
Bibb Co.
Monroe Co.
To Macon
G-Exxon Mrthn
F-Sweet Sue Tea Room
TAKE EXIT 15 FOR BOLINBROKE ARTS & CRAFTS - 3/4THS MILE EAST OF I-475. DON'T MISS SWEET SUE'S, THE FOOD IS EXCELLENT - SEE PAGE 132
I-75
Bolingbroke
15
Rt 41 Bolingbroke
Old 4
N
I-475 milepost numbers start here
177
Macon Bypass - take exit 177 (2 right lanes) - follow signs for "I-475 to Valdosta"
If visiting Macon, stay in left 2 lanes - see map on page 196
Old 58
Welcome Center
Information: 8:30-5:30 daily
Restrooms: 7:30-11:30
53 miles (85 kms) to the next Rest Area
G-BP Shell
F-Subwy
181
Rumble Rd Smarr
Old 59
WHY NOT TAKE A FEW HOURS AND VISIT MACON - STORY ON PAGE 132, DETAILED MAP SHOWING YOU AN EASY WAY TO REACH MACON'S FASCINATING MUSEUMS - PAGE 196
Caution - left lane ends
41
G-Amoco
F-Shony
L-Comfrt
EXIT 186 - THE WHISTLE STOP CAFE & FRIED GREEN TOMATOES - STORY PAGE 131 - MAP ON PAGE 61
185
Rt 18/Gray
Old 60
G-BP Chevn Shell
F-DQ Waffle
L-Ambasdr Hmptn H/Inn
186
Tift College Dr Julliette Rd
Old 61
G-Amoco Citgo Conco Exxon Texco
F-BKing CaptD Hrdee McDld Pizza Subwy Taco Waffle Wendy
L-Days Plantn TrdWd
L-Econo NFsyth Regency
187
Rt 83/Forsyth Monticello
Old 62
EXIT 186 - INSIDER TIP - THE GRITS CAFE - SEE PAGE 130
FORSYTH
Pop: 4,400
GEORGIA
Monroe County
Florida
NORTH
-1-
-2-
-3-
-4-
-5-
-6-
-7-
-8-
-9-
-10-
-11-
-12-
-13-
-14-
-15-
-178-
-179-
-180-
-181-
-182-
-183-
-184-
-185-
-186-
-187-
-188-
1,500
1,000
500

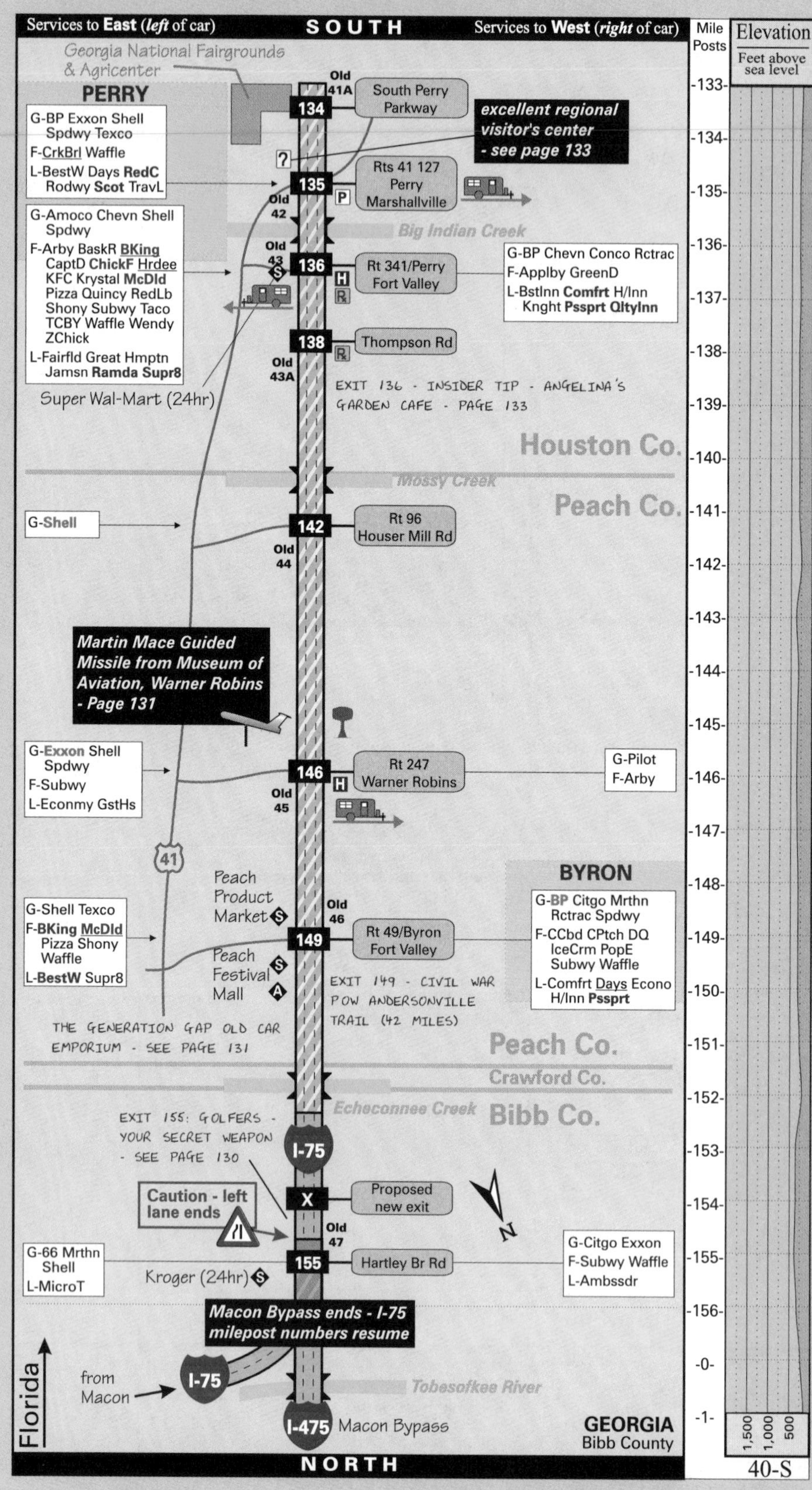

Services to East (left of car)
SOUTH
Services to West (right of car)
Mile Posts
Elevation
Feet above sea level
Georgia National Fairgrounds & Agricenter
PERRY
G-BP Exxon Shell Spdwy Texco
F-CrkBrl Waffle
L-BestW Days RedC Rodwy Scot TravL
Old 41A
134
South Perry Parkway
excellent regional visitor's center - see page 133
135
Rts 41 127 Perry Marshallville
Old 42
G-Amoco Chevn Shell Spdwy
F-Arby BaskR BKing CaptD ChickF Hrdee KFC Krystal McDld Pizza Quincy RedLb Shony Subwy Taco TCBY Waffle Wendy ZChick
L-Fairfld Great Hmptn Jamsn Ramda Supr8
Big Indian Creek
Old 43
136
Rt 341/Perry Fort Valley
G-BP Chevn Conco Rctrac
F-Applby GreenD
L-BstInn Comfrt H/Inn Knght Pssprt QltyInn
138
Thompson Rd
Old 43A
Super Wal-Mart (24hr)
EXIT 136 - INSIDER TIP - ANGELINA'S GARDEN CAFE - PAGE 133
Houston Co.
Mossy Creek
Peach Co.
G-Shell
142
Rt 96 Houser Mill Rd
Old 44
Martin Mace Guided Missile from Museum of Aviation, Warner Robins - Page 131
G-Exxon Shell Spdwy
F-Subwy
L-Econmy GstHs
146
Rt 247 Warner Robins
G-Pilot
F-Arby
Old 45
41
BYRON
Peach Product Market
Old 46
G-Shell Texco
F-BKing McDld Pizza Shony Waffle
L-BestW Supr8
149
Rt 49/Byron Fort Valley
G-BP Citgo Mrthn Rctrac Spdwy
F-CCbd CPtch DQ IceCrm PopE Subwy Waffle
L-Comfrt Days Econo H/Inn Pssprt
Peach Festival Mall
EXIT 149 - CIVIL WAR POW ANDERSONVILLE TRAIL (42 MILES)
THE GENERATION GAP OLD CAR EMPORIUM - SEE PAGE 131
Peach Co.
Crawford Co.
Echeconnee Creek
Bibb Co.
EXIT 155: GOLFERS - YOUR SECRET WEAPON - SEE PAGE 130
I-75
Caution - left lane ends
X
Proposed new exit
N
Old 47
G-66 Mrthn Shell
L-MicroT
155
Hartley Br Rd
G-Citgo Exxon
F-Subwy Waffle
L-Ambssdr
Kroger (24hr)
Macon Bypass ends - I-75 milepost numbers resume
Florida
from Macon
I-75
Tobesofkee River
I-475 Macon Bypass
GEORGIA
Bibb County
NORTH
-133- -134- -135- -136- -137- -138- -139- -140- -141- -142- -143- -144- -145- -146- -147- -148- -149- -150- -151- -152- -153- -154- -155- -156- -0- -1-
1,500 1,000 500

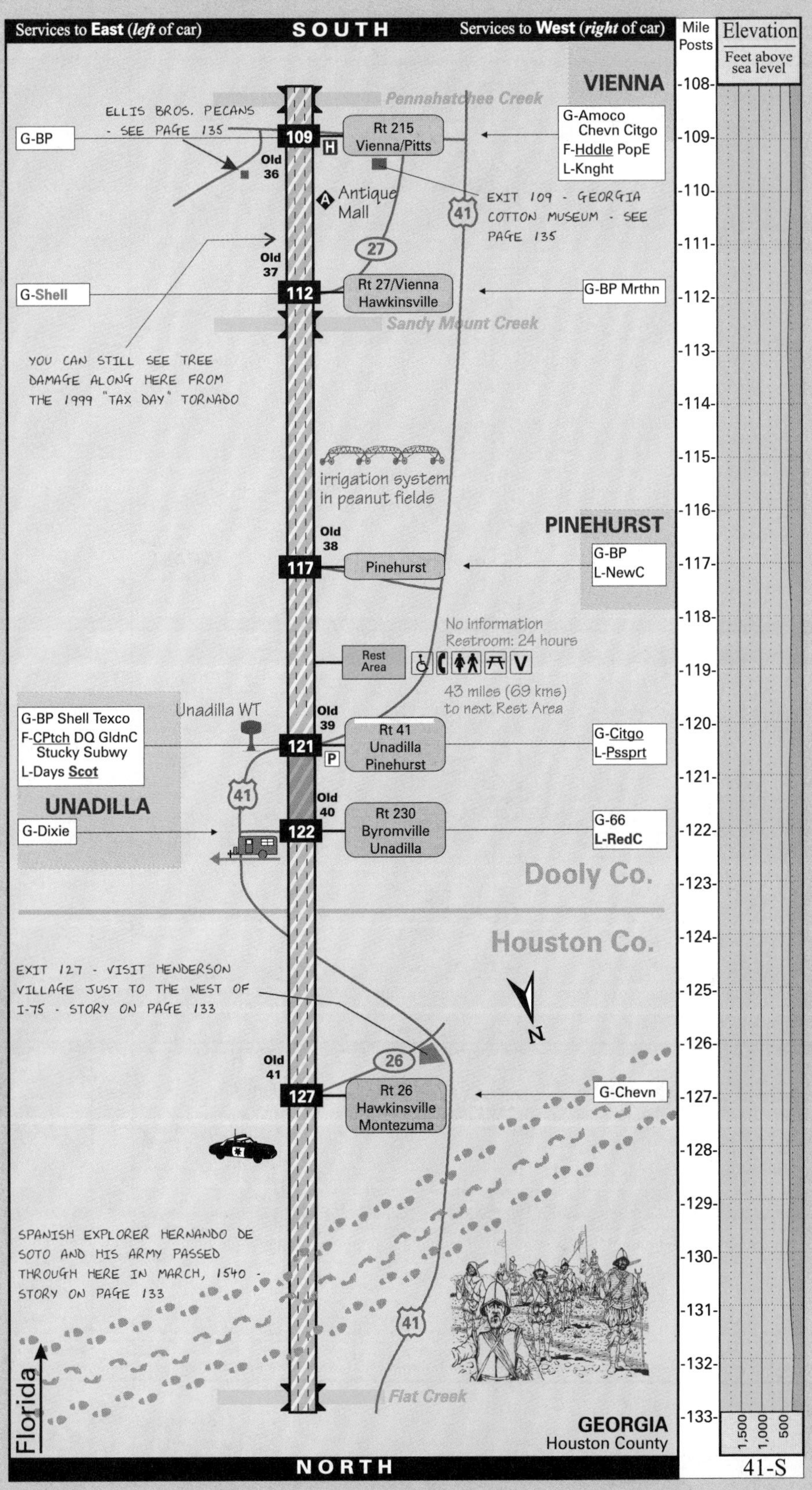

Services to **East** (*left* of car)
SOUTH
Services to **West** (*right* of car)
Mile Posts
Elevation
Feet above sea level
VIENNA
Pennahatchee Creek
ELLIS BROS. PECANS - SEE PAGE 135
G-BP
109
Old 36
Rt 215 Vienna/Pitts
G-Amoco Chevn Citgo
F-Hddle PopE
L-Knght
Antique Mall
EXIT 109 - GEORGIA COTTON MUSEUM - SEE PAGE 135
41
27
Old 37
G-Shell
112
Rt 27/Vienna Hawkinsville
G-BP Mrthn
Sandy Mount Creek
YOU CAN STILL SEE TREE DAMAGE ALONG HERE FROM THE 1999 "TAX DAY" TORNADO
irrigation system in peanut fields
PINEHURST
Old 38
117
Pinehurst
G-BP
L-NewC
No information
Restroom: 24 hours
Rest Area
43 miles (69 kms) to next Rest Area
Unadilla WT
G-BP Shell Texco
F-CPtch DQ GldnC Stucky Subwy
L-Days Scot
Old 39
121
Rt 41 Unadilla Pinehurst
G-Citgo
L-Pssprt
UNADILLA
Old 40
G-Dixie
122
Rt 230 Byromville Unadilla
G-66
L-RedC
Dooly Co.
Houston Co.
EXIT 127 - VISIT HENDERSON VILLAGE JUST TO THE WEST OF I-75 - STORY ON PAGE 133
N
26
Old 41
127
Rt 26 Hawkinsville Montezuma
G-Chevn
SPANISH EXPLORER HERNANDO DE SOTO AND HIS ARMY PASSED THROUGH HERE IN MARCH, 1540 - STORY ON PAGE 133
Flat Creek
Florida
GEORGIA
Houston County
NORTH
-108-
-109-
-110-
-111-
-112-
-113-
-114-
-115-
-116-
-117-
-118-
-119-
-120-
-121-
-122-
-123-
-124-
-125-
-126-
-127-
-128-
-129-
-130-
-131-
-132-
-133-
1,500
1,000
500

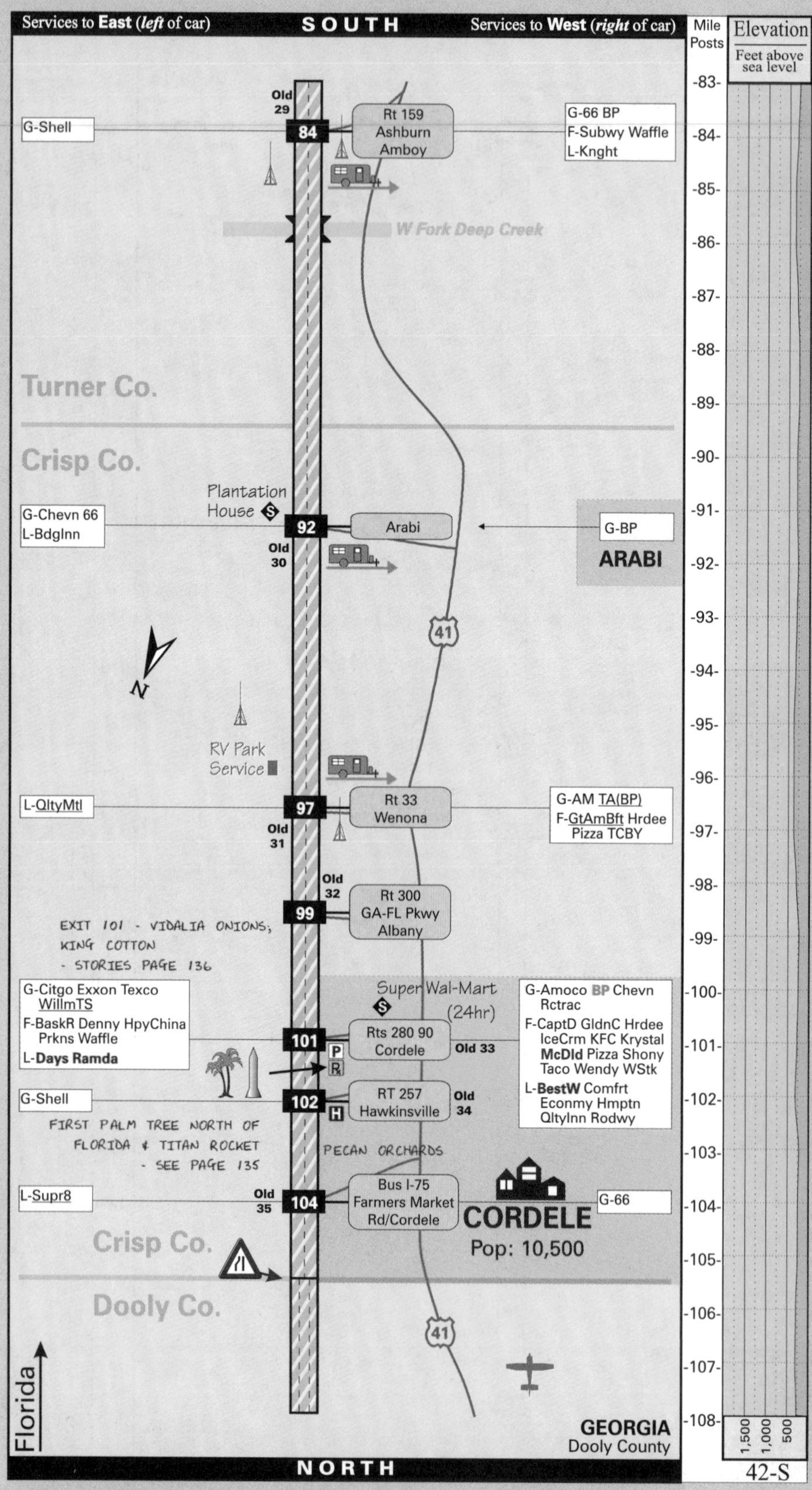

Services to East (left of car)
SOUTH
Services to West (right of car)
Mile Posts
Elevation
Feet above sea level
G-Shell
Old 29
84
Rt 159 Ashburn Amboy
G-66 BP
F-Subwy Waffle
L-Knght
W Fork Deep Creek
Turner Co.
Crisp Co.
Plantation House
G-Chevn 66
L-BdgInn
92
Arabi
Old 30
G-BP
ARABI
41
N
RV Park Service
L-QltyMtl
97
Rt 33 Wenona
Old 31
G-AM TA(BP)
F-GtAmBft Hrdee Pizza TCBY
Old 32
99
Rt 300 GA-FL Pkwy Albany
EXIT 101 - VIDALIA ONIONS; KING COTTON - STORIES PAGE 136
Super Wal-Mart (24hr)
G-Citgo Exxon Texco WillmTS
F-BaskR Denny HpyChina Prkns Waffle
L-Days Ramda
101
Rts 280 90 Cordele
Old 33
G-Amoco BP Chevn Rctrac
F-CaptD GldnC Hrdee IceCrm KFC Krystal McDld Pizza Shony Taco Wendy WStk
L-BestW Comfrt Econmy Hmptn QltyInn Rodwy
G-Shell
102
RT 257 Hawkinsville
Old 34
FIRST PALM TREE NORTH OF FLORIDA & TITAN ROCKET - SEE PAGE 135
PECAN ORCHARDS
L-Supr8
Old 35
104
Bus I-75 Farmers Market Rd/Cordele
G-66
CORDELE
Pop: 10,500
Crisp Co.
Dooly Co.
41
Florida
GEORGIA
Dooly County
NORTH
-83- -84- -85- -86- -87- -88- -89- -90- -91- -92- -93- -94- -95- -96- -97- -98- -99- -100- -101- -102- -103- -104- -105- -106- -107- -108-
1,500 1,000 500

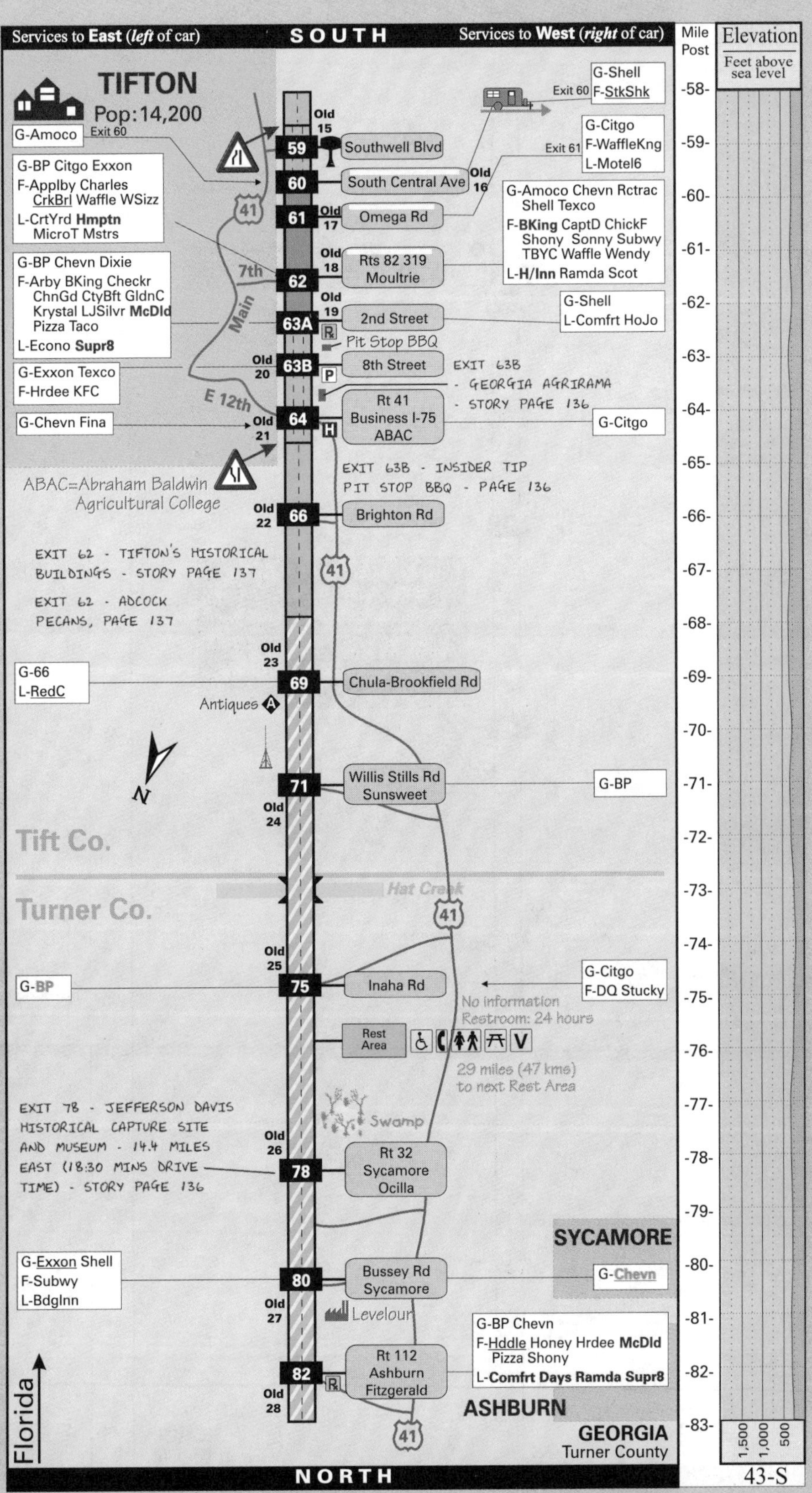

Services to East (left of car)
SOUTH
Services to West (right of car)
Mile Post
Elevation
Feet above sea level
TIFTON
Pop:14,200
G-Amoco
Exit 60
G-BP Citgo Exxon
F-Applby Charles CrkBrl Waffle WSizz
L-CrtYrd Hmptn MicroT Mstrs
G-BP Chevn Dixie
F-Arby BKing Checkr ChnGd CtyBft GldnC Krystal LJSilvr McDld Pizza Taco
L-Econo Supr8
G-Exxon Texco
F-Hrdee KFC
G-Chevn Fina
G-Shell
F-StkShk
Exit 60
G-Citgo
F-WaffleKng
L-Motel6
Exit 61
G-Amoco Chevn Rctrac Shell Texco
F-BKing CaptD ChickF Shony Sonny Subwy TBYC Waffle Wendy
L-H/Inn Ramda Scot
G-Shell
L-Comfrt HoJo
59 Southwell Blvd Old 15
60 South Central Ave Old 16
61 Omega Rd Old 17
62 Rts 82 319 Moultrie Old 18
63A 2nd Street Old 19
Pit Stop BBQ
63B 8th Street Old 20
EXIT 63B - GEORGIA AGRIRAMA - STORY PAGE 136
64 Rt 41 Business I-75 ABAC Old 21
G-Citgo
7th
Main
E 12th
41
ABAC=Abraham Baldwin Agricultural College
EXIT 63B - INSIDER TIP PIT STOP BBQ - PAGE 136
66 Brighton Rd Old 22
EXIT 62 - TIFTON'S HISTORICAL BUILDINGS - STORY PAGE 137
EXIT 62 - ADCOCK PECANS, PAGE 137
69 Chula-Brookfield Rd Old 23
G-66
L-RedC
Antiques
N
71 Willis Stills Rd Sunsweet Old 24
G-BP
Tift Co.
Turner Co.
Hat Creek
75 Inaha Rd Old 25
G-BP
G-Citgo
F-DQ Stucky
No information
Restroom: 24 hours
Rest Area
29 miles (47 kms) to next Rest Area
Swamp
EXIT 78 - JEFFERSON DAVIS HISTORICAL CAPTURE SITE AND MUSEUM - 14.4 MILES EAST (18:30 MINS DRIVE TIME) - STORY PAGE 136
78 Rt 32 Sycamore Ocilla Old 26
SYCAMORE
80 Bussey Rd Sycamore Old 27
G-Exxon Shell
F-Subwy
L-BdgInn
G-Chevn
Levelour
G-BP Chevn
F-Hddle Honey Hrdee McDld Pizza Shony
L-Comfrt Days Ramda Supr8
82 Rt 112 Ashburn Fitzgerald Old 28
ASHBURN
GEORGIA
Turner County
Florida
NORTH
-58- -59- -60- -61- -62- -63- -64- -65- -66- -67- -68- -69- -70- -71- -72- -73- -74- -75- -76- -77- -78- -79- -80- -81- -82- -83-
1,500 1,000 500

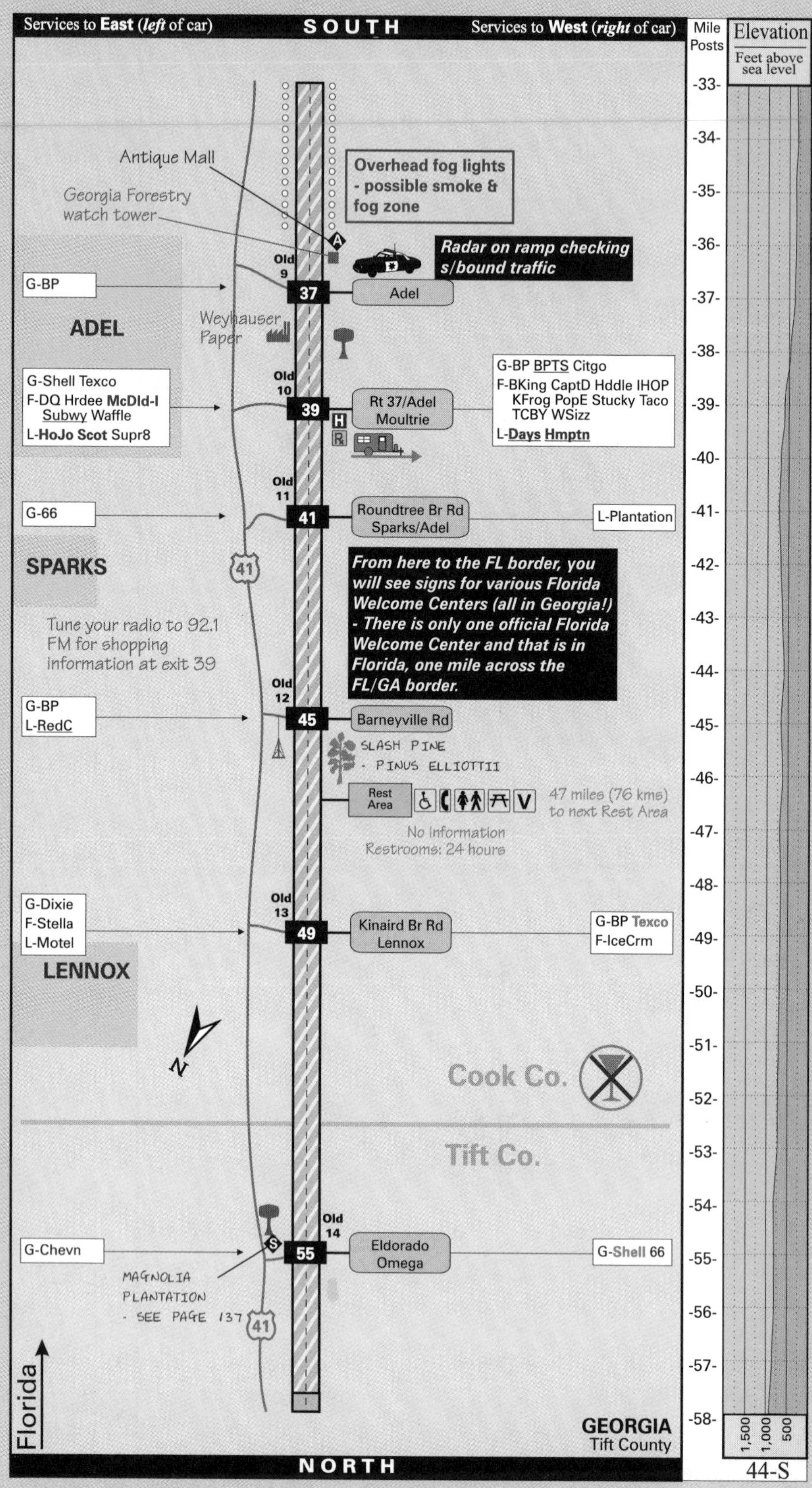

Services to East (left of car)
SOUTH
Services to West (right of car)
Mile Posts
Elevation
Feet above sea level
Antique Mall
Georgia Forestry watch tower
Overhead fog lights - possible smoke & fog zone
Radar on ramp checking s/bound traffic
Old 9
G-BP
37
Adel
ADEL
Weyhauser Paper
G-Shell Texco
F-DQ Hrdee McDld-I Subwy Waffle
L-HoJo Scot Supr8
Old 10
39
Rt 37/Adel Moultrie
G-BP BPTS Citgo
F-BKing CaptD Hddle IHOP KFrog PopE Stucky Taco TCBY WSizz
L-Days Hmptn
Old 11
G-66
41
Roundtree Br Rd Sparks/Adel
L-Plantation
SPARKS
41
From here to the FL border, you will see signs for various Florida Welcome Centers (all in Georgia!) - There is only one official Florida Welcome Center and that is in Florida, one mile across the FL/GA border.
Tune your radio to 92.1 FM for shopping information at exit 39
Old 12
G-BP
L-RedC
45
Barneyville Rd
SLASH PINE - PINUS ELLIOTTII
Rest Area
47 miles (76 kms) to next Rest Area
No Information
Restrooms: 24 hours
Old 13
G-Dixie
F-Stella
L-Motel
49
Kinaird Br Rd Lennox
G-BP Texco
F-IceCrm
LENNOX
N
Cook Co.
Tift Co.
Old 14
G-Chevn
55
Eldorado Omega
G-Shell 66
MAGNOLIA PLANTATION - SEE PAGE 137
41
Florida
GEORGIA
Tift County
NORTH
-33- -34- -35- -36- -37- -38- -39- -40- -41- -42- -43- -44- -45- -46- -47- -48- -49- -50- -51- -52- -53- -54- -55- -56- -57- -58-
1,500
1,000
500

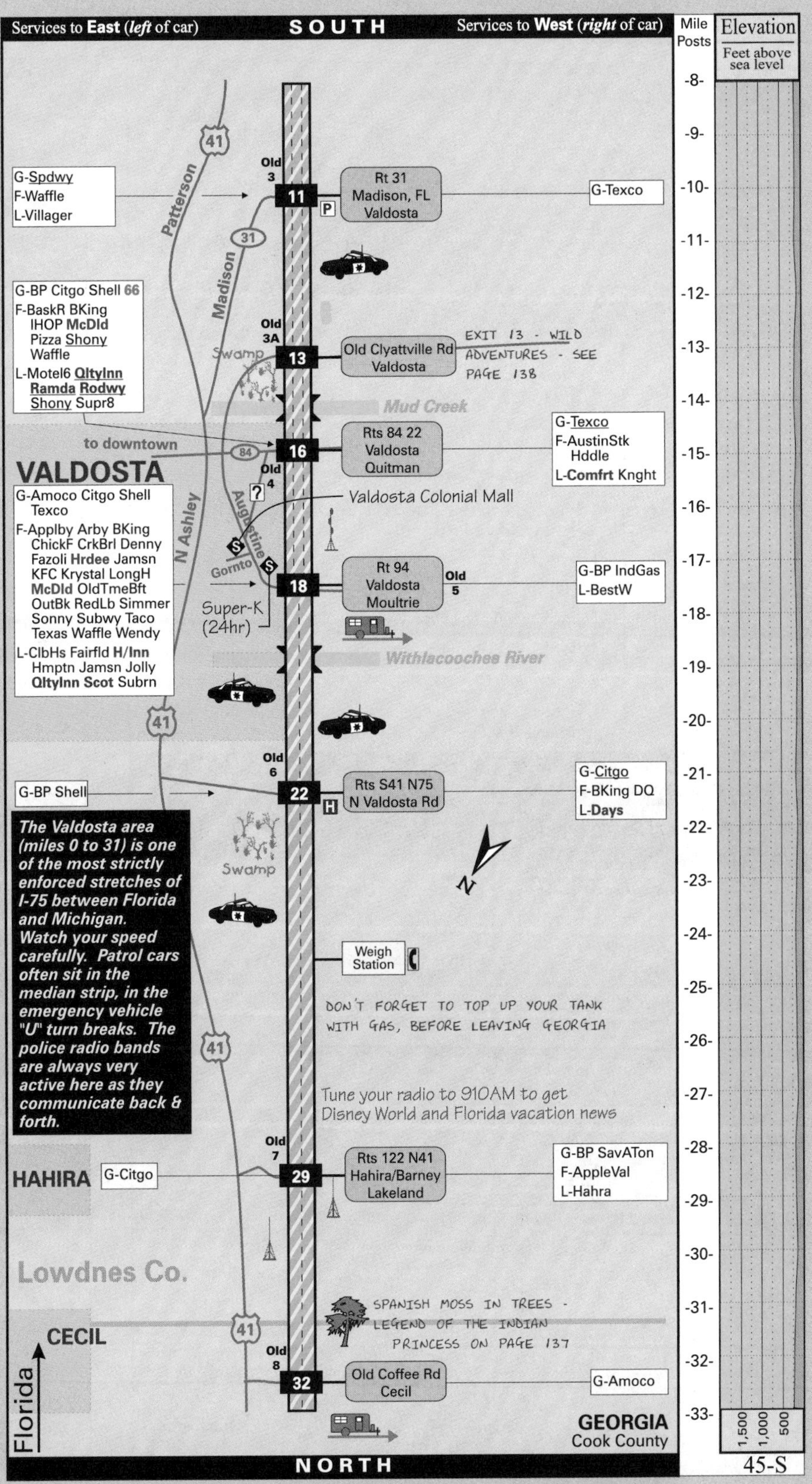
Services to East (left of car)
SOUTH
Services to West (right of car)
Mile Posts
Elevation
Feet above sea level
Old 3
11
Rt 31
Madison, FL
Valdosta
G-Spdwy
F-Waffle
L-Villager
G-Texco
Patterson
31
Madison
41
G-BP Citgo Shell 66
F-BaskR BKing
IHOP McDld
Pizza Shony
Waffle
L-Motel6 QltyInn
Ramda Rodwy
Shony Supr8
Old 3A
13
Old Clyattville Rd
Valdosta
EXIT 13 - WILD ADVENTURES - SEE PAGE 138
Swamp
Mud Creek
16
Rts 84 22
Valdosta
Quitman
G-Texco
F-AustinStk
Hddle
L-Comfrt Knght
to downtown
84
VALDOSTA
Old 4
Valdosta Colonial Mall
G-Amoco Citgo Shell
Texco
F-Applby Arby BKing
ChickF CrkBrl Denny
Fazoli Hrdee Jamsn
KFC Krystal LongH
McDld OldTmeBft
OutBk RedLb Simmer
Sonny Subwy Taco
Texas Waffle Wendy
L-ClbHs Fairfld H/Inn
Hmptn Jamsn Jolly
QltyInn Scot Subrn
N Ashley
Augustine
Gornto
Super-K
(24hr)
18
Rt 94
Valdosta
Moultrie
Old 5
G-BP IndGas
L-BestW
Withlacoochee River
41
Old 6
22
Rts S41 N75
N Valdosta Rd
G-BP Shell
G-Citgo
F-BKing DQ
L-Days
The Valdosta area (miles 0 to 31) is one of the most strictly enforced stretches of I-75 between Florida and Michigan. Watch your speed carefully. Patrol cars often sit in the median strip, in the emergency vehicle "U" turn breaks. The police radio bands are always very active here as they communicate back & forth.
Swamp
N
Weigh Station
DON'T FORGET TO TOP UP YOUR TANK WITH GAS, BEFORE LEAVING GEORGIA
41
Tune your radio to 910AM to get Disney World and Florida vacation news
Old 7
HAHIRA
G-Citgo
29
Rts 122 N41
Hahira/Barney
Lakeland
G-BP SavATon
F-AppleVal
L-Hahra
Lowdnes Co.
SPANISH MOSS IN TREES - LEGEND OF THE INDIAN PRINCESS ON PAGE 137
CECIL
41
Old 8
32
Old Coffee Rd
Cecil
G-Amoco
Florida
GEORGIA
Cook County
NORTH
-8- -9- -10- -11- -12- -13- -14- -15- -16- -17- -18- -19- -20- -21- -22- -23- -24- -25- -26- -27- -28- -29- -30- -31- -32- -33-
1,500 1,000 500

HAVE A SAFE TRIP TO YOUR FLORIDA DESTINATION. DON'T FORGET TO STOP AT THE WELCOME CENTER AND GET YOUR FREE ORANGE OR GRAPEFRUIT JUICE DRINK! ALSO, PICK UP YOUR DISCOUNT COUPON BOOKS FROM THE BOXES NEAR THE VENDING MACHINES

Dave

FLORIDA DESTINATIONS - Routes & Mileage

DESTINATION	ROUTE	MILES/*Km*
ORLANDO	FL Border (I-75)>Wildwood (FL Tpk)> >Orlando	210/*338*
TITUSVILLE	FL Border (I-75)>Wildwood (FL Tpk)> Orlando>Orlando (Rts 528/427)>Titusville	250/*402*
JACKSONVILLE	Fl Border (I-75)>Lake City (I-10)>Jacksonville	113/*182*
DAYTONA BCH	FL Border (I-75)>I-10>I-295>I-95>Daytona	188/*303*
FT LAUDERDALE	FL Border (I-75)>Wildwood (FL Tpk)> >Fort Lauderdale	407/*655*
MIAMI	FL Border (I-75)>Wildwood (FL Tpk)>Miami	422/*679*
TAMPA	FL Border (I-75)>Tampa	226/*364*
St. PETERSBURG	FL Border (I-75)>St. Petersburg	247/*397*
FORT MYERS	FL Border (I-75)>Fort Myers	346/*557*
NAPLES	FL Border (I-75)>Naples	388/*624*
KEY WEST	FL Border (I-75)>Wildwood (FL Tpk)>Miami> >Miami (FL Tpk/US 1)>Key West	578/*930*

Services to **East** (*left* of car) — **SOUTH** — Services to **West** (*right* of car)

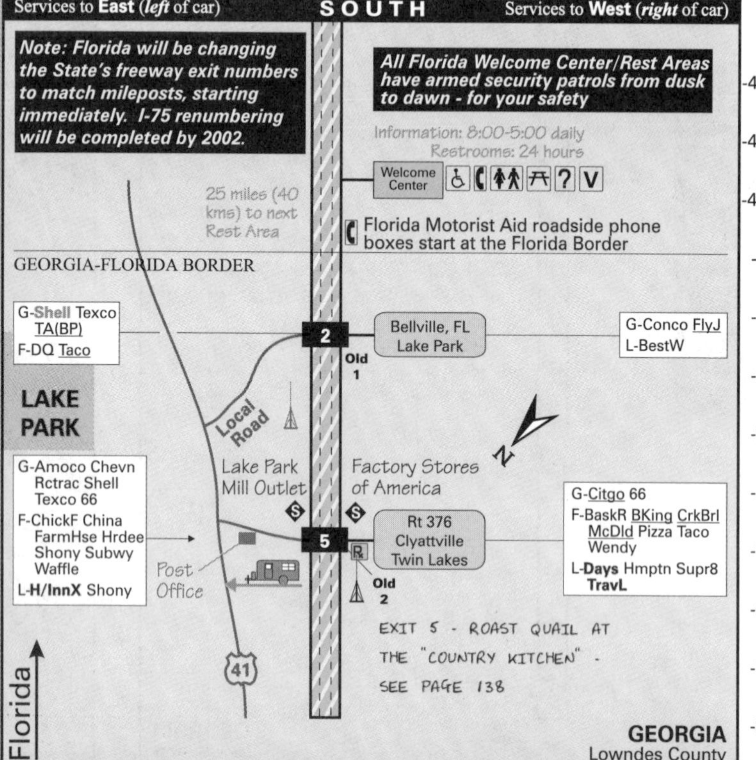

NORTH

Mile Posts: -469- -470- -471- -0- -1- -2- -3- -4- -5- -6- -7- -8-

Elevation — Feet above sea level: 1,500 1,000 500

Off The Beaten Path

One of the enjoyable aspects of a journey along I-75 is the abundance of interesting places you can visit within just a few minutes of an interstate exit. Yet many travelers don't take advantage of this because of the fear of becoming lost in unfamiliar territory.

On the following pages we provide you with some short side trips you can take - perhaps as a brief evening tour after checking into your motel, or as a short excursion in your day's drive.

Enjoy . . . after all, getting there is half the fun!

BATTLE OF THE RAISIN RIVER

Monroe, MI; West of I-75 Exit 14

During the 1812 War between Britain and the USA, a fierce battle took place just to the west of I-75, on the banks of the Raisin River. After the battle, Indians over ran Frenchtown where the US wounded were quartered, and massacred the soldiers.

I-75 maps: 9-S, 190-N Story: page 64

Distance from I-75: 1/2 mile
Time from I-75: 3 minutes
Min. time to visit: 30 minutes
Admission: Free, donation appreciated
Phone: 734-243-7136
Hours: Memorial - Labor Day
- 7 days a week, 10am - 5pm
Labor - Memorial Day
- Sat & Sun only, 10am - 5pm

Woods
Dixie Hwy (Old Hull Rd)
Militia & Indian
British Attack
Regulars
Orchard and Hollow
Site of old Frenchtown
Militia & Indian
Detroit Avenue
Battlefield Visitors Center & Museum
Sterling Is
East Elm Ave
Raisin River
14
over 60 soldiers massacred by Indians here
US soldiers retreat to woods south of river and surrender
SOUTH 75
0 ¼ ½ mile

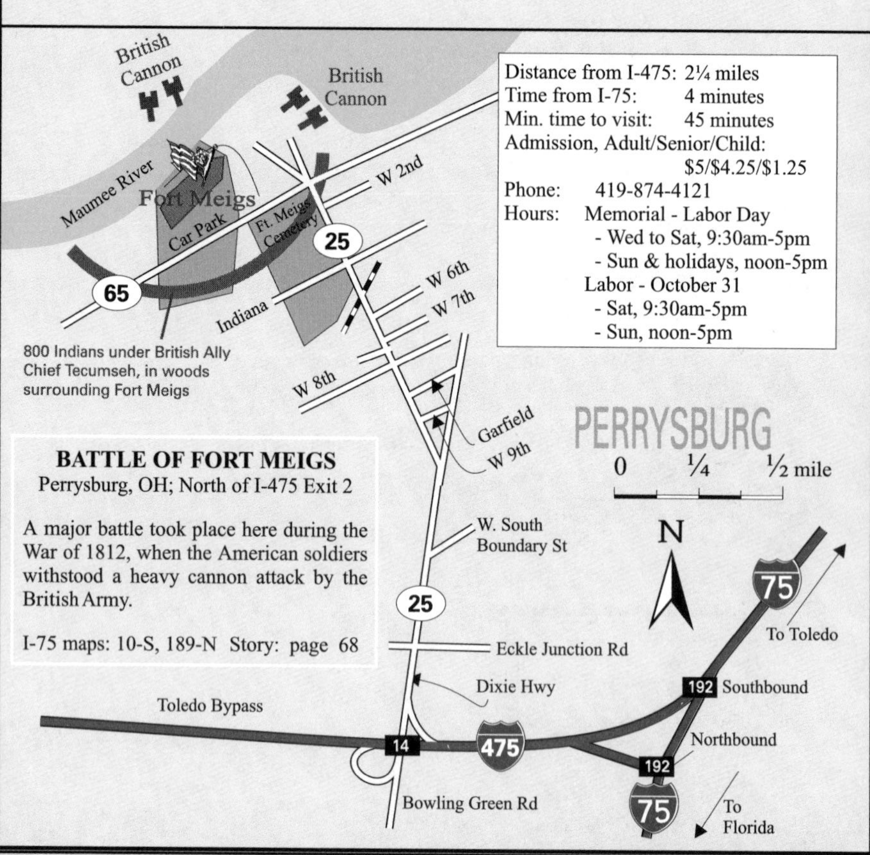

Distance from I-475: 2¼ miles
Time from I-75: 4 minutes
Min. time to visit: 45 minutes
Admission, Adult/Senior/Child: $5/$4.25/$1.25
Phone: 419-874-4121
Hours: Memorial - Labor Day
- Wed to Sat, 9:30am-5pm
- Sun & holidays, noon-5pm
Labor - October 31
- Sat, 9:30am-5pm
- Sun, noon-5pm

BATTLE OF FORT MEIGS

Perrysburg, OH; North of I-475 Exit 2

A major battle took place here during the War of 1812, when the American soldiers withstood a heavy cannon attack by the British Army.

I-75 maps: 10-S, 189-N Story: page 68

USAF MUSEUM

Dayton, OH; I-75 Exits 58 & 54C

The oldest and largest military airforce museum in the World. Follow the story of flight from Kitty Hawk to the Space Age with more than 300 exhibits.

I-75 maps: 15-S, 184-N
Story: page 78

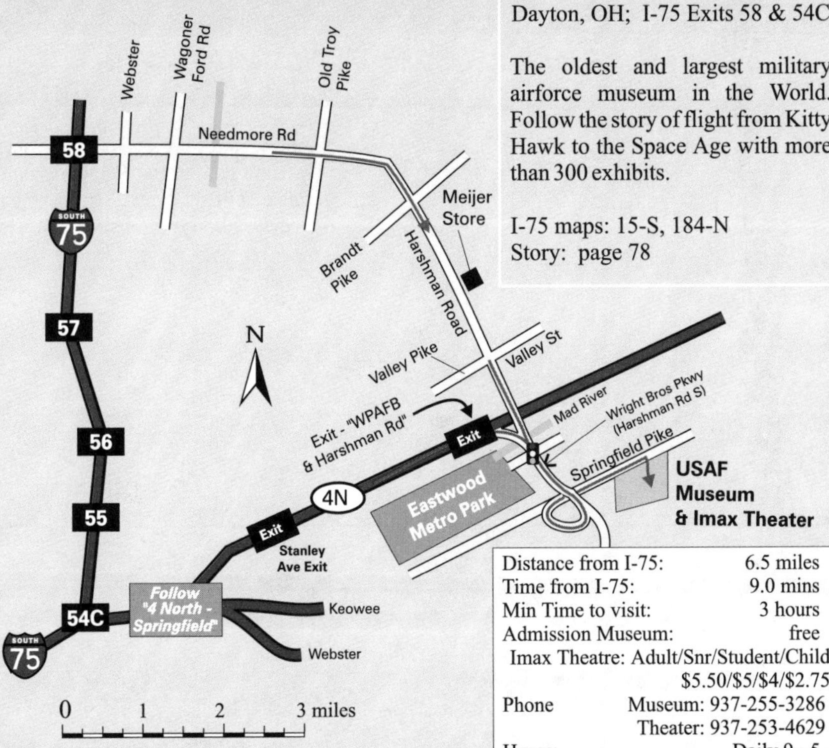

Follow "4 North - Springfield"

Distance from I-75:	6.5 miles
Time from I-75:	9.0 mins
Min Time to visit:	3 hours
Admission Museum:	free
Imax Theatre: Adult/Snr/Student/Child	$5.50/$5/$4/$2.75
Phone	Museum: 937-255-3286
	Theater: 937-253-4629
Hours:	Daily 9 - 5

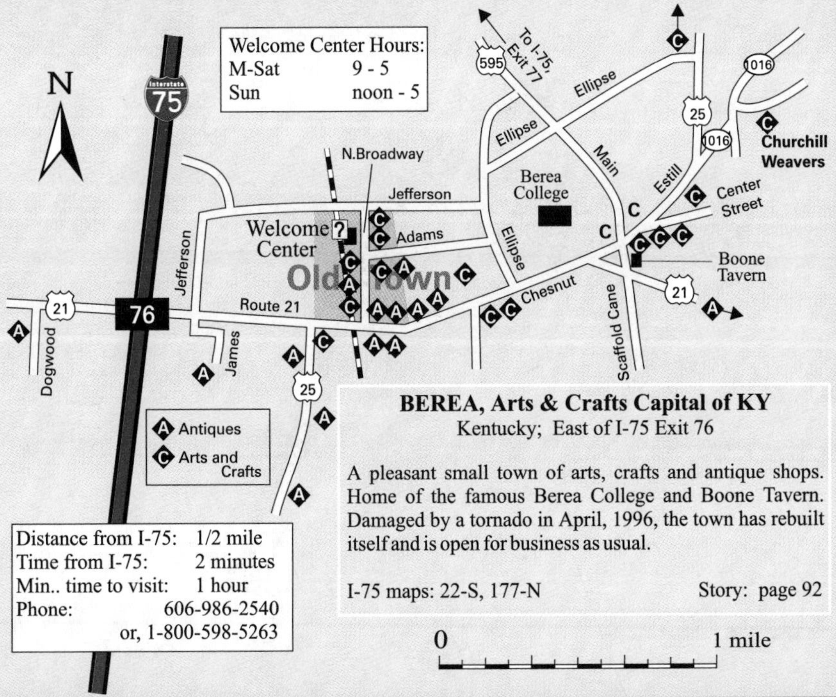

Welcome Center Hours:	
M-Sat	9 - 5
Sun	noon - 5

A Antiques
C Arts and Crafts

BEREA, Arts & Crafts Capital of KY

Kentucky; East of I-75 Exit 76

A pleasant small town of arts, crafts and antique shops. Home of the famous Berea College and Boone Tavern. Damaged by a tornado in April, 1996, the town has rebuilt itself and is open for business as usual.

I-75 maps: 22-S, 177-N
Story: page 92

Distance from I-75:	1/2 mile
Time from I-75:	2 minutes
Min.. time to visit:	1 hour
Phone:	606-986-2540
	or, 1-800-598-5263

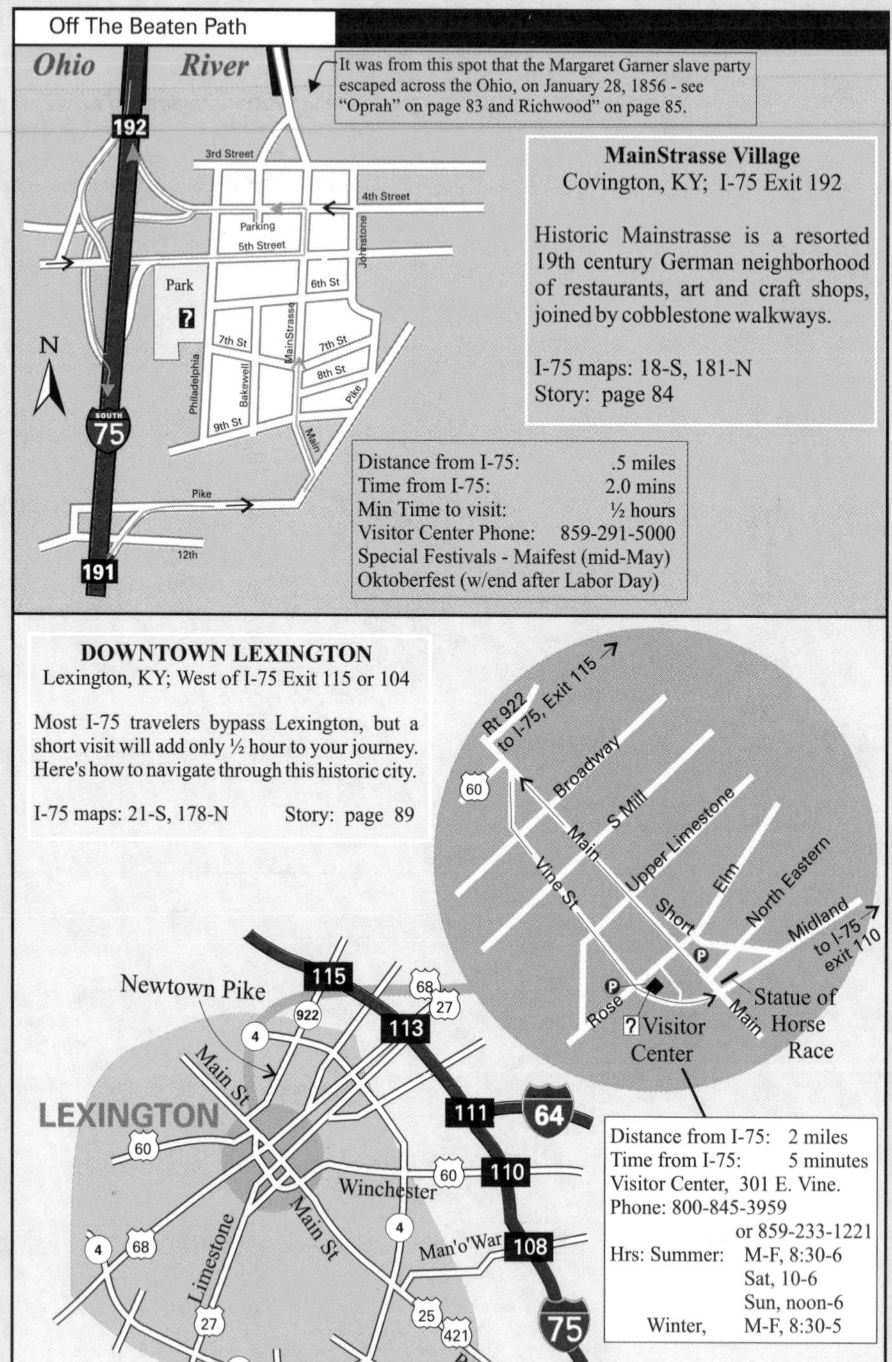
Ohio River
It was from this spot that the Margaret Garner slave party escaped across the Ohio, on January 28, 1856 - see "Oprah" on page 83 and Richwood" on page 85.
MainStrasse Village
Covington, KY; I-75 Exit 192
Historic Mainstrasse is a resorted 19th century German neighborhood of restaurants, art and craft shops, joined by cobblestone walkways.
I-75 maps: 18-S, 181-N
Story: page 84
192
3rd Street
4th Street
Parking
5th Street
Johnstone
Park
6th St
7th St
MainStrasse
7th St
8th St
Pike
Philadelphia
Bakewell
9th St
Main
N
75
Pike
12th
191
Distance from I-75: .5 miles
Time from I-75: 2.0 mins
Min Time to visit: ½ hours
Visitor Center Phone: 859-291-5000
Special Festivals - Maifest (mid-May)
Oktoberfest (w/end after Labor Day)
DOWNTOWN LEXINGTON
Lexington, KY; West of I-75 Exit 115 or 104
Most I-75 travelers bypass Lexington, but a short visit will add only ½ hour to your journey. Here's how to navigate through this historic city.
I-75 maps: 21-S, 178-N
Story: page 89
Rt 922 to I-75, Exit 115
60
Broadway
Main
S Mill
Upper Limestone
Vine St
Elm
North Eastern
Short
Midland
to I-75 exit 110
Rose
Main
Statue of Horse Race
Visitor Center
115
Newtown Pike
922
68
27
113
4
Main St
LEXINGTON
111
64
60
60
110
Winchester
Main St
4
Limestone
4
68
Man'o'War
108
27
25
421
75
4
Richmond Rd
New Circle Rd
104
N
0 1 2 3 4 miles
Distance from I-75: 2 miles
Time from I-75: 5 minutes
Visitor Center, 301 E. Vine.
Phone: 800-845-3959
or 859-233-1221
Hrs: Summer: M-F, 8:30-6
Sat, 10-6
Sun, noon-6
Winter, M-F, 8:30-5

WHITE HALL

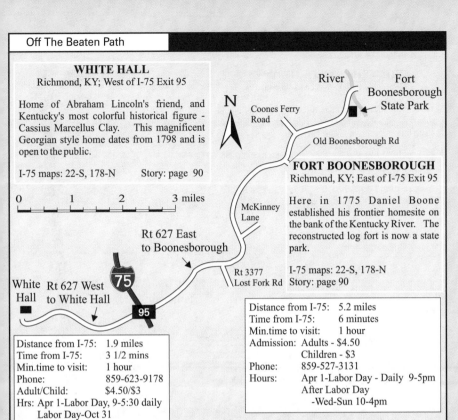

Richmond, KY; West of I-75 Exit 95

Home of Abraham Lincoln's friend, and Kentucky's most colorful historical figure - Cassius Marcellus Clay. This magnificent Georgian style home dates from 1798 and is open to the public.

I-75 maps: 22-S, 178-N Story: page 90

Distance from I-75:	1.9 miles
Time from I-75:	3 1/2 mins
Min.time to visit:	1 hour
Phone:	859-623-9178
Adult/Child:	$4.50/$3
Hrs: Apr 1-Labor Day, 9-5:30 daily Labor Day-Oct 31	

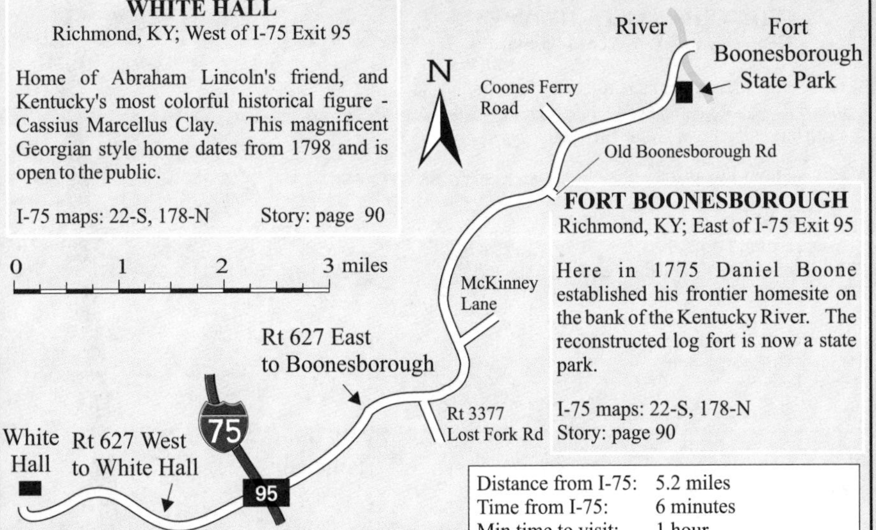

FORT BOONESBOROUGH

Richmond, KY; East of I-75 Exit 95

Here in 1775 Daniel Boone established his frontier homesite on the bank of the Kentucky River. The reconstructed log fort is now a state park.

I-75 maps: 22-S, 178-N
Story: page 90

Distance from I-75:	5.2 miles
Time from I-75:	6 minutes
Min.time to visit:	1 hour
Admission:	Adults - $4.50 Children - $3
Phone:	859-527-3131
Hours:	Apr 1-Labor Day - Daily 9-5pm After Labor Day -Wed-Sun 10-4pm

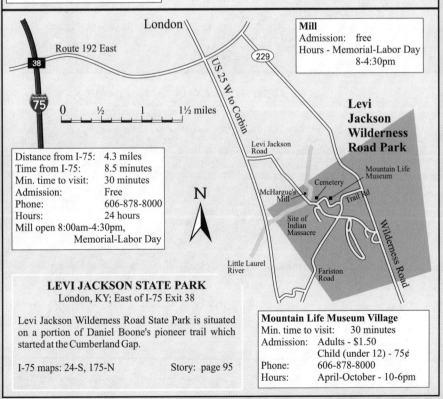

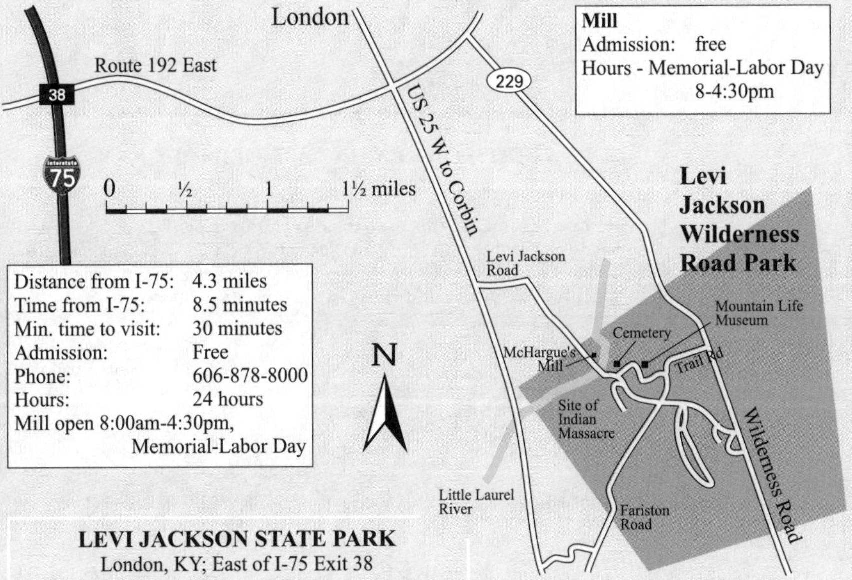

Mill
Admission: free
Hours - Memorial-Labor Day 8-4:30pm

Distance from I-75:	4.3 miles
Time from I-75:	8.5 minutes
Min. time to visit:	30 minutes
Admission:	Free
Phone:	606-878-8000
Hours:	24 hours
Mill open 8:00am-4:30pm, Memorial-Labor Day	

LEVI JACKSON STATE PARK

London, KY; East of I-75 Exit 38

Levi Jackson Wilderness Road State Park is situated on a portion of Daniel Boone's pioneer trail which started at the Cumberland Gap.

I-75 maps: 24-S, 175-N Story: page 95

Mountain Life Museum Village

Min. time to visit:	30 minutes
Admission:	Adults - $1.50 Child (under 12) - 75¢
Phone:	606-878-8000
Hours:	April-October - 10-6pm

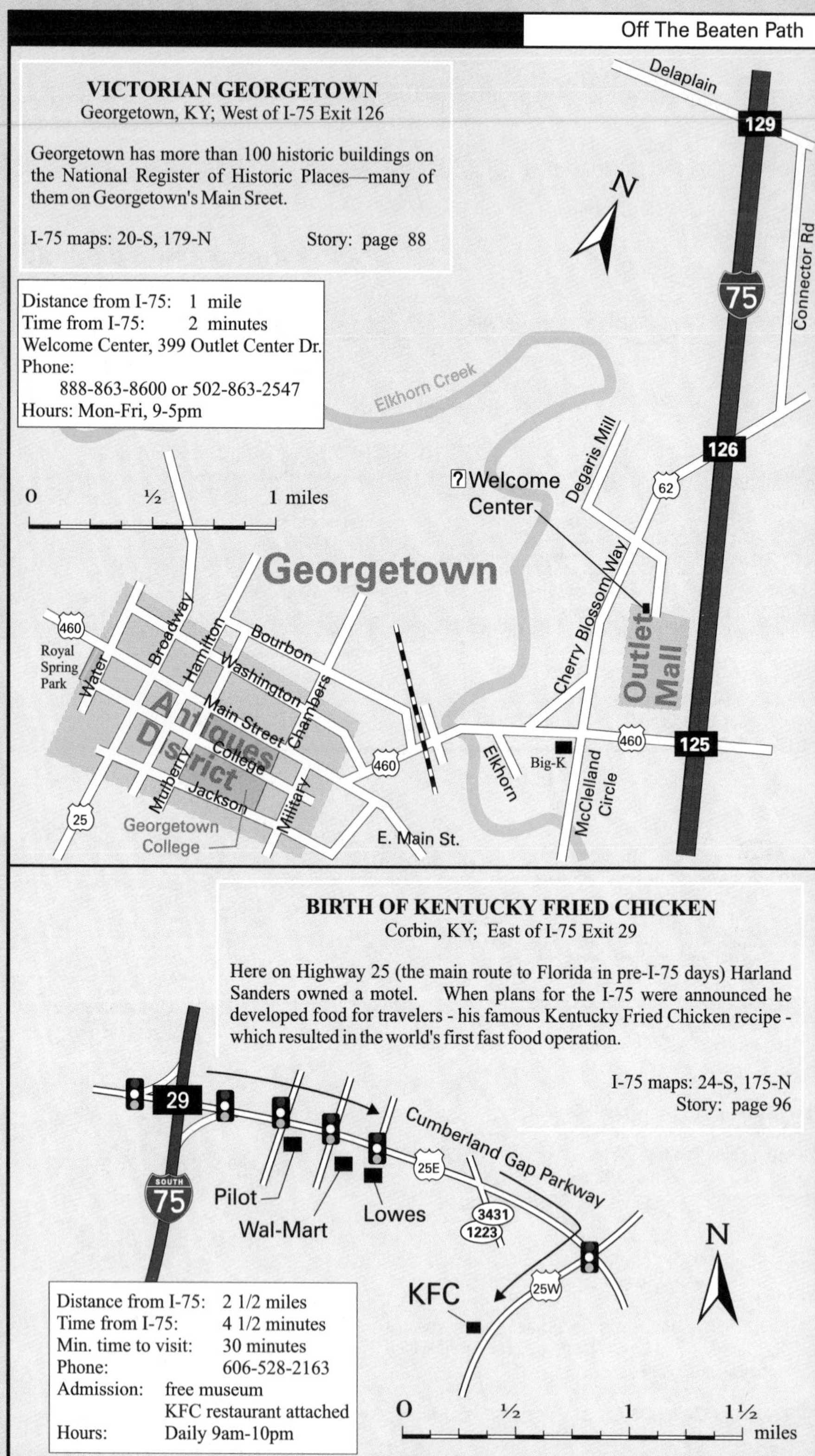

VICTORIAN GEORGETOWN

Georgetown, KY; West of I-75 Exit 126

Georgetown has more than 100 historic buildings on the National Register of Historic Places—many of them on Georgetown's Main Sreet.

I-75 maps: 20-S, 179-N

Story: page 88

Distance from I-75: 1 mile
Time from I-75: 2 minutes
Welcome Center, 399 Outlet Center Dr.
Phone:
888-863-8600 or 502-863-2547
Hours: Mon-Fri, 9-5pm

BIRTH OF KENTUCKY FRIED CHICKEN

Corbin, KY; East of I-75 Exit 29

Here on Highway 25 (the main route to Florida in pre-I-75 days) Harland Sanders owned a motel. When plans for the I-75 were announced he developed food for travelers - his famous Kentucky Fried Chicken recipe - which resulted in the world's first fast food operation.

I-75 maps: 24-S, 175-N

Story: page 96

Distance from I-75:	2 1/2 miles
Time from I-75:	4 1/2 minutes
Min. time to visit:	30 minutes
Phone:	606-528-2163
Admission:	free museum KFC restaurant attached
Hours:	Daily 9am-10pm

CUMBERLAND FALLS

Corbin, KY; West of I-75 Exit 15 or 25

One of the natural treasures of Daniel Boone National Forest, Cumberland Falls is well known for its "Moonbows," rainbows created in its mist by the light of the moon.

I-75 maps: 25-S, 175-N Story: page 96

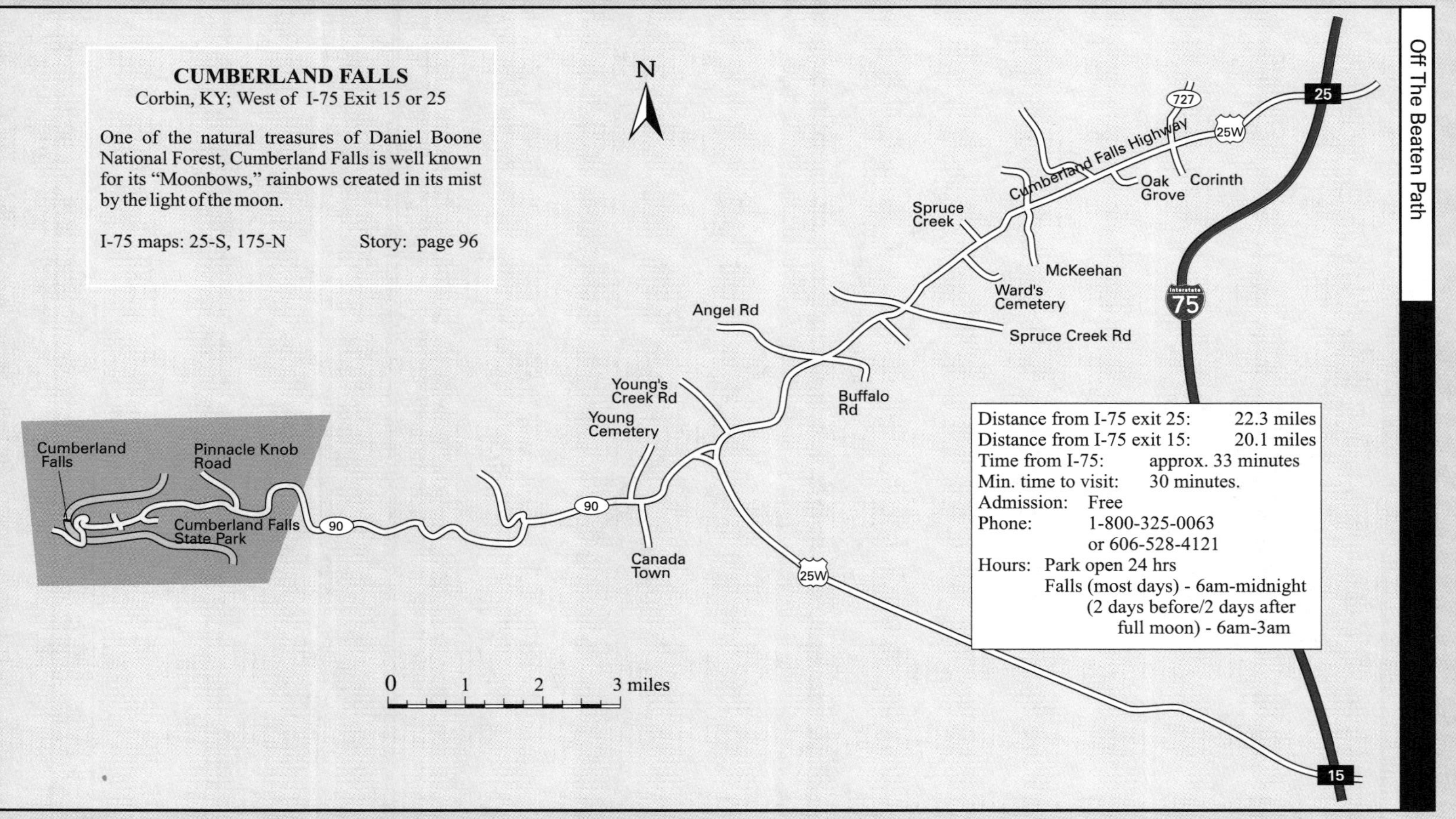

Distance from I-75 exit 25: 22.3 miles
Distance from I-75 exit 15: 20.1 miles
Time from I-75: approx. 33 minutes
Min. time to visit: 30 minutes.
Admission: Free
Phone: 1-800-325-0063
or 606-528-4121
Hours: Park open 24 hrs
Falls (most days) - 6am-midnight
(2 days before/2 days after full moon) - 6am-3am

ELK VALLEY

Tennessee - S/Bound: exit 160
N/Bound: exit 141

A pretty, alternative route to the I-75. Runs on winding road and through tunnels of trees in the valley immediately to the west of I-75. Caution - a great drive on a good day but do not use in bad weather or if you do not enjoy narrow twisting roads.

I-75 maps: 26-S, 173-N Story: page 98

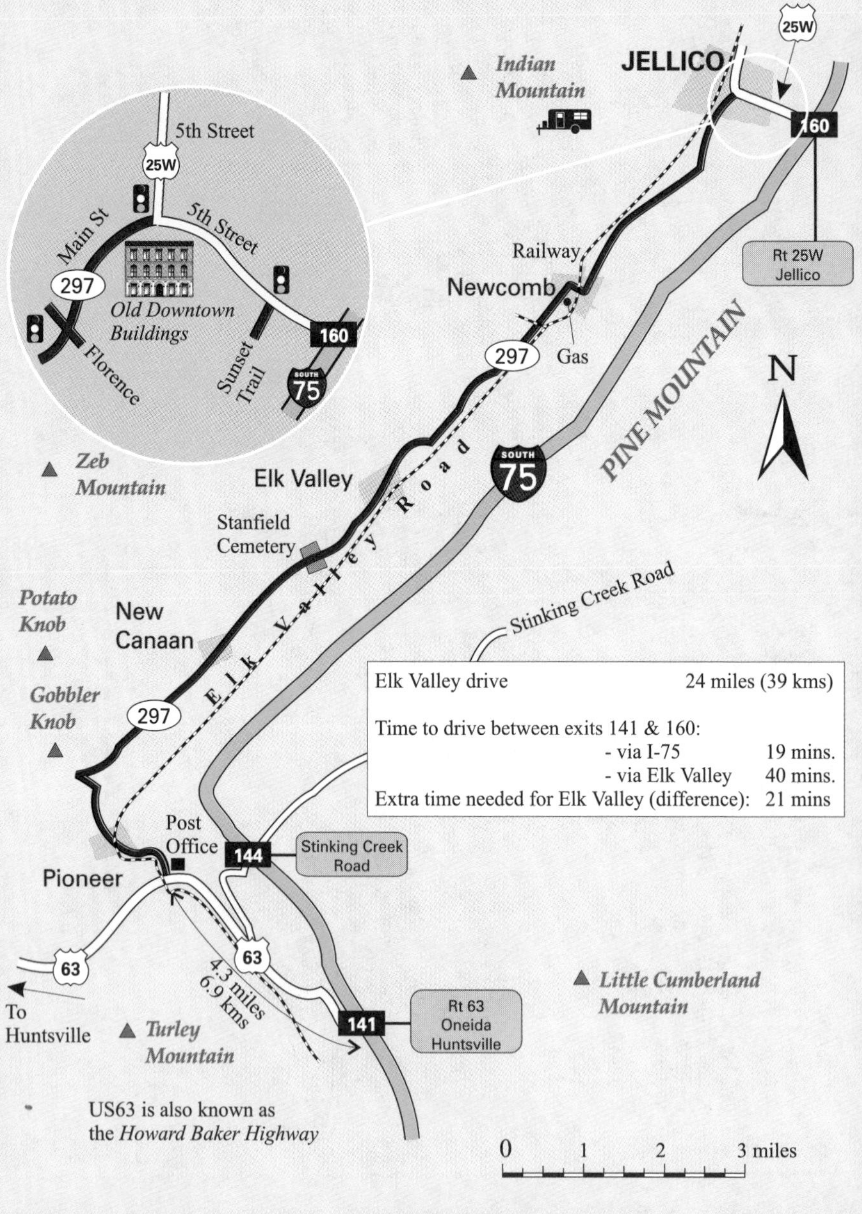

Elk Valley drive 24 miles (39 kms)

Time to drive between exits 141 & 160:
- via I-75 19 mins.
- via Elk Valley 40 mins.
Extra time needed for Elk Valley (difference): 21 mins

US63 is also known as the *Howard Baker Highway*

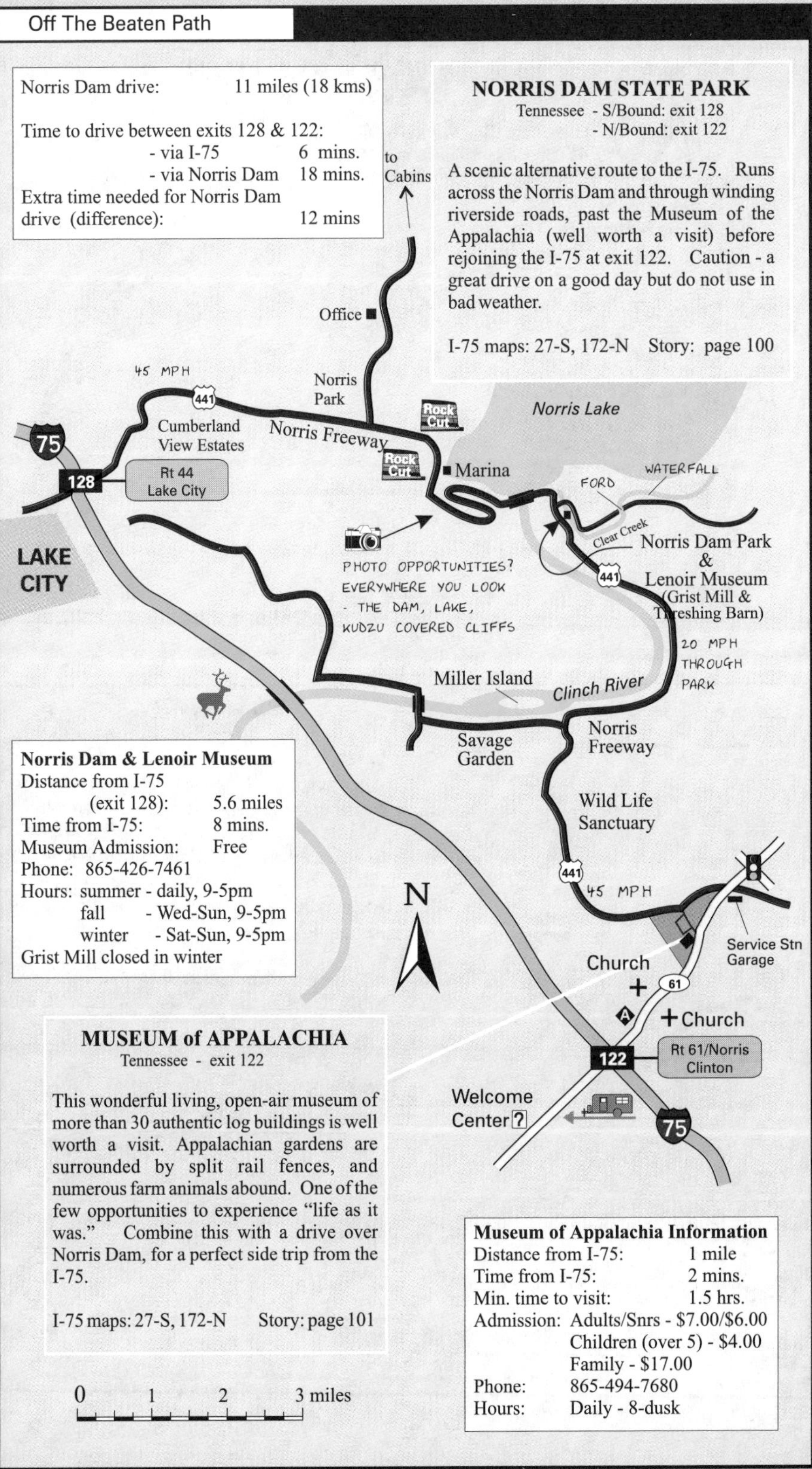

NORRIS DAM STATE PARK

Tennessee - S/Bound: exit 128
- N/Bound: exit 122

A scenic alternative route to the I-75. Runs across the Norris Dam and through winding riverside roads, past the Museum of the Appalachia (well worth a visit) before rejoining the I-75 at exit 122. Caution - a great drive on a good day but do not use in bad weather.

I-75 maps: 27-S, 172-N Story: page 100

Norris Dam & Lenoir Museum

Distance from I-75 (exit 128): 5.6 miles
Time from I-75: 8 mins.
Museum Admission: Free
Phone: 865-426-7461
Hours: summer - daily, 9-5pm
fall - Wed-Sun, 9-5pm
winter - Sat-Sun, 9-5pm
Grist Mill closed in winter

MUSEUM of APPALACHIA

Tennessee - exit 122

This wonderful living, open-air museum of more than 30 authentic log buildings is well worth a visit. Appalachian gardens are surrounded by split rail fences, and numerous farm animals abound. One of the few opportunities to experience "life as it was." Combine this with a drive over Norris Dam, for a perfect side trip from the I-75.

I-75 maps: 27-S, 172-N Story: page 101

Museum of Appalachia Information

Distance from I-75: 1 mile
Time from I-75: 2 mins.
Min. time to visit: 1.5 hrs.
Admission: Adults/Snrs - $7.00/$6.00
Children (over 5) - $4.00
Family - $17.00
Phone: 865-494-7680
Hours: Daily - 8-dusk

CHICKAMAUGA BATTLEFIELD

Georgia; West of I-75 Exit 350

One of the Civil War's bloodiest battles. Here in early September, 1863, 62,000 Union soldiers met 65,000 Confederates. The results? 34,600 killed, missing or wounded and a very costly victory for the South.

I-75 maps: 32-S, 167-N
Story: page 112

Distance from I-75:	7.7 miles	Visitor Center phone:	706-866-9241
Time from I-75:	20 minutes	Admission (theatre):	Adults - $3
Min. time to visit:	1 hour		Seniors - $1.50
Hours:	Memorial-Labor Day		Children - $1.50
	8-5:45 pm	Battlefield Tape:	Rental $3.00
	Rest of year	Battlefield:	- Free
	8-4:45 pm		- 8am to dusk

N
27
Battlefield Parkway
Forrest Rd
Reed's Br Rd
Dietz Road
Three Notch Road
2
75
KOA
350
Welcome Center
Chickamauga Battlefield
Lafayette Road
Georgia Wines
0 1 2 3 miles

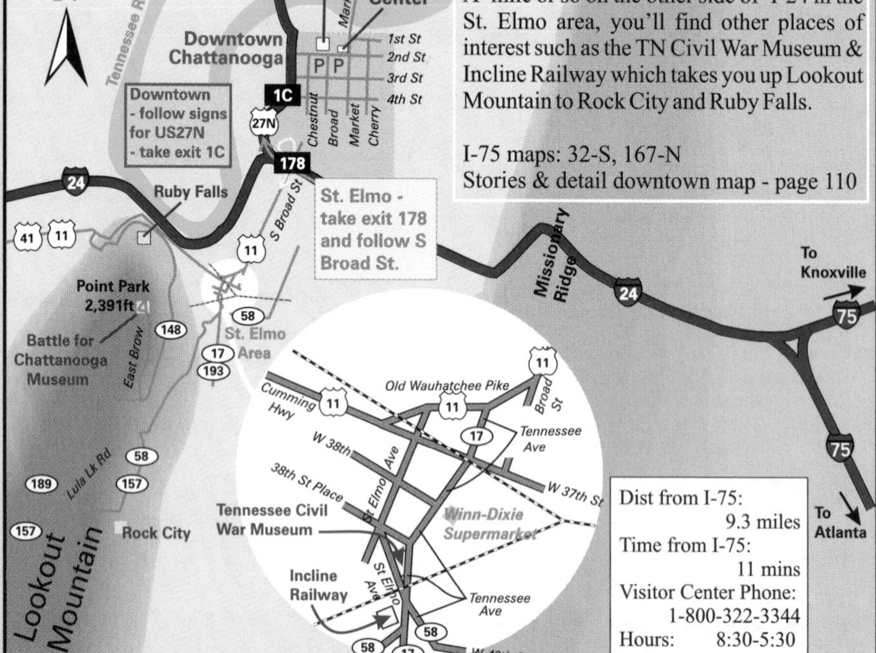

CHATTANOOGA

I-75 Exit 2

Often missed by Interstate travelers, this city's recently renovated downtown area is full of interesting places to visit and explore. A mile or so on the other side of I-24 in the St. Elmo area, you'll find other places of interest such as the TN Civil War Museum & Incline Railway which takes you up Lookout Mountain to Rock City and Ruby Falls.

I-75 maps: 32-S, 167-N
Stories & detail downtown map - page 110

Dist from I-75: 9.3 miles
Time from I-75: 11 mins
Visitor Center Phone: 1-800-322-3344
Hours: 8:30-5:30

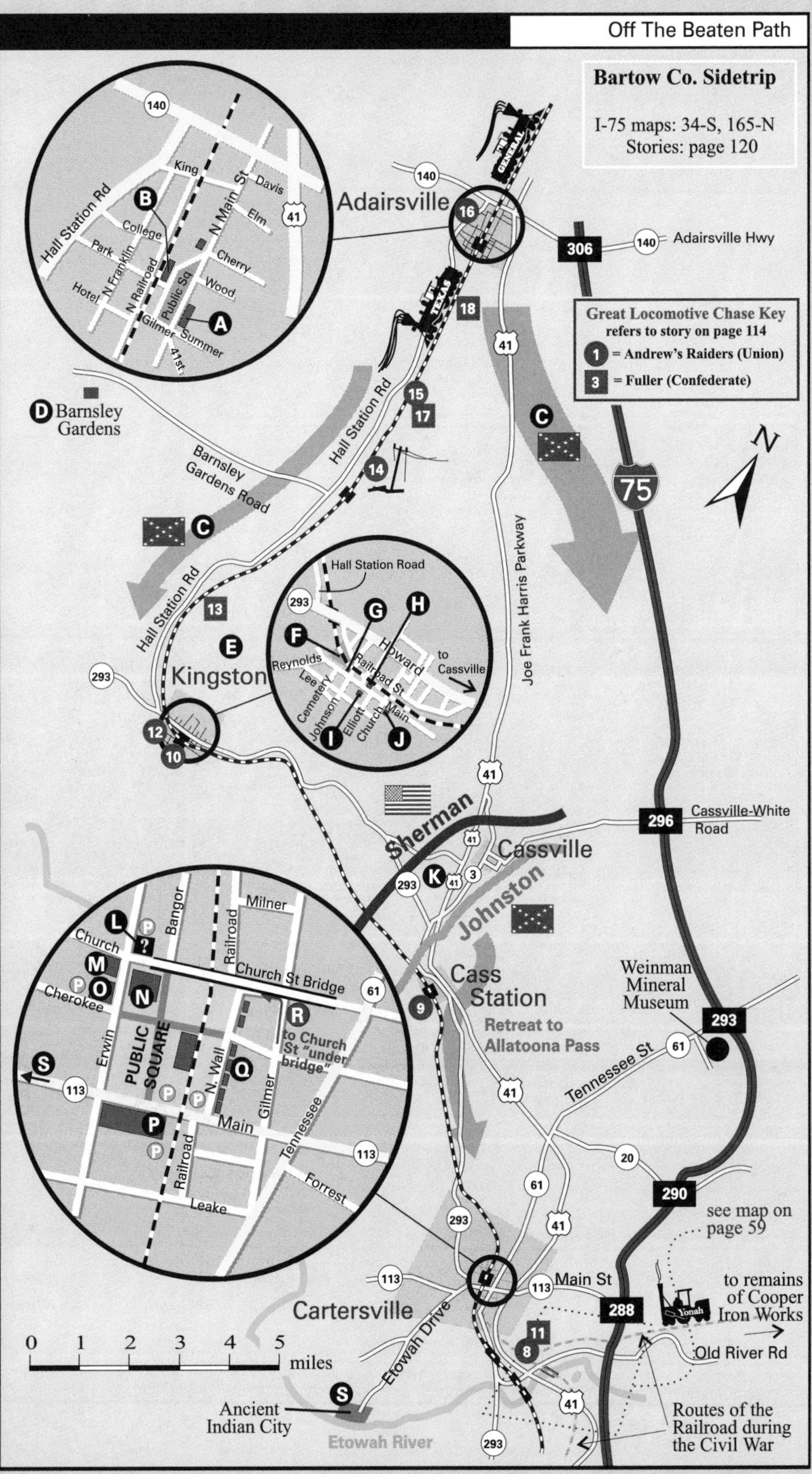
Bartow Co. Sidetrip
I-75 maps: 34-S, 165-N
Stories: page 120
Great Locomotive Chase Key
refers to story on page 114
1 = Andrew's Raiders (Union)
3 = Fuller (Confederate)
Adairsville
Adairsville Hwy
Hall Station Rd
King
Davis
N Main St
Elm
College
Cherry
Park
N Franklin
N Railroad
Public Sq
Wood
Hotel
Gilmer
Summer
41st
Barnsley Gardens
Barnsley Gardens Road
Joe Frank Harris Parkway
Kingston
Hall Station Road
Reynolds
Howard
Railroad St
to Cassville
Lee
Cemetery
Johnson
Elliott
Church
Main
Sherman
Cassville
Cassville-White Road
Johnston
Cass Station
Retreat to Allatoona Pass
Weinman Mineral Museum
Tennessee St
Milner
Bangor
Railroad
Church
Church St Bridge
Cherokee
Erwin
PUBLIC SQUARE
N. Wall
Gilmer
to Church St "under bridge"
Main
Tennessee
Forrest
Leake
see map on page 59
Main St
to remains of Cooper Iron Works
Yonah
Old River Rd
Cartersville
Etowah Drive
0 1 2 3 4 5
miles
Ancient Indian City
Etowah River
Routes of the Railroad during the Civil War

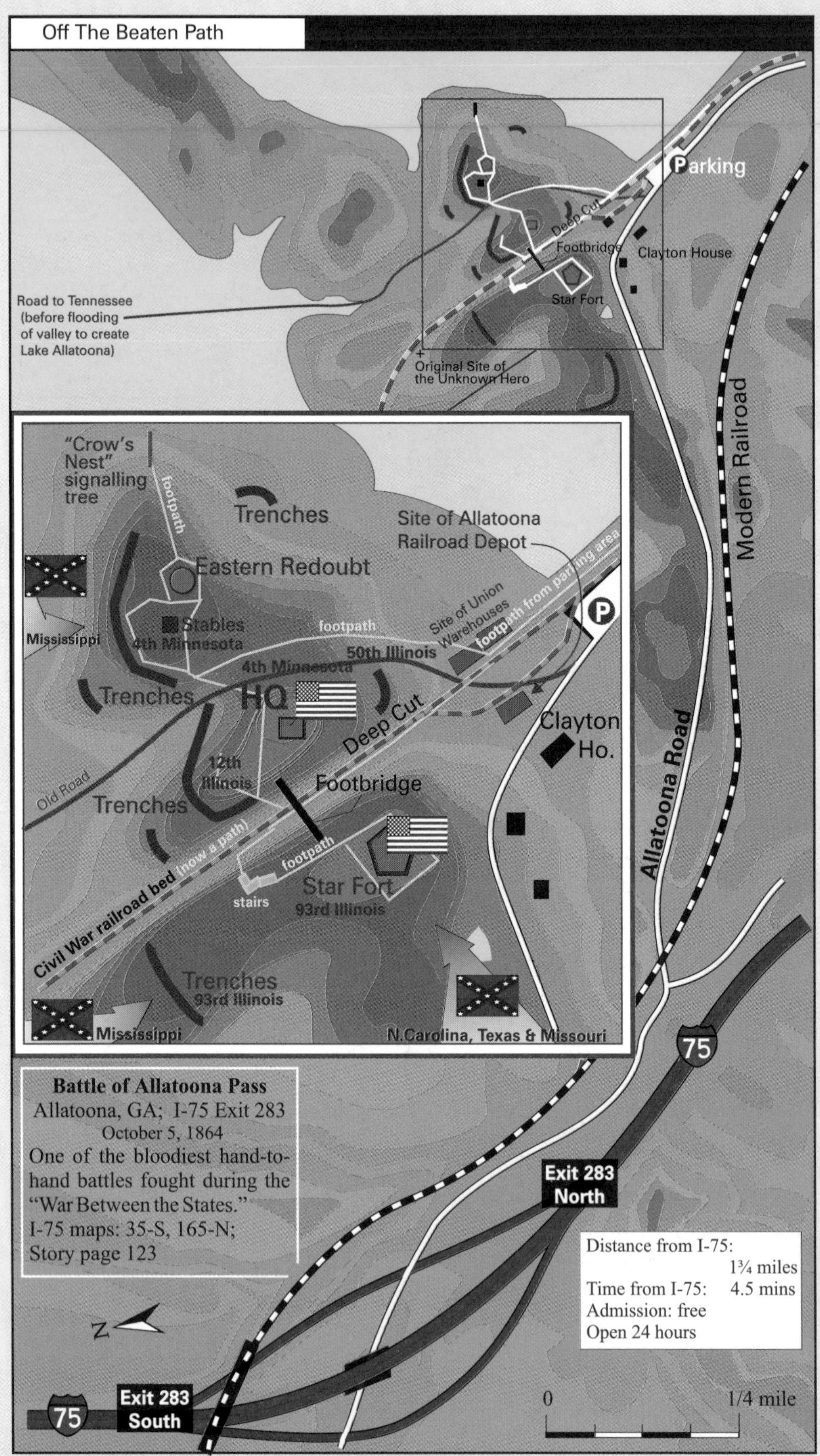

Parking
Deep Cut
Footbridge
Clayton House
Star Fort
Road to Tennessee (before flooding of valley to create Lake Allatoona)
Original Site of the Unknown Hero
Modern Railroad
Allatoona Road
"Crow's Nest" signalling tree
footpath
Trenches
Site of Allatoona Railroad Depot
Eastern Redoubt
footpath from parking area
Site of Union Warehouses
Mississippi
Stables
4th Minnesota
footpath
50th Illinois
4th Minnesota
Trenches
HQ
Deep Cut
Clayton Ho.
Old Road
12th Illinois
Footbridge
Trenches
Civil War railroad bed (now a path)
footpath
stairs
Star Fort
93rd Illinois
Trenches
93rd Illinois
Mississippi
N.Carolina, Texas & Missouri
75
Battle of Allatoona Pass
Allatoona, GA; I-75 Exit 283
October 5, 1864
One of the bloodiest hand-to-hand battles fought during the "War Between the States."
I-75 maps: 35-S, 165-N;
Story page 123
Exit 283 North
Distance from I-75: 1¾ miles
Time from I-75: 4.5 mins
Admission: free
Open 24 hours
N
75
Exit 283 South
0
1/4 mile

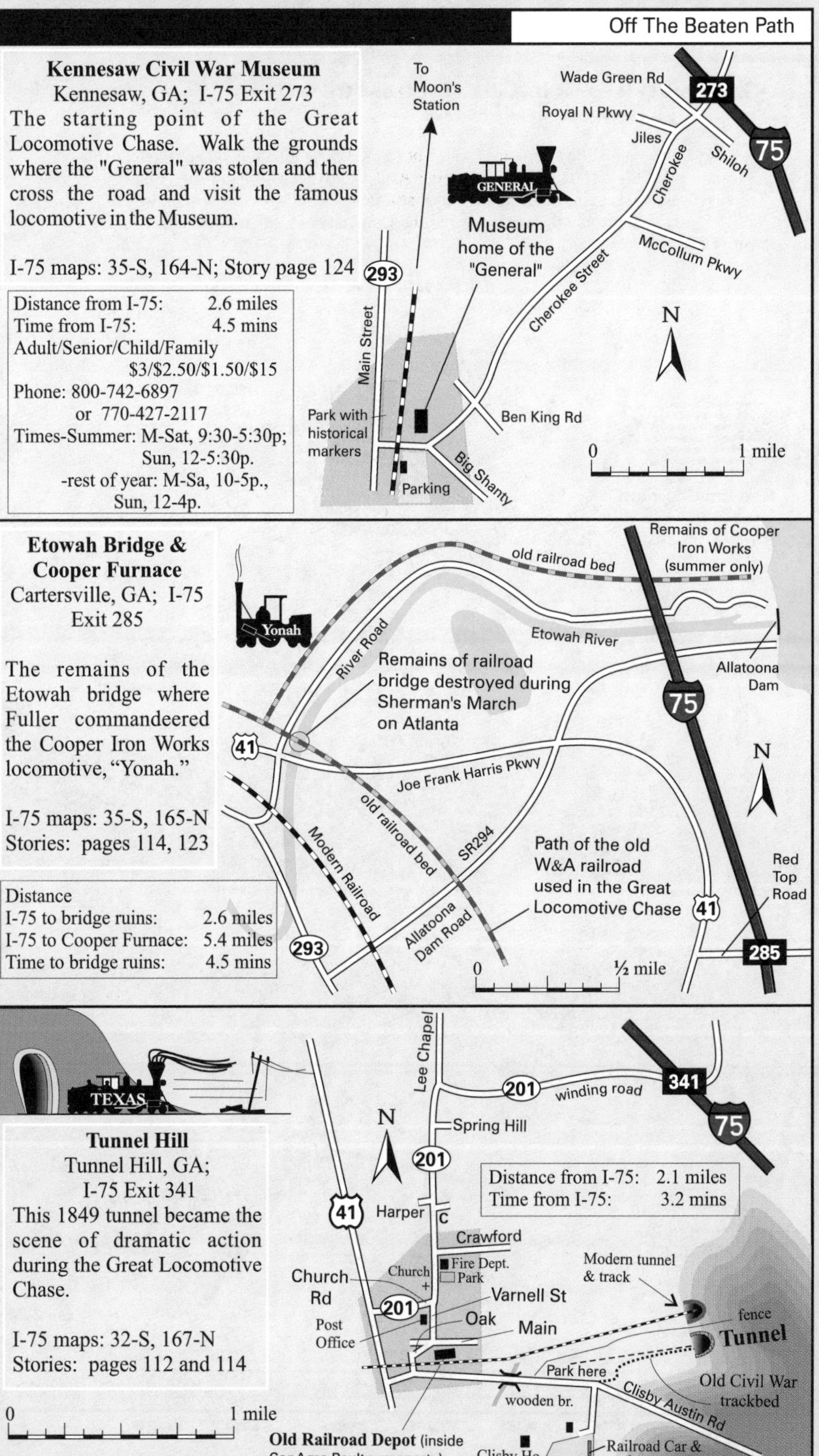

Kennesaw Civil War Museum
Kennesaw, GA; I-75 Exit 273

The starting point of the Great Locomotive Chase. Walk the grounds where the "General" was stolen and then cross the road and visit the famous locomotive in the Museum.

I-75 maps: 35-S, 164-N; Story page 124

Distance from I-75: 2.6 miles
Time from I-75: 4.5 mins
Adult/Senior/Child/Family $3/$2.50/$1.50/$15
Phone: 800-742-6897 or 770-427-2117
Times-Summer: M-Sat, 9:30-5:30p; Sun, 12-5:30p.
-rest of year: M-Sa, 10-5p., Sun, 12-4p.

Etowah Bridge & Cooper Furnace
Cartersville, GA; I-75 Exit 285

The remains of the Etowah bridge where Fuller commandeered the Cooper Iron Works locomotive, "Yonah."

I-75 maps: 35-S, 165-N
Stories: pages 114, 123

Distance
I-75 to bridge ruins: 2.6 miles
I-75 to Cooper Furnace: 5.4 miles
Time to bridge ruins: 4.5 mins

Tunnel Hill
Tunnel Hill, GA;
I-75 Exit 341

This 1849 tunnel became the scene of dramatic action during the Great Locomotive Chase.

I-75 maps: 32-S, 167-N
Stories: pages 112 and 114

Distance from I-75: 2.1 miles
Time from I-75: 3.2 mins

RESACA CIVIL WAR BATTLEFIELD and CEMETERY

Resaca, GA; Cemetery east of I-75 Exit 320

A bloody Civil War battle (5,547 men killed or injured) was fought here, between the 13th and 15th of May, 1864, as the Confederate Army was beaten back towards Atlanta. To help you understand the scope of this large battlefield, the mile markers are shown on the I-75. Directions and distances refer to the Confederate Cemetery which is well worth visiting.

I-75 maps: 33-S, 166 Story: page 117 and Civil War Sidebar, page 118

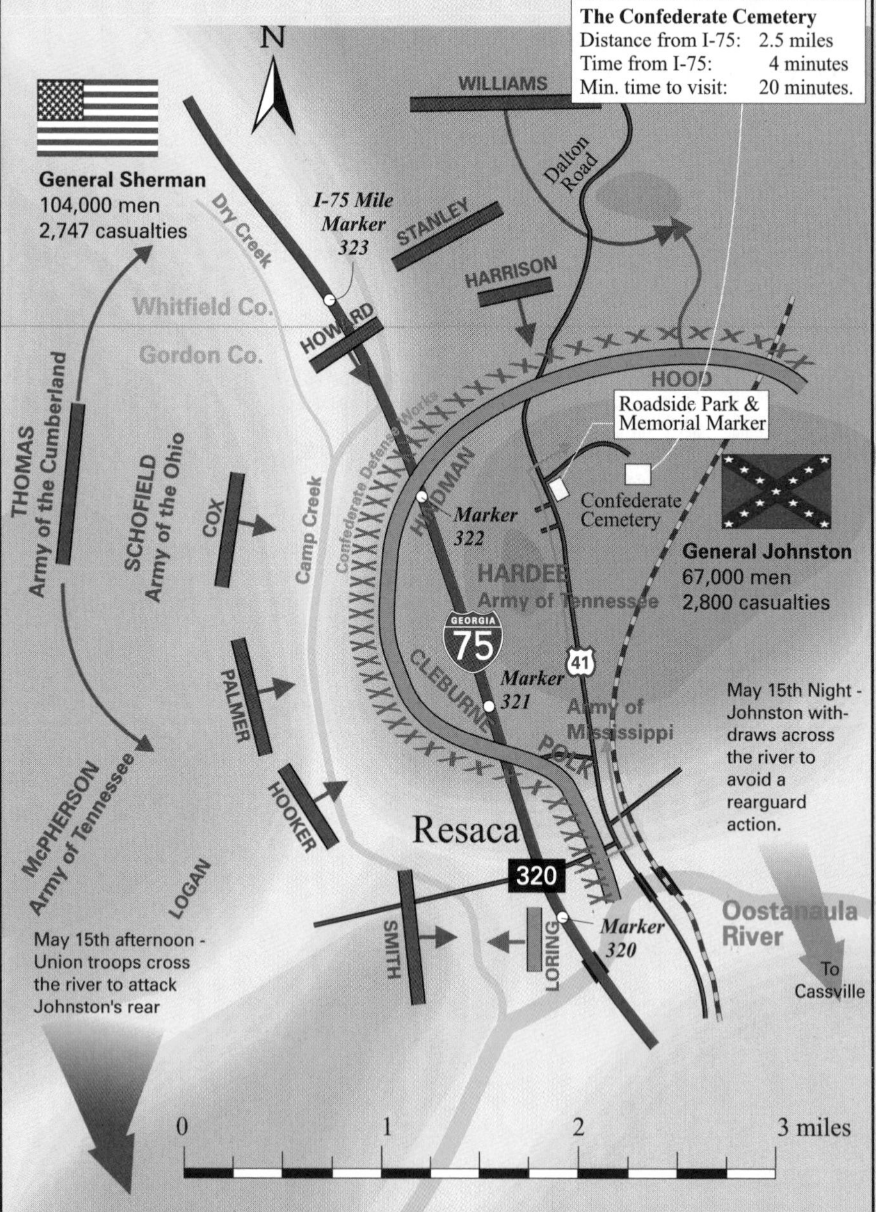

WHISTLE STOP CAFE

Juliette, GA; I-75 Exit 186

Made famous in the movie, *"Fried Green Tomatoes,"* the Whistle Stop Cafe & neighboring antique and craft shops are well worth the drive.

See *"the pond that flew away,"* Smokey Lonesome's Lil' house . . . and the infamous BBQ pit.

I-75 maps: 39-S, 161N
Story: page 131

Thanks to Dean & Betty Clements for help with the map

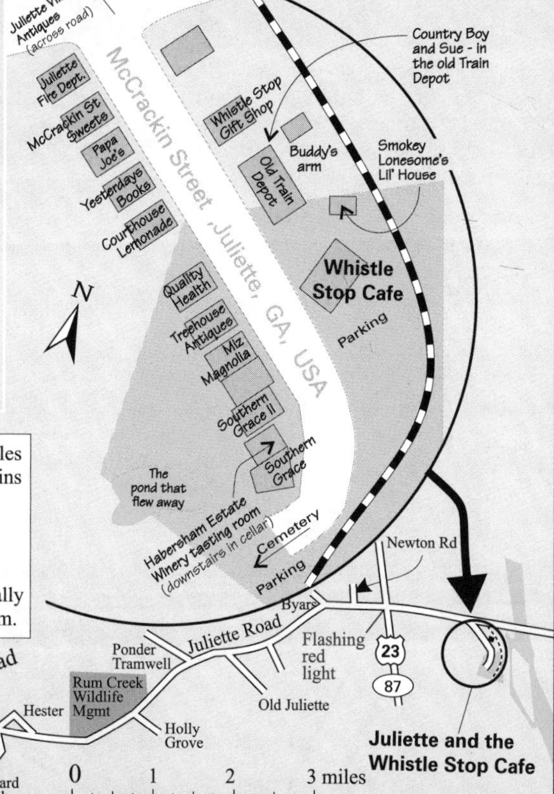

Distance from I-75:	9.3 miles
Time from I-75:	11.2 mins

Cafe phone: 912-994-2770
Cafe hours: M-Sat: 8am - 2pm
Sun: noon - 5pm

Juliette's store hours vary but normally all will be open between 11am - 4 pm.

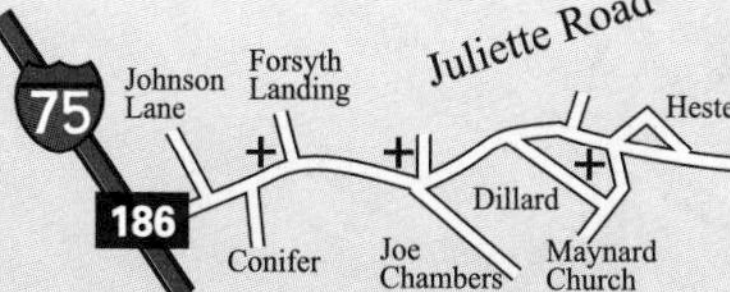

KNOXVILLE, TN BYPASS

N/bound exit 376; S/bound exit 122

A pleasant alternative to the rat race of hectic interstates around Knoxville. The bypass route runs through the Clinch River Valley with the Walden Ridge of the Appalachian Mountains to the north, and into Oak Ridge .

I-75 maps: 27-S, 171-N
Bypass story on page 101
Oak Ridge story on page 104

Oak Ridge Visitor Center,
302 S. Tulane Ave, Oak Ridge
at American Mus of Science & Energy
Phone:
800-887-3429 or 865-482-7821
Hours: M-F, 9-5pm
Sat, 10-2pm

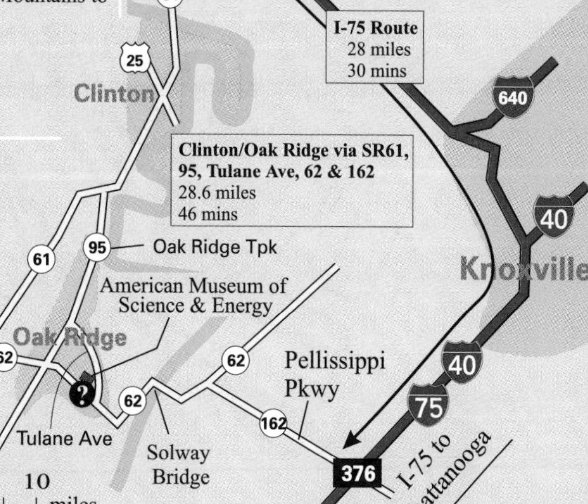

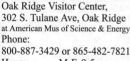

Detroit's Ambassador Bridge to Canada - and Back

Finding the Ambassador Bridge to Canada from I-75 is easy - just take exit 47B, drive across the lights at Lafayette and you are at the bridge toll booths. Watch for trucks on your left as you enter the Toll Plaza - they have to cross to get to the right hand lane.

Getting back onto I-75 South is not so easy. This is nothing to do with Customs or Immigration, it is more to do with finding I-75 again (incidentally, this section of I-75 is called the *"Fisher Freeway"*). The signs are quite confusing and depending upon the season, covered by foliage in some cases. We have included this map to help you.

Finding the I-75 South

1. After clearing Customs, drive across the lights at Porter. Do not go down the I-75 ramp to your left - it goes north!
2. Move into left turn lane after passing Bristol (a small side street on your right).
3. Turn left at the Vernor intersection lights.
4. On Vernor, move immediately into the left turn lane as you cross the bridge over the I-75.
5. At the next lights, turn left onto Fisher Freeway W. Ignore sign at the corner that says "Bridge to Canada."
6. Stay on "Fisher Freeway West" - past Bagley, Lambie, Howard, 25th St, to the lights at Grand Boulevard.
7. Pass Vinewood, Hubbard and Scotten. Immediately after the lights at Clark, move to the left lane and go down the ramp onto the I-75 South.
8. If this ramp is closed for construction, continue on along the service road - there are at least 3 more I-75 Southbound ramps ahead.

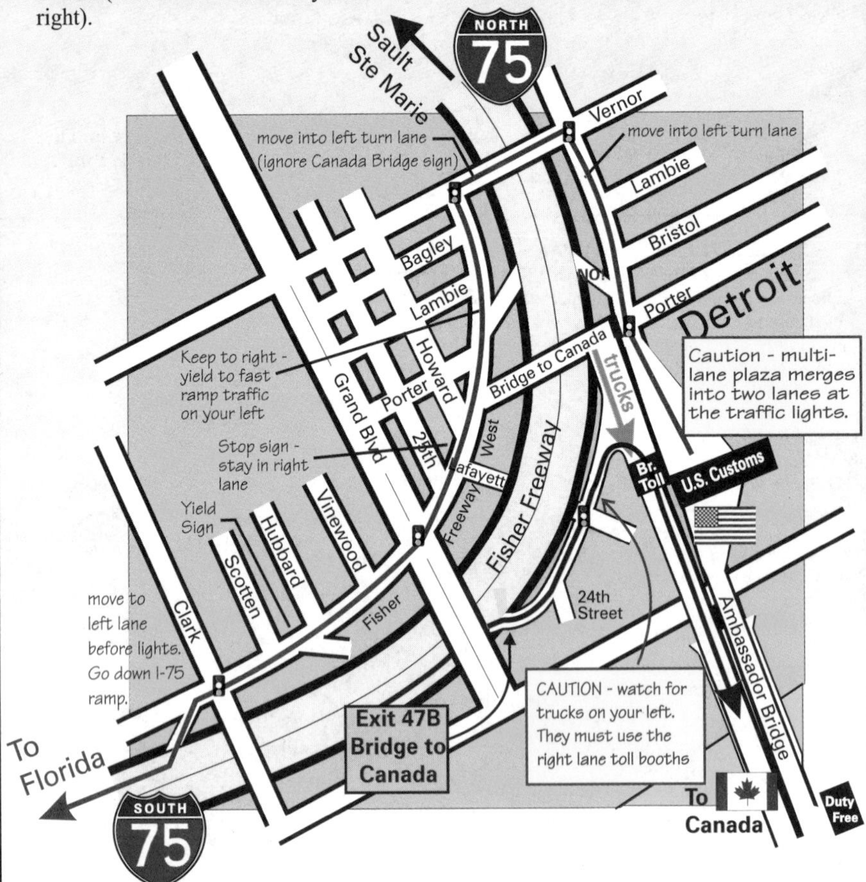

Mile by Mile on I-75

A journey along Interstate-75 can either be a boring, fast-paced ride between two points, or an exciting adventure–a chance to learn more about one of the most fascinating and historically rich areas in North America–much of it right alongside the highway.

For instance, did you know that as you drive the freeway you will pass the site of a War of 1812 massacre, drive through the center of a major Civil War battlefield and pass by two others, cross a two hundred year old pioneer path, traverse an area which not long ago was a swamp infested with rattlesnakes and panthers and travel across the bed of an ancient tropical sea?

Reflecting a more modern era, you will pass by stealth bombers, moon rocks, an electronic road surface and a plant building the F22 Raptor - the US fighter aircraft for the 21st Century. You will also pass by the "Kryptonite" room— a room so secret that only a few people are authorized to enter.

These are just a few of the wonders described in the following pages. Mile-by-mile, we take you down I-75 from Detroit to Florida, revealing the secrets, sights and attractions along the way.

As we travel through these pages, **"Special Reports"** will provide detailed information about sights of particular interest along the way, **"Insider Tips"** will share special local knowledge about interesting restaurants and other roadside "secrets." And our tried and true **$aving Tip$** will save you money . . . many of our readers have told us that these alone have saved them enough money to pay for this book, several times over!

We know you will find this section one of the most enjoyable in this book.

INSIDER TIPS

Throughout the following sections, you will find our famous "Insider Tips"—hints of special significance to help you save money and have a more enjoyable journey. In some instances, we recommend specific I-75 facilities which, from our personal knowledge (often first brought to our attention by our readers–see page 203) offer exceptional value or an unusual (and worthwhile) experience. None of these establishments have paid for this recommendation–we accept no commercial advertising in this guide. In fact, none of them knew they were being inspected at the time of our visit.

Here is where you get the <u>REAL</u> local knowledge.

Interstate 75 is dedicated as the
"Blue Star Memorial Highway"

MEMORIAL HIGHWAY

A tribute to the Armed Forces that have defended the United States of America

Most travelers use interstate-75 as a convenient means for getting from one place to another. In wintertime, its southbound lanes carry northern "snowbirds"who wish to exchange the freezing climates of their home towns for the sunny beaches of Florida. Once school is out, summertime finds young families heading south to enjoy off-season food and lodging bargains while visiting North America's most popular tourist destination, Walt Disney World.

Year round the northbound lanes carry southerners driving north in a quest for skiing, camping or fishing . . . or perhaps just to visit friends and relatives in Michigan, Ohio or Ontario, Canada.

But to me, I-75 is a destination in itself. Unlike the trans-continental interstates which developed from pioneer trails carrying early settler families on their journeys towards the west, I-75 has been criss-crossed by a thousand years of history. Prehistoric cities hid within its shadow. Armies, from the ancient Spanish explorers, the Blue and the Grey of the Civil War, and mechanized movements of the more recent military have traversed its countryside, pioneer explorers and frontiersmen such as Daniel Boone and Kit Carson roamed the lands now covered with its tarmac pavement.

These and many other secrets will be revealed to you in the following pages as we take you on a mile-by-mile journey of discovery, southbound on one of the Nation's most interesting highways.

MI Exit 15-Monroe & General Custer: This exit leads to one of the oldest communities in Michigan, the historic town of Monroe (settled by the French in 1780). General George Custer (of Civil War and Little Bighorn massacre fame) lived here for many years before joining the army and making a name for himself in the Cavalry.

There are more than 23 sites and buildings associated with General Custer in Monroe. The Monroe Museum produces a brochure listing all the sites. Unfortunately, many are not open to the public.

One of the most interesting is the privately owned Nevin Custer farm, just west of Monroe on the north bank of the Raisin River. George and his brother, Nevin, purchased the farm in 1871, five years before his death at Little Bighorn. George's favorite horse, Dandy is buried in the orchard near the barn. Visitors to the farm have included Buffalo Bill Cody and Annie Oakley.

Today, Monroe remembers Custer with a bronze statue of him astride his restless horse, Dandy, while pensively scanning the hills ahead. You will find this superb statue in downtown Monroe at the corners of Elm and Monroe Streets.

MI Exit 14-Battle of the Raisin River (map on page 48): Just west of this exit on the north bank of the Raisin River, lies the site of

WHAT'S IN A NAME?

Indian terms, historical characters, national heroes, town site descriptions–place names weave a colorful tapestry as we journey along Interstate-75. In some cases, early pioneers and settlers from east coast regions transferred the names of their original home towns to their new settlements (e.g.. Milford, Ohio), thereby perpetuating British and European names in the U.S. interior.

Throughout the following pages, we explain the meanings behind some of the more interesting place names encountered as we travel southbound to Florida:

Insider Tip
Signature Inns - Friendly and Clean

It is small wonder that the regional motel chain (Ohio & Michigan) of Signature Inns is the preferred choice of many corporations and travel agents. Started in 1981, this chain focuses on safe, quality accommodations at a reasonable price—all corridors are internal and access is past the front desk only. This safety theme is carried to the rooms which have electronic door locks. The rooms are large, exceptionally clean and well appointed.

Front desk service is always excellent, friendly and helpful. A free Breakfast Express, an all-you-can-eat buffet of fresh fruit, baked pastries, cereal, juices, coffee, etc., is included with your overnight stay, as is a free "USA Today" or "Wall Street Journal." Incidentally if you travel on business, they provide fax service and modem ports for in-room computer use - most also have a microwave and fridge.

When comparing motel rates, don't overlook these extras. For instance, if you buy a morning paper and have breakfast "on the road," you are probably spending another $10 per couple - a stay at Signature Inns saves you these added costs.

And a final point, many organizations claim to excel in "customer service" and many of them do until a problem arises . . . then watch out. Several years ago, we watched Signature Inn staff deal with a major "house" problem caused by a bad lightning storm. We were very impressed by the manner in which they resolved the situation to *everybody's* satisfaction, turning upset guests into "happy campers." This is REAL customer service; we heartily recommend Signature Inns, for this and all the other reasons.

an early settlement called Frenchtown. It was here that one of largest battles between the British and American Armies took place during the War of 1812.

On the evening of January 18, 1813, Frenchtown was occupied by an American force detached from an army recruited in Kentucky during the previous summer. The seven hundred men had faced a small British force earlier that day and, after hours of tree to tree fighting, had driven them back north towards Detroit. Several days later their leader, General Winchester, arrived with the remainder of the troops, bringing the army to a strength of 934 men.

In the quiet pre-dawn of January 21st, a huge British force of 597 British soldiers supported by 800 Indians, crept towards Frenchtown to take their revenge. The attack lasted less than twenty minutes before the American right (closest to the I-75) was outflanked and the men retreated to the river. Of the 400 men who fled, over 200 were killed and 147 were captured - including General Winchester.

The remaining 500 Kentuckians, fighting from behind picket fences at Frenchtown, were unaware of the collapse on their right, and successfully drove off three fierce British attacks with their rifles. When they saw a British officer come towards them with a white flag, they thought that the British were going to surrender. They were surprised when the officer gave them orders from their own General, now a prisoner of the British, to surrender.

After the surrender, the British withdrew and the Americans gathered their dying and injured to the settlers' homes in Frenchtown. The following morning, the Indian forces attacked, burning and plundering the homes and scalping the American wounded. Over 60 were killed–the action became known as the

MICHIGAN - *an old Indian word of unknown origins. It could come from Mishi-mikin-nac or "swimming turtle," a descriptive term used to describe the shape of some of Michigan's land, or from Mitchisawgyegan (michi gama), an Indian term meaning "Great Lake."*

DETROIT - *from the French word "d'etroit" (of the strait). Founded on July 24th, 1701, by French explorer Antoine Cadillac, the early settlement lay on the stretch of land between Lake Erie and Lake St.Clair.*

The 500 Mile Day - Breaking it Up

What is the best way of breaking up your driving day so that you don't become overly tired and yet travel a reasonable distance? After many trips along the I-75, we have adopted the following 500 mile/day approach which might also work for others, especially if like us they are "morning" people. It takes advantage of low traffic periods and the time-shifting of meals (it might not work well for families traveling with children) to avoid long delays at restaurants. Here's how the day goes:

Wake up at 6:30 a.m. and plan to depart at 7:30 (get a cup of coffee at the motel if possible, or make it on your portable coffee maker).

Drive 1 hour (7:30 - 8:30 am) advantage - traffic is very light.

Breakfast (8:30 - 9:15 am).

Drive 2 hours (9:15 - 11:15 am).

Coffee break (11:15 - 11:30 am).

Drive 2 hours (11:30 am - 1:30 p.m.) advantage - lighter traffic.

Lunch (1:30 - 2:15 p.m.) advantage - faster service, main lunch rush is over.

Drive 1¾ hours (2:15 - 4:00 p.m.).

Coffee break (4:00-4:30 p.m.) start planning night stop (about 90 miles ahead).

Drive 1½ hours (4:30 - 6:00 p.m.) - Stop for the night around 6:00 p.m.

"Massacre of the Raisin River."

The massacre shocked and enraged settlers throughout the Old Northwest Territory (today's Michigan). Ten months later, American troops chased the British army from Detroit to London, Ontario where a major battle took place on the banks of another river–Ontario's River Thames. During this battle, the famous Indian chief and friend of the British, Tecumseh, was killed. The American battle cry at this engagement? "Remember the Raisin!"

Hours and other details on page 48.

MI Milepost 10 (N/bound)-Monroe Welcome Center: When traveling northbound, I always make a point of stopping here for great information about the road ahead. Manager Lucy and her staff greet everybody with warmth and a smile. Even if you don't need travel information, it's worth pulling off here just to say "hi" to Lucy. She's truly a traveler's friend away from home.

MI Exit 9-Lake Maumee: We cross through the plains south of Monroe giving little thought to the scene a million years ago when melting glaciers hundreds of feet thick formed an ancient lake which ran right across this section of Michigan and down as far as Exit 159 (Findlay) in Ohio. Geologists named it Lake Maumee and its water surface was about 230 feet above the present position of our car. How can scientists tell? They found the beach ridges of the lake permanently etched into rock at an elevation of 800 feet above sea level (we are driving at 570 feet above sea level). The lake finally broke through the Grand River Valley in Michigan and as its water level fell, the current shoreline of Lake Erie appeared.

Ohio Exit 210-Toledo and the Ohio-Michigan war: It is 1835 and this is where we find our forgotten war. The land between this exit and Ohio Exit 199 is disputed territory and both Ohio and Michigan have laid claim to it. That large crowd of men over there marching down the road with flintlock muskets slung over their shoulders is Michigan's Army led southward by Governor Mason (the stout,

The 500 Mile Day - Drive by the Page

"Honey, let's drive three more pages and then stop at that Cracker Barrel shown in Dave's book at exit 373. It's on the left side of the road."

This is one of the most interesting things about *"Along the I-75"* — we have found that you start thinking of your day's drive in terms of the pages you're going to drive . . . rather than miles. Unlike other maps which vary in scale, our maps are designed to the same scale of 25 miles (40 kms) per page. This allows you to relate distance to pages very specifically.

For instance, if you are planning to follow the 500 miles per day plan described on the previous page, this becomes a 20 page day as follows:

Two pages before breakfast—five before morning coffee break—five pages before lunch—four before afternoon coffee—four pages before stopping for the night.

Somehow, this approach seems to make the large distances along the interstate easier to manage . . . and the day go much faster, too. One of our readers, an experienced I-75 driver of many years said, *"the miles seem to whiz by as we turn the pages."*

Traveling with children? - see next page.

black hatted fellow on the roan horse). They are on their way to attack the small settlement of Toledo and settle this question once and for all. They don't know yet but before the week is out, they will capture one of Toledo's founding fathers and hold him as a prisoner of war. Congress will finally have to intervene. The war that has broken out will be resolved by awarding the territory to Ohio, and granting Michigan full statehood in 1837 along with all the copper and iron rights in the peninsula to their north.

The issue of "who owns Toledo" will not go away. As recently as the summer of 1992, an editorial appeared in Toledo's principal newspaper. The Blade, questioning the ownership of Toledo by Ohio. Many still would like to cede the city to Michigan.

OH between Exits 198 & 163- The Black Swamp: You wouldn't have wanted to be here 125 years ago, for this entire region (about the size of Connecticut) was the dreaded Black Swamp. A dense, dank, gloomy forest populated mainly by deer, panthers, rattlesnakes, wolves and bear. The ground was an evil boggy quagmire of black muck which sucked pioneers down to their knees and if the animals and insects did not get them, then malaria probably would. In 1850, farmers decided to try to drain the area, and by 1890 more than 22,000 miles of ditches had drained the land and revealed the rich fertile farmland beneath. In 40 years, the stinking swamp had been transformed into the productive farms of today's Ohio.

OH Mile 195-southbound: - Beware of the Ohio *"Bear in the Air"*–all the way south to Cincinnati. Ohio leads the nation in traffic tickets issued by Highway Patrol aided by aircraft. Every time we drive through here when the weather is clear, our police radio scanner provides us with the most fascinating entertainment.

"Unit 37, this is Eagle 2. Red Camaro overtaking the southbound RV at marker (mile marker) 188. Clocked at 82."

"Vascar 82 . . . Roger."

OHIO *-early French explorers discovered the Ohio River, and used Iroquois words such as Oheo (beautiful) to describe it. The explored territory later acquired the name.*

TOLEDO - *because of its industrial heritage, named after the Spanish town of Toledo famous throughout history for "Toledo Steel."*

Sure enough, looking up through our sun roof is a speck of a high-winged single engine plane circling the interstate ahead at about 2,000 feet . . . and from the scanner radio speaker, the sound of a siren as a patrol car gets up to speed after the recalcitrant vehicle. Sure enough, a few miles further on, we pass the two sitting on the side of the road "doing business."

OH Exit 192-Fort Meigs (map on page 48): After the massacre of the Kentucky troops at the Raisin River in January, 1813 (see Michigan, Exit 14), fighting between the British and the Americans came to a temporary halt due to severe winter weather. U.S. Major General Harrison decided to build a new fort on the south banks of the Maumee River, named after the Governor of Ohio, Return Jonathan Meigs.

Originally designed as a temporary supply depot, it quickly becomes central to the protection of Ohio from the British Army. Fort Meigs has achieved major strategic status, for if it falls, Michigan and Ohio will become conquered territory of the British. At its peak it housed more than 2,000 American regulars from Ohio, Kentucky, Pennsylvania and Virginia. Let's go back in time and visit the fort.

It's late April, 1813; the fort is badly undermanned with twelve hundred troops of which only 850 are fit for duty–and of these, half are untrained. Will they be able to withstand the coming British attack? To protect his forces, Harrison orders long embankments of earth built across the fort parade grounds so his troops can burrow down into the muddy

The 500 Mile Day - Traveling With Children

"Children, we are going to drive three more pages and then stop at the McDonalds on page 27 with the playground . . . why don't you read me the stories about the next stretch of the interstate as I drive?"

Traveling with children has its own special challenges, and over the years I have received many letters from young parents who have given all sorts of great advice. On page 67, I described the method of "driving by the page" to make the distance go by quickly. Here's a special adaptation of that technique for the younger set:

- Pack the car the night before and let the kids sleep in the clothes they will be traveling in.
- Up at 5:30am - get yourself ready - wake up children and put them in the car. They'll go off to sleep again.
- Drive 4 pages (target 8:30), stop for breakfast - change clothes, brush teeth, etc.
- Drive 4 pages (target 10:30), stop for a rest room break and a run around or outside play time.
- Drive 4 pages (target 12:30), stop for lunch. Fast food facilities with playground areas are shown in red on our maps.
- Drive 4 pages (target 2:30), stop for a rest room break and a run around or outside play time.
- Drive 4 pages (target 4:30), stop for the night. Choose a motel with a pool so they can burn off some energy. Dinner 5:30-6pm. Off to bed early ready for the next day.

Another idea - rotate the car seating arrangement so that mom or dad spends some time in the back seat, and the children get an equal share of the front passenger seat. One safety item to consider though, don't place young children in a car seat where they could be injured should an air bag activate.

earth, behind them.

At 11 a.m. on May 1st in chillingly wet weather, a British force of two thousand lays siege to Fort Meigs, pounding its muddy earthworks and wooden blockhouses with 20-30 artillery pieces, for four days. Twenty-four pound cannon balls, red hot 12 pounders, mortar shells and fragmentation bombs rain down on the fort sending deadly iron and wood splinter fragments in all directions. Over the duration of the siege, thousands of such iron missiles will pound the fort and yet cause surprisingly little injury.

Six days later, reinforcements under Brigadier-General Green Clay arrive in the fort and although the buildings and earthworks have been badly mauled, the American flag still flies and the garrison has held tight. So the siege is lifted and the British withdraw and return northward into Ontario to the disappointment of their Indian allies under Chief Tecumseh, who had been waiting to take the fort and enjoy another "Frenchtown" massacre.

Two months later, the British Army makes another attempt to take the fort—which also fails.

Today, you can wander around this historic eight acre stockade overlooking the Maumee River, peer into the gloomy interiors of the log blockhouses and cast your mind back to the heroes who held this fort against a far superior force. Guides in period costume explain the actions which took place, and demonstrate some of the crafts of the time. Exhibits illustrate the 1812 War.

Hours and other details on page 48.

Escape Routes-The Old Road to Florida: By now, you will have noticed that our maps show not only the I-75, but parallel side roads so that should the traffic become heavy ahead, you know how and where to get off the interstate to bypass potential problems.

Most of these "escape" routes follow the traditional north-south route used by Florida snowbirds long before I-75 was built. US 25–the "Old Dixie Highway"–in the North and US41 through the South.

During the interstate's construction, many lands and buildings were expropriated to make way for the "super slab." Some survived physically but died as business disappeared. Later on when we reach exit 29 in Kentucky, I'll explain how a local motel owner took advantage of this situation to start the world's first "fast food" business.

Radar

When compared to national highway safety statistics, the I-75 is a very safe freeway. State police mean to keep it that way by actively monitoring speed and issuing tickets for infractions as little as 5 mph over the limit.

Now, I *know* you have absolutely no intention of speeding as you head along the interstates, but solely for academic purposes I thought you might like to update yourself with the new technology waiting to trap the unwary. In the next few pages, I will give you a look at the various devices used by the police to measure car speed and the counter measures available to the public. Radar detectors are legal (for passenger vehicle use) in all the I-75 states but we will also have a quick look at the VG-2, the device used by Highway Patrol to detect the illegal use of detectors in those states where they are banned — the so called, "detector detector."

OH Mile 186-RWIS: I bet you thought that the road surface beneath your wheels was just that - a road surface. Not any more! In this section of Ohio, and in sections north of Cincinnati and on Atlanta's I-75 in Georgia, the road surface acts as part of a giant input device which feeds information to traffic computers. Wire loops in the road record information, cameras and other roadside devices send other types of data to a central computer. This is all part of Ohio's multi million dollar Traffic Information System (OTIS).

In fact, you are just about to pass one of the input devices at mile marker 186. The pole with the weather vane and wind cups (known as an anemometer) in the median strip and the coils of wire you've just passed over are gathering all sorts of information and sending it electronically to the Road and Weather Information System (RWIS), all part of OTIS.

Now here's the amazing part. If you have a computer which can be hooked up to the

Money Saving Tip

After entering a new state, stop at the Welcome Center and get copies of the free motel coupon books - the green Traveler Discount Guide (the old Exit Information Guide) and the red Market America Motel Discount Guide. They can usually be found lying in a pile on the counter or a rack inside the door. Ask the staff, if you don't see them.

These publications will save you many $$$$ on your overnight accommodation. They are chock full of discount coupons for motels (independents as well as major chains) along the way. Typically, you will find discounts in the 20-45% range. Bargains we have seen recently were $65 rooms discounted to $36, and $42 rooms to $28. We use the books all the time on each trip (including our vacation stays in Florida) and save literally hundreds of dollars.

Here's how they work. Every day, each motel listed in the coupon books sets aside a certain number of discount rate rooms based on their occupancy experience from the previous night. The discounts are provided on a first-come first-served basis to travelers with the discount book coupons. What are your chances of getting a discount room? We normally pull off the road around 6 p.m. and in all our years of traveling have only been turned down three times at a motel of our choice. We quickly found another one nearby which accepted their coupon from the book.

The Traveler Discount Guide has now made it easier to get discount coupons for the motels you want. If you have Internet access and sign on to their website - www.roomsaver.com, you can actually choose the motels you wish to stay at before you leave home, and print out the coupons on your computer printer. Several readers who have done this told me that the coupons were accepted without question, saving them many dollars on their trip to Florida and back.

internet you can connect your unit to the OTIS computer and get instant information about the road surface (dry, rain, ice, snow, etc), construction and the weather on Ohio's I-75. The World Wide Web address is a bit of a "mouthful" so enter it carefully and then save it (i.e., "bookmark" it) for future use:

http://webapp2.dot.state.oh.us/otis/rwis

By the way, if you missed the sensor at this mile marker, you have a chance to see another one in the median strip just after exit 168.

OH Exit 181-BGSU: As we run southward, we pass the stadium and campus of Bowling Green State University. Founded in 1914, BGSU has developed into a major college campus of more than 100 buildings spread over 1,300 acres, and providing a diversity of programs to approximately 18,000 students.

OH Milepost 178-Ohio Welcome Centers: I always make a point of pulling into the Welcome Center at mile 178 to say hello to the knowledgeable counter staff of Blanca, Marian and Quinn. As Marian says, they have excellent information about Ohio's state parks . . . and of course, are fully briefed about any construction ahead.

If you are northbound, then you will have the pleasure of saying "hello" to Kate, Mary and Rose. They are our Toledo and Northwest Ohio experts.

OH Milepost 178-Interstate Defense System: As you pulled into the rest area, you may have noticed a historical marker which refers to the interstate as the *"National System of Interstate and Defense Highways."* Here's the story behind this long title:

Just after World War I, the War Department in Washington decided to "wave the flag" and thank the people of America who had generously supported the war effort in many ways. The Department felt that a convoy of America's military Might - tanks, trucks, field guns - driven across the continent from Washington to San Francisco would be a suitable event. The convoy would visit various towns and villages on the way and give the public a closer view of the equipment which had help win the European war.

They turned to a young lieutenant colonel to organize and lead this mission which he did with much enthusiasm. The convoy set off in the summer of 1919. From the first day it was a disaster. The heavy tanks often collapsed the wooden rural bridges and trucks frequently mired to the axles in mud. Two months after the journey started, at an average speed of 6 mph the convoy limped into Oakland, California.

The officer recorded in his memoirs,

"efforts should be made to get our people interested in producing better roads."

Others were also concerned about the state of the nation's roads and in the late 1930's during Roosevelt's administration, plans were finally being laid for a national grid of high speed freeways.

And then came another war in Europe - World War II. The young Lt. Colonel who led the 1919 convoy had risen in rank and become the Supreme Allied Commander with responsibility for coordinating the invasion of "Fortress Europe." He and his generals watched in horror as Hitler was able to rapidly deploy his troops via the German super-freeway Autobahn system.

The commander of course, was Dwight Eisenhower who in 1953 became President of the United States. On June 29, 1956 - the "official birth date" of the Interstate system - he signed legislation which created a ***"National System of Interstate and Defense Highways"*** – an extensive multi lane limited-access freeway system designed not only to move people quickly from one place to another, but serve as a vital element of defense during a national emergency, so armies can swiftly move along its arteries.

Insider Tip
Cracker Barrel's Talking Books

Tired of the radio and need something different to pass the time as you drive? Then stop at the nearest Cracker Barrel Store (see the maps for the closest "Cracker Barrel" exit to you) and rent a selection from their "Book on Audio" program. After you've finished listening to it, drop it off at your next Cracker Barrel stop and pick up another. Your total cost if you return it within a week? Three dollars!

These "tape books" cover the full gamut of interests. On a recent trip to Florida, we rented a current John Grisham novel *"The Testament,"* Robert Waller's *"Bridges of Madison County,"* a Daphne DuMaurier classic and *"The Eleventh Commandment,"* by Geoffrey Archer (total cost for all this entertainment – $12). There were even tapes of the latest selections from Oprah Winfrey's popular TV book club.

Dozens of other "books" are available, from Zane Grey to Agatha Christie . . . from P.G. Wodehouse's *"Jeeves"* series to many current non-fiction best sellers, such as Phil McGraw's *"Life Strategies."* There is also an excellent selection of children's stories — including current offering such as *"The Secret Garden"* read by Julie Christie— what better way to keep the younger travelers quiet and occupied? Cracker Barrel often adds new titles to keep the selection current.

Here's how the Cracker Barrel tape-book program works. Go to the revolving tape-book stand in any Cracker Barrel store and choose the tapes you want. The price of the tape-book is on the back ($12.99 for a single cassette book and $18.99 for a double, $23.99 — three cassettes and $27.99 for four). You pay the Cracker Barrel staff the full price, and they give you a special receipt for this amount. After enjoying the book on your journey you stop at another Cracker Barrel, turn the tape-book in and receive your money back less three dollars (per week) to cover the rental.

Oh, by the way – while you are there enjoy one of their marvelous country style meals. Their baked potatoes and fresh vegetables are scrumptious. We also enjoy browsing the well stocked country store before or after meals. The merchandise is always unique and reflects the home style atmosphere of this excellent restaurant chain.

VASCAR Speed Measurement

VASCAR, or **V**isual **A**verage **S**peed **C**omputer **A**nd **R**ecorder, is an older non-radar method of speed measurement. It is gaining in popularity again due to radar operator health concerns. VASCAR uses the "distance/time" equation, **S**peed = **D**istance/**T**ime - if you know the distance between two points and can precisely measure the time taken to travel between them, you can easily calculate the speed of the object making the passage; .

VASCAR is used frequently in all I-75 states, but in particular by air patrols (Ohio writes the most VASCAR measured tickets). An officer flying at 2,000 feet will see a car traveling at excessive speed. As the car passes a known reference point on the road, the officer flips a switch on his VASCAR unit. As the car passes the second measurement point, the officer flips another switch and the unit calculates the speed and displays it on the VASCAR screen. It should be noted that the distance between the two points is always pre-measured and entered into the unit - they are not necessarily the white "T" symbols you see painted on the road surface, but may be natural landmarks unknown to you. Details of the measurement are quickly relayed by radio to a ground patrol car, to make the "stop" (see page 67).

You should note that its most common application is in a moving patrol car with "distance"

information being inputted to the unit with a hookup to the car's odometer. The measurement can be made from a patrol car following you or even ahead of you.

Today however, national defense is less of a concern and the public at large is the beneficiary of what became a miracle of modern engineering . . . the largest coordinated public works program in the entire history of mankind (estimated to be much bigger than the building of the pyramids in Egypt, the construction of the extensive Roman road system in ancient Europe and Asia, or the excavation of the Suez Canal).

Defense isn't entirely forgotten though; sections of interstates have been designed to serve as tactical airstrips during times of crisis. During the 1960's, there was a concern that Soviet forces might attempt an invasion of the US mainland via Cuba. Sections of I-75 in lower Georgia would have been converted to airstrips to help meet this threat.

Prior to the Interstate System, traveling long distances could be painful; a trip from Detroit to Florida would take 5 to 6 days. Primary roads did not always go in straight lines - they often meandered around the countryside. Frequently they were single lane and at every community along the way, traffic lights, stop signs and local cross traffic slowed the journey. Today, however, I-75 makes the drive to Florida a comfortable and pleasant experience.

Insider Tip
Coffee Thermos Fill-up

Did you know that Cracker Barrel will fill your coffee thermos for $2.00? We've also heard that if you eat there, some Cracker Barrel's will waive the charge.

OH Exits 167, 164 & 157-Ancient Ridge Highway: As the ancient Lake Maumee slowly receded to existing lake levels, it left beach ridges and sand dunes which can still be seen. Since these were on high ground, the Indians used the ridges for their trails through areas such as the Black Swamp. Pioneers cut their paths on top of Indian tracks, and these eventually evolved into the early roads and then the highways of today. I-75 crosses three highways which have been built on the backs of ancient Lake Maumee beach ridges–Route 18 at Exit 167, Route 613 at Exit 164, and Route 12 at Exit 157.

OH Exit 161-I-75's Antique Roadshow: Those who watch this popular TV program will know that valuable treasures can still be found hiding among the bric-a-brac of antique malls and flea markets - and I-75 is particularly rich with such places.

Insider Tip
Bistro on Main, Findlay

Several readers' letters led me to this lovely restaurant housed in an old Victorian building on Main Street in Findlay. From the moment you pass under the green awning and enter the warm interior with its mellow wooden booths, etched glass, old brickwork walls and tin ceiling, you know you are in for a treat. But it doesn't stop with the decor. The staff is friendly and welcoming . . . and the menu of Northern Italian food is out of this world.

Owner Alisa McPharon loves cooking and her passion is to please her patrons. If it's not on the menu, she suggests you ask for it and will even go as far as going out to get the ingredients if it isn't on hand. Alisa's father, Edward, will probably seat you when you arrive. The night we were there, Kathy and I enjoyed sweet breads with creamy honey butter, a salad with raspberry vinegarette dressing, baked penne followed with my favorite of all desserts, a magnificent creme caramel.

All entrees are reasonably priced and the menu is supported with an excellent wine list. The Bistro is open for lunch 11-2:30 and dinner 5-10:30, 6 days a week (closed Sunday) ☎ 419-425-4900.

Bistro on Main is easily reached from I-75 exit 157: travel east along W Main Cross St (Rt12) for 1.2 miles; turn right onto S. Main St and drive south 2 blocks. Bistro on your left at number 407. Say "hi" to Alisa and Edward for me when you arrive . . . and enjoy.

To the right at this exit is Jeffrey's, Ohio's largest antique mall. Over 700 feet long (2 football fields end to end) and occupying 40,000 square feet. It is home to 300 dealers who are there from 10-6pm daily, year round.

OH Exit 159-Findlay: This is not exactly on I-75 but since so many people break their journey for an overnight stop at Findlay, I thought I would mention something that has fascinated me since I started writing *"Along the I-75"* in 1992.

At that time, because of an accident I was routed off I-75 and had to drive down County Road 220 which eventually runs into Findlay's Main Street. That's when I saw it! It's has to be the most grotesque and yet beautiful Victorian house in the world . . . best viewed in the evening as the sun is slowly sinking behind it in the west. A perfect Halloween property . . . go and judge for yourself.

The house was built in 1883 on part of a 300 acre farm owned by the Bigelow family and has only had three owners since. It has seven fireplaces and many of the original gas jets, including one on the staircase newel post shaped like a dragon, which breathes actual fire through its nostrils! The beautiful main staircase of carved butternut wood, curves up to the second story in front of a magnificent stained glass window.

The *"House on the Hill"* is so impressive that master magician David Copperfield used it as a setting for his spectacular "burning house" illusion, in his 1995 TV special.

To find "my" house, take exit 159 east (Trenton Avenue) for 1 mile until you reach Main Street. Turn left at the lights and go north 1 mile until you reach the point just above the Bigelow Avenue traffic lights where Main Street changes from two lanes to one–the house is immediately to your left. Catch it silhouetted in front of a sinking sun and you'll never forget it.

Some other notes of interest about Findlay. It was originally founded when natural gas was discovered in the area during the 1800's. This period was known as the great Ohio Natural Gas

FINDLAY - *after James Findlay and a fort he built in this area during the 1812 war with Britain. Findlay later became the Mayor of Cincinnati for two terms and a Brigadier-General with the state militia.*

Hi Tech Mapping in your Car

Did you know that you can have mobile colored digital mapping for $150? But you'll need a laptop computer (with a CD-ROM drive) which will run in your car.

Delorme Mapping sells a product called "Earthmate." It's a tiny GPS receiver (about the size of a deck of cards) which plugs into your laptop's serial port. The product also includes a CD-ROM called Map n Go (produced in conjunction with the AAA) and together, this provides the software to display a colored map of your exact location—anywhere in the USA. It also plots your path as you move.

In cities, it even displays side streets — invaluable if you are in a strange area. You can even download up-to-date weather and construction data prepared by the AAA, from a special Delorme site on the Internet.

The tiny Earthmate receiver sits on your dashboard and receives signals from satellites through the windshield, so no special installation is needed beyond plugging it into your cigarette lighter and your laptop.

And here's the incredible part–once you have entered the start, finish and intermediate stopping points of your trip into the computer, it will actually talk to you and tell you when you are approaching a turn, and how many miles it is to the next stage of your journey. So there is no need to look at the colored map on the computer screen as you drive.

Best of all, the Earthmate and accompanying AAA Map'n'Go CD-ROM only costs $149.95 . . . an absolute bargain!!! You of course, provide the laptop. Give Delorme a phone call at 1-800-569-8313 if interested. You can order the device over the phone with VISA or MASTERCARD. It is also available from many AAA clubs.

Boom (no pun intended!).

Mile 157-The Flag Tank: Findlay also bills itself as the "Flag City, USA"—a "tip o' the hat" to the patriotism of Findlay's citizens. A drive down Main Street in the summertime will attest to Findlay's claim since virtually every building is dressed with a flag or red, white and blue bunting.

And a "tip o' the hat" to Marathon Oil, whose magnificently painted oil tank beside I-75 leave no doubt that Findlay really is "Flag City."

OH Mile 150-Foxtrot Delta Yankee: Just to the east of I-75 at mile 150 is a round squat building with radio antennas on top. This is a signpost of sorts–an electronic signpost for aircraft called a VOR, or VHF Omnidirectional Range. It sits there transmitting its identification code, FDY in morse to anyone tuned into its navigation frequency.

Why does it do this? Just as interstates guide our car from city to city, aircraft are guided from place to place along invisible highways in the sky called, "airways." And just as interstates are given "I" numbers, airways are given "V" numbers, and their intersections are marked with VORs and other radio aids to navigation, to keep the aircraft on course.

For instance, if we were to travel the major air-route from Toledo to Cincinnati, which over-flies I-75 or just to its east for most of the journey, our flight plan would be as follows:

Take off at Toledo and join the airway **V47** at the **Victor-Whiskey-Victor** VOR - fly 30 miles to the **Foxtrot-Delta-Yankee** VOR (the one beside you at mile marker 150) - continue airway V47 for 42 miles to **Romeo-Oscar-Delta** VOR–and continue V47 for 82 miles to the **Charlie-Victor-Golf** VOR and Cincinnati's air traffic control zone.

As the journey proceeds, the pilot tunes in the frequency of the next VOR on the plane's navigational equipment, and displays indicate the distance away, the bearing towards, and whether the plane is on (or off) course for the next VOR—"highways in the sky."

And if you wish this sort of assistance was available for cars on the ground, well it is. For five years now, I have been navigating the interstates with a special navigational computer in

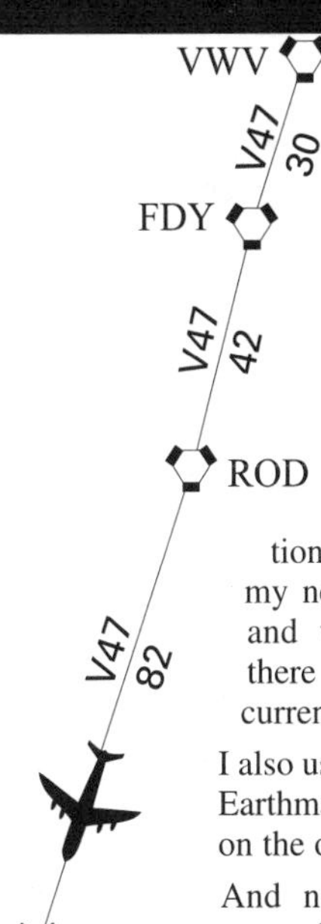

our car (called a GPS system - available at many marine supply stores for less than $500) which picks up radio signals from satellites in space and tells me exactly where I am, how fast I am going, which direction and how far away is my next destination point and when I will arrive there given the speed I am currently traveling.

I also use the Delorme/AAA Earthmate system described on the opposite page.

And now let's step back several hundred years in terms of navigation . . .

OH Mile 142-Yesterday's Virginia: What a difference a few hundred years make. If it had been possible to travel the I-75 route southward in 1784, you would now be leaving Connecticut and entering Virginia ... and after leaving Virginia 300 miles south of here, you would enter the Carolinas before arriving at the Florida border.

According to a map drawn in 1784 by Abel Buell, the four Atlantic states of Connecticut, Virginia, North and South Carolina stretched westward from the sea to the Mississippi River. Territorial disputes led to much of this land being designated as *"Northwest Territory"* (present day Michigan, Indiana, Ohio, Kentucky and Tennessee) in 1787.

Thomas Jefferson, a Virginian Congressman at the time, proposed that the land be sliced into fourteen new states, with names such as Cherronesus, Assenesipia, Illinoia, Michigania and Polypotamia. Congress rejected this proposal however and granted statehood to Kentucky and Tennessee in 1792 and 1796, respectively. In 1803, the eastern part of the remaining Territory gained statehood — with the Iroquois Indian name for beauty–"Ohio."

OH Mile 142-GROB: I bet you are wondering what the impressive GROB plant right beside Bluffton Airport, is all about. GROB (pronounce the "O" like in "sew") is a German company that services aircraft and does machine tooling.

OH Mile 141-Wildflowers: If we were driving through here in the summertime, we could not help notice the masses of wildflowers along the banks and median of the I-75. Blues, mauves, pinks and whites. Like many other states, the Ohio Department of Transportation has an active wildflower planting program which provides motorists with a rainbow of colors at more than 200 sites throughout the State.

Begun in 1984, the Ohio program now annually plants more than 2,000 pounds of wildflower seed along the roadsides. In addition to providing carpets of red, blue and yellow flowers, the program helps preserve native vegetation and reduces costs along the way. But today is January, and the plants lie asleep beneath their blanket of snow, awaiting the warm breath of spring to awaken and bloom once again.

Between mile markers 137 and 138, the Ohio Department of Transport have placed a sign

Insider Tip
"I apologize officer, if I was doing anything wrong . . . "

What to do if you get stopped for speeding? Remain calm, remove dark sunglasses if wearing them, roll down your window and keep both hands on your steering wheel. When he or she asks for your license, take it out of your purse, wallet or holder before handing it over.

Never offer excuses, admit to speeding or protest ignorance-instead, apologize to the officer and ask if he/she would issue a warning instead of a ticket. If you know you were going fast, accept the officer's decision gracefully-it's probably overdue.

If you feel you were not speeding, don't protest but do ask what method was used to measure your speed. Try and establish the make and model of equipment used. If the officer is not cooperative, do not pursue it. As soon as possible, join the National Motorists Association (608-849-6000); it has lots of helpful information about fighting unfair tickets.

announcing their Tree Source program, which is a similar initiative—planting trees for Ohio.

OH Mile 133-Lincoln Highway: On an overpass above us is US Highway 30–the Granddaddy of all of our super-roads–the old "Lincoln Highway." It is the route which taught the young 29 year old Dwight Eisenhower that America's roads were inadequate for heavy transportation (see *"The National Interstate Defense System"*–page 70). The first of the transcontinental roads, it was originally a Dutch settler's trail called the "Old Plank Road" starting near Philadelphia and linking with Indian paths through Ohio and the mid-west. It connected with the Oregon Trail in the Platte Valley and then ran through the mountains and past Salt Lake for the Overland Stage Route into California.

In 1912, Carl Fisher, a visionary from Indianapolis, tried to raise funds to develop this route into the first proper road across the nation–but little progress was made. Eventually, Fisher's dream came true as the Federal Government began its freeway building program, and the Old Lincoln Highway became the US 30 and I-80, a continuous modern route from Philadelphia to San Francisco.

OH Exit 127-US Plastics Corp: As you approach exit 127, you cannot miss the huge US Plastics Corporation plant on the right-hand side of the interstate. We decided to go in and have a closer look, and found ourselves in an incredible world of plastic. The US Plastics retail outlet covers 18,000 square feet and according to one of their sales staff, has the largest assortment of plastic goods in the world. If you have a plastic product need . . . no matter how unusual . . . you will probably find it here.

To reach US Plastics, go west at exit 127 and turn right on to Neubrecht Road. Run north parallel to I-75 for ½ mile and US Plastics is on your right. It's well sign-posted. Store hours are M-F, 8-5:00pm. ☎ 800-537-9724 or 419-228-2242.

OH Mile 124 -Lima's Kryptonite Room: A mile or so to the west of I-75 is a manufacturing factory of General Dynamics Land Systems Division, the Lima Army Tank Plant. Here they build, unarguably the best army tank in the world—the famed M1 Abrams Main Battle Tank. During the Gulf War, this sophisticated machine proved itself with top honors—in fact, it was found to be unstoppable and virtually indestructible.

In one incident, the crew abandoned a tank mired in mud and were ordered to destroy it. A nearby M1 fired two 120mm rounds into it with no effect. Then the abandoned tank's ammunition was detonated. The end result was very little damage—in fact, the tank was finally recovered and found to be operational with the exception that its gun sights needed to be realigned. The secret of this super strength armor is just beyond the I-75, and this brings us to Lima's "kryptonite" room.

In his excellent book, "Armored Cav," Tom Clancy takes us for a tour of the plant and gives insight into the M1 manufacturing processes. Based on a British innovation called Chobham armor, the M1's outer shell uses interleaved layers of high quality steel alloys and ceramic. But that's not all, using a deep secret "black art" process in the Kryptonite room, a layer of depleted uranium is somehow bound to the armor shell, more than doubling its effectiveness. Superman would be proud!

OH between Miles 116 and 91-Ohio's Ice Age: A glance out of the side window at the snow laden landscape gives a sense of what it must have been like during the Pleistocene Ice Age. At that time, huge glaciers rumbled southward from Canada dragging boulders, rocks and other debris which slowly ground the Ohio countryside down under their massive weight. As the earth warmed and the glaciers melted and receded, the rubble was left in large ridges known as "end moraines" - gigantic piles of debris which were slowly assimilated into the surrounding landscape. The interstate between Lima and Piqua is rich with such moraines–a good view of a typical

LIMA - *pronounced "lime-er" . . . although named after Lima, Peru.*

WAPAKONETA - *possibly named after a Shawnee Chief.*

glacial moraine can be seen by looking behind your car and to the right (northward) at Mile 114.

OH Exit 111-Neil Armstrong Air & Space Museum: If you are older than 35, I am sure you remember the hazy TV pictures on July 20, 1969, of Neil Armstrong climbing down the ladder of the Lunar Exploration Module, "Eagle," and saying–"That's one small step for a man; one giant leap for mankind." Neil Armstrong was the first human to set foot on the moon.

Neil was born and raised in Wapakoneta, just to the west of the I-75. Here he used to build model aircraft and work part time at the local pharmacy.

Today, there is a magnificent museum just to the west of I-75, to honor his achievements and showcase exhibits from America's space program. Built by the state of Ohio, the museum is housed in the low gray concrete building that looks like it has a white golf ball on top. Inside, there are seven galleries devoted to the history of space exploration. Exhibits include moon rock and meteorite samples, rocket engines, space suits, actual space rockets and spacecraft.

A special display records the early days of space exploration, including many personal items and Russian space artifacts.

Aspiring astronauts can try their hand at the new space shuttle landing simulator. This unit uses actual computer programs designed to help train the shuttle crew. After a short training session, you take over the controls and have command of the shuttle on its final approach.

The Neil Armstrong Air and Space Museum is very easy to find. Simply take exit 111 west; turn right at the first road and you are in the museum parking area. The museum is open from March to November, Mon-Sat 9:30-5pm; Sun, noon-5pm. Closed major holidays. Admission for adults/seniors/children is $5/$4.50/$1.25. ☎ 800-282-5393 or 419-738-8811.

OH between Mile 104 & 99-Lost River Teays: Ohio is rich in its ancient geological history. Between these mile markers, you are crossing the location of the lost River Teays. It was a major North American river of pre-glacial times and its valley was as much as 400 feet deep below the present position of the I-75. But the glaciers spelled its death. The rubble they dragged along blocked the course of the Teays, burying the valley–erasing it from the landscape forever.

OH Exit 102-Jackson Center-Airstream Trailer tours: If you are an RVer (Recreational Vehicle owner, to those who aren't), you will probably be interested to note that the famous Airstream Trailer plant is located 7 miles east of I-75 at this exit, in the town of Jackson Center. Each weekday at 2 p.m. (year round except during their July plant closing) they give a free tour of their plant, and an opportunity to see how these beautiful classic aluminum trailers are built. ☎ 937-596-6111.

OH Exit 74-S/Bound Construction Zone Bypass: Ohio DOT has planned a two year lane widening construction project (completion date, Oct., 2003) for I-75 between miles 74 and 69. It may or may not present a problem since ODOT plans to keep both lanes open but just in case, our friend Major Dick Hale - Dayton's WONE-980AM ace "Air Watch" traffic reporter "The Dixter"- has

Victorian Troy

Built on the banks of the Great Miami River in 1807, Troy has much to offer in the way of interesting architecture. In fact, some of the homes have been lived in for more than 150 years. The focal point is the Troy Public Square where routes 41 and 55 intersect. Here you will find many historical buildings listed on the National Register of Historical Places, such as the lovely red brick Dye building, fronted with the fountain and flower beds.

Where Market Street meets the Square are some excellent restaurants and antique & collectible shops.

The Miami County Visitors Bureau is located at 405 SW Public Square, Suite 272 ☎ 800-348-8993; pick up their map of the downtown area . . . and stroll around for a while.

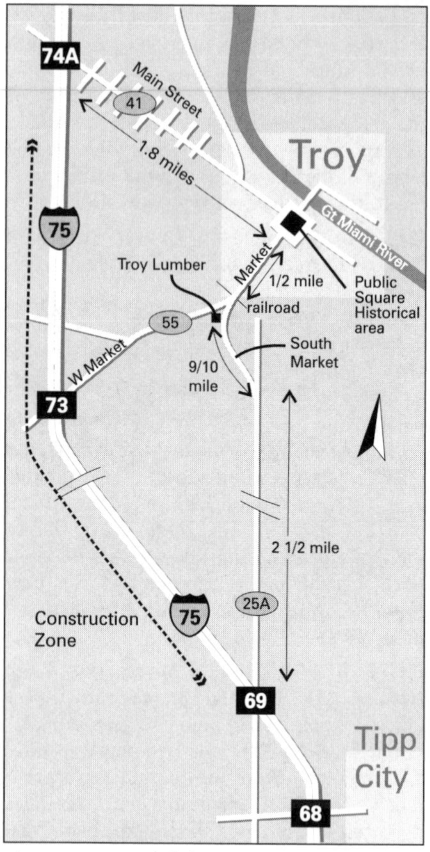

given me a special detour to share with you.

Dick suggests that should I-75 start to back-up, bypass the problem by leaving the freeway at exit 74 (see map above) and traveling east through the lovely Victorian town of Troy, heading south at the town square and rejoining the interstate at Tipp City. There are a number of traffic lights on the route into Troy, but they all appear to be synchronized and we drove through seven or eight of them without hitting one red light. The route is suitable for passenger cars and small RVs.

OH Exit 68 or 69-I-75 N/Bound Construction Bypass: If you are following this text on a northbound drive, skip ahead to my notes at Exit 74, and follow the route and map in reverse.

OH Exit 61-Dayton Construction Bypass: The Dayton stretch of I-75 is also undergoing major construction (between miles 53 and 51) with a planned completion date of October, 2001. Ohio DOT suggests you exit at 61 and detour around Dayton by using I-675, but this will add many miles to your journey. If you are driving a mid to large RV or planning to go through Dayton in peak traffic periods, we suggest you follow this detour . . . but for "four wheelers," we have a better solution.

We asked Dayton traffic reporter Dick Hale what the locals are doing and he suggested a much better detour route. We tried it and quite frankly, it's a very pleasant drive alongside the Great Miami River. In retrospect, I'd recommend it as in interesting change of pace even if there wasn't a construction zone ahead. The route Dick described to me is shown on page 79.

Mile 60-Dayton: As we negotiate the traffic of Dayton's freeway on our journey south, we should give some thought to the huge role this Ohio city played in the world of aviation.

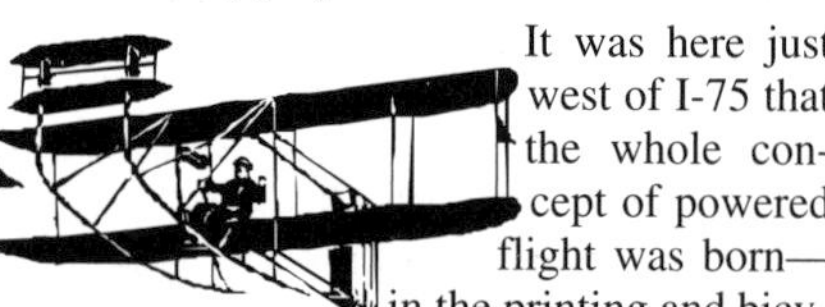

It was here just west of I-75 that the whole concept of powered flight was born—in the printing and bicycle repair shop of Orville and Wilbur Wright. Incidentally, the above noted construction bypass route will take you within several blocks (about a thirty second drive) of this historical site.

The Wright Brothers certainly put the "Birthplace of Aviation" stamp on Dayton since it was here that built their first airplane capable of sustained (20 miles) flight, the first airport and the first permanent flying school.

A few miles to the east of the interstate is the USAF Museum which contains the largest collection of military aircraft (ancient and modern) anywhere in the world, and finally, a few miles down I-75 is an airport from which a replica of the Wright Brothers' original design is still flown. Let's spend a few minutes off the interstate to visit some of these fascinating places.

OH Exit 58 (N/bound-54C)-USAF Museum (map on page 49): You must visit this awesome museum if you have any interest in

PIQUA - *the French explorer derivation of the name of a local Shawnee Indian tribe, from which the famous Indian Chief Tecumseh rose to fame.*

TIPP CITY - *from the Tippecanoe River. Tippecanoe comes from the Potawatami Indian name (Kithtippecanumk) for the "Buffalo Fish" which populated the river.*

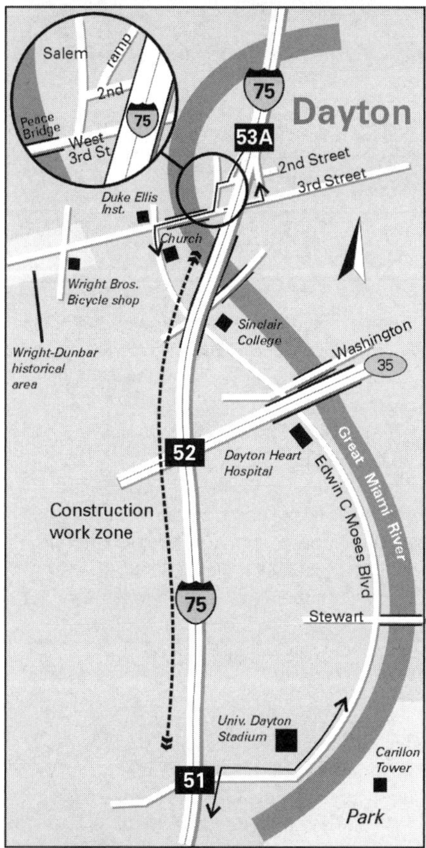

man-made flight. Nearly 300 military aircraft and missiles fill three halls, and range from very early "string and paper" efforts such as the Wright Flyer and Bleriot plane from 1909, to the most modern non-secret and experimental aircraft around. Some exhibits that particularly caught my interest were the original Wright wind tunnel, a space suit made by Litton in 1955 and the F-117 angular *Nighthawk* stealth fighter of Gulf War fame.

Among the technology on display in the Modern Flight Hanger is the awesome XB-70 *Valkyrie* experimental Mach 3 bomber with its long overhanging nose and cockpit. It looks so secret and yet it was rolled out 32 years ago in 1966; it makes you wonder what they are flying now that they **cannot** display?

In the Air Power Gallery you will find several exhibits which will make you stop and think about how fragile life was during the "Cold War" period. Atomic and thermonuclear bomb casings–about the size of a large office desk–give a new meaning to "do not touch."

Don't miss the Presidential Aircraft Hanger, and in particular, Boeing 707, tail #26000. This was the jet airliner which served Presidents Kennedy, Johnson and Nixon as Air Force One (see Special Report on page 80).

Number 26000 is open for public display and you may actual walk through the cabins which have been restored to the configuration used during President Kennedy's time. As soon as you arrive at the Museum, pick up your free pass from the information desk so you can drive your car over to the Presidential Aircraft Hangar, where you may also see President Roosevelt's C-54 "Sacred Cow," President Truman's VC-118 "Independence," and President Eisenhower's VC-121 "Columbine III."

New exhibits this year include the Holocaust exhibit, Berlin Airlift and a diorama of WWII Berlin bomb ruins.

Chillingly, you enter the Holocaust exhibit under the stark wrought iron sign - *"Arbeit Macht Frei"* meaning *"Work Brings Freedom."* Nazi Rudolph Hess required that these words be installed over the entrance gates of Auschwitz, and other concentration camps. Beyond is a very rare concentration camp uniform, which was worn by prisoner 114600 Moritz Bomstein.

Nearby, a display case contains an old violin, and with it a rather poignant story. In November, 1938, 15 year old Robert Kahn of Manheim, Germany, was forced to stand on the balcony of his home and play Nazi songs on it while his family was rounded up for shipment to concentration camp. Robert managed to escape, but only after he hid the violin inside the building.

He reached the USA and joined the army where he was able to serve in the forces which helped liberate Europe. After the war, he recovered the violin which had survived the bombings in its hiding place.

In another section of the building, a diorama shows bomb ruins in Berlin. Amidst the rubble lies a golden eagle with its outspread wings - the icon of the Nazi party. This eagle was one of two which stood either side of the entrance to Hitler's office in the Reich Chancellery. Several feet away, is a battered bust of Hitler, with bullet holes through the head.

Elsewhere, you will find one of the Defense Support Program"Star Wars" satellites which

Air Force One - Tail Number 26000

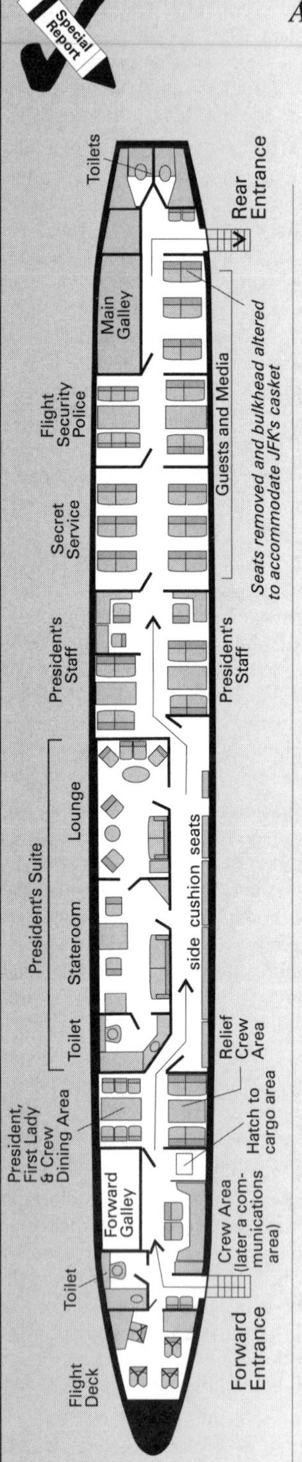

"Wright-Patterson, this is Sam 26000." This is the air traffic message which heralded the arrival of one of the nation's most famous aircraft to the USAF Base at Dayton, in 1998.

Boeing 707(Air Force designation C-137C), number 26000 was *"Air Force One"* for Presidents Kennedy, Johnson, Nixon from 1962 to 1973 . . . and on one occasion when his official airplane was unavailable, President Clinton. This aircraft took Kennedy to Dallas in November, 1963 and returned his body to Washington, DC., following his assassination. Sections of the bulkhead at the rear entrance (opposite the main galley) had to be cut away so that Kennedy's casket could be carried into the plane and set on the floor in the rear seating area. Mrs. Kennedy stayed with her husband for the trip back, sleeping on the floor beside him. On that fateful day, Johnson was sworn in as the 36th President in the main cabin area as 26000 sat on the ground at Love Field, Dallas.

In later service, Number 26000 carried Nixon to meet the Apollo 11 crew after their trip to the moon (1970), took Henry Kissinger to Paris for secret meetings with the North Vietnamese and conveyed Nixon on his historic "journey for peace" to China (1972). In 1981, 26000 transported former Presidents Nixon, Ford and Carter to Cairo for the funeral of Anwar Sadat, and flew Britain's Queen Elizabeth to the West Coast during her 1983 visit to the USA.

Presidential aircraft are proudly flown by the 89th Airlift Wing of the USAF. The aircraft are only designated *"Air Force One"* if the President are actually on board–otherwise, a code name and the tail number is used. While on Presidential service, 26000 carried two complete flight crews and could accommodate a maximum of 60 staff and guests. She can fly at 604 mph and has a cruising range of 6,000 miles.

Some interesting notes about 26000 as *"Air Force One."* Originally the color scheme was silver. Jacqueline Kennedy suggested the distinctive robin egg blue color scheme which is still in use today in modified form.

President Kennedy liked to board by the rear door; Johnson and Nixon boarded via the front door.

Johnson substantially altered the layout. Solid bulkheads were replaced with clear material so Johnson could see and address all who were on board; he also had a desk and chairs which could be raised or lowered electrically so he could sit higher than those he was meeting. The current presidential suite was moved to the center of the airframe in 1983.

help form part of a protective umbrella over North America, and the very latest of fighter technology, the F22 Raptor.

But a visit to the USAF Museum is more than just wandering around and admiring the hardware. I urge you to make time for the emotional experience of the IMAX theater. With its high six-story, wide screen, you feel as if you are actually strapped into the cockpit and it is here that you can come the closest to experiencing flight as you ride with the Blue Angels or glide over the glorious peaks of Hawaii.

See phone, hours, and details on page 49.

OH Mile 52.5-The Wright Cycle Company: As shown on the Dayton detour map, just to the west of I-75 is one of the most important aeronautical sites in the World–the Wright brothers bicycle and printing shop. It's hard to imagine that this 19th century building on a quiet side street was the birthplace of aviation as we know it today. And yet it was here that Orville and his brother, Wilbur, ran their printing and bicycle repair business, and by the evening's oil-lamp light developed the concepts of powered flight. It was here at 22 South Williams Street - the fourth of five locations for the brother's cycle business - that they read about some flying experiments in Germany. They felt that the concepts were wrong, and built a wind tunnel on the premises to test out a different theory which eventually led to their famous Wright Flying Machine, and the inaugural flight at Kitty Hawk, NC, in 1903.

As we leave this "cradle of flight," it is eerie to hear the rumble of a jet far overhead as a modern airliner climbs away from earth and up into the stratosphere.

OH Exit 52-Shawnee War Parties: Two hundred years ago you would be in the heart of Indian country, for the main Shawnee camp of Old Chillicothe lay on the banks of the Little Miami River, just thirteen miles to the east. The Shawnee were the most fierce of the Ohio tribes. Their war parties ranged the countryside down to the mountains in South Kentucky (Cherokee lands), often attacking the white settlers who were invading their lands from the east.

In 1778, the famous frontiersman Daniel Boone was captured by the Shawnee Chief Black Fish, and for four months lived as a member of the Shawnee tribe at Little Chillicothe. Learning of an Indian plan to attack his home at Boonesborough (just east of exit 95 in Kentucky) he escaped and made his way through the country alongside today's I-75 route, to warn the Boonesborough settlers.

OH Mile 42-N/Bound Construction Zone Bypass: If you are following this text on a northbound drive, skip to my notes at Exit 61, and decide whether you should take the I-675 bypass or follow our "local knowledge" detour route and map in reverse.

OH Exit 38-Crafter's Heaven: It would probably be easier to list handcrafts that are not carried–leathercraft and woodworking, for instance–but supplies for virtually everything else are carried in this huge warehouse retail outlet just west of the interstate. Pick up a free catalog just inside the door . . . and if you are reading it in your motel room that evening and find something else you need–they have a mail order service.

Factory Direct Craft Supply is at 315 Conover Drive. As you leave I-75, turn west onto State Route 73 and then immediately left onto Conover Drive. The craft supply outlet is halfway down on the right. Hrs: M-F 10-7; Sat 10-6; Sun 11-5. ☎ 1-800-252-5223 or 513-743-5855.

OH Exit 29-Flea Market Paradise: If you enjoy flea markets, then the north-east and north-west sides of exit 29 must be pure paradise. Trader's World (to the east) and Turtle Creek (to the west) markets are open on weekends from 9-5pm, all year round.

Exit 29-Tim Horton: Canadian travelers will be delighted to find one of the first I-75 outlets of their favorite Tim Horton coffee and doughnut chain, right here just east of exit 29. Named after the Toronto Maple Leaf hockey star, the Tim Horton chain was purchased by

DAYTON - *named in 1796 after General Jonathan Dayton, a soldier in the Continental Army of 1776, and later a statesman. In 1795 he served as Speaker in the House of Representatives and between 1799-1805 was a U.S. Senator. During his senatorial term, he was implicated in the conspiracy of Aaron Burr.*

Insider Tip
The White House Inn

Just a few miles west of exit 19 is a wonderful inn, serving excellent lunches and dinners in an "old world" setting. Owner/Chef Michael welcomes you to enjoy his *"heartland cooking and fireside spirits"* (entrees $7.50-$18.95) and the ambience of this lovely house surrounded by sweeping lawns, flower beds, herb gardens, patios and gazebos - six acres of heaven in Ohio.

The White House Inn is 2 miles from I-75. Go west at exit 19 (Union Center Rd), turn left at the traffic lights by the Marriott, through the lights at Allen Road and International Boulevard. Pass the Totes-Isotoner plant (no retail outlet) on the left and the pale blue "Butler Co." tank on your right. Up the hill passing the homes of Meadowridge on your right; in half-a-mile, turn right into the White House Inn driveway.

The Inn is open M-Sat, 11a-11p; Sun, 4-9p. ☎ 513-860-1110

Wendy's International in 1995–so of course, the Tim Horton is right alongside the Wendy's!

Mile 28-Welcome Center: Need a friend miles from home? Then go on in and say "hi" to Beverly, Joyce or Sheila at the southbound welcome center.

On the northbound side of the road, Carlene, Jerome or Serena will also help you on your way. They all know this book and love chatting with my readers.

OH Mile 24-Voice of America (VOA): On your left once stood the tall towers and curtain antenna arrays of the former VOA transmitter station. For more than 50 years, this station transmitted its signals to the World.

During WWII, the station played a major part beaming messages of freedom into the heart of Nazi Europe. As you drive by now, it's strange to think that this tiny parcel of land east of I-75 once incensed Hitler so much that he screamed in a Reichstag speech, about *"the propagandists in Cincinnati."*

OH Mile 25-Cincinnati's Traffic System: If you have a phone in the car, now is the time to dial 211 (Mon-Fri) for Cincinnati's ARTMIS Advanced Regional Traffic Management & Information System, and decide whether to take the bypass (coming up in nine miles) or continue on I-75 through the city.

If you don't have a cell phone, don't despair, an electronic overhead sign just past mile marker 20 will help you with your decision. You can also reach the same service by dialing 211 from a touch tone phone within the area or 513-333-3333.

After dialing 211, follow the prompts. Dial 751* (when prompted) to get information covering the traffic situation from mile 22 down to mile 4. Also dial 275* for the bypass. All traffic information is updated hourly.

OH Exit 21-West Chester Village: Just east of I-75 less than half a mile down the Cin-Day Road lies a small community where time seems to have stood still since founded in 1805 - the village of West Chester. Several antique stores and craft shops make this home in original West Chester buildings - there's even a piano restoration studio.

A pleasant place to take a short break from the sprawling antique malls along the freeway.

OH Miles 20 to 14-Ohio's Tropical Sea: You are now traveling across the ancient bed of a warm, shallow tropical sea (see Geology chart on page 92; Paleozoic Era–Ordovician Period–400 million years ago). The shale and limestone outcrops along I-75 are rich in fossils, particularly around Miles 20.5 to 19.5 and 14.8 to 14.3. As the teeming sea-life of small animals (examples, trilobites, primitive fish) and other life forms died, they settled to

MIAMISBURG - *after the Miami Indians, a tribe of the Algonquins who lived in this area, until driven by settlers westward to Indiana, Kansas and Oklahoma. The name probably originates from the Objibway word "Oumaumeg" meaning "People of the peninsular."*

CINCINNATI - *settled in 1788 and called Losantiville, the Governor of the then Northwest Territories renamed the village after a Revolutionary War officers' association called the Society of Cincinnatus, which in turn was named after Lucius Quinctius Cincinnatus (519 B.C.), a Roman dictator and soldier who was also a keen farmer.*

the bottom and slowly over millions of years, became the familiar layered (geologists call it sedimentary) rock that you see in exposed roadside rock cuts on your journey down the I-75. Often, the ancient animals' hard shells and skeletons remained intact in the rock, creating the fossils of today.

OH Exit 16 (S/bound)-RVs and Cincinnati: This isn't sign posted very well but if you are driving an RV or pulling a trailer, unless you are intending to stop in Cincinnati you must now take the bypass (I-275 East) at exit 16. This is a new rule to minimize the "heavy vehicle" traffic using Covington Hill in Kentucky.

OH Exit 14-Sneaky Pete: As you approach the concrete pillars of the overpass by exit 14, watch your speed *very* carefully. The pillar near the slow lane soft shoulder is a favorite hiding place for radar equipped patrol cars. The officers park their cars hidden behind the pillar and beam their radar guns at the oncoming southbound traffic as it leaves the 65 mph zone and enters the 55 mph speed reduction.

OH Exit 4 - Doris Mary Ann Von Kappelhoffen: Doris Kappelhoffen was born in 1924, about four miles east of here. She loved to dance and wanted to become a ballerina. In 1936, she and her dance partner Jerry Doherty won a local competition which enabled them to go to Hollywood. When she returned to Cincinnati in 1938, she was seriously injured when a train hit the car she was riding in, severely damaging her right leg. Any thoughts of a dancing career were over so her mother suggested she take singing lessons and this led to a singing engagement on Cincinnati radio station WLW-AM.

Local band leader Barney Rapp "discovered" her and the first song she sang with his band was "Day after day." Rapp suggested that if she was going to have a show career that "Kappelhoffen" would not be a great draw on a marquee. So remembering her first "professional" song, she changed her surname to "Day."

The rest is history. Doris Day went on to tour with Les Brown's band for $75 per week, and gained the fame which moved her back to Hollywood and the world of movies. "Que sera, sera - whatever will be will be."

Mile 0-Oprah's *"Beloved"*: Speaking of movies, have you seen the intensely powerful Oprah Winfrey movie, *"Beloved?"* If you have you will know the non-supernatural part of the story is based on a true incident involving a party of escaped slaves. But did you know that the slaves were owned by a man whose estate was at Richwood in Kentucky (see "Richwood" story on page 85) and that the escape took place across the great Ohio river, just to the east of here.

An historical marker on the south bank of the river records the event:

> *"On a snowy night in January, 1856, seventy slaves fled at the foot of Main Street* (in Covington, Kentucky) across the frozen Ohio River. A Margaret Garner was in the group. When arrested in Ohio, she killed her little daughter rather than see her returned to slavery. This much publicized slave capture became the focus of national attention because it involved the issues of Federal and State authority"*

**Editor's note: see map on page 50*

This incident happened 143 years ago, eight years before the start of the Civil War. Here is the story behind the escape.

A 22 year old slave called Margaret or Peggy Garner (Oprah Winfrey's Sethe in the film, *"Beloved"*) worked in the cookhouse of owner Archibald Gaines' estate, Maplewood in Richwood, Kentucky. Rather than remain in bondage, Margaret decided to escape to the "free" state of Ohio.

Accordingly, Margaret and her husband, Robert, gathered their four children and met with twelve others at the Richwood Presbyterian Church, where they used a large sled drawn by two horses to gallop through the snowy night, northward to Covington. Here they abandoned the sled and crossed the frozen Ohio on foot.

The Garners sought the "safe" house of a former slave, Kite. This was their undoing since the slave owners were in hot pursuit and quickly discovered that the Garners were hiding at the Kite home (the other slaves went elsewhere and were able to escape via the "Underground Railroad" to Canada. Surrounded by a posse of men, a battle commenced at the Kite home during which one of the deputies was shot. The door was broken down and seeing there was no escape, Margaret took a knife and killed her youngest daughter, Mary, so she would never have to suffer the horrors of slavery.

The trial that followed raised many legal and moral questions about slave ownership since one of the key arguments was that Margaret and her children were not slaves, but free due to earlier circumstances. Sadly however, the Court's decision was to return her to slavery in Kentucky. She died in 1858, still a slave.

KY Exit 192-MainStrasse (map on page 50): Just across the Ohio River in Covington, North Kentucky, lies a rather unusual community—MainStrasse Village. Covering approximately five blocks, this restored 19th century German neighborhood includes parks, antique, art and craft shops, and of course, restaurants serving fine Bavarian food such as sauerbraten, schnitzel and wurst, washed down with German lager.

The village people are proud of their heritage and offer old world service. Summer or winter, it's fun to wander the cobbled walkways and visit establishments such as the Linden Noll Gift Haus or MainStrasse Arts. Or sit under the trees near the Goose Girl fountain watching others go by while listening to the glockenspiel tower playing its 43 bell carillon in the nearby park.

Insider Tip
The Gatehouse

Renowned locally for its prime rib, the Gatehouse Bar & Restaurant is a castle complete with a moat!. Meals are a little more expensive than run from $16.95-$21.95), but they include a salad bar, and the quality is excellent.

The Gatehouse is 1/2 mile east of I-75 at exit 186. Turn left into the old Oldenburg Brewery property (this, and the Burbanks Restaurant have been sold and are now closed). Where the driveway curves back to the right (towards the old Brewery building), continue straight on into the Drawbridge Estates, as if you are going back to I-75. The Gatehouse will be ahead of you - surrounded by its moat. Hrs: 5:30pm-10:00

☎ 859-341-3800

If you are driving on I-75 at lunch time, you might consider a quick detour to either the MainStrasse Pub, the Strasse Haus or Wertheim's as a change from your normal fast food stop. Evening fine dining is provided by Wertheim's Gasthaus Zur Linde, whose menu specializes in German food but also caters to other tastes.

To find MainStrasse from the southbound I-75, immediately after crossing the Ohio River (Brent Spence Bridge), take exit 192 and turn left onto Fifth Avenue; follow map on page 50. I suggest you turn right at Philadelphia Street and visit the Visitors' Center which you will find within the park at Philadelphia and Sixth Street.

KY Mile 192-"Death" Hill: If you are prone to a "lead foot" and frustrated after the slow traffic of downtown Cincinnati, take our advice and do not speed up (or down) Covington Hill—known locally as, "Death Hill" for very good reasons. It's unsafe and famous for its aggressive speed control policing.

Incidentally, you'll be pleased to know that the number of trucks using Covington Hill

KENTUCKY - *a Wyandot Indian name "Kentahteh" meaning "land of tomorrow," or as early settlers used to call it - Caintuck.*

Money Saving Tip

Pickup your free copies of the green Traveler Discount Guide (old EIG) and the red Market America motel coupon books at the Kentucky Welcome Center (mile 177). Coupons in these books can save you as much as 45% off of regular motel rates.

has been greatly reduced. All "through 18 wheelers" must now use the I-275 bypass.

KY Exit 185 (N/bound)-RVs and Cincinnati: This isn't sign-posted very well but if you are driving an RV or pulling a trailer and unless you are intending to stop in Cincinnati, you must now take the bypass (I-275 East) at exit 185. This is a new rule to minimize the "heavy vehicle" traffic using Covington Hill in Kentucky.

KY Exit 186-A NASCAR Museum?: Watch for exciting things to happen in the Oldenberg Brewery property about half a mile to the east on Buttermilk Parkway. We do know that the building has been sold and that the previous occupants (Oldenberg brewery and Burbanks Restaurant) have gone. The new owner, who also owns the new Kentucky Speedway is currently having the interior gutted and rumors abound about a possible NASCAR museum being located here.

We will keep our "ear to the ground" and as soon as we know something, will post it on our website, **www.i75online.com**.

KY Mile 192-*"Florence Y'all"*: Do you see the warm welcome on the side of the water tower to our right? Now . . . y'all know you are now in the "South;" on the sunny side of the famous Mason-Dixon line (if extended over this far west).

But there is an interesting story behind the greeting, *"Florence Y'all."* It was never intended as a sign of welcome to Northerners. Originally, a local company used the publicly owned water tower to advertise their nearby business, the Florence Mall. Other area retailers were upset that public property was being used for this purpose and convinced the authorities that the tower should be repainted removing the offensive advertising. But although it agreed, the City lacked the budget to pay for the work.

Then an enterprising city employee suggested removing the "M" from "Mall" and replacing it with a "Y" - and that's how it remains to this day.

KY Milepost 177-Welcome Center: Need Kentucky information or motel discount coupons? Here's the place to get them. While there, say "hi" to Don, Judy and the center's supervisor, Peggy. They would love to help you.

KY Mile 175-Richwood: At Ohio mile 0, I told the story of Margaret Garner, the slave who escaped across the Ohio River with her daughter on a cold January night, in 1856.

It's hard to imagine that this tranquil Kentucky countryside was once a stronghold of slavery, and yet 144 years ago, this is where the sad story of Margaret Garner's escape started.

The map below will lead you to Richwood Presbyterian Church where the slaves met on the cold January night of the escape. If you turn right at the stop sign and drive another 4/10ths of a mile, you'll see a historical marker on your right marking the site of Major John Gaines' Maplewood Plantation where Margaret was kept in bondage. The main plantation house burned to the ground in the 1900's but you can see the ruins of the cookhouse and the smokehouse (where Margaret worked) to the right of the modern building. Please be aware that the property is private

KY Mile 169-Advantage-75: Are you curious about the "Advantage-75" signs that you see at truck weigh stations? This is an electronic scanning system which uses computers to automatically identify the equipment rolling through the weigh scales. Introduced in 1994 at a cost of $150,000 per weigh station, it is now speeding trucks through the documentation process at many of I-75's

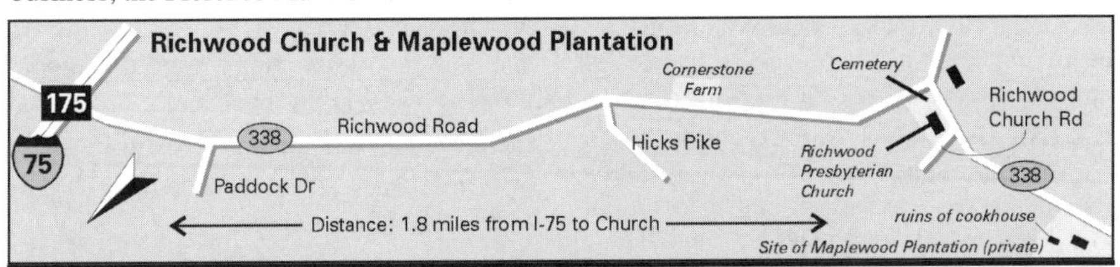

weigh stations.

This is the beginning of the elimination of interstate weigh stations. Eventually, all trucks will carry mini-transmitters (transponders) similar to those used by aircraft for traffic control purposes. A truck will roll down I-75 without slowing down, pass a road side scanner which reads the truck's load and destination data, drive over an electronic plate in the right lane road surface to record the load's weight, and get a green signal in their cab which indicates that they may continue—or a red signal to pull over for an inspection. Electronic sensors will monitor the other lanes to ensure that no trucks bypass this invisible data collection system.

Another technology used in many truck fleets today is the global position satellite (GPS) system which constantly records the exact location of a truck anywhere in North America. This information is uploaded from the

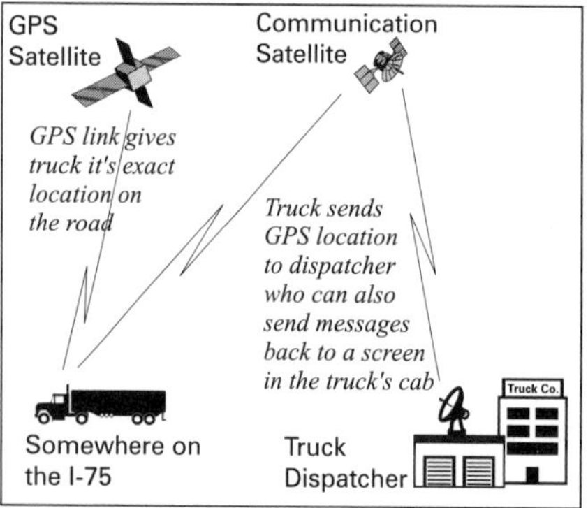

truck to a satellite in space (look for the flat round antenna usually on the cab roof) and then down to the truck company's central dispatch computer. This means that head office knows exactly where each truck is located at any time, how fast it is going and in which direction. This information coupled with data about the load, enables truck dispatchers to reroute their vehicles to maximize their transportation efficiency. Oh yes, truck drivers are instructed of such changes "on the roll" by a satellite pager system which gives them a visual message from their dispatcher right in their cab. No wonder, some companies are beginning to require a university degree for new truck drivers!

KY Exit 154-A Civil War Execution: Just a a quarter of a mile east of this exit is an historical marker commemorating a sad Civil War event which took place in 1864. Three Confederate soldiers were brought here from the Union prison in Lexington. At this spot, the three were hanged as a reprisal for the guerrilla murder of two Union sympathizers.

KY Exit 136-Blue Grass: Sixty miles back we passed over the mighty Ohio River and into Kentucky. Is it possible that the air temperature is a mite warmer? Certainly there is no snow here as we drive through the gently rolling Kentucky countryside. The scenery is very pleasant, but try as we might, we cannot see any famous bluegrass–and yet it is supposed to be all around us–but the grass is distinctly green!

So what is Kentucky Bluegrass? It is a type of grass which grows lushly in the State's rich limestone soil. It is not really blue–it's green, but in the spring, Bluegrass develops bluish-purple buds which when coated with early morning dew and viewed from a distance, appear as a rich, blue blanket cast across a meadow. Nobody knows where it came from but early pioneers found it growing in abundance when they crossed the Appalachian Mountains in their wagons. They shipped it back east and soon traders began asking for the "blue grass seeds from Kentucky" ... and the name stuck.

KY Exit 129-Toyota: Toyota Motor Manufacturing in Georgetown is huge. Its 1,300 acres property includes a test track, 8 million square foot plant and administration offices. Two vehicle production lines produce the popular Camry, Avalon and Sienna vehicles, as well as engine and axle components.

The Visitor Center conducts public tours of these facilities where you'll have a chance to see some of the 400,000 cars and 350,000 engines which are built here, annually. After an introductory video, you are taken on a guided tram ride through the stamping, body welding and assembly shops. Here is your chance to watch robots at work!

Drive east from I-75 towards the plant chimneys—you can't miss them. The plant's tours take place as follows:

June-August; Tues & Thurs; 8:30, 10, noon, 2 & 6 pm. Wed and Fri; noon and 2.

The plant is closed the first week in July.

Sept-May; Tues & Thurs; 8:30, 2 & 6 pm. Wed and Fri; 2pm only.

CB - I-75's Grapevine

There's an information grapevine along I-75 which runs 24 hours a day - 7 days a week and relays information faster than jungle drums. Better than continuous traffic reports on commercial radio, it reports with unerring accuracy abnormal (fog, snow, accident) road conditions ahead, the best lane to use, where the Highway Patrol are hidden and even inside information about restaurants. It's the soap opera of the radio waves and I guarantee that once you get hooked you will never have a dull or boring Interstate drive again.

Oh yes . . one other thing . . you also have to be able to understand the language. For instance, do you know what the following means? *"Hey 4 wheeler on my backdoor, hope y'all got your ears on 'cause I'm backin' it down"* or, *"South bounders, Smokey taking pictures at marker 114."*

Yep, it's good ole CB radio (Citizen's Band to the uninitiated) that indispensable communication medium of the long-distance trucker's world . . . and we wouldn't drive I-75 without it.

CB not only provides scads of information as you travel the Interstate but also peace of mind. You will never be alone at the side of the freeway should you experience a breakdown. With CB on board, you can summon help from your fellow travelers, and in most I-75 areas, state police and emergency organizations (such as REACT, or **R**adio **E**mergency **A**ssociated **C**itizens **T**eams). These agencies monitor the designated **highway emergency and general calling channel – channel 9**, and will respond to vehicles requesting assistance.

Finally, if this is your first venture into CB, we suggest a passive approach. Tune in to the trucks (channel 19 on I-75) and enjoy the ride. When you are ready to get your feet wet "on the air" try and call a fellow I-75 traveler heading in the same direction — *"Break, for a southbounder."*

Try channel 9 first—if you make contact, switch to another channel that you both agree upon since channel 9 should not be used for general conversation. If you have no luck on channel 9 then try the trucker's channel because this is probably where all the *"4 wheelers"* (private car) are listening— but again, switch to another channel right away after making contact since the truckers like to keep this channel for themselves.

SPECIAL NOTE - Kentucky and Tennessee Area Code Changes:

Since our last book, there have been two telephone number changes affecting I-75 areas.

In Kentucky, some **606 area codes have changed to 859**; in Tennessee, some **423 area codes have changed to 865**. Please note however that not all 606/423 codes are affected.

Insider Tip
Great Food! - Country Grill

Just a few seconds west of I-75 at exit 159, is a clean, family run restaurant which makes a very pleasant change to the larger chain "food factories." It is easy to spot the Country Grill as you come off the interstate. It sits on the side of a small hill (which gives its dining room a nice panoramic view of the lush Kentucky countryside), on the south (your left) side of the road. Ample parking is provided both in front of the restaurant and in a lower level (inc. RV parking) just below the building.

All meals are prepared on the premises from fresh ingredients by Chef Edward Smain. Table service is wonderful; Edward and Greg Melcher are the new owners and intend to maintain this restaurant's fine reputation. Greg will probably seat you at your table. The Country Grill is a rare find—I know you will enjoy it—we do and heartily recommend it. Hrs: M-F, 7-9; Sa & Su, 8-10; ☎ 859-824-6000

Reservations are necessary so phone ahead to get your tour times. Children must be at least 8 years old. ☎ 502-868-3027 or 1-800-866-4485.

KY Exit 126-Georgetown (map on Page 52): Just west of I-75 at this exit is the pleasant community of Georgetown. If you have a few minutes to spare, a drive down and back up Main Street is well worthwhile (I-75 is easy to rejoin). Brick sidewalks, old-fashioned lamp posts and more than 100 buildings listed on the National Register of Historic Places make this short sidetrip a visit to a bygone era of America.

Incidentally, an historical marker at the west end of Main Street tells us that the first Bourbon whiskey was distilled here using the fine limestone water from nearby Royal Spring.

Named after Bourbon County, Georgetown founder, Rev. Elijah Craig, set up a still at the spring in 1789 and brewed the first batch of this potent potion. Ironically, Scott County (in which Georgetown lies) is a "dry" county!

You can still visit the spring which is in a small park just behind the Historical Marker. The park also contains the 1874 log cabin of former slave, Milton Leach, and an interesting "statue" of Elijah Craig, carved out of a tree trunk.

KY Exit 120-Kentucky Horse Park: Kentucky is famous for its horses and horse breeding, and Lexington is at the heart of horse country. If you enjoy anything to do with horses (and even if you don't) then you owe it to yourself to stop at the Kentucky Horse Park (exit 120, Iron Works Pike–go east for ¼ mile).

Here you will be welcomed by a statue of that most famous horse of all–Man O'War (see story at Kentucky, exit 108), who is buried at the park. The Visitor Center has a spectacular film presentation, "Thou Shalt Fly Without Wings." Journey through time and trace the history of horses from prehistoric to modern times, along the spiral ramp of the International Museum of the Horse.

Afterwards, take the park shuttle, horse-drawn carriage or horseback (in snowy winter, horse-drawn sleigh) and enjoy the beautiful Kentucky park with its many horse related activities. The park houses an educational department where students are trained in skills to enter careers in the horse industry, so there is always something going on.

The park is open from 9-5pm. Parking $2. Apr to Oct, open every day; Nov to Mar, open Wed to Sun. Admission, includes the American Saddlebred Museum: adult/senior/child (summer) $12.50/$12.00/$6.50 (winter) $9.00/$8.50/$5.50.

☎ 800-568-8813 or 859-233-4303.

KY Exit 120-Ironworks Pike: An interesting note of history here. This road got its name from the early 1800's transport route which ran from the Slate Creek Ironworks about 40 miles east of Lexington, to Frankfort on the Kentucky River. War materials from the Ironworks were carried along this road for shipment by river down the Mississippi to Andrew Jackson in New Orleans during the War of 1812.

KY Exit 113-A Scenic Diversion: If you have a little time on your hands and would like to see some of the lush Kentucky horse farm land close up, you might enjoy a country drive east of this exit, along Paris Pike–route 68. Designated a "Scenic Route" you will travel past the stone walls and white fenced meadows of horse farms such as Walmac International, Bittersweet, Clovelly, C.V. Whitney, Elmendorf, Normandy, Spendthrift and Domino Stud. Many of these farms have bred thoroughbred champions running in major events around the world, most notably in the USA and France. Man o' War's sire, Fair Play and dam, Mahubah, are buried on Normandy Farm. CV Whitney's Farm is

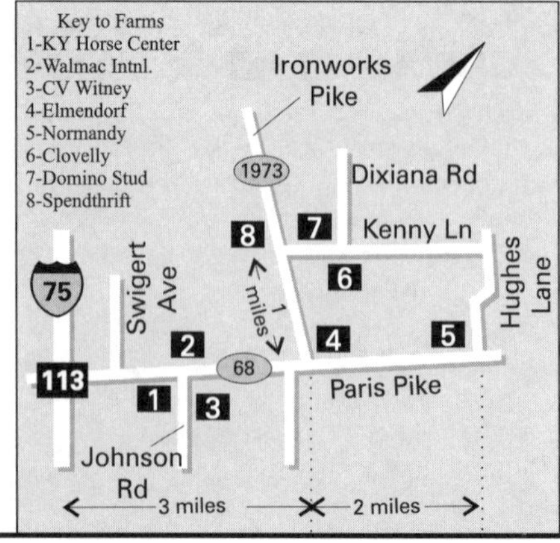

often host to film stars, international business and political figures.

The drive takes you 3 miles to the junction of Rt 1973 (Ironworks Rd), a further 2 miles takes you to Hughes Lane where you turn left. Turn left again in one and three-quarter miles onto Kenny Lane and left again onto Ironworks Road in 2 miles. One mile down Ironworks Road brings you back to the Paris Pike, where you turn right to drive the 3 miles back to I-75. Total? Thirteen miles of wonderful Kentucky countryside–twenty minutes of pure pleasure.

If short of time, just drive the 3 miles to the junction of Rt 1973, carefully turn around and drive back to the interstate.

KY Exit 115-Lexington Downtown area (map on page 50): One and a quarter miles south on Newtown Pike (route 922) will bring you to the Lexington downtown area. Lexington was a settlers' campsite in 1775 and yet had become a bustling commercial center within twenty-five years. Turn onto West Main Street, bear right onto Vine (one way), cross Broadway, S Mill, Upper, Limestone and stop at the Visitor Center at Vine and Rose (301 E. Vine St; ☎ 800-845-3959 or 859-233-1221.

I suggest you pick up a map and a guide book here for there is lots to see and do in Lexington.

While at the Visitors Center, pick up a copy of "Bluegrass Country Driving Tour," which includes the "Lexington Walk & Bluegrass Country Driving Tour." It has some wonderful short tours in the countryside around you, including some alongside I-75 in the direction you are traveling.

While there, walk over to Thoroughbred Park and see what I consider to be one of the most fascinating statues in the world! If you are in your car, you can park in the area just behind the statue - (see map on page 50).

This bronze statue by Gwen Reardon is of a "frozen" horse race, and you can easily spend a half-hour wandering around between the horses just looking at the expressions on the horses and riders' faces. Colored in subtle earth tones, you can see the supreme effort on the faces of the leading jockeys as they attempt to eek out just one more inch of horse flesh on the finish line. And don't miss the

Lexington's superb horse race statue

look of desperation on the face of the tail end jockey who already knows that he has lost. Take your camera . . . the close-ups you take will be memorable.

KY Exit 108-Man O'War: Man O'War Boulevard is of course, named after the famous Kentucky thoroughbred - foaled in 1917 - who put many new records into the book. Man O'War (World War I was taking place at the time) was said to have had a 25 foot stride and was once clocked at 43 MPH during a workout. He was only beaten once in his racing career, ironically by a horse named, *"Upset."*

In retirement, Man O'War and his groom, Will Harbot, became inseparable friends for 17 years. Will died in 1947; Man O'War died one month later . . . many said of a broken heart.

Lexington is thoroughbred horse country. The lush grass meadows growing on limestone soil make ideal horse grazing conditions. As you travel the I-75, the neat horse farms to the east with their trim plank fences–Kingston, Shandon, Winter Hill and Meadowcrest–are a delight to the eye. Check our I-75 maps–we have named them for you.

KY Exit 108-Mega shopping? Check out an I-75 mega shopping experience. Hidden from the freeway but just west of this exit, Hamburg Pavilion contains many "big box" stores, anchored by a huge Meijer 24 hour superstore and Target. A Barnes & Noble super bookstore is here (need another copy of this book? B&N have it in stock!) . . . and so are many other well known stores such as Office Max, Radio Shack, Old Navy, Garden Ridge, etc. A multi screen movie theatre (Regal Cinema) has opened and with all sorts of new lodging facilities across from the mall, this exit is fast becoming one of the favorite

LEXINGTON - *named in 1775 after Lexington, Massachusetts, by a group of colonial hunters who camped close by after the first skirmish with British troops during the War of Independence.*

stop-over spots for the Florida bound "snowbird."

KY Mile 98-Hawks: As we cross the Kentucky River, the road becomes more hilly for we are in the region known as the Kentucky Knobs. Geologists refer to this area as the Jessamine Dome, an area of sedimentary rock which was uplifted millions of years ago.

Two or three hawks glide above us, riding the air currents of the ridges, their sharp eyes focused on the ground looking for the tiny, almost imperceptible movement of a delectable field mouse or baby rabbit. Suddenly, one of them swoops down–sharp talons extended earthward– dropping like a stone. You look away knowing that once again a small animal has given its life to ensure that in death, life goes on. Such is Nature's food chain.

KY Exit 95-Fort Boonesborough (map on page 51): Just five miles east (about an eight minute drive) along route 627 lies Fort Boonesborough–a reconstruction of the wooden fortified settlement built by Daniel Boone in 1775. As you wander around inside the wooden stockade you may visit the settlers in their period costumes and watch them make soap, spin wool, and practice many other frontier arts and crafts. Most of the products made at the fort can be purchased in the adjacent gift shop. It's a great way to learn more about the hard life of a pioneer.

In 1778, Boone escaped from an Indian village in Ohio (Little Chillicothe–Ohio exit 52) and returned here to warn the settlers of an impending Indian attack. With the help of the British Army, the Indians lay siege to this fort for ten days. Heavy rains and the strong defense by Boone and his men broke the siege. On the tenth day the Indians gave up, disappearing into the trees around the fort.

As you peer through the half opened gateway into the dappled sunlight of the still green forest beyond, its easy to imagine that the cawing sound you just heard was not a bird but one of a Shawnee war party signaling the band to move closer to the stockade walls.

Hours and other information are on page 51.

KY Exit 95-White Hall (map on page 51): In the opposite direction just 1.9 miles (3½ minutes) to the west lies the famous White Hall. This magnificent Georgian and Italianate building was the home of Cassius Clay, namesake of Mohammed Ali. Clay is one of Kentucky's most colorful and historical figures–a noted abolitionist, politician, publisher, Minister to Russia, and friend of Abraham Lincoln. White Hall is really two houses in one. The original Georgian building–Clermont–was built in 1798, by Clay's father, Green. In the 1860's while Clay was on service in Russia, his wife, Mary Jane supervised the construction of the second house, over the original Clermont building. The transformed building designed by prominent architects Thomas Lewinski and John McMurtry became known as White Hall.

Hours and other information are on page 51.

KY Exit 90A-Richmond: Another attractive I-75 community which has managed to protect its 19th century heritage. Its downtown Main Street heritage area lies just over two miles east of the interstate, from this exit.

Route 169 (Tates Creek Road) runs west out of Richmond where in about 12 miles it reaches the Ohio River and the famous Valley

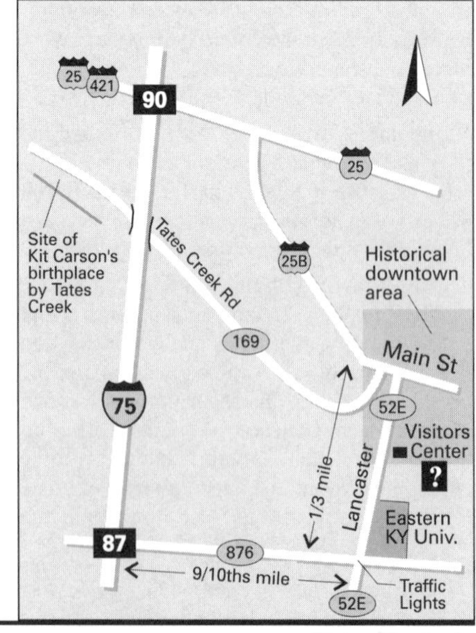

TEA-21, and all that . . .

Here are some interesting facts about the Interstate Highway system.

Usage—there are 4 million miles of roads in the USA. The interstates account for 45,744 miles or about 1.1%, and yet interstates carry 23% of the total traffic. The standard interstate should have four 12' wide lanes and 10' wide shoulders, although due to heavier traffic patterns, many states are now expanding old four lane sections to six.

Administration—Freeways are administered by the U.S. Department of Transportation, Federal Highway Administration (FHA), Washington, DC, in coordination with each State's Department of Highways (DOT). As the owner, each state is responsible for the construction and maintenance of sections of the Interstate system; the Federal Government reimburses the state 90% of its costs.

TEA-21—In June, 1998, recognizing that maintenance and expansion of the interstate system was not keeping up with current and future needs, President Clinton signed new legislation—the *Transportation Equity Act,* known as TEA-21—which will release billions of dollars to the states between now and 2003, to provide funding to improve all transportation systems. Much of this extra funding will be spent on the nation's interstates, it's estimated that Federal spending on highways will increase by about 10 billion dollars during this period.

Numbering—Interstate highways are numbered with two digits according to their route direction. North-South routes are odd numbered, starting in California with I-5 and moving eastward toward the Atlantic coast where we find the I-95. East-West routes are designated with even numbers and start in the south with I-4 in Florida and finish in the North with I-96 in Michigan. This system was chosen to avoid confusion with the older highway numbering system which started with US1 in the East and finished with U.S. 101 in the West.

Even the three digit Interstate extensions and beltways numbers have significance. If the ***first digit is even***, the route is a ***beltway***, bypass or loop around a city (e.g. I-275 around Cincinnati or I-475 around Macon). Incidentally, these beltways were not always designed as bypasses for the convenience of travelers. Planned during the Cold War period, some were designed as a means of allowing the military to bypass the rubble of a nuclear devastated city!

If the ***first digit is odd***, the route is a ***spur*** from the main route into a nearby area (example: I-575 at I-75 exit 268 [old 115] above Marietta, GA).

Signage—Interstate signs are not cheap. The entire system has signage worth over $200 million. An average interchange sign (about 150 sq. feet) costs around $5,000, and overhead suspended truss signs such as those used to signify major divides in an interstate highway can run as much as $35,000. Interstate signs are color coded. Green & white give directions; blue & white signs inform about roadside services (e.g. rest area). The signs are designed to be read 1,000 feet away. At 70 MPH, a vehicle takes 9.7 seconds to cover this distance. Some signs need fast readers!!!

Incidentally, those Lodging-Food-Gas service signs you see as you approach an exit do not necessarily list ALL the services available at the exit. Companies must pay the state to be listed - some decide not to.

Exit Numbers—the FHA recommends that exits be numbered from a state's southern/ western borders, in step with the distance in miles from the border. After Florida completes its exit number change in 2003, all I-75 states will be in compliance with this recommendation.

Safety—Interstate highways are generally 2½ times safer than other roads. Why? Multiple lanes smooth the flow of traffic, divided roads with median barriers reduce or eliminate headlight glare and head-on crash situations, fenced right-of-ways control access by animals and pedestrians, absence of stop signs and traffic lights eliminate sudden stopping situations, and finally, controlled access of all intersections so that the cross route goes over or under (rather than through) the Interstate, eliminate dangerous cross-traffic hazards.

Geology and Dinosaurs along I-75.

The I-75 winds its way across an ancient land with many rock cuts revealing the geology of very early times.To help you understand the age of the land around you and the life forms which were present at that time, here is a simplified chart of the Geological Time Scale.

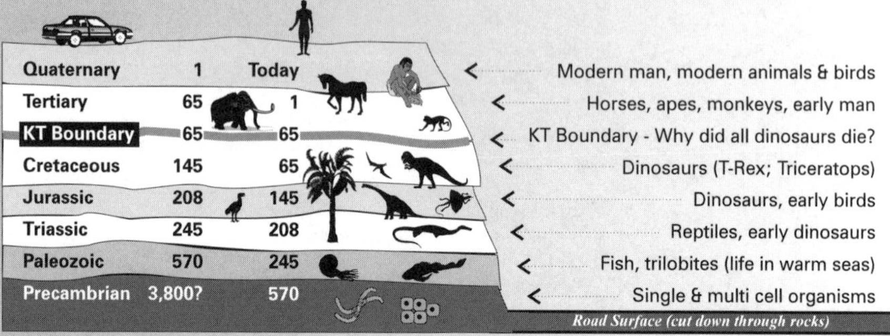

Think of the Time Scale as an eight layer cake; each layer representing a period of time (numbers are in millions of years). The oldest layer is at the bottom and the newest (today) is at the top:

Incidentally did you notice that according to the chart, Tyrannosaurus Rex, the huge flesh eating monster in the movie "Jurassic Park" was not around in the Jurassic period? It did not appear until the Cretaceous Period, 63 million years later–the movie should have been called, "Cretaceous Park."

continued top or next page

View Car Ferry, Kentucky's oldest continuous business.

It's along this road that the famous pioneer and explorer, Christopher "Kit" Carson was born in a small log cabin beside Tates Creek, on Christmas Eve, 1809. Kit Carson, went on to become a living legend as a frontiersman. His skill as a hunter and rifleman was thought by many to be second to none. The publication of his adventures during his 1842-1844 exploration of the West was widely read in the eastern cities and spurred many on to life on the new frontier.

Mile 86-Sedimentary Rock: We pass through an interesting cut of stratified limestone–successive layers of sedimentation from an ancient tropical sea which have been heaved up by the Earth's colossal, mountain folding forces. In summer, this cut is particularly pretty–topped with stands of young lush trees and carpets of wildflowers.

KY Exit 76-Berea (map on page 49): Literally seconds off the I-75, the small town of Berea just to the east is a hidden jewel that many drive by in their haste to reach Florida. If you enjoy crafts and antiques, make sure you plan an overnight stop here for Berea is exciting and vibrant. In 1988, it was designated the *"Craft Capital"* of Kentucky by State Legislature.

The largest concentration of working studios and craft galleries can be found in "Old Town Berea," located near the Berea Welcome Center on North Broadway.

I suggest you go to the Welcome Center first and get a copy of their excellent Berea guide and fold-out map–it's a great help in navigating around the town. You'll find the Center housed in the town's original 1917 L&N

RICHMOND - *named by early settlers after the capital of Virginia, which in turn was named after Richmond, Surrey, England.*

Special Report–continued from top of previous page

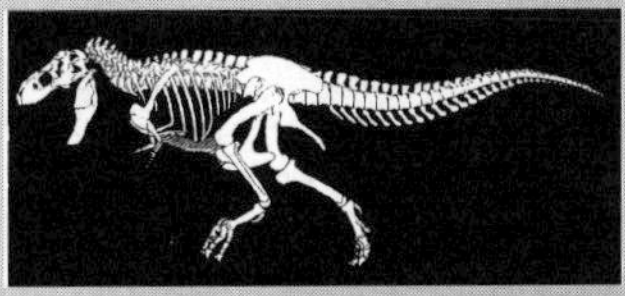

Dinosaurs disappeared 65 million years ago, possibly as the result of a major natural catastrophe. Geologists have identified a dark narrow band of material called the KT Boundary, which appears in rock strata of that time. This layer contains iridium, an element rare on earth but common in asteroids. It also contains tectites, small beads of glass fused under tremendous pressure and heat (most powerful nuclear bomb times 500,000). One theory is that a 6 mile wide asteroid collided with the earth (the Chicxulub Crater) in the ocean off the Yucatan Peninsula, Mexico, causing a massive, earth circling cloud of sulphur fog and debris. This blocked the sun plunging the world into a dark cold ice age, killing all land animals in the process. The KT Boundary may consist of debris from this cloud which settled back onto the earth's surface and was gradually covered by later geological layers.

As we drive along I-75 we travel over an ancient section of landscape, for time has seen many of the more recent geological layers eroded away. Today, the surface geology is often the rocks of the seventh Paleozoic period–a time when warm tropical salt seas covered the land. During that period, sediment suspended in the sea water continually dropped to the bottom accompanied by dead fish, shell invertebrates and vegetation debris. Over time, the ocean bed hardened layer by layer into sedimentary rock such as limestone and shale; the trapped fish and shell remains became the fossils which can be found today in the sedimentary (many-layered) rocks of the cuts along the I-75. All the way from Ohio, through Kentucky and Tennessee and down into Georgia, the surface geology is of this Paleozoic period.

But what about the Dinosaurs? Did they ever stalk the lands through which the I-75 now runs? Not according to the surface geology for this is too old. But marine dinosaur bones of the late Cretaceous period have been found in southwest Georgia.

Railroad Depot building. Hours and other details are on page 49.

Don't miss the historic Boone Tavern located in the heart of College Square along with numerous galleries and shops. At last count, Berea is home to over 25 craft shops & galleries and 14 antique shops or malls.

Several readers have written to me recommending the Wanpen restaurant (Chinese and Thai). I haven't reviewed it yet; if you would like to try it, turn right at at the first lights - Brenwood.

Berea is also home to Berea College, a liberal arts establishment where students receive a free education in return for work in the school's various departments and programs. Interesting student-guided tours of the campus are offered daily, departing from the Boone Tavern.

Historic Berea, where the bluegrass meadows meet the rugged mountains, is truly a living celebration of the Appalachian culture. Stop for a night and enjoy it.

KY Mile 73-Rock Springlets: We are approaching the Cumberland Mountain region of Kentucky, an area rich with timbered ridge scenery, dense stands of forest, and interesting rock cuts. A favorite of mine is on the west side of the interstate at Mile 63. The face of the cliff is covered with vines and the rock often weeps from hidden springlets of ground water. In the warm sunlight of a spring day, it is magical.

KY Exit 62-Renfro Valley: Renfro Valley Entertainment Center is one of Kentucky's best kept secrets. Just 15 miles south of Berea, the beautiful Valley is known as "Kentucky's Country Music Capital."

Fiddling, banjo picking, singing, clogging, bluegrass, and vaudeville comedy make up the best country music and entertainment show this side of Nashville. The two barn theatres host eleven live shows weekly, plus a full schedule of Headliner concerts and special events. Many stars have graced the Renfro Valley stages . . from Red Foley to the

BEREA - *for the Biblical city in ancient Syria.*

Osborne Brothers, or Loretta Lynn to John Michael Montgomery. Enjoy the Renfro Valley Barn Dance, Jamboree, Mountain Gospel Jubilee and traditional Festivals.

Another claim to fame is the Renfro Valley Gatherin' - a radio show continuously produced since 1943 and broadcast to more than 200 stations across North America each week. It is said to be the second longest running show on radio (the Grand 'Ole Opry is the longest).

While here, take some time to visit the new Historical Cabins & Craft village, tour John Lair's Theater, and enjoy down-home cooking at the log Lodge's famous Boarding House suppers, or snacks at Old Joe Clark's eatery. On the premises you'll discover a new RV Park and miniature Golf.

The Valley's musical venues run from March to December. From May to October, the entertainment of various forms, runs from Wednesday to Sunday. The programs and stars vary, so its best to call ahead at 1-800-765-7464 for your reservations. At the very least, there is a Barn Dance every Saturday night and a Sunday Gatherin' every Sunday morning at 8:30 am.

KY Mile 61-Interstate Engineering: As we drive through more rock cuts, we cannot help wondering about the massive engineering and construction task presented to I-75 road builders. The roadbed was built through anything which stood in its path. At times, I-75 cuts deep into the side of a hill and at others, it traverses a short valley on top of an embankment.

At this mile marker, you notice how the rock face on both sides of the road has been blasted and cut back in steps. If you look carefully, especially when the sun casts shadows across the rock, you will often see evidence of the original explosion shafts running vertically down the rock face. These were drilled down through the earth a few feet apart, along the line of the rock face. Dynamite charges dropped down each hole were set off at the same time, slicing the earth away from the face where it could be gathered and trucked away at the road bed.

The building of America's Interstate system is often quoted as the largest public works project of all human times–larger than the building of the Egyptian Pyramids; broader in scope than the digging of the Suez Canal–this truly must be so. As we whiz by on our way to Florida, we take our hat off to you, the builders of I-75. Thank you all for your Herculean work.

KY Mile 56-Daniel Boone National Forest: We are about to cross a stretch of the Daniel Boone National Forest. From the I-75, it doesn't look very big but most of it lies to the east and west of us. In fact it covers 21 counties and over 670,000 acres of rugged terrain - steep slopes, narrow valleys, picturesque lakes, rocks and cliffs. It is a primary recreation area with many miles of hiking trails and opportunities for outdoor activities such as picnicking, camping, fishing and water sports.

There is even a hunting area where only pioneer weapons such as muzzle loaded flintlocks or long bows may be used. All modern firearms are banned.

As we cruise down the freeway on automatic control at 65 MPH, we often think about the hard life of the early pioneers as they pushed their way inland from the settlements of the Atlantic shore. The Appalachian (pronounced locally as, "App-er-latch-urns") Mountains blocked their path and until the Cumberland Gap was discovered, the journey by ox-drawn wagon laden with all their household possessions was next to impossible. Measuring their forward progress in days–not minutes–they overcame obstacle after obstacle to achieve Utopia ... that wonderful land just beyond the next misty horizon.

And the difficult terrain of their journey was not the only hazard. As the War of Independence raged on the Atlantic Coast the British Army incited the warlike Indians of Ohio and Kentucky to attack the pioneers and turn them eastward again. Soon small bands of Miami, Wynadot, Shawnee and Cherokee braves were treading the paths in the forests beside which we now travel, to ambush the settlers and tomahawk them to death.

In 1775, a man called Henderson formed the Transylvania Company and purchased the lands we now know as Kentucky from the Cherokee Indians–his wish was to sell land grants to white settlers from the east, and he hired Daniel Boone to help with this mission.

The country we are now passing through is named in honor of Boone, for it was he who blazed the original Cumberland Gap trail in 1775. Later, with 30 axemen, he broadened the trail cutting trees down below wagon axle height, so that settlers could follow his Wilderness Trace through the Cherokee lands into the Land of the Big Meadow– "Cain-tuck." He and his men opened the entire trail in less than three weeks!

In the next few miles, as I-75 curves, you will actually cross Daniel Boone's original pioneer's trail twice (see I-75 map pages 24-S and 175/176-N). Half a mile beyond mile marker 47, the "Wilderness Trace" comes from the northeast and runs parallel on the east (left) side of the I-75, until it crosses over to the west at Mile 45.5. It runs immediately adjacent to the I-75 on the west (right) side, until it re-crosses just south of Mile 44.

The modern terrain matches the 200 year old frontier trail well. It is still easy to imagine those deerskin clad woodsmen with their wide brimmed beaverskin hats and their flintlock muskets crooked over their arms. We can still hear the rumbling of the wagon wheels and the snorting of the pack horses as the first settlers move northward on their journey to Boonesborough, Kentucky.

KY Exit 38-Levi Jackson State Park (map on page 51): Nine minutes to the east of this exit lies the Levi Jackson Park. Levi Jackson was born in 1816, the son of an early pioneer. Through the years, the Jackson family acquired many acres of land including a section of Daniel Boone's original trail. In 1931, Jackson's son donated large sections of his holdings to the State, to be protected as park land named in honor of his father.

Within the park lies the site of Kentucky's worst Indian massacre–Defeated Camp. Dur-

Insider Tip
We find the Perfect Motel

It's the little things which turn a good motel room into a great one, and I may have found the perfect match to my expectations . . . at the Baymont Inn, west of the I-75 at Kentucky exit 29.

Here are my first impressions on opening the door with the plastic security card: — a fresh, clean smell in the air—well decorated room with high ceilings—separate vanity-bathroom areas (very important for traveling couples and fast morning get-aways)—modular shower with excellent shower head and a GREAT steam extractor fan—lots of lights (5 x 100w + vanity area fluorescent)—large 25" screen TV with remote control unit—very, quiet even although next to the interstate—soft, full reclining chair—heavy noise-killing drapes—coffee maker with full supplies.

But I've saved the best until last. I had been driving northbound in a freak winter storm which caused snowy and icy conditions all the way from Atlanta. Coming over Tennessee's Pine Mountain in next to impossible winter conditions was another story and all I wanted to do was get off the road with minimum fuss and into a swimming pool . . . and forget the drive. Imagine my delight when I found that the Baymont maintains its pool at a tepid 97°F (36°C), and that an even warmer bubble-spa is right alongside. Incidentally, the pool is housed inside a large glass enclosure which allowed me to swim in the tension-relaxing warm water while watching the traffic fight the snowy interstate outside.

We ate dinner at the Cracker Barrel restaurant next door. The following morning, we enjoyed a free breakfast and paper in the special "breakfast room," enabling us to make an early start (on a cleared road). This motel is highly recommended.

The Baymont Inn's direct phone number is 606-523-9040.

Special Report

Birth of the World's Fast Food Business

Hidden in the valley just to the east of the Interstate in south Kentucky is a gem of a discovery–the birth place of America's (and the world's) fast food industry. For this is where Harland Sanders ran his Sanders Court Motel and Restaurant for many years (long famous with travelers for its clean rooms, country hams and pecan pie), right alongside the main route to Florida - Highway 25 (see map on page 52).

Imagine Mr. Sanders' consternation in 1956 when he learned about the Government's plan to build a super highway (the I-75) to Florida just two miles to the west of his property. Sixty-six year old Sanders decided that his reputation for good wholesome food could continue to attract customers so he set about developing a new type of food for the traveler which they could take along on the road with them–deep fried chicken.

The rest, of course, is history. His 11 secret herbs and spices combined with pressure frying techniques, developed into his famous Kentucky Fried Chicken, the first fast food business in the world. Later, the Commonwealth of Kentucky honored him by granting him the title of Colonel, and the name "Colonel Sanders Kentucky Fried Chicken" was born.

How much money did Harland Sanders' Motel and Restaurant make? Here are his financial results for 1945:

RESTAURANT	- Food Sales	$1,847	
	- Cost of Sales	1,081	
	- Net Food Sales	$766	
	- Expenses	777	
	- **LOSS**	$10	**$11**
MOTEL	- Revenue	$906	
	- Expenses	542	
	- PROFIT	**$364**	**364**
TOTAL PROFIT FOR 1945			**$353**

Today, you may visit the free museum which includes a typical Sanders Court motel room, the Colonel's office and the kitchen where he developed his special recipe. You can sit in the original restaurant which was restored and re-opened in September 1990, and eat where it all began! Order the Colonel's original recipe from the adjoining modern KFC (Kentucky Fried Chicken) store.

ing the night of October 3, 1786, under a hunter's moon, the McNitt party became the victims of a bloody Indian massacre in which at least 24 of the travelers were killed.

The group of approximately 60 pioneers, representing 24 families, had been traveling for over a month and had stopped for the night on the Boone Trace near the Little Laurel River.

Indians, Shawnee and Chickamauga were in the area to observe religious ceremonies. A war band may have become disturbed when it observed the settlers singing and playing cards at their overnight camp–also a sacred Indian place beside the river.

The scalped bodies were found later by local settlers, who buried the remains by the camp. During the raid, up to ten pioneers were taken prisoner, including 8 year old Polly Ford who spent nearly 15 years living with the Indians before being rescued.

Hours and other details are on page 51.

KY Exit 29-KFC (map on page 52)

KY Exit 25-Cumberland Falls (map on page 53): If you have time to explore some of the rugged Kentucky countryside, then I heartily recommend this side trip to the Cumberland Falls. Realize however that it will take just over an hour to drive there and back, and you will need a minimum of 30 minutes to enjoy the scenery when you arrive.

Cumberland Falls State Park is part of the Daniel Boone Forest, and is very typical of the unspoiled countryside of pioneer times. The Falls themselves are quite spectacular–a 125 foot curtain of water plunging 60 feet into the boulder strewn gorge below. The mist

ROCKCASTLE RIVER - *named for the castle-like rock formations along its course.*

CORBIN - *named after James Corbin Floyd, a circuit judge (traveling magistrate who rode the district by horse, dispensing justice within the various rural communities).*

of Cumberland Falls creates the magic of the "moonbow," a rainbow only visible on a clear night during a full moon. This unique phenomenon appears nowhere else in the Western Hemisphere. Phone the park number provided on the map for moonbow viewing dates and times. Hours and other details are on page 53.

KY Mile 8 & 3-Mountains: Soon we will be crossing the Kentucky–Tennessee border and climbing from Jellico up into the sky. At Kentucky Miles 8 and 3, the freeway ahead gives us a glimpse of what is to come–a panoramic view of the mountain ridges to the south. Taylor, Patterson, Vanderpool, Chestnut Oak, Walnut and Brushy Mountains march across the horizon and recede into the bluish hazy distance.

KY Mile 1 (N/bound)-Welcome Center: Say hello to Debbie, Wilma, Claude or Jeff if they are at the counter.

Tennessee Mile 161 (N/bound)-Graveyard: Many people notice the tiny graveyard beside I-75 just before this mile marker. Here is stark evidence of the way the interstate planners slashed the new freeway across landscape, dividing businesses, farms, homesteads, and in this case - separating the local folk from their departed loved ones. The graveyard is lovingly maintained by the Gibson, Hyslope, Corbin and Parrott families; the cemetery is always well groomed and the flowers fresh and bright.

Tennessee-the State that almost wasn't: Did you know that Tennessee would have been called *Franklin* if a Rhode Island delegate to an early Congress had not been too late to vote? Here's what happened:

In 1769, settlers from Virginia illegally migrated across the mountains and moved into the protected lands of the Cherokee, settling along the banks of the Watauga river.

Neighboring North Carolina refused the settlers appeals for help against the Cherokees who attacked the settlers so, four years before the American Revolution, they formed the Watauga Association, wrote the first American constitution (the Watauga Compact) and later in 1784, created the State of Franklin (after Ben, of the same name).

In 1788, the state approached the Philadelphian Congress requesting entry into the Union as the 14th state, but the motion was lost by a single vote (remember that tardy delegate from RI?) and the State of Franklin disappeared forever . . . except in the hearts of Tennesseeans. For being

Insider Tip
Cumberland Inn - "Our Tranquility Base"

Cumberland Inn is such a great find that I am almost reluctant to share it.

Less than two minutes east of the I-75 at exit 11, Cumberland Inn was built—with absolutely no expenses spared—by Cumberland College to serve as a conference center for its many faculty and alumni programs. The College often makes extra rooms available to the public starting at $69.00 year around. General Manager Steve has offered a special discount to *"Along Interstate-75"* readers if the Inn is not too busy, so be sure to mention this book when you check in. The inn's phone number is 800-315-0286 (606-539-4100).

And the rooms are exactly what you would expect at an up-scale conference facility. Quiet, wonderfully clean and very well equipped. Hair drier, iron and ironing board, coffee equipment, an electronic calendar on the TV–no detail is missed, even the shower curtain rings have bearings! But would you expect less? In the past, two U.S. Presidents have visited the Cumberland Lodge.

The Athenaeum dining room is superb–friendly service by the college's students, real table linen, napkin rings, shining silverware—and great food. Surrounded with library shelves bearing more than 400 books and entertained by an automatic grand piano, I can't think of a better way to spend an evening after a day on the interstate. The price? Our evening meal for two people came to just more than $25, less tip.

The Lodge setting is so peaceful—it really is a wonderful way to break your interstate journey—this is truly our "Tranquillity Base" in Kentucky.

Kudzu

Special Report

If it is summer and you look across to the northbound lanes at Tennessee mile 78, you will see an incredible stand of Kudzu (pronounced *cut-zoo*, with the stress on the first syllable). This prolific vine (Pueraria) grows rapidly, covering everything in its path. You often see it in South Tennessee or Georgia covering telephone poles, fences and surrounding trees. Brought to America from Japan in 1876, it was first grown in the Japanese Pavilion at the Philadelphia Centennial Exposition and then became popular as a house plant.

Until 1955, it was used to stop soil erosion in the South, but it escaped and rapidly became a menace to the point where it has been described as a "national disaster." Growing as much as a foot a day in hot weather, the vine develops roots wherever its leaves touch the ground. In one season, it can easily grow 100 feet away from its original stem, enveloping everything in its path. The good news, however, is that cattle like to eat it, and it has been used for its herbal and medicinal properties. Recently, it has been found to be very useful in alcohol addiction therapy.

Money Saving Tip

$$$$$$$$$$$$ $SAVE$ $$$$$$$$$$$$

Pickup your <u>free copies</u> of the green Traveler Discount Guide and the red Market America motel coupon books at the Tennessee or Kentucky Welcome Centers (mile TN 166 or KY 1). Coupons in these books can <u>save you as much as 45%</u> off of regular motel rates.

a descendant of a Watauga Association settler is as revered in Tennessee as a proven genealogy back to the *Mayflower* is in Massachusetts.

Over the next few years, Congress annexed Franklin to North Carolina, then designated it as part of the "SW Territory." The settlers finally achieved statehood in 1796, when Tennessee was admitted as the 16th state. The first Governor was John Sevier, one of the leaders of the original efforts for statehood.

Tennessee Mile 161-Welcome Center: It's always a joy to stop at this well maintained Welcome Center. Say hello to Rick, Barbara, Joyce or Debbie, who are usually at the counter helping travelers with their journeys through Tennessee.

TN Exit 160-Jellico: The small town of Jellico guards the northern gateway to the southernmost range of the massive Appalachian Mountains chain which sweeps across the northeast U.S.A., from New Brunswick, Canada to the Carolinas and Tennessee. Jellico, possibly named after the mountain Angelica plant which was used by settlers to brew an intoxicating drink called "Jelca," was settled in 1795 and incorporated in 1883. Some say the town was incorporated to provide a legal means of selling Tennessee whiskey.

It is remembered for a terrible train crash which occurred here during WWII. A speeding train hauling 15 cars loaded with over 600 soldiers on their way to army camp, derailed and crashed into the deep gorge of the Clear Fork River, about 1½ miles to the east. More than 35 men were killed.

Elk Valley (map on page 54): If you have time (this will only take you an extra 21 minutes) and the weather is reasonable, I suggest you turn off I-75 at exit 160, drive through Jellico and take the Elk Valley road which parallels the interstate. It rejoins I-75 at exit 141. For those who ply the freeway year after year, this might be a refreshing break. As you drive through the Jellico main street, note the old storefronts on either side. This is an unusual opportunity to see some really old buildings in their original state. Although they are designated as historical landmarks, they have not been renovated.

TENNESSEE - *after the major Cherokee Indian town of Tanasi, located on the river which is now known as the Little Tennessee, in the eastern part of the State.*

JELLICO - *named after the Angelica plant which grew in these mountain areas. Early settlers were said to have made an early moonshine from it— an intoxicating drink called, "Jelca" or "Gelca."*

Route 297 continues on past the buildings and becomes a very pleasant country byway through leafy tunnels formed by overhanging trees, winding corners and occasional vistas to the east of I-75 as it climbs over Pine Mountain (not recommended for RVs).

TN Mile 159-Pine Mountain: The road seems to climb forever as it starts its four mile ascent toward the highest point on our southward journey. We are climbing the Pine Mountain Ridge with Elk Fork Valley and Jellico Mountain to our right; the Cumberland Mountain range to our left. The interstate tops at Mile 147, and then, as it starts its descent to Caryville, we come across one of the most famous exit signs on our journey - the one that every I-75 traveler remembers:

TN Exit 144-"Stinking Creek Road": With all the names available to county planners, how did "Stinking Creek" ever get its name? As usual, the answer is rooted in history.

Many years ago, there was a very harsh winter in the Tennessee mountains and wildlife were unable to forage and find food. They gathered at the local creek where water and sustenance had always been plentiful but the creek was frozen; eventually the animals died of starvation and thirst. In the Spring, all the carcasses thawed out and soon a horrible stench pervaded the area. So with great imagination, the creek was named "Stinking Creek."

Moonshiners: (note-don't try this without a local map or GPS system in your car). On past trips I have wandered around the backwood tracks leading off of Stinking Creek Road-among the hills, valleys and hollows with their sweetwater creeks and room for a small corn patch. It's not difficult to imagine smell and sounds of a different time-wood smoke, sour mash and the hiss of a copper still. The clink as another wide-mouthed Mason jar is set aside after receiving its potent fill of "white lightning," which trickles from the still's copper pipe.

Many say that stock car racing owes its roots to these early moonshine activities since the moonshiners were often outracing the Revenuers, in their constant battle of outwitting each other. Soon, bragging rights for the fastest car were established by racing each other . . . is this how NASCAR was born?

Sergeant York: A famous World War I hero lived and hunted in the mountains just beyond Elk Valley to our west - Sergeant Alvin York. He grew up with guns and as a boy, was a crack shot and had the reputation of making every single bullet he fired, count.

Drafted into the Army in 1917, he struggled with the moral issue of shooting humans, but all this changed in Europe's Argonne Forest, on a cool day in October, 1918.

While attempting to move forward, York's platoon was trapped and surrounded by a large German force of machine gunners. In the next few minutes, York single-handedly took out 35 machine gun nests and captured 132 enemy soldiers - all in one action and with only 18 rifle shots and 6 shots from his .45 Colt pistol.

At one point, he was charged by a German Major and six men with fixed bayonets. York coolly picked them off one by one with his pistol, starting at the rear so the men in front weren't aware of their fallen comrades. He then captured the lone survivor, the Major!

Insider Tip
Louie's on the Lake

Less than half-a-mile just to the east of Tennessee exit 134 is the Cove Lake State Park which in itself is well worth the short break in my interstate journey. But my mission is to try the offerings of a new family style restaurant crowning a hilltop overlooking the lake–*"Louie's on the Lake."*

Open for lunch and dinner, the menu is interesting and reasonably priced. Kathy and I enjoyed 'Tater Skins and Spinach Artichoke Dip, followed by Delmonico Steaks. A nice change from the fast food "factories" along the interstate.

Kids foods are also provided for the younger travelers and patio service is available during warmer weather.

Louie's is open year-round, from 11am–9pm, 7 days a week. ☎ 423-566-6676 for further information.

The "New Deal" and Tennessee Valley Authority (TVA)

As you travel through Tennessee, you will encounter the massive works (Norris Dam & Chickamauga Dam, for example) of the Tennessee Valley Authority, the TVA . . . what's it all about?

In the 1930's, the country was hurting from the effects of the Great Depression, and nowhere was this more evident than in the state of Tennessee. Newly elected President Franklin Roosevelt decided that the answer was to put the country back to work, and in 1933 proposed a "New Deal" which created many public works agencies and projects thus producing employment, and jump starting the economy.

In Tennessee and surrounding states, a major need was electrical power so work projects were implemented to build dams and generating plants on the Tennessee River. Whole towns, such as Norris, TN were created to house the workers for these projects. Senator George Norris of Nebraska led a fight to create an agency to keep such projects out of private hands, and the Tennessee Valley Authority (TVA) was born.

During the Second World War, the TVA's ability to produce massive amounts of electrical energy was fundamental to the development of the atomic bomb (see Oak Ridge story on page 104). Today, the TVA is a powerful agency controlling all water issues such as power generation, flood control and navigation on the state's river system.

Sergeant York was awarded the Medal of Honor for his heroic stand. Every single shot from his rifle and pistol had counted . . . a legacy from his hunting days in these mountains beside I-75.

TN Mile 137-Devil's Racetrack: About 1/4 mile to the east of the interstate is a cone-shaped hill with vertical runs of sandstone rock up its sides. This is the "Devil's Racetrack," a formation of Pennsylvanian rock (late Paleozoic Age–see the geological strata diagram on page 92), about 340 million years old. People come from miles to explore this unique geological feature, rich with fossils.

TN Exit 128-Norris Dam; map on page 55): Here is another opportunity to take a short scenic trip off the I-75, for very little extra investment in time. This side trip across the picturesque Norris Dam will only add an extra 12 minutes to your journey, and bring you back to I-75 at exit 122.

For a really interesting time, you might wish to visit the Lenoir Museum at the Norris Dam State Park or the Museum of Appalachia (see Insider Tip), before rejoining the interstate.

During the summer, Kathy and I stopped at the Grist Mill, just below the Museum on the east side of the dam, and chatted with a Park Ranger. She told us that the road below the Grist Mill led to a ford and waterfall . . . so off we went. We discovered a narrow leafy road which ran alongside Clear Creek. After driving slowly through the shallow ford, we found the waterfall. Below it, the creek meandered across a bed of small rocks and pebbles, in a small valley speckled with yellow winged butterflies–a beautiful sight on a warm, sunny day. The whole adventure only took fifteen minutes; if you would like to repeat our adventure, just follow our "waterfall" road on the Norris Dam map in the "Side Trip" section.

Just to the west of Norris Dam lies the Norris Dam State Park. I was intrigued to find that you can rent cabins within the park–10 of them are labeled deluxe, or "AAA," 19 are rustic, or "AA." More about this in the Lodging–Section 6–of this guidebook.

TN Exit 122-Museum of Appalachia: see page 101.

TN Exit 122-New Welcome Center: Right next door to the Golden Girls, is a new log cabin Welcome Center. Stop by and say hello to Connie. If you decide to take the Knoxville bypass via Clinton (see following item), she will be able to help you. Hours are M-Sa, 9:30-5:30; Sun (summer only), 12:30-5:30. ☎ 865-457-4542

NORRIS - *named after George William Norris, Senator and a great champion of public electric power. Norris was instrumental in promoting the Tennessee Valley Authority (TVA) as the agency to harnessing the power of water. The town of Norris was built to house the builders of the Norris Dam.*

Insider Tip
Museum of Appalachia - A Mountain Man's Gift to the Future

When you arrive at the Museum of Appalachia and enter the main building, you know that you have come to a special place. The smell of warm, freshly baked bread wafts by as you purchase your tickets. You follow the signs to this huge outdoor museum, passing the brick fireplace where a flaming log pops and snaps on ancient andirons. These are all good omens.

As you move out into the bright mountain sunlight, it's as if you have stepped back into time. Nestled close to some rounded stacks of hay are several sheep while a small herd of Scottish Longhorn cattle drink by a small pond. Across the meadow, come the sounds of fiddle and banjo as a group on the verandah of an old mountain house, enjoy a few moments away from field chores.

For this is a living mountain village–the Museum of Appalachia. A wonderful experience of 34 original mountain buildings, displayed in such a way that you would believe the inhabitants have just stepped out back for a few minutes.

A well organized indoor museum displays many artifacts and examples of Appalachian mountain living. Of particular interest are the many different types of musical instruments, including a long horn which was used by Grandma for warning everybody within miles, about "revenue men" in the valley.

To John Rice Irwin, founder of this wonderful museum, it has been an ongoing labor of love. And this dedication shows in the detail around you. John Rice's friend, Alex Haley, paid him the greatest compliment when he said,

> *"This museum is evidence of John's love of the land, his love of his mountain culture, his love of the mountain people who came before him. One cannot walk these grounds and through these cabins without savoring the spirit and strength of a people rich in culture and heritage. You can feel them here, and this is the unique dimension that makes the life work of John Rice Irwin so extraordinary."*

John Rice has created a true gift for future generations–we heartily recommend it.

See map on page 55 for phone number, hours and other details.

TN Exit 122-Bypass Knoxville via Oak Ridge (map on page 61): Sometimes it would be great to get off I-75 for a little while . . . and Exit 122 provides such an opportunity. Rather than continue running south and through the sometimes heavy traffic of Knoxville's I-40, you might want to consider "cutting the corner" and taking the "country route"—Route 61—over to Oak Ridge (see Tennessee exit 376A for the story of Oak Ridge and the Atomic Bomb), and then down

Insider Tip
Golden Girls Restaurant

No, not the TV *"Golden Girls"* but the four Golden family sisters who really know how to operate a great restaurant.

Owners Ann & Jeanné, and sisters Becky and Kathy run a restaurant that is very popular locally. Excellent food, attentive service and reasonable prices add up to superb value.

You know its good when you see the many police cars parked outside at meal time.

Go west at exit 122. The Golden Girls restaurant is a log building (set back a bit) on your right hand side. Hours are 6am-10pm. ☎ 865-457-3302

Insider Tip
Great American Buffet

If you love buffets, then this is for you. Three hot tables with over 35 different items, two salad tables with over 28 items - and a huge dessert table. And the prices don't hurt either - $6.49 for lunch and $8.49 for dinner (knock off a $1 if you are a senior). It's no wonder that the Great American Buffet is so popular.

Go west at exit 108 and look for the restaurant on your left.

The hours are M-Th, 11am-10pm; F-Sat, 11am-11pm; Sun brunch, 9am-noon; Sun noon-10pm. ☎ 865-687-8773

Route 62/162 to rejoin I-75 west of Knoxville at I-40/I-75 Exit 376.

The route crosses the Clinch River 3.6 miles from I-75 just east of Clinton, and then winds around a bit as it follows the northern bank of the Clinch River with the Walden Ridge of the Appalachian Mountain chain to the north. 5.3 miles from I-75 you will go through local traffic on East Clinch Avenue in downtown Clinton, but this quickly passes. Five miles west of Clinton, join Route 95 (Oak Ridge Parkway) and drive 5.5 miles into the town of Oak Ridge where you join Route 62 (Illinois Avenue). South of Oak Ridge after 5.2 miles, you cross the Clinch River on the Solway Bridge; a mile further take Route 162—Pellissippi Parkway—for 6.2 miles down to rejoin the I-40/I-75 as it runs towards Nashville/Chattanooga. The total distance is 28.6 miles (about 40 minutes). If you stay on I-75, your distance will be about the same but depending upon traffic, should only take you 30 minutes.

If you would like to take this alternative route, follow the sidetrip map on page 61.

TN Exit 108-The Map Store: If you love maps, books on maps, globes, instruments and anything else to do with the world of cartography as I do, then I've discovered "heaven" for you just 1.7 miles east of I-75. You will find large scale, small scale maps of the mountains around you, your home state and just about every country in the world.

My favorites are the plastic molded relief maps made by Hubbard Scientific; their maps of I-75 as it winds its way through the 3D mountains and valleys of Tennessee are works of art. Ask George or Ron to help you; they both love maps and know the store's stock well. Here's how you reach the Map Store:

Take exit 108 - go east for 1/10th mile - turn right onto Central at the lights. Go south on Central - pass Cracker Barrel on your right - through traffic lights at Inskip - bear left after 9/10ths mile. Through traffic light at Brushin Road (the road you are on is now Dutch Valley Rd) - The Map Store is on your right 4/10ths mile after the last lights.

The Map Store's address is 900 Dutch Valley Drive; hrs: M-F, 8:30a-5:30p, Thurs: -7:00p; ☎ 865-688-3608 (888-929-6277, US only).

TN Mile 107-Southbound Driving Notes: As I-75 swings down and around Knoxville, it briefly joins and assumes the mile marker numbers of other interstates.

First we join the westbound branch of the I-640 (the Knoxville northern "ring road") for a few miles. Take care as you approach I-75's exit 3 where it appears the main road (2 lanes) goes off to the east. You don't want that! Instead, stay well over in the right lane (the I-75) which becomes a single lane ramp for ½ mile until you join the high speed traffic of the I-640.

After three miles, you again bear right as the I-640/I-75 combination joins the I-40 west to Nashville/Chattanooga. On the ramp, the two lanes quickly become one, so move left as soon as possible—and move left again once on the I-40 since the single ramp lane also disappears. The mile markers change once again—this time to a 380 series. Watch for police along this stretch since it is actively patrolled for out of state speeders (the "locals" seem to whiz by at excessive speeds with complete immunity).

TN Mile 383-The Body Farm: Now, if you are squeamish (or just about to stop for a meal), please skip the following paragraphs.

KNOXVILLE - *originally called White's Fort, in 1791 it was renamed after General Henry Knox (1750-1806), a soldier during the American Revolution. General Knox was the army Commander in Chief (1783-84) and the Nation's first Secretary of War under President Washington (1785-95). The main depository of the Nation's gold bullion, Fort Knox, is also named after him.*

Insider Tip
The Best BBQ Ribs on I-75 (north of Georgia)?

For year's at great personal risk (to my waistline), I have been searching for the "Best BBQ Ribs on I-75." For a while, Burbank's in Florence, KY, held the honors but this restaurant has relinquished its lease at the Oldenberg Brewery . . . and the ribs at the Cincinnati Burbanks just don't seem to be the same.

Now, we know where to find the best ribs in Georgia (I'll share that with you in an Insider Tip, later), but where can they be found north of the "Peach" state? From my own taste tests and from the many readers' letters I've received, there are three restaurants in the Knoxville area which are constantly mentioned - Calhouns, Corky's and Hops. Ironically, all are within a few miles of each other; two are at the same exit . . . so why don't you be the judge? Let me know how your own personal taste test turns out; record your vote on the "Help me write . . ." page at the back of this book (page 203) and I'll announce the results in next year's book.

Calhouns: locals flock to Calhouns which claims to be the "Home of America's Best Ribs." As soon as you step through the front door, you know that manager Lisa Clark is ready for our challenge. Food is fresh, service is warm and friendly; it's a popular spot for the locals and was rated ★★★★ by the Knoxville media. Calhoun's is just 2 minutes off the interstate and easy to find-take exit 376B (I-140E-Pellissippi Parkway) and leave it after 6/10th mile at exit 1A (Kingston Pike N, US11E, US70). Go through traffic lights at Mabry Hood, and Calhoun's - a wooden barn-style building with dark red roof - is immediately on your right. Calhouns - 10020 Kingston Pike, Knoxville, TN 37923;Hrs: Mon-Thu, 11:00a-10:00p; Fri-Sat, 11:00a-11:00p; Sun, 11:00-9:30 ☎ 865-673-3444

Corky's Ribs & BBQ: according to the their sign, Corky's Ribs has racked up more awards for its BBQ and sauces than any other restaurant, and manager Randall Proffitt wants to add ours to his list. Here you'll find St. Louis pork ribs slowly smoked for hours in hickory fired pits - basted, seasoned and served in C's famous BBQ sauce - 14 ribs to a full rack. They also serve Memphis style ribs.

The decor is modest but interesting; brick arches; high warehouse ceilings - booths and tables. Corky's is very close to I-75. Take exit 378 (S. Cedar Bluff Rd) and immediately swing over to the left turn lane. At the lights, turn left-Corky's is immediately on your left. Corky's Ribs - 260 N. Peters Road, Knoxville, TN 37923 Hrs: M-Th, Sun, 11:00a-9:30p; Fri-Sat, 11:00a-10:30p ☎ 865-690-3137

Hops Restaurant and Brewery: "Hops" manager Bryan Tesh is banking on having an in-house Brewmaster to tip the balance in his direction. For the primary focus here is micro-brewed beer - a fact hard to ignore since there is a huge copper brew kettle in the center of the restaurant. Among the beers brewed on the premises are Alligator Ale, Hops Special and Hammerhead Red. Brewmaster Billy Phelps suggests you order his tasting special, in which you can sample four of his brews. I haven't personally tasted the ribs here but many of my readers have . . . and they come highly recommended.

To reach Hops, take exit 378 (S. Cedar Bluff Rd) and stay in the right lane. At the lights, turn right on to Peters Road. You'll see Hops red sign on your right after driving 1/3rd mile. Hops - 338 N. Peters Road, Knoxville, TN 37922; Hrs: M-Th, 11:00a-10:30p, Fri-Sat, 11:00a-11:30p, Sun, 11:00a-10:00p ☎ 865-692-1430

If you continue to read, I make no apology for the subject matter . . .

About 2 miles south-east of where you are right now is the 3 acre Bass Anthropological Research Facility. Also known by its initials BARF (I kid you not!), or the "Body Farm." Made famous in crime writer Patricia Cornwell's novel of the same name, the Body Farm is a highly secured area where corpses are placed in various situations (in the open, buried under leaves, in water, etc.) and in different environments (burnt out cars, old trunks,) . . . and in the interests of forensic science, left to deteriorate.

Operated and monitored by the Tennessee University, the facility is famous in the world of crime detection. Organizations such as the FBI and regional police authorities use the Farm's findings to determine how long a corpse might have been dead (given climate and environment of the discovery site).

How is this done? Well, out of a belated sense of propriety I'm not going to tell you unless you ask me in person; that way I can access your ability to handle such sensitive information . . . or better still, read Patricia Cornwell's best selling book. You'll find the answers in lurid detail.

Oh! by the way, you cannot visit the Body Farm . . . it's not an "attraction" and is surrounded by razor wire fences. However, since this book claims to be a complete guide to I-75 . . . I just wanted you to know it was there.

TN Exit 376A-Oak Ridge (map on page 61): 12.3 miles to the north of the I-40/I-75 lies a city built in 1942, for the workers of Clinton Engineering Works. A city so "secret" that it was on no map and anybody asking casual questions about it would be investigated by the FBI as a possible spy.

In 1939, the US Government realized that the Nazis in Germany understood the possibilities of an atomic bomb. Their scientists had recently succeeded in splitting atoms of uranium at Berlin's Kaiser Wilhelm Institute. An atomic bomb in the hands of the Nazis would have guaranteed world dominance by the Germans so it was important that the USA protected its interests by similar development as quickly as possible.

President Roosevelt, through a new organization known as the Manhattan Engineering District (MED) authorized a full-scale bomb development program. The MED identified three secret sites to perform various functions in the research. Site W at Hanford, WA was chosen as the plutonium production location; site X in Tennessee chosen for uranium production, and site Y was a lonely mesa in New Mexico called Los Alamos . . . here the various components from "W" and "X"would be assembled under the direction of Robert Oppenheimer, and the finished bomb tested.

In 1942, the Manhattan Project–the development of the World's first atomic bomb commenced operations under the leadership of MED's Colonel (later Major General) Leslie Groves.

Site X was a series of three valleys northwest of Knoxville, named after one of its ridges– Black Oak Ridge. It was chosen for the manufacturing operations required to extract radioactive uranium (U235), because of the availability of huge amounts of hydro-electricity generated by the TVA dams; the valleys offered shelter to adjacent operations should one of the plants explode, and finally, it was very sparsely populated by farmers who could be easily relocated. Its remoteness also helped with the security issues.

So the secret city of Oak Ridge was born; very few residents were allowed to leave it and until 1949 it could only be visited by special permit. Three plants with code names K25–uranium extraction and enrichment, X10–atomic pile and Y12–uranium atom separation were built in parallel valleys under another secret organization, the Clinton Engineering Works. The entire area, including the town of Oak Ridge with housing and amenities for all the workers, was enclosed by a barbed-wire fence with access controlled by seven gates. Life in the area was very basic and made difficult by the ever present mud.

Today things are much different, an excellent visitors' center and several attractions—the American Museum of Science and Energy, New Bethel Church (where the Project scientists used to meet), the Graphite Reactor and the K-25 visitor overlook — are well worth a visit for those interested in the birth of the Nuclear Age.

The operations at Oak Ridge continue to do the impossible. Whenever an answer to an "impossible" but essential project is needed, business and the military turn to the Oak Ridge National Laboratory for answers. While there in 1998, the Museum was displaying ORNL's latest success, a completely sterile surgical operating room which could be parachuted to the ground, in a folding package no larger than 10' x 10' x 10'.

The Visitor Center and Museum of Science & Energy phone numbers, hours and other details are on page 61.

TN Exit 373-Farragut: see page 105-Insider Tip for the Apple Cake Tearoom at this exit.

Also at exit 373, is an interesting antique shopping mall–Campbell Station Antiques. Located in the Station West Center next to Cracker Barrel, this 10,000 square foot antique emporium has everything from antique clothing to rare books. Open daily, M-Sat, 10-6; Sun, 1-6. ☎ 865-966-4348.

TN Exit 368-Driving Notes: Here I-75 leaves the I-40, and continues south towards Chattanooga. I-75 mile marker numbers resume.

TN Mile 81-Rock City: Those who drove to Florida in the pre-I-75 days will remember the classics of roadside advertising—*Burma Shave* and *Rock City*. Most of these were discontinued when federal legislation required the removal of all private roadside signs along the interstates, but several have survived.

"Rock City" signs were very prolific and adorned the roofs of barns, outhouses, and farm buildings throughout the South (Rock City is an attraction in Chattanooga), announcing the number of

Insider Tip
Apple Cake Tea Room

One of the most pleasant luncheon experiences between Detroit and Florida is to be had at the Apple Cake Tea Room, just to the south/east of I-75/I-40 at exit 373, on Campbell Station Road. Housed in a cozy log cabin, the minute you enter the door you know this is going to be a special dining occasion; pine wood and tasty home cooking aromas greet your senses and prepare you for the meal to follow.

But before you order, take a look around the carefully decorated interior. The Henry family has lived in Farragut for many generations and with great pride, Apple Cake owner Mary Henry furnished the interior with many of her treasured family photos, antiques, quilts and other mementos. If it's not too busy and the room is not in use, ask Mary to show you the private bridal reception room upstairs. On display setting the scene is a wedding gown that was discovered in Mary's grandmother's attic. It's worth the climb up the winding staircase.

The other thing that is evident about the Apple Cake is the wonderful service. Mary's enthusiasm is shared by her staff who all care that you have an enjoyable visit. It couldn't be better.

But now to the menu. First, a very presentable French Onion soup and then on to the main course. There are a number of sandwich choices; I enjoyed the grilled chicken sandwich on a fresh croissant. Side orders of honey butter, cheese toast and banana nut bread help round out the course. And then our server talked me in to trying the Cornucopia for dessert . . . a wonderful blending of vanilla ice cream, sauteed bananas and homemade chocolate or butterscotch sauce (I chose Chocolate) nested in a pizzelle basket (made from crunchy pancake mix). Scrumptious!

And now a word to the guys . . don't be put off by the words, "Tea Room" in the restaurant's name; I'm sure you'll enjoy the experience as much as your wife. The food is excellent, helpings plentiful and prices reasonable. I will certainly be back.

To find the Apple Cake Tea Room, take Exit 373, south/east towards Farragut. The Apple Cake is in Appalachian Log Square plaza on the left side of Campbell Station Road, almost immediately opposite the Pilot gas station. Hours: Mon-Sat. 11am-2:30pm ☎ 865-966-7848

FARRAGUT - *"Damn the torpedoes - full speed ahead!" was the famous command of Rear Admiral David Farragut, as he led his Union fleet to a Civil War victory through the mines in Mobile Bay on August 5, 1864. The town of Farragut is named in his honor.*

LOUDON - *after a very unsuccessful Commander in Chief of British forces during the French and Indian wars - John Campbell, 4th Earl of Loudon (1705-1782).*

miles you had to travel to *"See Rock City."* If you look very carefully to the left at mile marker 81, you will see a barn with an original *"Rock City"* sign painted on its roof.

Tennessee Wineries: You don't have to go to Sonoma or Napa Valley in California to enjoy free winery tours and wine tastings. Southeast Tennessee is fast becoming known for it fine American wines and there are three wineries where you can enjoy these pleasures within minutes of the I-75.

Recently, Tennessee vineyards have taken bronze, silver and gold medals in national and international competition. The fine wines of this area are slowly becoming "known" through the wine growing world. Today, more than 200 wine growers practice their art throughout the state continuing a long standing Tennessee tradition.

And you don't have to be a "wine snob" to enjoy these tours either. Nobody is going to worry if you can't tell the difference between a Chardonnay and Seyval Blanc—your hosts only wish is that you enjoy yourselves and leave with a better understanding of their excellent products.

Let's stop now, and enjoy a visit with some of these wine growers:

A word about wine tastings—we know that drinking and driving don't mix but on a normal winery tour you will rarely consume more than a glass of wine in total, even though you may try many different varieties.

Your host will recommend you start with dry reds and whites, and proceed through the tasting to sweet and dessert wines. He or she will pour a small amount into a clean wineglass.

Experienced wine tasters hold the glass up to the light while gently rocking it to see wine's color and viscosity ("body"), sniff each wine while rolling it around in its glass to appreciate its smell ("bouquet"), sip it and swill it around their mouth and then spit the sample out into a wine spittoon. In this manner, they can appreciate all the attributes of several wines without absorbing much alcohol.

Tasting can take as long or as little time as you please, but we recommend ½ hour as being reasonable.

TN Exit 76-Loudon Valley Winery: Just over 2 miles to the east of I-75's exit 76 (Sugar Limb Road), nestled on a crest overlooking the great Tennessee River is this Gold Medal winery. Owner Stan Dylewksi and his assistant, Brenda, enjoy managing the ten acres of vineyards—containing fifteen varieties of American, French-American hybrid and European (Vinifera) grapes—meeting people and showing them around this impressive estate.

In addition to the tour and tastings, you might enjoy stretching your legs after a long drive by going on a short nature trail hike through the virgin tree stands and down to the river. In the spring and summer, the many wild flowers along the path make this a particular treat. Take along a picnic and delight in the riverside tranquillity.

To find the winery, take exit 76–Sugar Limb Road and on the south side of I-75, immediately turn right onto Hotchkiss Valley Rd, travel west for 1.7 miles and turn left onto Huff Ferry Rd. Within 200 feet, turn left onto a winding gravel road which in 1/3rd mile takes you to a bluff where you'll find the Loudon Valley Wineries Tasting Room overlooking the Tennessee River.

The winery is open for tours and tastings, from 10-6 p.m., Monday to Saturday, and from 1-5 p.m. on Sunday. ☎ 865-986-8736.

TN Exit 76-TN Valley Winery: A quarter of a mile to the west of I-75 exit 76 (Sugar Limb Road) lies the entrance to the Tennessee Valley Winery. Here, the Reed family—Jerry, Tom and Chris Reed—continue practicing the Tennessee wine making tradition, producing more than 12,000 gallons of table wines each year from their 32 acres of plantings at the Wildwood Vineyards, located 15 miles south in Roane County. Wine-maker, Tom, is proud of the fact that the family's estate has won medals and awards from all over the United States.

Tours, tastings and picnic facilities are all available here; Tom invites you to stay a while and enjoy a picnic lunch on the sundeck. Enjoy the winery tours and tastings, from 10-6 pm, Mon-Sat, and from 1-5 pm on Sunday. ☎ 865-986-5147

TN Exit 60-Lost Sea: Seven miles to the east of I-75 (9 1/2 minutes along Route 68) lies North America's largest underground lake–the "Lost Sea." Listed in the Guinness Book of Records, the huge body of water lies within the Craighead Caverns, and covers 4.5 acres. A trip across its surface in a glass bottomed boat allows you to see the many huge speckled trout in the crystal clear water below.

It is an eerie experience as you glide across the mirror lake in the dimly lit limestone cavern; unusual rock formations, mineral deposits and strange cave flowers heighten the mystery.

During the Civil War, the caves were a source of saltpeter for gunpowder. Close your eyes and imagine smoky lanterns casting their flickering shadows on the cavern walls as Confederate soldiers swing their pickaxes. Listen to the ring of metal against stone. These are spooky surroundings.

If you decide to tour the caves, dress warmly because below ground, the air is a constant 58 degrees summer or winter. Also wear solid shoes–the tour includes a walk of about 3/4 mile.

Hours: 9-dusk, daily; Admit-Adult/Child: $9:00/$4:00; ☎ 423-337-6616.

TN Exit 60-Coca Cola shop: Do you collect Coca Cola memorabilia? If you do, then don't miss the Coca Cola shop tucked in behind the huge flea market building, just to the west at exit 60. Apart from all the Coca Cola paraphernalia, there are shelves holding hundreds of bottles of Coke from just about every place or venue where commemorative bottles were produced. Need an unopened bottle of Coke from the Atlanta Summer Olympics or the 1986 World Series - they've got it.

TN Exit 60-Orr Mountain Winery: Just east of the entrance to the Lost Sea lies Orr Mountain Winery. Lying on a peaceful hillside with a spectacular view of the valley between Mount Le Conte and Starr Mountain, owners Sue and Harry Orr invite you to enjoy the "grape experience from vine to wine." In the spring, "be thrilled at the new shoots bursting forth," and at all times, "see the process of turning great grapes into fine wines as they go from press, to vat, to tank, to bottle."

One mile past the Lost Sea attraction, turn right (at the blue Winery sign) onto CR-117, go one mile and turn right onto CR-121, and follow the signs for 500 yards.

Hours: W-Sa, 10-6, Sun, 2-6, closed Jan/Feb; ☎ 423-442-5340.

TN Mile 52-"The World's Best Ice Cream: Once again, I put on my reporter's hat and left I-75 at Tennessee's exit 52 (Mt. Verd Road) and followed route 305 eastwards for 4.3 miles (6.9 kms) through pleasant countryside towards Athens, to visit Mayfield Dairy Farms and sample their "World's Best Ice Cream."

Mayfield Dairy is well marked on the left side of the road, you can't miss the big round brown and yellow billboard at Mayfield Lane stating *"Mayfield Dairy Farms–Home of the World's Best Ice Cream."*

Full of anticipation I headed right for the Visitor Center's ice cream parlor to interview the staff and sample the wares.

I'm impressed! The "World's Best" accolade was awarded by no less an authority than Time Magazine, in an article published on August 10, 1981. Now I have not tasted all the ice creams in the world so am really in no position to judge, but I've got to tell you that their thick, creamy, smooth, yellow vanilla ice cream (the flavor most often ordered by adults) was up to expectations . . . and far beyond.

Just to make absolutely sure (after all, somebody has to do it), I also checked the newest Mayfield's flavor, "Hog Heaven," a fabulous blend of vanilla cream and caramel toffee flavors, with dark chocolate "melt-in-your-mouth" chocolate chunks spread throughout. It's to die for!

"Monkey Business," a banana based cream, with peanut butter swirl and chocolate came in a respectable second.

My host, Chad, mentioned that once again, this year's favorite with the children is "Superman," vanilla with yellow, blue and pink swirls - so I had to try that too. I wonder if we are many years away from a Harry Potter flavor?

If you have extra time, you might like to take the very interesting tour of the ice cream and milk processing plant. Ever wonder . . . "How *do* they put the stick inside the ice cream bar?" "How they make the different flavors of ice cream?" After a film presentation, you'll see the bottling of milk and production of ice cream and other food items and all will be explained.

The ice cream parlor at Mayfield Dairy is open May to October: Mon-Fri, 9am-5pm, Sat, 9am-2pm - closed Sundays and major holidays. November to April: Mon-Sat, 9am-2pm. Ice cream prices are very reasonable, starting at 75¢ for a mini-scoop, $1 for a single scoop, $1.50 double and $2.00 for a triple.

Plant tours are held every half-hour–Mon-Fri, 9am-5pm (last tour 4pm); Sat., 9am-2pm (last tour 1pm)–closed Sundays and major holidays. The ice cream plant is not operational on Saturdays; the milk plant is not operational on Wednesdays. Admission is free; comfortable slip-resistant shoes are recommended for the plant tour. Further information? ☎ 423-745-2151 or 1-800-629-3435.

TN Miles 46 & 45-McMinn Information Counters: Need information about this area, or Tennessee in general? The southbound rest area at milepost 46 and the northbound one at milepost 45 have excellent information counters. While there, say hello to manager Betty. She'll probably be at one or the other.

TN Mile 44-Electronic Fog Detection and Warning System: You are about to enter a "high-tech" portion of the freeway. Born out of tragedy - the Hiwasee River Valley electronic Fog Detection and Warning system.

Man-made fog is a frequent problem on this five mile section of I-75, caused primarily by industry east of this location . . . and it can be deadly.

Since the original opening of this stretch of highway in 1973, there have been 18 fatalities and 130 injuries in more than 200 fog related crashes. In December, 1990, a terrible traffic accident of massive proportions was caused by fog rapidly enveloping I-75. On the southbound downgrade towards the River, (mile markers 38-36) 83 cars and trucks piled into one another due to the poor visibility. The end result? Thirteen killed and 50 injured.

This tragedy provided the impetus needed to deal with this deadly section of I-75, and the fog advisory system was born. The Fog Detection and Warning system uses eight fog sensors and 44 speed detectors to constantly monitor visibility and traffic flow. In the same manner as an optical smoke detector, the fog sensors measure the clarity of the air between its detection cells - if you look closely you will see the two arms of the sensors on some of the roadside poles.

Data from the monitors are then relayed to a central computer at the Highway Patrol Office in Tiftonia, where software analyzes the incoming flow of data and translates the result into variable messages and actions. These include warning messages on the overhead electronic signs, reduced speed limits and highway radio messages. In extreme cases, the system can even activate swing barriers at six I-75 entry ramps, thereby closing off a fog shrouded freeway to traffic. Since the system's installation in late 1993, there have been no fog related accidents or fatalities within the system's area.

Incidentally, if you rely on a radar detector, you might as well turn it off through this stretch since the fog system emits signals in the "X" band frequencies and your detector will go off as you pass each sign pole. In fact, the police use this to their advantage and often set up their radar trap towards the end of this stretch–just when most drivers assume that their detector is emitting another false alarm.

TN Mile 42-Spanish Explorers: And now for a change of pace. In May, 1539, the Governor of Cuba, Don Hernando de Soto landed in Tampa, Florida, and started an extensive exploration of North America with an army of 600 men.

For more than four years, he traveled over 4,000 miles while searching for gold and silver . . . and a north passage to China. Ranging up the US mainland through Georgia, he led his army into the Carolinas, Tennessee . . . and as far away as modern Chicago, until he turned southward through Missouri and into

HIWASSEE RIVER - *Cherokee Indian word meaning "meadow."*

BRAINERD - *named after David Brainerd, a pioneer missionary among the Cherokee Indians.*

Arkansas where he died in 1542.

Extensive journals were kept documenting his exploration. Since most of the Indian sites mentioned are known today and many modern roads are built over early Indian trails, the track taken by his expedition is well known today. The path of the modern I-75 crosses the path of de Soto and his army in two places–Athens, Tennessee and Perry, Georgia.

From his journals for May, 1540, we know that while in Tennessee he spent a night at Madisonville. The next day an Indian chief visited him and led him to Athens. Here he was joined by a scouting party he had sent up the Tennessee Valley towards Knoxville, where they discovered Indian mines.

He and his army then traveled to, and camped on, Hiwassee Island, at the confluence of the Hiwassee & Tennessee Rivers. Examination of the terrain indicates that he would have crossed the modern path of I-75 in the vicinity of this mile marker.

TN Mile Marker 18-Radar Alert: Be careful here just in case the traffic ahead of you suddenly brakes! The interstate runs downhill and gently curves to the left—thick trees line the median zone.

At the bottom of the hill (and curve) an emergency vehicle path cuts through the trees between the south and northbound I-75 lanes, and here the police love to hide with radar beamed up the hill. Cars cannot see them until they are right on top of the radar trap and speeders violently brake to avoid a ticket (it doesn't work).

Watch the traffic ahead of you as you descend this hill. We don't want you to rear-end a speeder.

TN Mile 6-Construction: Good news! According to Tennessee Department of Transport, the heavy construction from here to mile 4 will be completed by December, 2000. So there is a chance that when you reach this point, you will be able to sail through with no delays.

TN Exit 5-Knife Museum: Just a few seconds east of I-75 is the home of the National Knife Collectors Association, with a museum of more than 12,000 knives and swords neatly displayed and labeled. It's easy to drive by the museum without realizing it, so watch for the windowless building on your left at 7201 Shallowford Road. Hours are M-F, 9-4 year round. Closed on weekends.

Admission is $2.00 for adults; children and those over 65 are free. ☎ 423-892-5007.

TN Exit 4 - Chattanooga Choo-Choo: As a kid, I used to love the distinctive smell and noise of steam locomotives as they chugged their way through the countryside. Now you can experience it (again . . . if you are over 40 years old!) with a ride on the Tennessee Valley Railroad.

You board your coach at the Grand Junction Station and travel to downtown Chattanooga behind ex-Southern Railway #4501, ancient Central Georgia #349 or perhaps locomotive #610 or #630. Follow the Civil War track of the Tennessee & Georgia Railroad, a vital supply link first for the Confederacy and then for the Union as the tides of war shifted in 1863. You can sense the Civil War atmosphere as the train winds through the Chattanooga country and into the darkness of the 1858 Missionary Ridge tunnel.

Afterwards, enjoy the audio-visual show and railroad exhibits, visit the repair shop or browse the gift store.

To find Grand Junction Station which is 3.8 miles from the interstate, take I-75 exit 4 (Chickamauga Dam) and follow Route 153 north to the fourth (Jersey Pike) exit. Follow the "TVRM" signs to Cromwell Road.

The Railway runs on full service (10am-5pm) June to August, and partial service (10am-2pm) April, May, Sept, Oct and November. It's charters and school groups only from December to March, but phone them anyway, there may be an group scheduled with

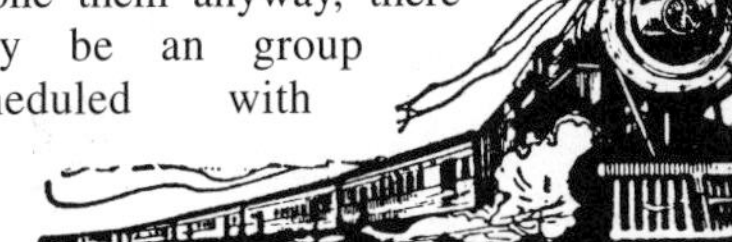

CHATTANOOGA - *probably from a Cree Indian word meaning "rock rising to a point" (Lookout Mountain).*

space available when you are in the area. Fares are adults/children: $8.50/$4.50. ☎ 423-894-8028.

TN Exit 2-Chattanooga (main map on page 56, downtown map below): Many people bypass Chattanooga because it seems such a long trek to the west of I-75, but for those that make the effort, the drive to the downtown area is quite scenic and interesting as the road winds down the face of historic Missionary Ridge. Besides, the trip from I-75 exit 2 is not that long–9.3 miles; about 11 minutes–and over the last few years downtown Chattanooga has experienced a renaissance and grown into a wonderfully interesting place for visitors.

To reach downtown, take I-75 exit 2 (I-24 West). At exit 178 (Downtown) take US27 North to exit 1-C (4th Street), turn left at the second traffic light (Broad Street)–ahead of you is the Tennessee Aquarium with the Visitors Center to its right. You'll find parking lots on either side of the street just before these buildings as well as in front of the Visitors Center.

Tennessee Aquarium: Gone are the days of dark, dank rooms with small thick glass apertures separating fish and viewer. The Tennessee Aquarium is a "4th generation facility, an aquarium which tells a story as you wander down through its thematic galleries.

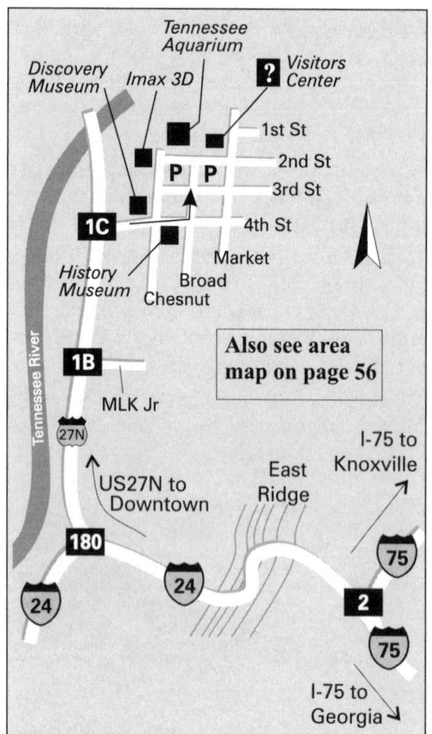

You start your self-guided tour by following the flow of the Tennessee River, from its beginnings in the Appalachians, into the great Mississippi and onward towards the salt waters of the Gulf of Mexico. Fabulous vistas of birds, animal and marine life accompany your journey as you descend through the aquarium building. First, the Appalachian Cove Forest with its dripping rocks, ferns, moss covered trees, mountain streams and otter pool. Then to the Tennessee River Gallery where you examine (above and below water) the huge "Nickajack" and "Reelfoot" lakes. "Discovery Falls" takes you through an interactive educational gallery where children (and adults) may examine various specimens at close range. And finally, on to the Mississippi Delta—a recreated cypress swamp where snakes, alligators and other fearsome reptiles live—and the Gulf of Mexico, the aquarium's only salt water tank.

The Aquarium hours are: May 1-Labor Day: M-Th, 10-6; F-Sun, 10-8 Rest of year: 10-6 daily. Admission is adults/children $10.25/$5.50 – children under 3yrs are free.

The Aquarium also has an Imax 3D theater showing nature oriented films with images that leap off the screen. Tickets are $6.75/$4.75. Combination aquarium & theater are also available at $14/$8.50. ☎ 800-262-0695 or 423-265-0695.

Other downtown attractions: Here are some other downtown attractions you might enjoy; pick up information from the Visitors Center (see map):

- Creative Discovery Museum
- Hunter Museum of Art
- Medal of Honor Museum
- Regional History Museum
- Tow & Recovery Hall of Fame
- An interesting place to eat – Sticky Fingers, (cor. Broad & 5th).

St. Elmo and Lookout Mountain (see map on page 56): On the other side of I-24 rises Lookout Mountain, peaking at 2,391 feet. On the mountain you'll find other Chattanooga attractions - Battle of Chattanooga Museum, Incline Railway, Ruby Falls and Rock City. The drive up the mountain (see map) to the Point Park at the top is well worth the effort.

But for me, the best of area attractions is near the foot of the Incline Railway, on St.Elmo Street. The Tennessee Civil War Museum houses an excellent collection of exhibits and information about the *"War Between the States."* The museum is open daily from 10am-6pm. ☎ 423-821-4954.

Chattanooga and Coca-Cola: As we head towards the Georgia border, I have to remind Kathy that we will soon be entering "Coca-Cola Country." Kathy is such a Pepsi fan, she's liable to ask for diet Pepsi in the *"World of Coca-Cola"* museum in Atlanta! But Coca-Cola is so strongly identified with Georgia that in days gone, the State's Welcome Centers handed out free Coca-Colas to greet incoming tourists.

Few people know however, that Chattanooga has extremely strong Coca-Cola connections as well. For it was here that changes were made to the marketing of the drink which helped Coca-Cola change from being a soda fountain drink, to the huge international success it is today.

In 1899, two Chattanooga businessmen - Benjamin Thomas and Joseph Whitehead sat in Coca-Cola owner's - Asa Chandler - Atlanta office, explaining how they would like to take the drink and sell the brown liquid in little green straight-sided bottles. Chandler laughed and said it would never work. He was convinced that Coca-Cola's future lay in drug store soda fountain sales, so he sold the two men the rights to bottle and distribute Coca-Cola within the USA, for $1!

Thomas and Whitehead set up the first bottling plant in Chattanooga on the ground floor of a pool hall, and the rest is history.

Bottling a drink to increase sales may sound like basic common sense today, but in the late 1800's it was a novel approach for a soda fountain drink. Soon, the Chattanooga group sold bottling franchises to other businessmen across the Nation, became rich beyond their wildest dream . . . and Coca-Cola was on its way to become a national, and then international, success.

Chattanooga and the Supreme Court: The Supreme Court doesn't conduct criminal cases, does it? It did on one occasion. Lawyers among my readers may be surprised to learn that the first and only criminal trial ever held by the Supreme Court in history, was due to the inactivity of a Chattanooga sheriff and his deputies.

Here's what happened. In 1906, a young girl was raped and soon, Ed Johnson, a black man was captured, "railroaded" through court and sentenced to hang. But there were many unusual and unfair circumstances about this case and on appeal it quickly became apparent that Johnson was innocent of the crime. Supreme Court Justice John Harlan issued a stay of execution, while the case was re-examined and further arguments heard.

In Chattanooga, on hearing this news emotions ran high because a Federal agency had "interfered" with a local matter. A large mob broke in to the jail, captured Johnson and lynched him from a nearby bridge. Sheriff Joseph Shipp and his men stood by and did nothing to interfere with the mob's concept of "justice."

The Supreme Court was so enraged its orders had been ignored, that it decided to show that federalism was strong and here to stay. It brought contempt charges against the Sheriff, his deputies and members of the lynch mob.

This very unusual chain of events is the subject of a riveting book, *"Contempt of Court,"* by Curriden and Phillips.

Georgia Mile 353-Georgia Exit Numbers: As you've probably discovered by now, all interstate exit numbers start with the first exit on the state's southern border. Many found out to their surprise when they started driving home from Florida last spring that Georgia had changed its exit numbers from the old "sequential" numbering system to the federally recommended "mile marker" (or "mile log") exit numbering system used by most other states. Highway crews started this change in January and put up the last sign at Lake Park, Georgia on March 22, 2000.

All references to the old numbers were removed and according to the many phone calls we received, this caused much inconvenience for most returning "snowbirds."

We are proud to say that to our knowledge,

GEORGIA - *in honor of King George II of England, by early explorer James Oglethorpe who received a Royal Charter in 1733, to settle the area.*

Money Saving Tip

Pickup your free copies of the green Traveler Discount Guide (old EIG) and the red Market America motel coupon books at the Georgia Welcome Center (mile 352). Coupons in these books can save you as much as 45% off of regular motel rates.

the 2000 edition of *"Along Interstate-75"* was the only travel book which included both the old and new exit numbers. We had anticipated the change (which had been announce by Georgia DOT for several years) and ensured that our maps and stories reflected both the old and new numbers.

In this year's edition, we have left the "old" numbers on our maps, just in case a reader might wish to reference an "old" number.

GA Mile 352-Welcome Center: One of my favorite stops on our I-75 trips is to pull in here, chat with the excellent staff and find out what is new within the State of Georgia. Say hello to my friends, Betty, Jane, Janice, manager Jo Anne and Teresa if they are at the counter that day. They all know and love Georgia.

GA Exit 350-Georgia Winery (see Chickamauga map on page 56): The warm sunshine and distinctive soil of Georgia assures a strong wine industry which, in fact, has been around since 1730. Wineries such as Cavender Castle, Chateau Elan, Chestnut Mountain, Fox Wineries, Habersham Vineyards guarantee a good choice of varietal grape products . . . and the tasting room for one of the wineries, Georgia Wines, is just around the corner. Take exit 350 (old 141 - Battlefield Parkway) and travel 300 yards west until you see the KOA sign on your right. Turn right . . . and the tasting room is immediately on your right. Vineyard Master, Maurice, or Wine-maker, Patty, will help you with your choices. Georgia Wines is open Mon-Sat: 11-6pm. ☎ 706-937-2177

GA Exit 350-Chickamauga (map on page 56): After visiting Georgia Wines, you can continue westward along Battlefield Parkway to visit the well preserved battlefield of Chickamauga (about 20 minutes to the west). Phone, hours and other details on page 56.

For many miles south of Chattanooga, I-75 follows General Sherman's Union Army campaign to burn and destroy Atlanta–at Miles 338 and 323, the freeway runs right through the battlefields of Rocky Face Ridge and Resaca, respectively. And at Georgia Exit 122 (Unadilla), you can follow the Andersonville Trail to visit the Confederate's dreaded Andersonville Prisoner of War Camp. It lies about 42 miles southwest of I-75.

GA Exit 348-Ringgold & the Great Locomotive Chase (see special report on page 114, sidetrip maps on page 59, Bartow Co. map on page 57, and detail I-75 maps between GA exit 348 and exit 273): One of the best known adventures of the Civil War–made even more famous by a Walt Disney movie, "The Great Locomotive Chase," starring Fess Parker, and Buster Keaton's classic of the Silent era, The General - was exactly that . . . an epic chase where a steam locomotive stolen by Union soldiers, was chased through the Georgia countryside by its Southern crew, who used their feet, a push car, and three other locomotives before they successfully recaptured their errant ward.

But best of all, the route of this chase from Kennesaw in the south, to Ringgold in the north, criss-crossed the path of the modern I-75 as it winds its way from the Tennessee-Georgia border towards Atlanta. We have mapped this chase alongside the modern interstate for you on southbound map pages 32 to 35 & northbound map pages 164 to 167.

GA Exit 341-Tunnel Hill (map on page 59): Interesting things are happening at the famous 1850 railroad tunnel at Tunnel Hill, which played such a significant role in the Civil War's Great Locomotive Chase (see

Money Saving Tip

Fill up with gas as soon as you can–even if you only need a 1/4 of a tank. Georgia still has the cheapest gasoline in the USA.

CHICKAMAUGA - *a Cherokee Indian name whose meaning is either "sluggish or dead waters," or "boiling waters."*

RINGGOLD - *in memory of Samuel Ringgold, professional soldier and Indian fighter who died of wounds received in action during the Mexican War, 1846.*

page 114) and in General Sherman's 1864 Atlanta Campaign.

$875,000 has been allocated by Georgia DOT and Whitfield County to preserve the 1,477 foot tunnel and its imposing arches. Tunnel owner Ken Holcomb (who also owns and has restored nearby Clisby-Austin House) is working on plans for a historical park nearby, so all may enjoy this heritage site.

Clisby-Austin House is also a special Civil War site. It was used as a hospital during the war and later, as General Sherman's HQ during his campaign against Atlanta. After General John Hood lost his leg at the battle of Chickamauga, he and the limb were transferred to the House; the leg was buried in a nearby cemetery.

To find the tunnel, follow the map on page 59 to Tunnel Hill. Once you have driven across the bridge, park your car on the left of the road before the hill. You can walk right up the old rail bed (now a footpath) to the mouth of the tunnel.

Insider Tip
Born to Shop, Dalton Style

In case you didn't already know, there's excellent factory outlet shopping–the West Point Pepperill Mall - on the east side of Exit 333. And with great forethought Hampton built an excellent inn within easy walking distance right alongside the mall. So, you can park your car at the inn - shop–go back to your room–shop–go back to your room–shop, etc. Note: a ground floor room might be your best bet. The inn also provides an excellent free breakfast. An outlet shopper's dream come true!

GA Mile 339-Battle of Rocky Face Ridge: Ahead of you looms the craggy heights of Rocky Face Ridge, shielding the strategic town of Dalton behind. Here, for eight days starting on May 7th, 1864, Confederate General Joseph Johnston held off General Sherman's Army of the Ohio, under the command of Major General Schofield. The Rebs were well entrenched along the ridge (known locally as "Buzzards Roost") and as you can see, the terrain was very difficult for the attacking forces. In places, the men could only advance along its precipitous paths in single file; General Sherman described this gap as "the door of death."

While General Schofield pursued his attack, Sherman decided to outflank the Confederates and sever the railroad further south. On May 9th, he sent his Army of the Tennessee to the west through Snake Creek Gap and down towards the sleepy, Georgian town of Resaca (mile marker 320). On May 11th, realizing the assault on the Ridge was impossible, Sherman left a token attacking force and followed his main army down towards Resaca. Johnston found out about this flanking movement from prisoners a day later, and rapidly pulled his troops from the "Door of Death" and retreated to defend the railroad at Resaca.

GA Exit 333-Dalton: You have passed the signboards advertising carpet sales at Dalton on your journey south, but have you ever wondered ... why Dalton? Well Dalton bills itself as the Carpet Capital of North America, and it all started with one young farm girl, Catherine Whitener, supporting her family in the early 1900s by making tufted bedspreads and scatter rugs at home. Other women joined her and soon Dalton had a booming cottage industry, saving the area from the pangs of the Depression.

In these early days, one of the most popular designs incorporated two colorful peacocks facing each other. Since the women used to hang the newly made carpets and rugs on lines strung near the old US 41route to Florida, this local highway in Dalton became known as "Peacock Alley."

By the 1950s advances in machinery and dyeing opened the door to the modern carpet

continued on page 116

DALTON - *in honor of Tristram Dalton (politician & Senator from Maine), whose grandson was the engineer who laid out the town and donated land.*

Special Report

The Great Locomotive Chase

During the Civil War, the Western & Atlantic railway line between Chattanooga and Atlanta was of great importance to the Confederacy, moving freight and soldiers between these two important railway centers. This vital link was a single track railway with passing tracks at various stations along the route. Kentuckian James Andrews, a Federal spy, devised a plan to steal a train near Atlanta and destroy the track and bridges along this line as he traveled northward. Andrew's tiny band of Union soldiers became known as Andrew's Raiders, and the subsequent actions of Saturday, April 12, 1862—the "Great Locomotive Chase."

Note: This Special Report tells the story of the chase from the theft of the "General" at Big Shanty (Kennesaw–exit 273) to its conclusion at Ringgold (exit 348). The chase therefore ran from south to north. If southbound on I-75, I suggest you read this report first so you understand the significance of the various locations as you run south towards Kennesaw. The entire adventure is shown on the I-75 map pages covering the exits mentioned above, supported by special sidetrip maps on pages 57 and.59. Numbers in the report refer to the locations marked on the maps—numbers in circles represent Andrew's Raiders (Union) actions; numbers in squares represent Fuller's (Confederate) actions.

Kennesaw

Ringgold

1. 5:30 a.m.—on a wet, rainy day, James Andrews and 23 Union soldiers from Ohio ride from Marietta to Big Shanty (Kennesaw) as passengers on a northbound train pulled by the locomotive, General. William Fuller is the train's conductor
2. 6:00 a.m.—while the train stops for breakfast at Big Shanty, Andrews' Raiders capture the General and with three box-cars, head north towards Chattanooga. Andrews and two men ride the locomotive while the rest of the armed band are hidden inside the box-cars.
3. 6:10 a.m.—Fuller, disturbed at breakfast and believing that Confederate conscripts had stolen his train to get clear of Big Shanty's army camp and would shortly abandon it, decides to give chase on foot. The General's engineer, Jeff Cain and a railroad engineering foreman, Anthony Murphy run with him.
4. The General runs out of steam a few miles up the track from Big Shanty. Andrews did not realize that the boiler dampers had been closed while the crew were at breakfast. The dampers were quickly opened and fires re-stoked with oil-soaked wood while the Raiders cut trackside telegraph wires to prevent "intercept" messages going north.

   After a quick run north, the General arrives at Moon's Station, and the Raiders "borrow" an iron bar from a track repair crew. The Raiders intend to remove rail sections behind them to halt pursuit, but later find the bar is inadequate for the task.
5. A breathless Fuller and companions arrive at Moon's Station, and take a pole-car. The three continue their pursuit by poling the car northward at 7-8 mph.
6. After passing through Acworth Station, the Raiders stop and cut more telegraph wires and damage a rail section.
7. The General halts just below Allatoona to cut telegraph wires.
8. Andrews sees the Yonah, a work locomotive belonging to the Cooper Iron Works on the north banks of the Etowah River, with steam up. He is concerned since he knows that if a pursuit message gets this far north, there is now an operational locomotive and armed crew, to give chase. He does not stop since destroying the Etowah Bridge would not fill a purpose now.
9. The General pulls up at Cass Station (near Cartersville). Andrews convinces a suspicious railway worker that he is carrying much needed gunpowder north to the Confederate Army. The patriotic worker gives Andrews his only railway schedule so that Andrews can plan his northbound run to meet and pass southbound trains at appropriate stations.
10. The Raiders pull into Kingston Station, a major passing point on the railroad. Here they wait for a southbound train but when it finally arrives, they find that there are two unscheduled southbounds on the same track section. The Raiders are forced to

wait until the next section of track is clear. In the meantime, the station personnel are getting very suspicious of the northbound "gunpowder" train.

11. Fuller cannot stop the pole-car in time and it runs off the track at the broken rail section, dumping the crew and car down an embankment. Uninjured, they carry the car back up and resume the chase. After an epic pole-car journey of 20 miles, Fuller and crew arrive at the Etowah River and commandeer the Yonah.
12. After a wait of more than an hour, the General pulls out of Kingston to continue its northbound journey, just eight minutes before the arrival of Fuller aboard the Yonah. Andrews is now aware that pursuit is close since he has heard the frantic whistle of the Yonah as it approaches Kingston.
13. Fuller cannot get past the southbound trains so once again, he and his companions take to foot, running across the Kingston railroad yards to commandeer another locomotive, the William R. Smith. They give chase northwards towards Adairsville Station. To warn of obstructions, Fuller hangs onto the locomotive's cowcatcher while scanning the track ahead.
14. Aware that a chase is now on hand, the Raiders stop to cut wires and pile railroad ties across the track as a delaying tactic.
15. Several miles further, the Raiders stop to remove a rail section but find that their crowbar is too small to easily pull the spikes. By brute strength, the men manage to bend and snap a rail and throw it in the bushes.
16. Feeling safe once more, the Raiders pull into Adairsville Station where they find a long southbound train pulled by the locomotive, Texas. The suspicious engineer refuses to pull his train forward to clear the north switch of the passing track. After another delay, Andrews manages to convince the driver, and tries to send him southbound to either collide with their pursuers or derail on the broken section.
17. The William R. Smith is stopped in time to avoid being derailed by the missing section of rail. Fuller and company take off on foot for the third time, running up the track where they manage to flag down the southbound train pulled by the Texas.
18. They hear the engineer's story and commandeer the Texas for their chase—running in reverse. As they pass through Adairsville, Fuller, without stopping the train, uncouples the cars, runs ahead, turns the switch to a side track diverting the cars into it, returns the switch for the mainline movement, jumps back on board the Texas and the pursuit continues unencumbered by the weight of the cars.
19. The Raiders hear the whistle of the Texas to the south. They create as high a head of steam as possible by burning wood soaked in oil. The General careens up the railroad, leaning out and almost toppling on the curves.
20. The General and the last train southbound from Chattanooga pass at Calhoun Station without incident.
21. As the Texas steams through Calhoun a few minutes behind the General, Fuller spots a 13 year old telegraph boy, and grabs him onto the moving train. He writes a telegram to the Confederate commander in Chattanooga.
22. Desperately, the Raiders stop and attempt to remove a rail section but are only able to bend it slightly out of shape. They also cut the telegraph wire. They quickly scramble back on board when they see their pursuer for the first time–the reversed Texas with a full head of steam charging in their direction.
23. The Texas miraculously rides right over the damaged rail section.
24. Around a curve and out of sight, the Raiders uncouple a box car and let it run down a grade onto Fuller, who reverses his direction of travel to "catch" the box-car. He couples it to the Texas' tender and resumes the chase with the box car leading.
25. The Raiders do not have time to burn and destroy the covered Oostanaula River Bridge (a major target) so drop the second box-car in its center span hoping to slow down the pursuers. As before, the Fuller "catches" the box-car, couples it and later drops them both at a siding near Resaca Station.
26. A mile north of Resaca Station, Andrews cuts the Calhoun-Dalton telegraph wire and piles ties across the track.
27. The tactic of dropping railroad ties onto the track works to delay the Texas. Each time, the engineer must throw the locomotive into full reverse, skid to a halt while Fuller and his men jump down, clear the track and start on their way again. Seeing this, Andrews decided to punch a hole through the rear wall of the remaining box-car, and drop a succession of ties on the track behind him.

28. Aware their pursuers are close again, the Raiders stop to cut wires and pile railroad ties across the track as a delaying tactic. Just south of Green's Station (Tilton), the Raiders stop again and attempt to remove a rail. They can only pry it out of shape, however. Andrews puts another rail underneath the bent rail, to try and derail the fast approaching Texas.

29. Thinking the damaged rail will have stopped the pursuit, a mile north of Tilton, Andrews' Raiders stop to take on much needed wood and water, but have to cut this short when they hear the whistle from the fast approaching Texas again. For the second time that day, the Texas has managed to run over damaged railway track without derailing.

30. After two more miles, the General stops again. Telegraph wires are cut and the track obstructed.

31. The Raiders decide to speed through Dalton, a major Confederate camp. A mile north of Dalton, they stop to cut the telegraph wire to stop messages getting through but they are unaware that minutes behind them, Fuller has dropped off the boy telegraph operator, who manages to get a portion of the message through to Chattanooga.

32. A few miles ahead is the Tunnel Hill railroad tunnel, and the Raiders discuss whether to ambush the Texas or perhaps travel through the tunnel and then reverse the General locomotive back towards the pursuing Texas for a collision. They decide to speed on northwards.

33. The Texas approaches the smoke filled tunnel. They cannot see ahead and are aware of what the Raiders might plan. Fuller decides to plunge into the tunnel's darkness at full speed, regardless of safety.

34. To their horror, Andrews looks back and sees the Texas emerge from the tunnel hard on their heels. They are approaching a covered wooden bridge across the Chickamauga River so he orders the last box car set on fire and then uncoupled in the middle of the bridge. Wet wood and the driving rain of the hour prevents this last attempt to escape, from working.

35. After a frantic dash through Ringgold, the Raiders are out of wood and oil and the General is slowing down. Andrews orders his men to jump from the train and find their own ways back to Union lines.

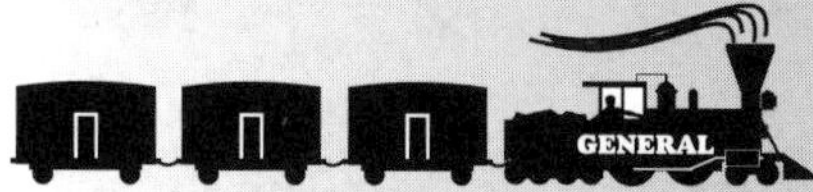

The mission failed because of the dogged pursuit by the General's conductor, William Fuller. Of the Raiders, sixteen were captured and eight were able to escape back to the safety of the Union. Of the captured men, eight were taken to Atlanta (including James Andrew) where they were hanged. Six were exchanged and two were "enlisted" in the Confederate Army. After the war, most of the surviving Raiders were awarded the Medal of Honor.

continued from page 113

industry. The entrepreneurial spirit of the local residents turned the cottage bedspread industry into multi-billion dollar carpet manufacturing. Today, more than 65% of the world's carpets are made in Dalton!

GA Exit 333-An Ancient Enigma: I love mysteries . . . especially if they are from an ancient era. If you travel east from this exit for 26.6 miles (42 minutes driving time), out of Dalton, through Chatsworth, and then up the scenic switchback road on the side of Fort Mountain which rises 2,840ft, you will find an ancient enigma in the state park at the top.

For its here that you will find an ancient stone wall built from non native rock, winding 855 feet in length and ranging in height from two to six feet.

Nobody knows who built it or what it was used for. The commonly accepted date of its construction is around 500AD (about the same time the European Vandals were sacking the ancient city of Roman).

Local Indian culture includes a legend recounting the visit of moon-eyed people who built the wall. The possible interpretation of this is that the area was visited by white men.

To visit Fort Mountain State Park, drive east from exit 333 down Walnut Ave., past the Walnut Square Mall and out of Dalton along US76 until you reach the junction of SR52 (8.0 miles), turn right and follow SR52 to the Chatsworth junction of US 411 at 3rd Street

RESACA- *originally called Dublin by Irish railroad workers, renamed after the Mexican town of Resaca de la Palma, by returning Mexican War veterans.*

(5.3 miles), go across lights and drive on the mountain road (routes 2, 52) to the park gates (8.2 miles), and then 5.1 miles inside the park to the ancient wall. Hrs: 7:00a - 10:00p;

☎ 706-695-2621 (800-864-7275)

GA Exit 320-Battle of Resaca (see map on page 60 and Special Report on page 118): At mile marker 323, you are just about to drive right across the Civil War battlefield of Resaca.

Nowhere can the atmosphere of that day in 1864 be better felt than at the Confederate Cemetery just a few minutes east of the I-75. The map on page 60 will help you find it.

The first time I visited this site it was dusk and I was by myself. It was lonely and yet somehow peaceful–just row upon row of old but tidy graves–in the soft fading light filtered through the leafy boughs of the trees above.

The United Daughters of the Confederacy had recently put tiny flags by many of the tombstones, so even 130 years later, the men are still cared for. Imagine the anguish of wives and daughters, of families left behind who didn't know where their men had gone. But we know where they went–their journey ended here.

GA Exit 317-New Echota and the Cherokee Nation: During the early 1800's, north Georgia was the heart of the sovereign Cherokee Indian Nation. By this time, the Cherokee was the most progressive Indian tribe in North America.

In 1821, they became the first American Indians with a written language, invented by Sequoyah. New Echota (pronounced "air-chot-er"), the Cherokee national capital, was located just half a mile from here (take exit 317 - and follow Rt 225 east for 1 minute). There, a constitutional government with

Insider Tip
Flammini's - An Italian Family Dining Experience

Have you ever been to an Italian family feast . . . one where everybody knows everybody, people wander around and talk to people at other tables, everybody is happy and smiling and laughter fills the air. Well, *Flammini's Cafe Italia* in Dalton is just like that. Even if you are far from home, the minute you poke your head through the door and past all the family photos, you are made warmly welcome by owner Pete, or perhaps his parents, Jack and Pat. You *know* you are going to have a wonderfully, enjoyable evening among new friends. Tiny lights twinkle throughout the dining area, and everybody–from the staff to the patrons is obviously having a good time.

The Flammini's are from the Marche region of Italy near the Adriatic Sea, and serve traditional foods from the small towns in the region . . . recipes which have been handed down through the generations of the Flammini family. Beef, seafood, veal or chicken in various preparations can be served with your choice of nine different pastas. And of course, they serve dining room pizzas. After our tasty main course of Veal Marsala (veal sauteed in marsala wine with mushrooms) and capellini (angel hair) pasta, Pat Flammini insisted that I sample a taste of traditional Tirami Su dessert (ladyfingers, soaked in rum, layered with mascarpone cheese and coffee whipped cream) . . . it's to die for! Incidentally, the Flammini's haven't forgotten those with dietary concerns, and offer a number of light and childrens' meals.

The entire dining experience at Flammini's is best summed up by their own menu notes . . . *"in our family, there is always plenty of food and room for one more at the table. At Flammini's there will be food in generous portions and we'll consider you as part of our family."* Believe me, they mean it! *Buon Appetito*

Flammini's Cafe Italia is at 1205 W. Walnut Avenue, Dalton. To find it, take exit 333 (old 136) and drive east along Walnut Avenue, through the lights at Tibbs Road–look for the yellow sign with black writing on your right–7/10ths of a mile from I-75. Open for lunch on Thurs and Fri only. Hours: Mon-Wed, 5pm-9:30pm; Thur-Fri, 11am-10pm; Sat, 5pm-10pm. Closed Sunday. ☎ 706-226-0667

Special Report

I-75 and the Civil War

As you drive through north Georgia, you will pass a number of nearby Civil War battlefields–Chickamauga and Chattanooga's Lookout Mountain. The I-75 follows the route of Sherman's march toward Atlanta with its resulting destruction by flame - and you will actually drive through two of the battlefields (see Resaca map on page 60).

Imagine the scene–it is May 13,1864. Strung out across the path of the southbound I-75 a few yards south of mile marker 323 is a thin line of young men crouched in hurriedly constructed trenches cut deep into the red Georgian earth. Banks of rubble have been thrown forward to give added protection from the whining Minie balls which zip overhead like angry hornets waiting to administer the sting of death. A fountain of red soil suddenly shoots skyward in front of them, followed by the vibration of the ground shock wave and deep crumping sound of a distant explosion. A Confederate field gun is ranging in on their position.

Sweltering under the hot Georgian sun in their heavy flannel uniforms of dark blue, they wait their officer's command to rise up and charge over the rough ground toward the wooded rise where they can see the gray hunched shapes of the Confederates behind log spiked palisades. Behind the wooden barriers, the distinctive saltire cross of the red and blue Battle Flag floats lazily overhead.

On closer look, the mud and sweat streaked faces are of very young men–frightened, quietly exchanging comments of bravado in nervous, throat-tightened voices. Many, only in their sixteenth or seventeenth year, will not see nightfall.

They are showing the strain of the Atlanta campaign–many escaped death only a few days earlier facing the same enemy in the battle of Rocky Face Ridge, 14 miles north of here. They were lucky, for they survived and flanked General Johnston's Gray forces who have now retreated southward to make yet another stand here–at Resaca–as the Rebels fall back toward Atlanta's

Continued top of next page

executive, legislative and judicial branches ruled the nation. Once the largest town in this area, New Echota consisted of houses, stores, taverns, a Council house, Supreme Courthouse, and a printing office which published a national bilingual newspaper, the Cherokee Phoenix.

In 1838, the Cherokee were rounded up at gun point and imprisoned by state and federal armies.

Later that year, these peaceful people were forced to what is now Oklahoma. Four thousand Cherokee died on the terrible march west known as the "Trail of Tears."

Today, you may visit New Echota where the State of Georgia maintains an excellent museum and seven of the original houses.

The historic site is open Tues.-Sat, 9-5, Sunday 2-5:30pm. Admission adults/children–$2.50/$1.50. ☎ 706-624-1321.

GA Mile 310-Mercer Air Field: Across the freeway beside the northbound lanes is a field containing vintage aircraft - the collection of local businessman, E.L.Mercer. Representing aircraft from WWII, the Korean War and Vietnam eras, sadly, they have deteriorated over the years and are probably not flyable now.

GA Exit 306-a sidetrip through historic Bartow County (map on page 57): Some of us are now going to leave I-75 and take a sidetrip to the west visiting some of the fascinating historical sites in Bartow County. If you would like to join us, turn to page 120. Those deciding to drive on I-75 should continue with the text below: We'll rejoin you at exit 288.

GA Exit 293-the end of I-75: For many years, this was the end of I-75 and cars driving to Florida had to divert westward down US41 until they could rejoin the next portion of I-75 near mile 273. The reason? Another Civil War of sorts . . . in 1965!

At issue was the building of I-75 in a straight line from Chattanooga to Atlanta, for it was

main defense line in a losing war.

These are the men and boys of the General Sherman's 35th Indiana, under the command of Brigadier General Stanley. Little do they know that the Confederates have already spotted a weakness to the left of their line and at 4 o'clock that afternoon, six divisions of General Hood's best Rebs will charge down the slope and drive them from their position. The situation will be saved by the 5th Indiana gunners firing double-shotted canister into the Grays, and the timely arrival of General William's Union Army of the Cumberland, currently positioned a mile to their right.

Before the end of this battle three days later, 5,547 men and boys will have been killed or injured, and the Confederates will be forced to pull back to make yet another retreating stand at Cassville, opening the door to Sherman's Union victories at New Hope Church, Kennesaw Mountain ... and ultimately, Atlanta.

All this action, which involved over 171,000 men, took place right across the ground you are traveling as you approach Exit 320. The map on page 60 relates the I-75 mile markers to the battlefield.

After driving through the 35th Indiana's Union line positions (just south of Mile 323), you pass through the Confederate defenses (just north of mile marker 322) of General Hood and then cross the Confederate encampment and back through the Rebel army's southernmost defense lines (just south of mile marker 321) manned by the troops of Generals Cleburne and Polk. At Exit 320, you are in no man's land between the forces of Cleburne and the Union attackers of Major Generals Loring and Smith. The Oostanaula River forms the southern boundary of the battlefield.

designed to go right through the center of Lake Allatoona and surrounding woodlands, on a causeway–and that's where the battle lines were drawn.

The resulting fight halted the completion of the first continuous Interstate to Florida's border. Twelve years later, with the last lawsuit dismissed and the road's path relocated somewhat to the west of its original plan, Georgia's Governor Busbee and U.S. Transportation Secretary Adams cut a red, white and blue ribbon and the traffic began to flow over the I-75's last (and most controversial) link. The date was Wednesday, December 22, 1977; 21 years after construction of the I-75 had officially begun.

As Governor Busbee said, *"it is now possible to drive from Canada to the Gulf of Mexico without stopping for a single traffic light or stop sign."* In a message to those present at the ceremony, President Carter called it *"the most important interstate route in the nation."*

GA Exit 293-Weinman Mineral Museum: If you enjoy rocks and precious stones, there is a treat in store for you just minutes off of I-75 at this exit–the William Weinman Mineral Museum.

More than 2,000 exhibits are displayed in three halls. The Georgia room contains many specimens native to the State, as well as a simulated cave and waterfall. Indian artifacts dated back to 8,000 BC and fossils as early as the Paleozoic Era (see chart on page 92) are displayed in a second room, while a third contains the international Mayo collections.

Children can touch the skull (replica) of a 30 foot Triceratops Horridus dinosaur or try their hands at gold panning and mineral classification while parents peruse the Gift Shop.

continued on page 123

OOSTANAULA RIVER - *Cherokee name, "place of the rocks across the stream," for a shallow place to ford.*

Special Report

A Sidetrip Through Bartow County

Let's take a few hours away from the interstate and travel through what I consider to be one of the most interesting counties in Georgia. Here in Bartow County we will discover heritage buildings, local restaurants, antiques, arts and crafts and many Civil War sites. To help, you'll find a map of our tour on page 57.

Total driving distance/time (not including the sidetrip to Barnsley Gardens and Kingston, is 33 miles/1 hr., 3 mins. Add on 3 miles/7 mins. for Barnsley, and 1 mile/3 mins. for the local drive through Kingston.

Leave I-75 at exit 306 and drive west, through the traffic lights at US 41. Just past the Citgo (1/10th mile), turn left to Adairsville Main St.

Adairsville, became a bustling supply depot during the Civil War-this ended abruptly when Sherman marched through on his way to Atlanta.

Today though, it's enjoying a renaissance and has become a great place to stop and relax for a while. The entire town with its many heritage buildings is listed on the National Register of Historic Places.

The **1902 Stock Exchange (A)** (124 Public Sq.) is a fine example of an historical restoration. Inside, you'll find antiques, gifts, crafts, used books, a cafe-style gourmet coffee shop and even an Antebellum dinner theater. Owner Rita Pritchard loves chatting with visitors and showing them her architectural treasure.

If the South had successfully ceded from the Union, I suspect that **Miss Hannah's Tru-South Old Fashioned Soda Fountain (A)**, Lunch Room and Candy Store (118 Public Sq.) would be exactly as you find it today. Miss Hannah's has an excellent menu of fine food, all made fresh on the premises. A bumper sticker sums up their view of current politics - *"Don't blame us, we voted for Jeff Davis."*

Once back in your car, drive west across the railroad tracks on Park St and past the **Train Depot (B)**. This played a role in the Great Locomotive Chase (see page 115, item 16), for it was here that the Conductor Fuller commandeered the southbound Texas and started chasing the stolen General backwards, towards the north.

Continue on Park, at the stop sign, turn left on to Hall Station Road. This road parallels the railroad track down to Kingston. A number of events during the **Great Locomotive Chase** took place along this stretch (see page 114) as Andrews' Raiders attempted to stop their pursuers.

The road was also witness to a **Civil War trap (C)**; it played a role in CSA General Johnston's innovative counter attack strategy which if successful, would have turned the tide against Sherman and possibly saved Atlanta.

Withdrawing from the Battle of Resaca (see page 60), Johnston decided to fool Sherman into thinking that the entire Confederate army was retreating down Hall Station Rd towards Kingston. He did this by noisily sending a third of his men - 24,000 soldiers, heavy artillery and wagons, down the road we are now on while his main force quietly moved down another route to the east.

Sherman fell for the ruse, sending most of his troops "chasing the Rebs" down this road. A much smaller force traveled the eastern route not realizing that the main Confederate army was just ahead.

On arrival, both Confederate armies regrouped north of Cassville and with superior numbers, made a stand across the east route. The plan was to quickly annihilate the small Union army and then swing around to the west to deal with the remainder of Sherman's troops.

But just before the trap was sprung, a small detachment of Federal cavalry was sighted to the right of the CSA; they assumed they were being outflanked by the main Union force. Abandoning their trap, they fell back to the long 2 mile ridge just southeast of Cassville.

That evening, several generals convinced

Johnston that the ridge was untenable. He agreed to withdraw which he did during the night, heading southward towards Allatoona Pass. This non-battle could have been a key turning point in the Battle for Atlanta; it later became known as the **Cassville Affair (K)**.

We will now visit - **Barnsley Gardens (D)** - the sort of place you would only expect to find in Georgia - beautiful Antebellum gardens, Civil War action, a ruined manor house, *"Gone With The Wind"* connections, and a ghost. In 5¾ miles, turn right off Hall Station Rd on to Barnsley Garden Rd, and drive 3¾ miles to the Barnsley Gardens gate; at the gatehouse, they will direct you to the gardens, the ruined manor house and museum.

In 1824, penniless Godfrey Barnsley, arrived in North America, where he rose to become a prominent and rich cotton planter. Needing an estate, he purchased this property and named it Woodlands. During his business travels abroad, Barnsley collected rare and exotic plants, brought them back and planted the famous Woodlands gardens–perhaps best known for their countless varieties of roses.

The untimely death of his wife, Julia and the Civil War bought an end to his fortunes, and sadly, Godfrey died as penniless as the day he arrived on these shores. Disaster struck again in 1906 when a tornado ruined the main house and nearby gardens.

Today, thanks to Prince Hubertus of Bavaria, we can enjoy Barnsley's roses, ferns, fruit trees, rockeries and woodland gardens–over 30 acres of cultivated delight surrounding the ruins of Godfrey's Italianate villa.

Don't miss the excellent museum to the right of the ruins. Here you will find Barnsley's knowledgeable historian, Clent Coker. I'll leave it to Clent to explain the stain from a large pool of blood on the floor of the old building.
Admission-Adults/Snrs/Children: $10/$8/$5; Hrs-Summer: Tu-Fri 10-6, Sat-phone to ensure no weddings, Sun 12-5; Winter: closes at 4pm; ☎ 770-773-7480.
Return to Hall Station Road and turn right to continue towards Kingston. In two miles, on your left you'll pass **Spring Bank (E)** famous for the limestone mined from the hills to the east. It makes such strong concrete that some of it was used to build the Brooklyn Bridge.

In another 2½ miles, we enter the historical town of **Kingston**. When you reach the junction of SR293, turn left. After crossing a railroad bridge, turn right and follow around onto Railroad St. which runs parallel with the tracks. Immediately to your right where the baseball park lies, is the site of the **Kingston Depot & railroad switching yard (F)** which played a major role in the Great Locomotive Chase (see page 114, items 10 and 12).

Turn right, cross the tracks at Johnson. At corner of Main is a sign marking the location of the Hargis Home, site of **Sherman's HQ (G)** during the Cassville Affair.

Turn left on Main Street, past the small but excellent **Museum (H)** on your left. Sat-Sun, 1:00-4:00p; $1 donation; ☎ 770-336-5540.

On your right you'll see a marble plaque marking the site of **Wayside Home (I)**, the CSA's first hospital (1861). The facility treated more than 10,000 sick and wounded during its 3 years of operation.

Continue along Main St. On the corner of Main and Church is the white **McGravey-Johnson Home (J)**. Here on May 12, 1865, the last CSA troops under arms were surrendered to the Union. Turn left onto Church St.

Drive up Church St., across the tracks turn right onto Railroad St.; drive to join Route 293, and then turn right towards Cassville. You are now coming into the Cassville area - an area rich with Civil War "finds." The developers of The Planters (3¾ miles from Kingston) recently unearthed swords, buckles and CSA insignia). Ahead of you in the distance lies Johnston's **Cassville Affair ridge (K)**.

We will now head towards Cartersville. Turn left onto Boyd Morris Drive, then right onto US41 South. Driving on US41 for 6 miles until you reach the traffic lights at ML King Jr cross street. Go through and move to the right lane before the next lights in ½ mile - Church Street. Turn right and drive across the Church St. Bridge until you reach Erwin. Turn right and into the parking area of the **Cartersville Visitors Center (L).**

Here you will find all sorts of information about this historic town. Many visitors incorrectly think that Cartersville was named after President Jimmy Carter. It was named after Colonel Farish Carter (1780-1861), an early landowner. Before leaving, say "hi" to Ellen, Regina, Susie and the Center's friendly staff - they love to meet & help visitors. ☎ 707-387-1357.

On leaving the parking area, turn left onto Erwin. Just past Church St. on your right is the **Sam Jones United Methodist Church (M)**, and on your left, the **old 1914 Post Office (N)**, now used as the City Hall. Next to the church is the "new" **1903 Bartow Co. Courthouse (O)** with a very interesting Civil War column and statute, on the corner of the property. If you have time, park the car and read the poem on the statue's base - it'll moisten the eyes of the hardiest soul.

Turn left at Main St. and park in the Public Square on your left. Opposite you'll see the Young Brothers Pharmacy. On its eastern outside wall is the **first outdoor Coca-Cola advertisement (P)** in the World, painted by a Coca-Cole syrup salesman in 1894.

Stroll along **North Wall St. (Q)** and enjoy the interesting shops and buildings. Across the tracks to your left is the **Cartersville Railroad Depot**.

To your right across Cherokee, you'll find the **1920 Grand Theater** - home of the famous Cartersville Opera Company (☎ 770-386-1552), **Etowah Art Gallery** (11 N. Wall; ☎ 770-382-8277) and the **Bartow History Center** (13 N. Wall; ☎ 770-382-3818); many have interesting gift shops which are worth browsing.

Continue along N. Wall Street, cross Cherokee and turn right into Church St. under the Bridge. You'll find two very special treats waiting for you in this unusual subterranean street which I call, **"Underground Cartersville" (R)**.

Wonderful lunch treat await you at the **Railside Cafe.** Owners Christy Bennett & Chef Jennifer Nichols serve wonderfully fresh and creative foods. In particular, I enjoy their crab cakes. Hrs: Tu-Sa, 11:30a-2:30p; ☎ 770-386-9130

Next door is a most unusual shop - **The Shaving Gallery**, owned and operated by a most unusual (in the nicest of senses) person, Lauren Cross. Lauren (an expatriate from New Zealand via London) is an expert at shaving men. She's done it for years and it is a wonderfully relaxing experience. She and her staff have many other services as well - most of them for the ladies.

Drop in and say "hello" to Lauren - tell her, Dave sent you! Hrs: M-Sa, 9a-5p: ☎ 770-386-9130

The **Ancient Indian City (S)** is 1,000 year old and lies on the bank of the Etowah River, 3 miles (11 minutes) back west from where you parked your car on Main Street. Follow Main St. westward (away from I-75). Continue forward on SR 113 where Bartow St. (SR293) leaves to the right. Watch for the branching of route 113 West and Etowah Drive. Take the left branch (Etowah Dr.) and follow the road until you reach the Etowah Indian Mound State Park. It's well marked along the route.

Dated from 1000–1500 AD, this entire area was once a huge Indian village. Today, you may explore the remains of three flat topped ceremonial mounds and a moat which encircled the town remain.

Archeological digs have yielded many finds which are on display at the park's Visitor Center. Libby, the Park Manager is very knowledgeable and can answer your questions about this mysterious site.

The park is open Tues-Sat, 9-5, Sun 2-5:30pm; Admission: Adult/Children; $3/$2; ☎ 770-387-3747.

Returning to I-75 from downtown Cartersville is easy. Just follow Main St. east (SR113N), past the Coca-Cola sign, cross Tennessee (SR61) and US41.

Shortly, you'll arrive at back at I-75, at exit 288.

continued from page 119

The Museum is closed on Mon. Hours for Tues-Sat are 10-4:30pm; Sun, 1-4:30pm. Admission is Adult/Senior/ Children (6-11); $4.00/$3.50/$3.00.

To find the museum, take exit 293 and go west for a few yards on route 411. Turn left onto Mineral Museum Drive which is just past the Holiday Inn. ☎ 770-386-0576.

GA Exit 288-Cartersville: Those who took the Bartow Co. sidetrip will rejoin I-75 at this point. If however, you decided to drive the freeway, it's not too late to visit the Cartersville sights described. Cartersville is just a few minutes to the west of this exit.

GA Exit 285-Etowah Bridge and Cooper Iron Works (map on page 59): Follow the map and visit remains of the Etowah Bridge where the locomotive, Yonah was commandeered during the Great Locomotive Chase.

GA Mile 283-The Georgia Gold Belt: Yep, you heard properly . . . gold! And there is still lode buried in this area - for it's all part of a band of rock which stretches across North Georgia, called the Dahlonega Rift.

Now, perhaps you didn't know that the nation's first gold rush did not occur in California, but in Dahlonega, Georgia, 93 miles east along Route 52 from I-75 exit 333 (old 136). In 1828, the area boomed and more than $6 million in gold coin was minted at the Dahlonega Mint before the Civil War closed it down.

Dahlonega is quite a distance to the east (54 miles) but if you decide to visit, you can pan for gold in several locations as well as visit one of the 19th century mines and an interesting Georgia State Park museum.

Mon-Sat, 9-5; Sun 10-5. Admission, adult/child–$3/$2. ☎ 706-864-2257.

But back to the ground you are currently driving over.

GA Exit 283-Battle of Allatoona Pass (see map, page 58: A small but significant battle in the War Between The States, took place about a 1¾ miles east of here. Known only to the locals, the battlesite is undisturbed with trenches, redoubts and a fort in situ. It has now been opened to the public by the Etowah Valley Historical Society and the Corps of Engineers, and you are invited to wander its wooded paths, but first let me take you back to 1864 and set the scene for you:

By early September, General Sherman had successfully captured Atlanta and the single track Western & Atlantic railroad running through North Georgia had become a vital link for bringing supplies to the occupied city. But Southern President Jeff Davis had announced that he intended to disrupt the route using Confederate raiders. One of the most vulnerable stretches of track was the section at Allatoona where it cuts through a 175ft deep, 360ft long man-made pass; it would be easy work for a small contingent of "Rebs" to block it at this point. For protection, Sherman posted a small detachment of men to fortify Allatoona. Trenches were dug and earthwork defenses built on the high ground either side of the cut - both camps joined by a wooden footbridge 170 feet in the air.

On October 4th, Confederate commander General Hood issued several conflicting orders to General Samuel French, one of which told him to "fill up the deep cut at Allatoona . . ." (an impossible feat of engineering given the 30 hours allowed for the task).

Sherman received early warnings of this as Confederate troop movements were reported in the area. He dispatched reinforcements to

Insider Tip
Doug's Place

People drive from miles around to eat here, but it's not what you would call a "fancy dining" place. You'll either love Doug's Place, or hate it - but it's certainly the favorite for all the locals.

Reminiscent of a restaurant from the '60s, the walls are covered with old family photographs, signs and country tools.

Service is fast and friendly and the food excellent; the leather furniture clean and the silverware comes in clear plastic bags. Owner, Doug Ferguson is often at the cash register, so say "hi" on the way by.

To reach Doug's Place, take I-75 exit 283, and drive west for 1.1 miles to Emmerson. The restaurant is on the opposite corner of the crossroads at the flashing yellow light. ☎ 707-382-9063; Hrs: Bkfst/Lunch- Mon-Fri, 6:00a-2:00p; Sat: 7:00a-2:00p; Dinner - Wed & Fri: 4:30p-9:00p.

Allatoona under the command of General Corse but due to railroad damage inflicted by the "Rebs," only a portion of them arrived. With the scene set for the battle, Corse had a total force of only 2,025 men to defend the Pass against French's force of 3,276.

What developed as the Battle of Allatoona Pass was one of the most vicious and deadliest of the entire war. Its intense hand-to-hand fighting produced many heroes. The Star Fort on the western side of the Pass was the scene of the most intensive action. The defenders under the personal command of Corse, fired their Henry 15 shot repeater rifles so fast that they became too hot to hold. As the fort ran out of ammunition, Pvt. Edwin Fullington crossed the footbridge three times as he was fired upon by enemy snipers, to resupply the defenders. Another defender, Pvt. James Croft, received the Medal of Honor for bravery during this battle. General Corse received a wound to his cheek in the heat of the attack.

At noon, General French received word that Yankee reinforcements were in the area and in view of the heavy casualties his forces had received, he decided to withdraw.

The cost of the day? Out of the 5,301 men engaged in the four hour battle, only 3,698 lived to tell about it - one of the bloodiest days of the entire war.

GA Mile 274-Larry McDonald Memorial Highway: You have probably just seen the roadside "Larry McDonald Highway" sign and may have wondered who he was. Lawrence Patton McDonald was a high profile, highly controversial Georgian Congressman, who was born and lived near Atlanta. He died in the tragic Korean Airline Flight 007, shot down by Soviet fighters in September, 1983. In 1998, the Georgia House of Representatives passed a resolution naming I-75 from the Tennessee border to the Chattahoochee River, in his honor.

GA Exit 273-Kennesaw Civil War Museum (map on page 59): After following the route of the Great Locomotive Chase backwards all the way down from Ringgold, you can now visit the actual restored locomotive, "General" and the place where she was seized on April 12, 1862. In fact, the parking area opposite the Museum is right at Big Shanty where the crew stopped the train for breakfast that fateful morning.

It is also worth noting that the other major locomotive involved in the Chase, the "Texas," is on display in Atlanta at the Cyclorama. ☎ phone 404-658-7625 for directions and information.

GA Exit 271-Speed Zone: Have you ever wanted to drive a race car, or pilot one of those drag strip monsters down the track? If so, Speed Zone is for you. As its brochure states, "you are about to enter a 12 acre park completely dedicated to speed, racing and competition. It is the closest thing to professional racing ever offered to the public."

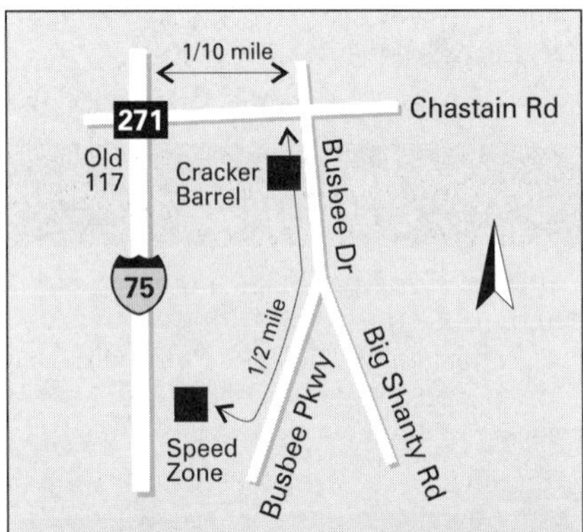

Insider Tip
Tune in to Captain Herb

Mile 281–Just a reminder, you are twenty six miles north of the point where the Atlanta bypass leaves I-75 to circle around the city to the west. Now is the time to start thinking about whether you are going to bypass Atlanta or stay on I-75 and go right through.

Why not tune in Captain Herb on 750 AM and get a traffic report? See page 193 for Atlanta rush hour times and page 195 for the bypass map.

The attraction offers a number of challenges - you can ride the powerful Eliminator dragsters (3 races for $15), drive the Turbo Track ($5 for 5 minutes), handle the Slick Trax ($5 for 5 minutes) or master the Grand Prix circuit ($2.50 per lap). A special ticket deal is also available which gives $30 of racing for $25.

Speed Zone is geared primarily to 18 to 35 year olds, but younger family members (42" or taller) may ride as passengers on the Turbo or Grand Prix tracks during daylight hours. Youngsters over 5' tall, may also drive a special car on the Turbo Track during daylight hours.

It seems to me that Speed Zone might be an excellent way to discharge all that youthful energy which can build up during a long car journey. Speed Zone hours are Sun-Thur, 11:30am-11pm; Fri-Sat, 11:30am-1:00am.

GA Exit 267B-Marietta Square: Marietta has a charming town square hidden away literally a few minutes west of the I-75. With angle parking around the perimeter and a round fountain in a parkland setting in the center, its a great place to just sit and relax under the shady trees, or perhaps go and browse the shops around its edge. Just one block to the west is the old railroad track and an excellent Visitors' Center inside the c1898 Western & Atlantic Passenger Depot. Say "hi" to Mary and the other volunteers - they do a grand job. Hrs: M-Ft: 9-5, Sa: 11-4, Su: 1-4; ☎ 770-429-1115.

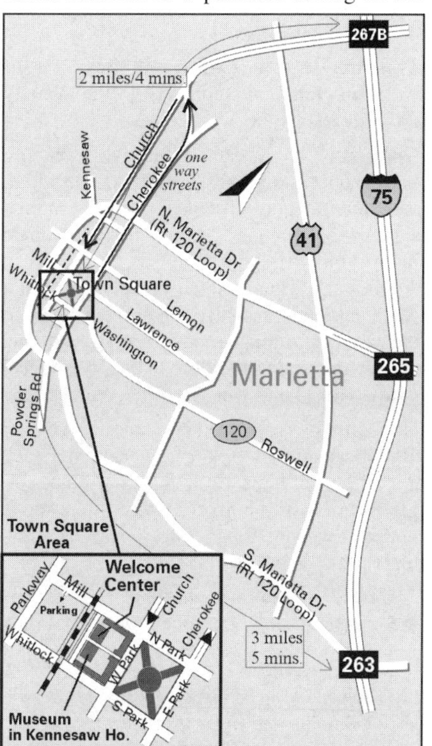

Next to the Center is an historical hotel - called Fletcher House during the War Between the States, and later changed to Kennesaw House. It was here that James Andrews' Raiders (Great Locomotive Chase - see page 114, item 1) stayed - in some cases, four to a bed - before boarding the train the following morning, which they would steal during breakfast at Big Shanty (Kennesaw). An excellent museum upstairs includes the room used by James Andrews. Curator Dan Cox loves to chat with visitors and tell stories of the past. Hrs: M-Sat, 11-4; Sun, 1-4; Admission: $3; ☎ 770-528-4982

F22 Raptor: A little farther south of here in Marrietta is Lockheed, the testing grounds for one of the Nation's most controversial aircraft, the F22 Raptor. Designed to continue the USA's combat dominance in the air for the first quarter of the 21st Century, the Raptor combines stealth, maneuverability (hovering, flying backwards, etc.), supersonic cruise speed without an afterburner and very advanced integrated avionics (aviation electronics).

The latter is very impressive indeed. Each F22 has computing power of two Cray Supercomputers, and has the ability to automatically link up with other aircraft in its flight and exchange data without pilot intervention. For instance, each fighter can quickly determine on its display unit, all characteristics of the other F22's in its flight - fuel loads, weapons available, target locks, etc. - all without voice communication. The first F22 Raptor took off from Dobbins AFB on September 7, 1997,

MARIETTA - *for Marietta Cobb, believed to have been the wife of Thomas Cobb, after whom Cobb County is named.*

and climbed to 15,000 feet in the skies over Marietta and I-75, in seconds.

At $83.6 million each, Congress has been watching this project like a hawk and releasing funds on a stage-by-stage basis. Currently, the first two Raptors, 4001 & 4002 are at Edwards AFB in California. Congress has now approved funds for four more F22's and these will shortly be seen in the air, once again climbing I-75 skies over Marietta.

GA Mile 260-Atlanta's Advanced Traffic Management System: You have just passed under one of the electronic gantry signs of Atlanta's Advanced Traffic Management System, or ATMS, billed as the most sophisticated traffic management system in the World.

Many technologies such as video cameras and road sensors feed information into a control center where the information is analyzed. Up-to-date traffic information messages are relayed back to travelers via the overhead signs (there are five over I-75 in the Atlanta area)—and to in-car navigational displays, hand-held "Palm" personal communication devices (for people walking), on-line computer services and cable TV. The overhead signs should be a great help in driving through or around Atlanta. They will also give you a final check on whether to take the bypass (coming up in another mile) or not.

GA Mile 258-Atlanta Express Lanes: To help traffic move on the crowded expressway through Atlanta, the city has designated the left lane from mile marker 258 to 237 as a restricted High Occupancy Vehicle (HOV) express lane.

The HOV lane is dedicated to public and emergency vehicles, and cars with two or more people on board. Unlike many other cities though, the Atlanta Express Lanes are ***restricted to this traffic 24 hours a day, 7 days a week.*** Watch for the black diamond sign and double dashed lines marked on the road, which identifies the restricted traffic lanes.

Incidentally, the signage reads "two person car pools" but we have checked with the Atlanta authorities and any private car (even with out-of-state license plates) with two or more people in it may use the express lanes. A special "car pooling" permit, as some readers thought, is not necessary.

A small word of caution. Since the express lanes occupy the freeway's left hand lane and the I-75 running through Atlanta has some exits which also exit to the left, be very careful that you don't accidentally leave I-75 at those exits. There are however, several points where due to the "basket weave" of other interstates joining and leaving I-75, the express lanes appear to leave the normal flow of I-75 traffic. The express lanes are clearly marked "I-75" with an arrow. Follow these with confidence since they rejoin I-75 a little further on. Just feel good about the fact that you are in the express lane and moving . . . whereas the rest of I-75 traffic is probably standing still!

On this year's maps I have provided separate Atlanta driving instructions - instructions (in red boxes) for those using the regular lanes and "black diamond" instructions for those in the HOV lanes.

The Varsity: at exit 249D lies one of Atlanta's famous landmarks - the Varsity drive-in restaurant.

Now there are several things you need to know about the Varsity before you decide to eat there. It can be crowded, noisy . . . in fact, sometimes raucous . . . but it's an Atlanta institution. Anybody who is anybody in Atlanta has eaten there. Presidents Carter, Bush, and most recently, Clinton have graced the Varsity dining rooms where you can choose the room according to the TV channel you would like to watch.

No matter how crowded it is - they serve over 10,000 customers and 17,000 hotdogs each day; they sell more Coke than any other single location in the World - the orders move quickly over the many sales positions along the 150' stainless steel counter.

"Whad'll ya have?? whad'll ya have??" is the constant cry. As founder/owner Frank

ATLANTA - *formerly named "Terminus" (in 1837 for the southern end of the Western & Atlantic Railroad), and changed to "Marthasville" in 1843 to honor Gov.. Wilson Lumpkin's daughter. Finally to "Atlanta" in 1845, suggested by the word "Atlantic" in the name of its most important industry, the W&A Railroad.*

CHATTAHOOCHEE RIVER - *Cherokee name probably, "marked rocks," for painted stones found in the river.*

A Short Latin Lesson for the South

As you visit museums and historic locations in the South, you will often encounter the terms *antebellum* and *postbellum*. These refer to the periods before the Civil War (also known as *The War between the States*, in the South) and after the Civil War, respectively. For instance, a plantation house might be described as Antebellum, meaning that it was built before 1861.

The terms come from the Latin, Ante meaning Before, Post meaning After, and Bellum meaning War. An easy way to remember these is to think of two other Latin terms familiar to everyone–a.m. meaning Ante Meridiem, or Before Noon (morning), and p.m. meaning Post Meridiem, or After Noon (afternoon).

Gordy says, *"Have your money in your hand and your order in your mind and we will get you to the game on time."*

Alternatively, you can sit in your car and one of the car-hops will come and take your order. Parking isn't always easy to find in the service area, but with a little patience you'll soon see a happy customer backing out.

You will either love or hate the Varsity, but it will be an unforgettable experience. Frank's daughter, Nancy Sims runs the Varsity along with her staff of very interesting characters - try and get Irvy Walker on the Express Counter to chant the menu for you.

If driving south on I-75, take exit 249D, turn left and the Varsity is immediately on your left just across the bridge. Pull into the first driveway (before the building) for car-hop service or regular parking.

When you leave, drive around the back out onto Spring St, cross the traffic lights at Ponce De Leon and across North Ave., stay left past the I-75 North ramp until you see the I-75 South sign - follow the I-75S ramp back down onto the freeway (also known as the Atlanta Downtown Connector).

If driving north, take exit 249D, cross Spring St and turn left when you reach West Peachtree, turn left again at North Avenue and you will see the Varsity across the road from you.

When you leave, follow the directions above for southbound travelers but take the I-75 North ramp instead.

Turner Field (Olympic Stadium): At mile 246, on your left is Turner Field (named after Atlanta's Ted Turner), site of the 1996 Summer Olympic Opening and Closing ceremonies. The stadium is home for the Atlanta Braves baseball team.

Just to the north of the Stadium is the distinctive open girder statue of the Olympic Torch, honoring the Games.

Mile 239-World's Busiest Airport: At mile 239, you might notice lights on top of stalks in I-75's median. These are the final approach lights of runway 27R, of the world's busiest airport, William B.Hartsfield International.

Built on land originally owned by Asa Chandler, the founder of The Coca Cola Company, as the site of his auto race track, Hartsfield was recently named the world's busiest airport by the Geneva based International Airport Council. Currently, Atlanta handles 73.5 million passengers a year, compared to Chicago O'Hare's 72.4 million.

GA Exit 237-Georgia Farmers Market: Just to the east of I-75 lies the huge Georgia Farmers' Market. To reach it, turn off at Exit 237 (old 78) and go east to the second traffic light. Turn left into the double gates and follow the left hand lanes marked Shed Area–"Georgia Farmers" (don't worry–it's open to the public even though it looks commercial)–follow the lanes around the building and there you will find sheds with stands selling–pecans, onions, tomatoes, peanuts–every type of fruit and vegetable you ever wanted.

Time for a meal? Don't overlook the market's popular Thomas Marketplace Restaurant. Open from 6am to 9 pm, 7 days a week, it's where many of the local folk eat. At peak

JONESBORO - *originally called "Leakesville," it was renamed after Samuel Jones, an engineer who revived the Macon & Western, a bankrupt railroad.*

MCDONOUGH - *in honor of War of 1812 naval hero, Commodore Thomas McDonough (1783-1825). During the 1812 naval campaigns on Lake Champlain, he fought and won the battle of Plattsburgh which caused the British forces to retreat back to Canada.*

Insider Tip
Tokyo Japanese Steak House

For a change of pace, you might enjoy dining Teppanyachi style at this restaurant where the chef prepares your steak, chicken or shrimps (and performs) right at your table. The special teppa tables with their hot cooking surfaces seat 8 people. With a friendly group, the show can be spectacular - so introduce yourselves to others when you arrive - you'll soon be having a great time! Meals are all inclusive and include soup or salad, entree, dessert and beverage.

The Tokyo Japanese Steak House is located at 3688 HIghway 138. Go east at exit 228; the restaurant is located in the last shopping plaza on your right just before you reach the I-675 ramp.

Hours: Mon-Thur 4:30-10pm; Fri-Sat 4:30-11pm; Sunday 4:30-10pm.
☎ 770-506-8866

times, you might find it a little noisy (it's a huge barn of a room) but the Southern home-style cooking, fried green tomatoes, fried chicken - is excellent.

GA Exit 224-Golf Heaven: see Insider Tip on page 129.

GA Exit 221-McDonough Square (see map): There's a lovely town square of a bygone era a few miles off I-75 at McDonough. In its center sits a white stone memorial to the "War between the States," shaded on all sides by old leafy trees. Sitting in the sun on one of the wrought iron benches at the side of the square, it is easy to close one's eyes and imagine that you hear the excited voices of an early Confederate muster at the beginning of the war when McDonough's youth were going to go up north to "whop them boys in blue" . . . or perhaps the concerned shouts of the city's merchants on the evening of November 15, 1864, when they heard that the 17th Corps of Sherman's Army was camped nine miles north of McDonough at Stockbridge, and intending to head in their direction the following morning.

Thanks to the skirmishing actions of the Kentucky 4th Mounted Infantry ("The Orphan Brigade"), the Feds decided to move off in another direction as part of Sherman's right wing of his devastating "March to the Sea" - saving McDonough from possible pillage and burning.

Today, the square is surrounded on three sides by interesting stores to poke around in. From the old general store - McDonough Hardware to various antique and gift shops. Southern food is served at the Gritz Family Restaurant. On the north lies the imposing Henry County Courthouse.

The McDonough Square is one of those small treasures which never gets adequate mention in the glossy travelbooks-enjoy a bygone era.

GA Exit 218-McDonough Visitors' Information: Need area tourist information? The McDonough Chamber of Commerce is at this exit about 3/4 mile down the road west of I-75. This new information center is brand new and even has computer hook-ups so you can get your e.mail messages.

GA Exit 201-Buckners, A Different Dining Experience: Buckners Family Restaurant and Music Hall is certainly an unusual dining experience, for they combine great southern cooking with gospel singing (Thursday, Friday and Saturday evenings).

The buffet meal (served at round communal tables with lazy susan food trays in the center) gives a choice of two entrees each day and is all inclusive. A typical day might include southern fried chicken, BBQ pork or beef, mashed potatoes, stewed tomatoes, cream corn, black-eyed peas —followed with peach cobbler for dessert.

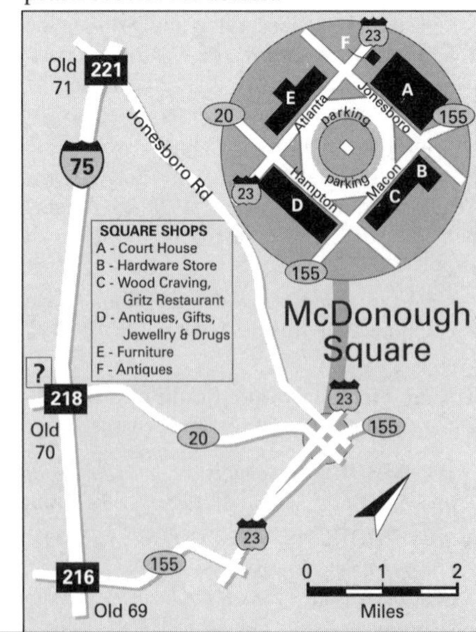

Insider Tip
Golf Heaven - The Inn at Eagle's Landing

We have a real treat for those of you who love to occasionally pamper yourselves with luxury, and it includes if you wish, a round of golf on one of the finest private courses in Georgia.

The management of the lovely gated Inn at Eagle's Landing (just south of Atlanta) has offered readers of *Along Interstate-75* a special weekend price which includes a large deluxe room with executive amenities, afternoon wine & hors d'oeuvres reception in the Tee Lounge, late night cookies & a hot beverage beside the brick fireplace in the sumptuous mahogany and leather living room and an excellent continental breakfast overlooking a world class golfcourse. Of course, you also have the use of their fully equipped fitness room and two swimming pools. An in-house spa and the private dining room in the golf Clubhouse are also available to you.

Now, the golf course is a world-class championship course designed by the acclaimed Tom Fazio and home to one of the LPGA championships. Here's a sample - hole 8, 207 yard, par 3 - "beautiful and treacherous, considered one of the most difficult par 3's in Georgia. Elevated tee to a long, narrow and rolling green menaced by a creek on the left."

Non-golfers might enjoy the clay and hard tennis courts, or simply sitting out on one of the Inn's balconies or perhaps the patio beside the goldfish pool, enjoying magazines or a novel and delighting in the fresh air of the surrounding woods.

If you would like to take advantage of this offer which is $100 per night (a 40% discount from the regular rates), please give Director of Sales John Couey a call at 770-389-3118; make sure you mention *Along Interstate-75*. Should you wish to arrange a round of golf, mention this to John and he will explain the various green fee options open to you. This very generous offer expires on October 31, 2001.

Although, reservations are preferred to avoid disappointment, the staff will do their best to accommodate you if you arrive without previous arrangements. Just press the bell at the gate and again, make sure you mention you are a reader of this book.

To reach the Inn, take exit 224 (Eagle Landing Parkway) and drive east for 1 mile, turn right just after the Publix plaza onto Country Club Drive. The gates to the Inn at Eagle's Landing are a short distance down the road on the left.

After your meal, wander around the tables and make new friends, for owners Glen and David Buckner encourage that type of informal, down-south atmosphere.

Buckners is closed on Monday and Tuesday. On other days they open from 11:30-8:00 pm. Please note that there can be line-ups on Saturday evening.

GA Exit 198-High Falls State Park: Less than two miles east of I-75 is a pretty place to pause—perhaps for a picnic beside the 100 foot waterfall—the High Falls State Park. Incidentally, an excellent overnight stop for RVers.

GA Exit 186-Juliette-Whistle Stop Cafe (see page 131; map on page 61).

Southern Grace, Juliette - I must mention my very special place here . . . the two rocking chairs on Betty's front porch or the two rockers down in the wine cellar where it is cooler. It's wonderful to sit here and chat with Betty and her son, Dean. Ask Dean about

FORSYTH - *for John Forsyth (1780-1841) who was Governor of Georgia in 1827 and Secretary of State between 1834-41, under Presidents Jackson and Van Buren.*

MACON - *after Nathaniel Macon (1757-1837), an American Revolutionary patriot and politician.*

ECHECONNEE CREEK - *from Creek Indian, "place where deer are trapped."*

Insider Tip
Falls View Restaurant

Visitors from the Magnolia State and local folk agree, *"this is the best catfish restaurant this side of the Mississippi."* Located across the road from High Falls State Park, it's tucked back in a wooded setting, with a real fireplace to provide comfort on the cooler days.

The menu offers many seafood items as well as steaks, chicken and hamburgers . . . the prices are very reasonable. Service is provided by owner Tommy Wilson, the Wilson family and their staff. Say "hello" to Tommy for me and tell him I sent you.

To find the Falls View Restaurant, take exit 198 (old 65) and drive 1.4 miles east towards High Falls Park. Watch for the restaurant parking area on your right, after passing Exxon.

Hours: Tue-Thurs, 4pm-9pm; Fri-Sat, 4pm-10pm. ☎ 912-994-6050

local history–he's very knowledgeable. Notice the clock behind the counter. Betty keeps "River Time" because she doesn't like to change it in the spring or fall . . . *"and the nearby Ocmulgee River keeps the same time year round."*

Mile 180-Macon Welcome Center (see map on page 196) "BJ" : I cannot go by here without stopping to say "hello" to that wonderful Southern lady, BJ, and her warm associates on the staff of the Macon Welcome Center. They are now in their brand new Center building, which I hear is going to be decorated shortly with the attractive Macon *"Song & Soul of the South"* theme.

BJ and I go back a few years (well . . . I do; she doesn't!). She has tried to teach me to pronounce "kudzu" in the Southern manner . . . but with my English accent getting in the way, I think she has given up!

Do try and visit Macon - it's a fine place. See my special report on page 132.

GA I-475 Exit 15-Bolingbroke: Virtually everybody heading south on the I-475 Macon Bypass misses Bolingbroke. This tiny village of antique, craft shops and a tea room lies just seconds off of I-475 east of exit 15. See Insider Tip—"Sweet Sue's Tea Room"—on page 132 for hours and other information.

GA Exit 155-Ironwoods Family Golf Center: Can't wait to get to Florida to swing a club, or perhaps you need a little practice without your southern golfing partners knowing? Here is everything you could wish for - automated driving range - putting practice green and even a practice sandtrap (although I know you'll not need this!).

The automated range is fascinating. At the Pro counter, you buy an electronic card for a predetermined number of balls, go up to one of the two tier driving range stages, insert your card in the control unit and drive away. There's no need to stoop, a new ball automatically arrives on your tee as soon as you have driven the previous one - you can even automatically adjust the height of your tee.

The ball costs vary but average about 8 cents per ball. For instance, you can buy a card with 56 balls for $5.

Money Saving Tip

$$$$$$$$$$$$ SAVE $$$$$$$$$$$$

If planning to spend the night in Macon, tell BJ (or other staff at the Macon Welcome Center), and let them make arrangements for you. Tell them what your budget is–they can often arrange much better rates (assuming availability) than you could by yourself.

Insider Tip
Grits Cafe

Several readers have raved about this unusual restaurant, for here you can dine in an early 1900s setting, under real gas lights (Fall & Winter only).

Regardless of its name, most of the items on the menu - crab, lamb, steak, etc - are not based on grits. Terri and gourmet Chef Wayne Wetendorf will ensure you have a fine meal and enjoyable experience.

Take exit 186 and drive straight ahead for 1 mile. The Grits Cafe will be on your left, on the "Square" at 17 W. Johnson St, across from the Forsyth Courthouse. Hours-Lunch: M-Sa, 11-2; Dinner: M-Th: 5-9: F-Sa: 5-10: Closed Sun. ☎ 912-994-8325

Special Report

Whistle Stop Cafe & Fried Green Tomatoes

Do you remember enjoying the wonderful movie, *"Fried Green Tomatoes?"* If you did, then you might like to visit the tiny village used as a backdrop for the film. And yes, the *Whistle Stop Cafe* really exists . . . the movie company left long ago but the spirit of Whistle Stop lives on in the warmth and charm of Juliette's people. *Whistle Stop Cafe* owner Robert Williams, Betty Clements and her son, Dean, of the *Southern Grace* country collectibles shop & Habersham Wines, Donna & Larry Pierce of McCrackin St. Sweets . . . and the many other fine people of Juliette are just as friendly and heart-warming as the folk in the movie.

The center of activity is the *Whistle Stop Cafe* (yes–they do serve fried green tomatoes as well as other Southern delicacies). The best time to visit is breakfast when all the local folk are coming and going, although .lunch can be fairly active too. Despite the success of the film which brought worldwide fame to Juliette, the town folk are determined to maintain this spirit and not let it become another "plastic" commercial tourist attraction.

Across the street, Betty not only runs the *Southern Grace* and two other stores next door, but also a wine and tasting room down the cellar steps. Here you can sample Georgia's *Habersham Estate* wines such as , Cherokee Rose, Belle Blush, Granny's Arbor, Scarlett, Peach Treat . . . then there is *Miz Magnolia* and *Treehouse Antiques* (Ruth and Idgie's house in the movie), and so on up Juliette's main McCrackin Street until you reach the Firehall (see map on page 61). The twelve or so shops have varying hours but you should find them all open between 11-4 p.m.

Thirsty? Try Grandma Huber's wonderfully sweet and thirst quenching - "lemonade made right!" at McCrackin Street Sweets, just beside the Fire Hall. A photograph of Grandma (just inside the door as you enter) ensures that "all the makins' are right." Also try the cream fudge.

In today's hectic pace, a sidetrip to Juliette is a much needed break to recharge the soul—it's a short trip to another time and age and I heartily recommend it. Jessica Tandy's parting line in the movie mentions the Whistle Stop Cafe . . . *"It was never more than a little knockabout place but when I look back on it . . . it's funny how a tiny place like this brought so many people together."* Thanks to all the wonderful folk of Juliette, it still does.

Juliette, Georgia is 9.3 miles (11.2 minutes) east of I-75 at exit 186 (see map on page 61).

The facility is completed with a family miniature golf course, a pro shop, restaurant and games room.

Ironwoods is easy to find - from exit 155, travel east ½ mile, turn right at Skippers Rd, drive south ½ mile. It's on your right.

GA Exit 149-The Generation Gap: "Free Attraction - Old Car Emporium and Antique Mall" is what the sign says and I must admit I found the booths and displays inside, fascinating. Apart from being an excellent, clean (the restrooms are a delight) 35 booth antique mall, the focus of The Generation Gap is the sale of classic cars . . . and you are invited to wander around and enjoy them as if in a car museum. Inside the front door is a San Francisco Cable Car from the famed Market Street run. When we were there, nine other classic vehicles were awaiting proud new owners. As the owner of a 1951 MG TD in original showroom condition, I can appreciate the loving work which has gone into restoring these vehicles.

Owners Traci Stubbs and Bill Bonbrake obviously have a passion for antiques and classic cars: their "showroom" is a "must stop" for anybody else so inclined.

The Generation Gap is on the east side of I-75. Drive east ¼ mile until you see Peachtree Parkway, turn left onto this road which then curves back toward I-75 to run parallel to it. Look for the green Antique Mall and Auto Museum sign on your left. Hrs: M-Sat, 9-7; Sun, Noon-6. ☎ 912-956-2678

GA Exit 146-Museum of Aviation: A CGM-13 Martin Mace guided missile on the

Macon - the Song & Soul of the South

Special Report

Without a doubt, Macon is the *"Song & Soul of the South"* and yet so many travelers intent on getting to Florida, pass it by on I-475. Why not arrange to spend a night there. Located on the banks of the Ocmulgee River, it is full of history and things to do. Use the map on page 196 to orientate yourself. You'll find reasonably priced motels and inns at exits 171 & 169; many have discount coupons in the free motel books (see saving tips on pages 70 & 130).

The easiest way to travel downtown is to take I-75, exit 165. At this exit, you join interstate-16 traveling east towards Savannah. Leave I-16 in 2 miles at exit 2 (MLK Blvd). This will take you across the river and into the quiet and spacious downtown area of Macon.

Drive straight across Walnut St - the Tubman African-American Museum is on your right - and as you round the curve, my favorite of all the museums - the Georgia Music Hall of Fame - is on your left. Take care here because MLK Blvd goes off to the right at the intersection of Mulberry St. Stay in the left lane and bear left onto Cherry St Plaza, which becomes 5th Street in a few blocks.

At the intersection of Cherry St and Cherry St Plaza, the Sports Hall of Fame is on your right and immediately on your left is the imposing Terminal Station Visitor's Center. I suggest you park here (free parking to east of building) and pick up Macon brochures and maps, including a downtown restaurant map. The Center's hours are M-F, 9a-5:30p; Sa, 9a-5p. ☎ 912-743-3401.

For a short visit, I highly recommend you reserve a seat on the excellent Sidney's Tour of historic Macon. The costumed guide is superb and will give you an excellent overview of the city. You'll see major sites such as Sidney Lanier's (Georgia's foremost poet) cottage, Hay House, Cannonball House, Tubman African American Museum . . . all in an air-conditioned bus. Tours: 10am & 2pm daily except Sunday, ☎ 912-743-3401

If you enjoy ancient history, don't miss the Ocmulgee (pronounced: oak-mul-gee, like the "g" in "geese") National Monument Indian village park (dated back to 9,000BC), visited by Hernando de Soto in 1540. ☎ 912-752-8257

Insider Tip
Sweet Sue's . . . a Soda Fountain Experience

I tuned the radio to my favorite "oldies" station, WAYS 99.1FM in Macon, and settled back to the swinging cadence of that old Dinah Shore standard, *"gonna take a sentimental journey."* Little did I know that in a few minutes I would be taking my own sentimental journey by stepping back in time, into the "Norman Rockwell" interior of Sweet Sue's Tea Room, at Bolingbroke, Exit 15 on the I-475 Macon Bypass.

This is the perfect lunch stop. Not only is the food fresh and tasty but owners Beverly and Jim Mickle have made the soda fountain of old, a "house speciality." Jim is the resident *"fizzician"* and can whip up old fashioned delicacies such as lemon-lime, strawberry or cherry phosphates, fountain specialities such as coke and root beer floats, banana splits and traditional sundaes in a minute. But I've got ahead of myself—back to lunch!

You must try the home-made daily soup. You don't have to ask what it is (unless there are some things you just cannot eat), I know you'll enjoy it; subtle tastes of herbs and spices make this a wonderful taste experience. I followed this with a fresh garden salad and a bacon, lettuce and tomato sandwich on a croissant.

For the mid-afternoon crowd, Sweet Sue's serves either a Southern Afternoon (finger sandwiches, cheese wafers, nut bread & lemon curd tarts) or Lord Bolingbroke (cucumber sandwiches, scones, clotted cream, jam, lemon curd, shortbread) Tea Tray. Sweet Sue's is open Mon-Sat 11-4, with tea trays served between 2 - 4pm. If you decide to visit, say "hi" to Bev and Jim for me. They're a delightful couple.

south eastern corner of this exit highlights the fact that nearby Warner Robins is a USAF town. It is also home to the Museum of Aviation. With over 85 aircraft on display (and growing), it is the second largest Air Force museums in the USA.

The best part is that you can get close. In fact a number of the larger aircraft are parked outside and you can walk right up and around them. The collection covers all the years from the 40's, but is not dated. For instance, you can get within touching distance of an SR-71 Lockheed "Blackbird" and F-15A McDonnell-Douglas "Eagle." Although 34 years old, the SR-71 remains one of the fastest and highest flying aircraft (that we are told about!). It can fly 15 miles above the earth's surface at 2200mph, enough speed to cross the USA from coast to coast in one hour – awesome!

SR-71 "Blackbird"

The museum is 10.7 miles east of I-75 (driving time, 18 mins). Go east of I-75 at exit 146 and follow the signs to Warner Robins and the Museum - it's well marked. Admission to the museum is free; theater $2. Hrs: 10-5pm, daily: ☎ 912-926-6870

Insider Tip
Angelina's Garden Cafe

Angelina's is an attractive Italian restaurant, beside the Quality Inn at Exit 136 in Perry.

We stopped here for lunch and enjoyed hot soft rolls coated with cheese and sitting in a butter & garlic sauce, followed by a generous helping of an all-you-can-eat Italian salad.

Prices are reasonable; service friendly and with soft mandolin music in background, the ambiance is perfect. One note of warning though, you've got to (both) be garlic lovers - it is used liberally in the food preparation.

Look for Angelina's green awning as you drive west of I-75 - Maitre d' Jimmy Swiger will ensure you have a happy visit. Hrs-lunch: M-F, 11:30-2; dinner: M-Thur, 5-9:30; Fri-Sat, 5-10 ☎ 912-987-9494

GA Exit 135-Visitor Center: To the east of I-75 at this exit is an excellent Visitor Center for anybody spending time in this "Peach Festival" area. It is well stocked with maps and brochures, and friendly advice. M-Sat, 8:30-5. ☎ 912-988-8000.

You will also find the Georgia National Fairgrounds at this exit.

GA Mile 130-Hernando de Soto: At Tennessee mile 42, I explained how in 1539, Don Hernando de Soto, the Spanish explorer led his army of 600 men on a journey of exploration of the North American continent. As he moved northward through Georgia, his journal for March, 1540, records how he marched from Montezuma (about 15 miles west of I-75 mile marker 125), crossed Beaver Creek and arrived at an Indian village at Perry where he observed the women spinning silk from the fibers of mulberry trees. His army would have crossed the terrain of the modern I-75 around mile marker 130. Several days later, the army moved on towards modern Macon and crossed the "Great River"–the Ocmulgee.

GA Mile 133-an Epiphyte: Now we are south of Macon, the large sprawling industrial concerns of northern Georgia have disappeared. The stands of conifers in the sawmill pinelands and trees draped with Hanging Moss give a much more relaxed, laid back appearance to the roadside. To me, Hanging (or Spanish) Moss (Tillandsia Usneoides) is always the guarantee that you are beyond the most southern snowline. It is a peculiar plant, not a moss and not a parasite as many people believe. It is in fact an Epiphyte–a plant that does not grow in soil but clings to another plant or tree for support and lives on the air surrounding it.

GA Exit 127-Henderson Village: Barely one mile west of this exit is a fascinating alternative to the interstate motel - an 18 acre village of deluxe overnight lodging and fine dining complemented with formal gardens, fountains and a 3,500 acre hunting preserve (game shooting and wild boar hunting). Definitely not for the budget minded traveler, but perhaps the ultimate stopover for that special occasion. A fine way to celebrate a birthday or anniversary while on the road to or from Florida.

But let's talk about the restaurant . . . it's housed in the beautifully renovated Langston House (1838), decorated throughout with original antiques and divided into small intimate dining rooms. Renowned chef, Garry Kensley has been attracted from Europe where he earned the *"Restaurant of the Year"* award for two years in a row, as well as many other European accolades, including a gold medal for his bread.

The menu items change from day to day and might include such delicacies as honey and lime barbequed salmon filet or southern fried crabcakes; grilled swordfish with a creamy crab sauce or chicken with a lemon thyme and ginger mousse – the menu for the day is bound to be mouth-watering!

Incidentally, prices are quite reasonable with a two course lunch for under $12 or a three course dinner for under $28.

And now to the lodgings. Henderson Village is an assembly of old historical buildings from the area–local homes and tenant farmer cottages, all completely renovated and decorated in the finest fashion for a deluxe stay. Winding brick paths meander through the Village, moon lights in the trees and old fashioned gaslamps light the way during the evening.

I was really taken by the tiny square of six inward facing cottages. As you cross the verandah and enter the door of each, you immediately notice the wonderful aromas of cedar and bayberry.

All the old architectural features that make these buildings so endearing, have been kept. Some have wooden shingle roofs while others have tin, but all are completely modernized and weather-tight. Modern heating and air-conditioning is hidden away where you cannot see it. Beautiful old brick hearths (retrofitted with safe but very authentic looking gas fireplaces with glowing embers) along with functional antique furnishing ensure warm and comfortable interiors.

All buildings have at least one porch; some with porch swings, others with rocking chairs or wicker furniture. There is something special about sitting out and quietly rocking the time away, on a warm southern night.

Mornings are special too. I can just imagine staying at the Holland House (early 1900's) having breakfast on the porch served by the Langston House restaurant's silver tray room service. No expense has been spared in Henderson Village to evoke the atmosphere of a peaceful but bygone era.

General Manager Stuart Macpherson has kindly invited readers of *"Along I-75"* to take a break from the highway, to come and enjoy the grounds, relax and wander around this unusual community and perhaps, sample some of the delicacies at the Langston House. He has special lower rates for my readers.

And if that isn't a warm enough welcome, then wait until you meet Angus, Stuart's friendly Golden Retriever. Angus loves the Henderson Village guests and will willingly show you around if you wish. Stuart makes sure that Angus is always wearing a freshly ironed neckerchief each day - he is fun and very well behaved. Angus is a special friend; we hate it when we have to say *'bye*.

For a fully pampered and relaxing stay–away from the pressures of I-75 drive, Henderson Village has much to offer .

Restaurant hours are 7:00-9:30am for breakfast, 11:30-2:30pm for lunch and 6:00-9:00pm for dinner–Tues to Sat. Sunday brunch is from 11:30-2:30pm. For further information and reservations, phone toll free 888-615-9722, or 912-988-8696.

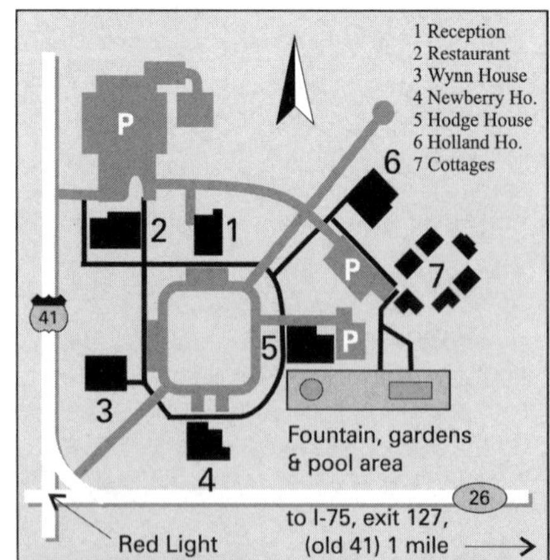

PERRY - *"We have met the enemy and they are ours" was the naval signal sent by Oliver Hazard Perry (1785-1819) after he beat the British fleet on Lake Erie during the War of 1812. Perry is named in honor of the war hero.*

Insider Tip
A Visit to Ellis Bros.—a family Pecan Farm

"We're Nuts . . . " is the slogan of Ellis Bros. Pecans, and if there's anything you want to know about this local nut, Elliott Ellis is your man. Just east of I-75 the Ellis family has been farming pecans for three generations. In fact, the pecan trees in the grove just to the north of their retail store were planted in 1918, just after the end of WWI. Pecans are harvested by air blasting them onto strips of ground kept clear of cover between the trees. Elliott took me for a tour of his shelling plant behind the store and I was surprised at the control he must maintain over the humidity. Quality control is very high in their process and he is very proud of the fact that in 1992 they won the Georgia Family Business of the Year Award.

In the store, you will find just about every type of coated pecan—coffee, honey, ginger and chocolate, to name a few. Irene Ellis has an in-house candy kitchen with four marble topped tables to supply this need. The Ellis' also grow and make the wonderful Mayhaw Jelly (see below) as well as sell almonds, cashews, peanuts—and five varieties of pecan incl. Stuart, Desirables, Papershells (Schley/Sumner).

To reach Ellis Brothers, take exit 109 east (old 36 - route 215) and take first left (Tippetville Rd) at the Ellis Bros. sign. Ellis Bros. is well marked, about ¾ mile on left. The store is open 7 days a week, 8am-7 pm; phone: 1-800-635-0616 or 912-268-9041.

GA Mile 115-Peanuts and Irrigation: The fields just to the west (right) of you here are peanuts. The large wheeled girder units are used for irrigation.

GA Exit 109-Georgia Cotton Museum: The history of Georgia and the history of cotton have long been closely associated, and now a new museum ½ mile west of I-75 tells all with some very attractive exhibits. Did you know for instance, that the first Georgia cotton was brought from England in 1733 and planted in the Trustees Garden in Savannah; or that Georgia was the first state to produce cotton commercially?

For more than 250 years, "King Cotton" as it was known played a major role in building the economy of Georgia—until it was almost wiped out by the Boll Weevil. But it has come back and today is a major Southern crop again.

The museum is more than just a collection of artifacts. It includes information about the slave issues. It demonstrates the tools used, including Eli Whitney's Cotton Gin (for removing seeds from the white cotton lint) and a weighing beam used to weigh cotton bales. Samples of cotton in various stages of growth are available so you can actually touch and feel Georgia's number one cash crop.

If you've ever wondered about cotton then you're in the right place. Museum custodian Margaret Hegidio knows cotton and loves to chat with her visitors.

Dooly County, Georgia is one of America's major cotton crop areas. As one early traveler to the area wrote, *"when you visit Dooly County in the Fall, you can enjoy the "snow of the South. The cotton is so thick and so white that it appears to be snow on the ground with bright green trees framing the view."*

Museum hours are: Mon-Sat, 9:15-4pm, closed Sunday. ☎ 912-268-2045

GA Mile 103-Pecan Orchard: If you didn't have time to stop and visit the Ellis Bros. at exit 109, here's your chance to see a grove of pecan trees beside the interstate. Look for an orchard of trees on the right (west) side as you travel south, between exits 104 and 102.

GA Exit 101-Cordele: Worthy of note–we are just passing the first palm tree north of Florida. It's to the right (west) of the freeway, halfway between I-75 and the Holiday Inn property.

If you take this exit to buy gas, you might be surprised to see a Titan Rocket. The Titan was an early rocket and contained many unusual and exotic materials–these have led to corrosion. In the late 1980's, engineers came from the air force desert "bone yard" at Davis- Monthan AFB, Arizona, to renovate this particular Titan.

GA Exit 101-Cotton: Just south of this exit on your right is a cotton field which may or may not be of interest depending upon whether you are a Northerner or Southerner. If you missed the Cotton Museum at exit 109, here's your chance to see a cotton field from your car.

Keep an eye on this field—green for most of the summer, it bursts into a field of thigh high cotton balls in mid-August.

GA Exit 101-Vidalia Onions: Vidalia onions are well known all over the world for their unusual sweetness and flavor. In fact they are so sweet they have a higher sugar (fructose) content than Coca-Cola. They are also tearless!

Why do they taste so different, after all they are an ordinary variety of onion? It's due to the local sandy, low-sulphur soil in the Vidalia area (85 miles to the east along Rt280 of this exit). This was discovered by accident in 1931 when local resident Mose Coleman planted some onion seeds from Texas, and could not believe the sweet, juicy results. They were so good that they could be eaten raw.

Today, Vidalia onions have grown into a multi-million dollar business. Just like fine wines, only onions grown in certain areas are allowed to bear the Vidalia logo. The best time to buy is in the spring. Genuine Vidalia onions may be found at many local supermarkets, but you might wish to shop at the Georgia State Farmers Market (exit 237) if driving north.

GA Exit 78-Jefferson Davis Capture Site: May 10, 1865–pity poor Jefferson Davis, ex-President of the Southern Confederacy. He had been on the run from his capital, Richmond in Virginia, since early April and had a $100,000 reward of gold on his head. With his wife, an escort of 20 men and $300,000 in gold and silver from the Confederate Treasury, the party decided to camp in a pine grove beside a stream.

Imagine their feelings when they were woken up in the early morning by two Federal cavalries shooting at each other and everything else in sight. A soldier aimed at Jefferson but his wife offered herself as a target instead. Jefferson surrendered quickly to save her life.

A colonel rode up and said, *"Well, old Jeff, we've got you at last."*

This action took place at the Jefferson Davis Park—15.6 miles (18.5 mins.) east of I-75 at this exit.

By the way, the Confederate Treasury disappeared and has never been found—but no digging is allowed in the park!

Sixteen miles may seem like a long way to drive for such a destination, but if you are a true Civil War buff, you will not regret it. For me, as I stand looking down the grass slope across the location of the Davis' encampment, and along the track of the old 1800's road with its log bridge across the creek, it is still possible to imagine the poignancy of the event 135 years ago as two groups of Union soldiers fought each other for the honor of capturing the scared group. Hrs: Tu-Sat, 9-5; Sun, 2-5:30, closed Monday. Museum admission: Adult/Child. $5/$2; ☎ 912-831-2335

GA Exit 63B-Georgia Agrirama: Two minutes west on Eighth Street, country life in the late 19th century is the focus of this living outdoor museum. The town's guides wear costumes from the period and practice the trades and skills which would have been required to live in this rural community.

Insider Tip
Pit Stop Bar-B-Que

By now, you probably know that my two loves when I travel are history and eating. In fact, some people have even subtitled this book, *"Dave eats his way to Florida!"* But I don't want you to miss this excellent Pit BBQ restaurant just to west of I-75 at exit 63B. After your meal, go and visit the smoke house at the back.

Hours: Tue-Thur, 11am-9pm; Fri-Sat, 11am-10pm; Sun, 11am-9pm; closed Mondays ☎ 912-387-0888

CORDELE - *after Cordelia Hawkins, daughter of Colonel Samuel Hawkins, president of the Savannah, Americus and Montgomery railroad.*

As you wander around the town, visit the steam-powered sawmill, water wheel grist mill, smokehouse, sugar cane mill and turpentine still, among other rural industries. All in all, a pleasant way to spend an hour or so, off the road.

Agrirama is open year round: Mon-Sat, 9-5. Admission: Adult/Senior/Child (4-16) \$8/\$6/\$4 ☎ 912-386-3344.

GA Exit 62-Tifton's Historical Buildings: Follow route 82 for 1 ½ miles east to Tifton's downtown area, where you will find twelve city blocks featuring old homes from the late 1800's to 1930's nestled among shade tree streets. See the neon lighted theater, historic churches and over 30 shops in restored buildings. Seventy percent of these buildings are on the National Register of Historic Buildings. This is ideal for a walking tour—an opportunity to get out of your car and stretch.

GA Exit 62 -Adcock Pecans: Just to the east of this exit is Adcock Pecans, the huge retail outlet of the Sunbelt Plantation company. I'm always impressed with the huge array of jellies, jams, relish, salsa, sauces and spreads on display. At the last count, there were 88 different varieties in stock, from pumpkin butter to guava jelly to chow chow-you never know what you'll find.

GA Exit 55-Magnolia Plantation: I can never seem to get my car (or my wife, Kathy) past the Magnolia Plantation without a mandatory stop to check out their large stock of local relishes, honey, jellies, jams or marmalades. We always come away with at least a few jars of Vidalia Onion relish.

GA Mile 43-Florida Welcome Centers?: By now you will have noticed roadside signs advertising Florida Welcome Centers at exits ahead. Some even advertise free or discounted Disney tickets. But common sense indicates that of course, an official Florida Welcome Center would be located in Florida, not Georgia - and it certainly would be on the southbound side of the road!

There is only one I-75 official Florida Welcome Center and that is at Florida mile-marker 471, or 44 miles ahead (see page 139).

Most of these other places are Orlando area condominium sales outlets. They want you to commit to spending several hours visiting their condo site in Florida after which, you are taken into a "gift" room where you can choose from items which often include discounted WDW tickets.

They will actually book a time and date at the "Welcome Center" and some even require a small deposit to ensure you turn up.

GA Mile 32-Spanish Moss: Another stand of Hanging (Spanish) Moss to the right of I-75 reminds me of the *"Legend of the Spanish Moss"* -

There's an old, old legend that's whispered by Southern folk,
About the lacy moss that garlands the great oak;
A lovely princess and her love, upon their wedding day,
Were struck-down by a savage foe amidst a bitter fray;
United in death they're buried, so the legends go
'Neath an oak's strong, friendly arms, protected from their foe;
There as was the custom, they cut the bride's hair with love
And hung its shining blackness on the spreading oak above;
Untouched, undisturbed it hung there, for all the world to see
And with the years, the locks turned gray, and spread from tree to tree.

Georgia Mile 27-Disney Radio: Turn on your car radio to 910 AM. You will know that you're close to the Florida Border because Disney is in the air.

Money Saving Tip

Before you leave Georgia, fill up with gas - even if you only need a 1/4 of a tank. Georgia still has the cheapest gasoline in the USA.

TIFTON - *for Nelson Tift (1810-91), an officer in the Confederate Army and U.S. representative from 1868-69.*

ADEL - *by homesick eastern settlers, second and third syllables from their home town name, "Philadelphia."*

GA Exit 16-Valdosta's Barber-House: Four miles and 10 minutes east of I-75 (turn left onto Ashley St.), you will find an old Southern home of the neo-classical style. Built in 1915 for one of the early bottlers and promoters of Coca-Cola, its marble steps, six Ionic columns and wide portico symbolize the Georgian Mansion of the deep south.

Today, it houses the County's Chamber of Commerce, and is open Mon-Fri, 9-5 pm. ☎ 912-247-8100.

GA Exit 13-Wild Adventures: West of I-75, 4.4 miles along the Old Clyattville Road, lions, tigers, a black bear, giraffes, alligators, zebras, 70 monkeys and other exotic animals await you at —Wild Adventures.

Owner Kent Buescher is fulfilling a dream by creating a theme park from his 170 acre property, originally a horse farm. Lions, tigers, a black bear and many more live animals provide realism to Wild Adventures safari rides.

But that's not all. For the young in heart, more than 20 amusement rides such as Pharaoh's Fury, Chaos, Tiger Terry and the Giant Wheel are guaranteed to provide an adrenaline rush. Slower rides such as bumper boats, swings and the Carousel keep the younger (and perhaps, senior) family members happy.

Finally, Wild Adventures is proud of its "Big Name" shows and concerts. Stars such as Chubby Checker and Waylon Jennings provide outstanding entertainment for the enjoyment of the lawn chair and "blanket-on-the-grass" audience. I suggest you phone ahead to find out who is "on stage" the day you plan to visit.

All of this comes with a one price admission for everything–animals, safari, amusements and shows. The all inclusive admission is: adults/snrs/children: $14.95/$12.95/$10.95;

Hours vary greatly according to season and day of the week. Phone for information. ☎ 912-559-1330.

Georgia Mile 2-Northbound Welcome Center: If you are traveling north from Florida don't forget to stop and say hello to the friendly staff at the Georgia Welcome Center. Manager Cathy and her staff of Barbara, Carole, Leigh and Missy are all very knowledgeable and will help make your journey north through Georgia, as interesting as possible.

Incidentally, please note that the restrooms close at 11:30 at night, and re-open at 7:30a.m.

Florida Mile 472-the Florida Border: You are now at the Florida border and the exit numbering system is about to change. Florida is the last of the I-75 states to use the "old" numbering system where exits are numbered sequentially from the southern end of the interstate.

But times are a-changing. Recently, Florida DOT announced plans to convert to the recommended "mile post" numbering system.

The change will commence on I-75 (and I-4) in July, 2002, with a planned completion date of June, 2003. Wisely, FDOT plans to leave the old numbers up for several years; they will be removed from I-75 (and I-4) signage between July, 2004 and June, 2005.

FL Mile 471-Florida Welcome Center: Don't forget to stop here for your free orange or grapefruit juice. Say hello to Patrick and

Insider Tip
Country Kitchen Quail

By now if you've been following my *Insider Tips*, you probably think that I have eaten my way to Florida! I admit, I do enjoy food so . . . when somebody mentions a restaurant in South Georgia that serves BBQ quail, I just have to go to check it out.

Now, a word of explanation . . . Quail is a wild game bird common in this area. In the Fall, hunting groups will often gather for organized shooting parties.

The Farmhouse Restaurant at Lake Park (Exit 5 - old 2) specializes in quail, although they buy their birds from a game farm, so they are not wild. They are always on the menu either grilled or deep fried, but from time to time, the Farmhouse also has an outdoor BBQ special.

If you are passing through this area, you might want to try this local delicacy.

VALDOSTA - *From "Val d'Aosta" meaning "vale of beauty." This was the name of the northern Italian estate of Governor George Troup.*

Money Saving Tip

Pickup your free copies of the green Traveler Discount Guide (old EIG) and the red Market America motel coupon books at the Florida Welcome Center (mile 471). Coupons in these books can save you as much as 45% off of regular motel rates.

Don't forget the special free Florida restaurant coupon books, either.

If the Welcome Center is closed, you'll find copies of all these books in the newspaper boxes, outside the vending machine area.

his staff of knowledgeable counter people. The information section is very well stocked, and open from 8am to 5pm, daily.

Incidentally, if you arrive here after hours, go over to the newspaper boxes outside the vending machine area-you will find a good supply of the free Florida motel and restaurant guides, and coupon books here.

Well . . . here we are. This is where I must now leave you and head back north. I've enjoyed riding along with you, sharing adventures and stories along the way.

Drive safely and enjoy your time in the sun.

FLORIDA - *named by explorer Ponce de Leon, who discovered the land on Easter Sunday (Pascua Florida), in 1512. Florida means "flowering" in Spanish. Ponce de Leon's original Florida claim encompassed all the land up to and including Newfoundland in Canada.*

$$$ Savings at Disney

Here are two essential books for those heading to Walt Disney World (WDW) in Orlando. Both books have won substantial awards because they do their jobs amazingly well! The first will save you so much time - almost a day if you had planned to stay for four. The second provides a wonderful keepsake of your visit which you will treasure for many years to come:

Bob Sehlinger's ***"Unofficial Guide to Walt Disney World,"*** is updated and published annually. Jammed full of so many good "behind the scene" time and money saving tips for your Magic Kingdom, EPCOT and MGM Studio visits, that it has quickly become an insider's "must have" for a Disney visit. It tells you where the best and worst food bargains are — which rides to go on first to maximize your attendance time — how to plan your day against the normal crowd patterns and avoid excessive line-ups . . . where and when to make special feature reservations . . . and much more. We have used it and fully endorse the author's statement that it provides the *"information necessary to tour WDW with the greatest efficiency and economy, and with the least hassle and standing in line."*

"Passporter Walt Disney World," by Watson & Marx is also updated and published annually to ensure you get the most up-to-date information. The ***Passporter WDW*** is quite a unique idea - it's five books in one - a travel guide, planner, organizer, journal and keepsake. Any family visiting WDW these days is going to spend a lot of money and the ***Passporter WDW*** protects that investment by providing an organized way to keep your memories, so you may treasure them later. It will payback its cost many times over in the years to come.

Most book stores have both of them in stock. If not, the store staff can easily ordered them for you(see details in *"Sources & Resources"* - page 197); both are also available on the internet at amazon.com. These books are not available within Walt Disney World so you should buy them before you leave home. To make the best use of them—study them—learn the best and the worst—plan your strategy—choose your tactics—and then comfortably "do" four days of Disney World in three . . . comfortable $$$ savings throughout the theme parks, as well!

NOTES:

Interstate-75 Lodging

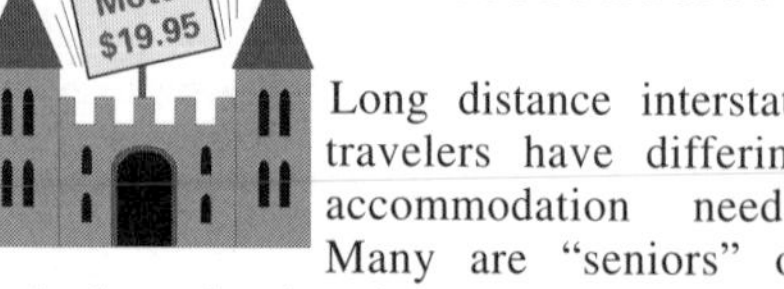

Long distance interstate travelers have differing accommodation needs. Many are "seniors" or retired people who might want to know if the "property" (this is what a lodging facility is called in the hospitality industry) has an attached restaurant (to save walking) or has facilities for the disabled. Some like to drive their car right to the unit door, others prefer the security of limited access properties where a door card is needed to open external doors. Young families on a budget vacation will try and save as much money as possible and will probably look at the "budget" chains such as Motel6, Red Roof or Super8. Still others might wish to relax in a swimming pool after a long day's drive, or just flop down and watch a movie on TV.

Whatever your needs, I-75 lodgings can cater to all tastes. Once you've determined your "style," the next thing is to locate a suitable property at your planned night's destination—and then get down to the fun task of obtaining the best rate for your stay.

Getting the Best Rates: I-75 has been around a long time and it has a lodging surplus along its length - except in March. Because of this, rates can be very competitive and some times, price wars will be apparent in their discounts. ***Hint:*** *use those free motel coupon books which are issued every 3 months (see page 70), to get the very best "price war" rates.*

When you go into a motel, do you ask them if they have a room for a night, and just leave it at that? If you do, you may not be getting the best rates available. After all, purchasing a motel room is no different to purchasing any other consumer product or service. It pays to shop around a bit, even if you do your shopping in the same motel—here's what I mean.

Rates within a property vary depending upon where a room is located (lower vs. upper floor; poolside or facing a highway, etc.) and how it is equipped. Generally, lower priced rooms are on upper levels, face the freeway and have one bed.

Once you've established room location, be aware that most properties usually have different rates for the same room; here's the structure: **a) the "rack" rate**—the standard rate which you get if you just ask for a room for the night, **b) the "senior" or "affiliation" rate** (at many motels the staff are not allowed to ask if you are a member of the AARP or AAA, you must volunteer this information), **c) the "discount coupon" rate**—this is often the easiest to get since discount coupon books are available everywhere (see page 138). But a motel might designate only a few rooms as "coupon" rooms, so it's on a "first come-first served" basis, **d) the "commercial" or "corporate" rate**—everybody, retired or not, can probably produce a business card or has worked for a corporation, use it, and **e) the "preferred" rate**—often the best, not always available.

When I approach the front desk of my selected motel, I first establish what the rack rate is for a standard 2P/1B (2 people/1 bed) room—this becomes my "yardstick"—and then ask for their best discounted, preferred rate. If not available, we then compare "corporate rates" to "discount coupon" and "affiliation" rates. We <u>never</u> pay the "rack rate."

Traveling with Pets: Traveling with pets can be difficult due to rules imposed by some motels - these run from "no pet" facilities to "pets welcome" on a no-charge or a pet deposit/surcharge (usually $2-$5) basis.

When questioned, we found that motel operators are not necessarily biased against pets; damage in not an issue (after all they do not surcharge for children who can cause more wear and tear on facilities than pets). They do have problems however with allergic reactions caused to guests staying in rooms previously occupied by pets, and must perform special cleaning to minimize this (it has been found that proteins in pet saliva can be a particular allergy problem).

As pet owners ourselves, we understand that pets are very much part of the family. We recommend the AAA book *"Traveling with Your Pet"* (see page 198).

To help pet owners, on our maps we have marked **in blue any motel which accepts pets** (they may require deposit or surcharge); exits with veterinarians & animal clinics are identified by this green "V" symbol.

V

I-75 Lodging Alternatives

The following sections describe some alternatives to motel lodging. Bed & Breakfasting is an adult alternative, but if you are traveling with children, "lodging in the rough" may be a fun family experience.

Bed and Breakfast: For many years, Kathy and I have enjoyed Bed & Breakfast (B&B) lodgings on our travels through North America. Some of the wonderful places we have stayed include an herb farm in Pennsylvania, a lobster fisherman in Massachusetts, a haunted house in Salem with a secret door in the wall of our room, a High Court Judge in Connecticut and in a beautiful "ginger-bread" Victorian home in Cape May, NJ. Each stay has been a valuable and unforgettably pleasant experience.

B&B may not be for everybody though. The homes may be a few extra miles off the freeway (but the drive is usually worth it); you usually have to reserve ahead and provide a deposit (charge card number) when you phone; prices tend to be higher than motel lodging; often bathrooms are shared between guests and since you are staying in someone's home, the restrictions you would experience staying with friends, normal apply.

Also, you must enjoy people - after all, the best part of the B&B experience is the interesting people (hosts or other guests) you meet. Spending time with them, chatting about common interests, learning about the local countryside or other parts of the country - is one of the most enjoyable things about B&B. If this is <u>not</u> for you, then stick to hotel or motel lodging.

Hidden in the countryside bordering the Interstate-75, are some unique B&B opportunities. Here are some recommended by our readers:

OHIO

Toledo - The Geer House B&B
Restored 19th century Victorian in historic area; Dbl: $45-75, ☎ 419-242-7065

Miamisburg - English Manor B&B,
12 room Tudor style south of Dayton; Dbl: $65-95, ☎ 937-866-2288

KENTUCKY

Georgetown - Pineapple Inn,
Four room Victorian Home, on Natl. Reg. Dbl: $65-95, ☎ 502-868-5453

Lexington - Riverside Cottage,
Overlooking the Kentucky River, wildlife Dbl: $95-125, ☎ 859-229-4988

Berea - Shady Lane B&B,
Secluded Colonial bird lovers paradise, Dbl: $55-70, ☎ 859-986-9851

TENNESSEE

Knoxville - Maplehurst Inn B&B,
European style Inn, historic district, Dbl: $79-199, ☎ 865-523-7773

GEORGIA

Marietta - Stanley House B&B,
Historic, early Victorian, AAA rated 3 diamond, Dbl: $100 ☎ 770-426-1881

Atlanta - Sugar Magnolia B&B,
Restored Queen Anne Victorian home, Dbl: $80-125, ☎ 404-222-0226

Byron - Memories Inn,
Restored southern home, five rooms Dbl: $75-95, ☎ 912-956-2498

Lodgings "In the Wilderness": Want to try something different while you travel? Then consider a cabin in the woods. These are available at some state parks, or at private facilities such as KOA Kampgrounds. Here's the information:

KOA Kamping Kabins - KOA facilities are primarily for RVer's, but many of them have log cabins for rent as well. Some are available year round, others are closed in the winter; many have heaters and/or air conditioning. All have lockable doors, electricity and can sleep 4-6 people in 1 or 2 room layouts. But it is really upscale camping - there are no cooking facilities except for a BBQ or fireplace pit outside - and washing/shower facilities are in a communal building. KOA supply the beds and mattresses; you supply bed linen (or sleeping bags) and towels. To learn more, pick-up a Directory at any KOA campground.

State Park Lodging - Many state parks have lodging facilities. Here are two to try:

Norris State Park, TN (see page 100) - this lovely Tennessee park nestled in the woods above Norris Lake has 10 deluxe and 19 "rustic" cabins for rent. The "deluxe" have

3 bedrooms, full furnished kitchens, TV, wood fireplaces, bath w/shower, heating & a/c - all linens are supplied. The "rustics" are similar, but smaller. The units normally rent by the week, but give the Park a call, they may have one or two available for one night stays. Reservations: 423-426-7461; toll free 800-543-9335.

Red Top State Park Lodge, GA (exit 285) - just 2 miles east of I-75 lies Red Top State Park with its famous lodge and restaurant. Surrounded with hiking trails winding through the pine trees, with glimpses of Allatoona Lake in the distance, the Lodge is a wonderful place to refresh the spirit.

Please drive slowly in the park - it's full of wild deer. Kathy and I stayed here in June (rooms are often available for Sun. to Thurs. nights, especially Fall & Winter) and at twilight, we spent an enjoyable hour just sitting quietly near the Lodge's front entrance watching families of deer grazing just south of the parking lot.

At time of writing the Lodge has just come under new management, so we have not reviewed it in this year's book.

The lodge's 33 rooms cost (Dbl) $69-79 depending upon day-of-the-week and season. They are often booked but with a little advance planning you could enjoy a peaceful night in the woods on the way to Florida. Reservations: 1-800-573-9658 or 770-975-0055.

Symbol	Motel	Toll Free No.
BHost	Budget Host	800-283-4678
Baymnt	Baymont Inns	800-301-0200
BestW	Best Western	800-528-1234
C/Ctry	Cross Country Inn	800-621-1429
ClbHse	Clubhouse	800-258-2466
Comfrt	Comfort Inn	800-228-5150
CtySte	Country Inns/Suites	800-456-4000
CrtYrd	Courtyard-Marriot	800-321-2211
CtHrth	Country Hearth	888-443-2784
Days	Days Inn	800-329-7466
Econo	Econo Lodge	800-553-2666
Evoy	Envoy Inn	800-227-7378
ExtStAm	Ext. Stay America	800-646-8000
Fairfld	Fairfield Inn	800-228-2800
H/Inn	Holiday Inn	800-465-4329
Hmptn	Hampton Inn	800-426-7866
HoJo	Howard Johnston	800-446-4656
Jamsn	Jameson Inns	800-526-3766
Knght	Knights Inn	800-843-5644
LaQnt	La Quinta	800-687-6667
MHost	Master Host Inn	800-633-3434
MicroT	Microtel	888-771-7171
Motel6	Motel6	800-466-8356
Mstrs	Masters Inn	800-633-3434
Pssprt	Passport Inn	800-251-1962
QltyInn	Quality Inn	800-228-5151
Ramda	Ramada Inn	800-272-6232
RedC	Red Carpet Inn	800-251-1962
RedRf	Red Roof Inns	800-733-7663
Rodwy	Rodeway Inn	800-228-2000
Rsdnts	Residence Inn	800-331-3131
Scot	Scottish Inn	800-251-1962
Shony	Shoney's Inn	800-222-2222
Signtr	Signature Inn	800-822-5252
Sleep	Sleep Inn	800-753-3746
Supr8	Super 8 Motels	800-800-8000
TravL	Travelodge	800-578-7878
Wingate	Wingate Inns	800-228-1000

Toll Free Reservation Phone Numbers

The chart to the left provides the 800 or 888 (no charge) reservation phone numbers for all of the popular motel chains along the Interstate. The advantage of the 800/888 number system is its convenience, but be aware of two drawbacks.

First, you cannot always use a discount coupon from a free coupon books (Exit Information Guide or Market America) when making an 800 number reservation - some will accept them but most don't. Most motels will however honor a senior (AARP) or AAA discount if you mention it to them over the phone. Make sure you mention it again when you check in.

Secondly, you may be told that the motel of your choice is full. If so, a phone call to the specific motel (get the number from the 800/888 operator) can often find you a room since most motels do not allocate all their rooms to their 800 number reservation system. They usually keep rooms available for last minute local needs.

Useful Information

Local Knowledge - if you have it you will always feel comfortable when you travel. Throughout this book, you will find all sorts of local I-75 knowledge. Here is some more to help you:

"Where can I get local traffic information on my car radio?"

"Is it OK to use my radar detector in Georgia?"

"Should I gas up in Kentucky or Tennessee?

"There's a tornado alert for Preble County - is that close?"

These are the sort of questions answered in this section. In fact, if you can think of other questions which need answers, let me know (see page 203), and I will try and oblige in a future edition:

INTERSTATE-75 RADIO GUIDE

Area (Southbound Sequence)	Best Traffic	Misc Music	Soft Top Pop	Oldies	Pops	Special Programming: Public	Classical	All Talk	News	Sports	Rock	Jazz	C&W	Religion
Detroit, MI	950AM	97.9	95.1	104.3	95.5	101.9	1310AM	760AM	950AM	1130AM	101.1	98.7	99.5	103.5
Toledo, OH	1370AM	105.5	101.5	93.5	92.5	91.3	91.3	1370AM	1370AM	1370AM	104.7	97.3	99.9	90.3
Lima, OH	102.1	103.3	98.1	107.5	92.1	90.7	90.7	1150AM	1150AM	102.1	98.9	90.7	102.1	97.7
Dayton, OH	980AM	107.7	99.9	95.3	92.9	90.9	94.1	1290AM	1410AM	1220AM	104.7	94.9	99.1	93.3
Cincinnati, OH	700AM	100.9	98.5	103.5	101.9	91.7	90.9	550AM	700AM	1230AM	92.5	88.5	105.1	93.3
Lexington, KY	590AM	104.9	99.3	105.1	94.5	88.9	88.9	590AM	590AM	1300AM	96.9	91.3	92.9	1380AM
London, KY	1400AM	92.3	103.9	--	107.3	90.9	--	1330AM	1330AM	--	100.3	--	103.9	103.1
Jellico, TN	1540AM	107.3	--	102.1	102.7	91.9	--	--	--	--	103.5	--	99.5	710AM
Knoxville, TN	990AM	98.7	97.5	102.1	95.7	91.9	91.9	670AM	850AM	990AM	103.5	98.7	107.7	96.3
Chattanooga, TN	107.9	97.3	92.3	107.9	--	88.1	90.5	102.3	1150AM	102.3	96.5	88.1	98.1	102.7
Dalton, GA	98.9	104.5	92.3	107.9	106.7	88.1	90.5	105.5	850AM	--	106.5	93.7	107.1	1530AM
Atlanta, GA	750AM	96.7	94.9	97.1	94.1	90.1	90.1	640AM	640AM	790AM	96.1	104.1	101.5	1080AM
Macon, GA	99.1	107.9	107.9	99.1	93.7	89.7	89.7	940AM	940AM	940AM	106.3	97.9	95.9	900AM
Cordele, GA	--	104.5	96.3	98.3	98.7	88.1	88.1	--	--	--	102.9	--	104.9	101.3
Valdosta, GA	910AM	93.9	96.7	1450AM	92.1	91.7	91.7	910AM	910AM	--	104.1	--	92.9	101.1

Note: all radio station frequencies are FM, unless otherwise noted.

Radio Along I-75

To the left is a selection of major radio stations which can be received at various locations on the interstate.

There are many other excellent stations which can also be received in each location, but this chart represents a good cross section of the more powerful ones, subdivided by the type of music or programs provided (in the radio business, known as the station's "format").

Where a station's format falls under several categories, we have listed it under the best "fit" for its main programming, or in those areas with only a few stations, under each of the appropriate categories.

Several comments follow:

Best Traffic - covers at least the morning & afternoon rush hours, with unscheduled traffic reports when trouble conditions occur. See also page 193 for the traffic "personalities" of the major urban areas.

Misc. Music - we have used the most popular local radio station here, either *"Middle-of-the-Road,"* or *"Urban Contemporary."*

Public - stations which are members of either the American Public Radio (APR) or National Public Radio (NPR) systems. Their programming tends to be classical or jazz.

All Talk - we've attempted to provide those stations which offer the popular nationally syndicated shows, such as Doctor Laura Schlessinger or Rush Limbaugh.

News - the station which is most likely to provide local breaking news content.

Religion - there are many choices on both the FM & AM bands. I have chosen the strongest local station, with religious music content.

Clear Channel AM Radio Stations

Radio signals travel much farther in the dark. To avoid interference, the FCC requires that many stations reduce their night "distance" coverage by performing an antenna "pattern" change at dusk. By agreement, some powerful (50,000 watt) AM radio stations provide nighttime extended coverage and their signals can cover as much as 750 miles after dark. This is useful to know if you are on a night drive since you can stay with the same station for many miles. Here are the powerful I-75 "Clear Channel" AM stations:

MI-WJR-760, **OH**-WLW-700, **KY**-WHAS-840, **TN**-WSM-650, **GA**-WSB-750

Police & Weather Phone Numbers; State Gas Taxes

Need to phone the State Police for advice, or do you want to check road conditions to your destination? Listed below are the phone numbers you will need. Use the police number if there is no phone service for road conditions. Please note that the state police numbers shown in the third column are for information only - ***use 911 in an emergency.***

State	Emergency No. Cellular/Reg.Phone	State Police Information	Weather & Road Conditions	Department of Transport Web Sites	Gas Taxes
Michigan	**911**	517-332-2521	800-337-1334 press 2	www.mdot.state.mi.us	19
Ohio	**911**	614-466-2660	(M-F) 614-466-7170	www.dot.state.oh.us	22
Kentucky	**911/800-222-5555**	502-277-2221	800-459-7623	www.kytc.state.ky.us	16
Tennessee	***THP/615-741-2060**	615-741-3181	800-858-6349	www.state.tn.us/transport/	20
Georgia	***GSP/404-624-6077**	404-657-9300	404-635-6800	www.dot.state.ga.us	7
Florida	***FHP or 911**	850-488-8676	800-475-0044	www.dot.state.fl.us	13

Cell Phone Users - 1-800-525-5555 will connected you immediately to the nearest state police dept.

Note 1 - there are no state phone numbers for construction. All Departments of Transport now have comprehensive reports on their Internet sites.

Note 2 - "Gas Taxes" are the cents each state collects at the pump from each gallon of gas pumped into your car. A Federal tax of 18.4 cents is also added to the "per gallon" price.

I-75 Traffic Laws

Traffic laws change from state to state. Here is a useful chart which summarizes some of the laws in the six states crossed by I-75.

STATE	* Minimum Driver Age	Right Turn on Red	Child Restraints	** Mandatory Seat Belt Usage	Radar Detectors
Michigan	18 (16)	Yes	under 4 years old	DR, FP + RP under 16	OK to use
Ohio	18 (16)	Yes	under 4 yrs or 40 lbs.	DR + FP	OK (exc. commercial)
Kentucky	16 (16)	Yes	under 41" tall	DR + all passengers	OK to use
Tennessee	16 (15)	Yes	under 4 years old	DR, FP + RP 4-12	OK (exc. commercial)
Georgia	18 (15)	Yes	under 4 years old	DR + FP	OK to use
Florida	16 (15)	Yes	under 5 years old	DR + FP + RP 5-16	OK to use

Notes * Figure in ( ) is minimum age for driver with conditional of probationary license

** DR = driver, FP = front seat passenger, RP = rear seat passenger

The Triple "A" for Help

One of the best investments you can make for a long distance drive is to join the AAA (or CAA in Canada). It doesn't cost a lot of money (annual membership fees vary from area to area but it is usually in the $50-70 range) and yet the peace of mind provided when traveling long distances is well worth the money. Should you experience a breakdown or other car emergency, they are only a national toll free 1-800 phone call away:

USA - 1-800-AAA-HELP Canada - 1-800-CAA-HELP

TORNADO WATCH

Special note: this section is not intended to alarm you - but to make sure that you are well informed and prepared should a Tornado emergency occur in your area, while traveling the I-75.

It was six o'clock in the evening. Kathy and I had checked into a motel in Miamisburg, Ohio, and were beginning to relax after a long day on the interstate . . . when we were interrupted by a loud banging on the door - *"Everybody to the basement - three tornados have been spotted in Preble County!"*

Where was Preble County? We had no idea. What should we do to minimize our risk? We didn't know. After the emergency was over, I decided to find the answers to these very important questions & share them with you.

Over the last few years we have certainly gained a heightened awareness of tornados

Tornado Safety Tips

If in a sturdy building:

- go to the lowest level, interior room in the building.
- take a flashlight and battery radio.
- stay away from large rooms, such as auditoriums, ballrooms,etc.
- avoid rooms with windows & outside walls.
- hide under something that is sturdy.
- cover yourself with blankets, pillows, coats (to protect from flying debris).
- protect your neck and head areas. Put on a crash or safety helmet, if you have one.

If in a weak structure or RV home:

- get out and seek a sturdy shelter.

If caught in the open:

- lay flat in a ditch face down (1st choice) or behind a sturdy hedge. Cover head with arms.

If in a car:

- get out, and if close to an overpass, crawl up into the "V" created by the concrete banks and the road above.
- If no overpass, find a ditch, hedge or sturdy structure.

Insider Tip
Your Personal Alert System

After this summer's experience, we do not travel the interstate without a Weather Radio with a weather alert feature - in the car or in our motel room. The best type to buy is a unit which receives all 7 of the National Weather Service (NWS) frequencies. It must be capable of receiving the NWS "Alert" signal - this will ensure that your unit will sound an alarm when a NWS alert signal is received. It should also have a built-in backup battery, for emergency use.

Your home unit should be capable of receiving the special *Specific Area Message Encoding (SAME) signal* - this signal (also known as the FIPS code) enables your unit to give you alerts for your specific area, rather than on a broad county basis. The 6 digit FIPS code for your area is obtained by phoning the toll-free NWS number 1-888-697-7263, and following the automated instructions. The resulting code is punched into your radio unit.

I have tested two Radio Shack units on the road, they meet all the requirements and work very well. During our test run, we actually experienced one Tornado alert, 2 flood warnings and 2 severe thunderstorm alerts. The portable unit we use in our car as we travel is Radio Shack model 12-246 (cost $29.99); it runs on 3 AAA batteries. The second unit has the *SAME* feature. It is Radio Shack 12-250 and costs $69.99. We use this as our "plug in" unit in our motel at night. If staying for any time in one location,I obtain the FIPS code for the area. The unit has a 9v backup battery and displays alert messages on a screen as well as indicating the alert severity. *(Canadians, please note: the SAME unit uses codes which only apply to land areas in the USA; it is only available in Radio Shack stores in the U.S.).*

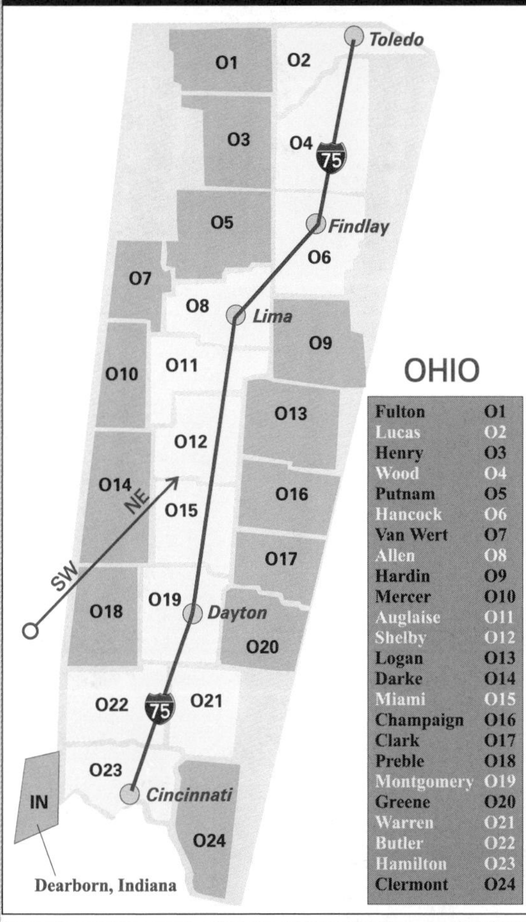

(or twisters, as they are often known), as we travel. In April, 1996, a section of the small town of Berea was devastated by a tornado which swept across the I-75 and slammed into the "old town" area. And of course, we are all aware of the terrible damage done by a tornado which touched down just east of Kissimmee, Florida during the 1997/8 winter. Here are some tornado facts:

Tornados tend to travel from the south-west quadrant of a storm system to the north east. Never try to outrun a tornado in your

County Maps

Tornado warnings are usually issued by county. I have shown all the **I-75 counties** (in yellow) through which you may travel, together with at least one other county either side (in green). The **southwest-northeast axis** is also shown in each case, since this tends to be the general path of tornado spawning storms.

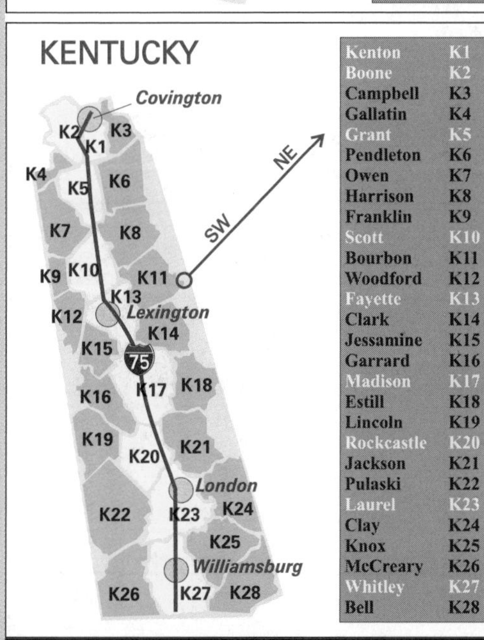

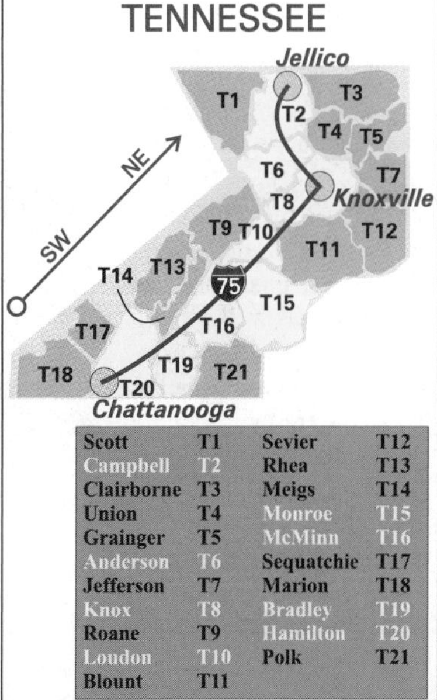

car, but if there is clear sky to your south-east, that is the direction to go.

A storm that can spawn tornados is often preceded with lightning, hail and heavy rain. They tend to happen in late afternoon, early evenings during the late-spring/early summer.

Most injuries are caused by flying debris. A tornado can come in many strengths, from one which damages light trees, branches or billboards (known as an F0) to a very rare F5 which can hurtle a wooden plank projectile at speeds up to 200 mph. Pressure differential in tornados does not play a big role in terms of damage. Forget the old wives tale about opening a window on the opposite side to the storm; experts say it makes no difference.

In terms of risk, here are tornado frequencies by state, compiled by the National Severe Storm Center in Kansas City: Texas-189 Kansas-92 Oklahoma-64 Michigan-21 Ohio-61 Kentucky-11 Tennessee-8 Georgia-19 Florida-60. I-75 is no more vulnerable to tornados than any of the other major corridor routes between the northern states and Florida. In fact, the tips in this story can be equally as well applied to your home area. I consider my home weather alert system as important as my smoke detectors or security system, and keep it running at all times.

I certainly hope you never encounter a tornado, but if you do at least you are well prepared.

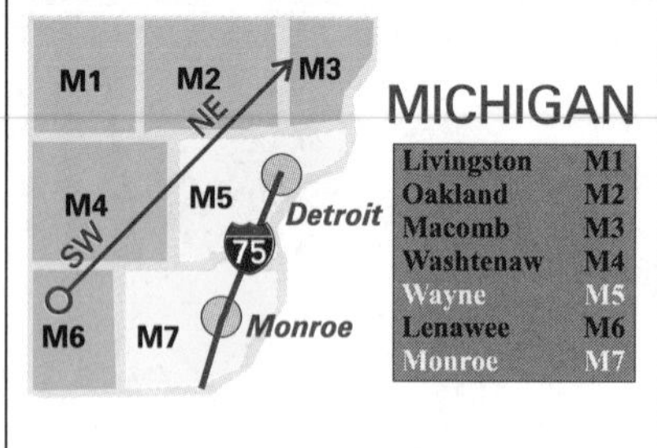

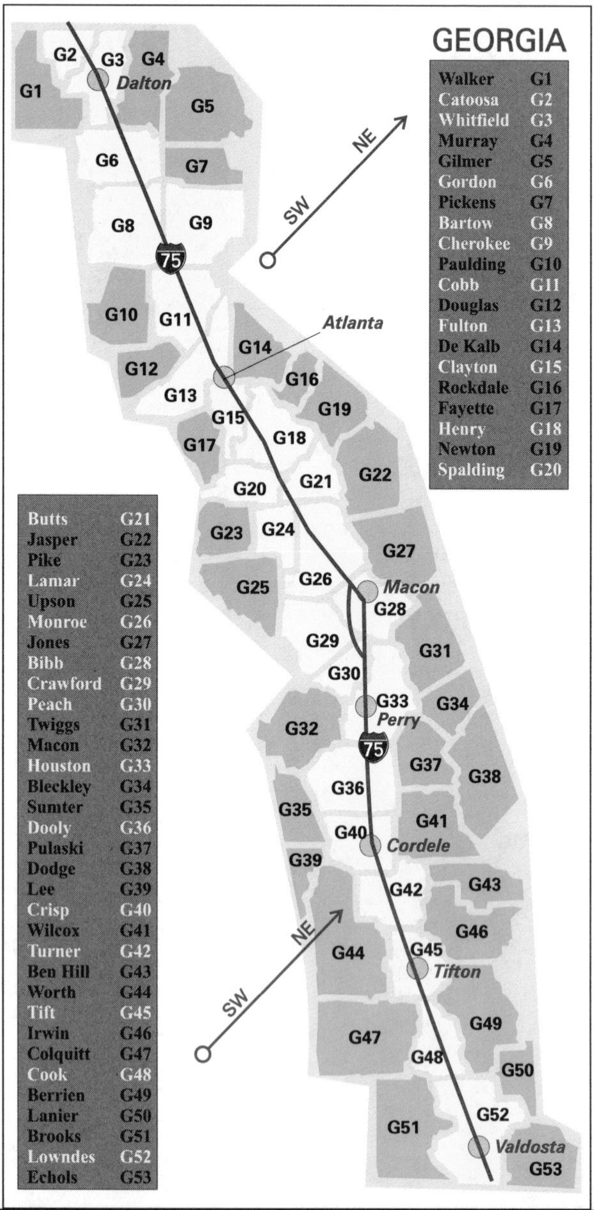

MICHIGAN
M1
M2
M3
M4
M5
M6
M7
NE
SW
Detroit
Monroe
75
Livingston M1
Oakland M2
Macomb M3
Washtenaw M4
Wayne M5
Lenawee M6
Monroe M7

GEORGIA
Dalton
Atlanta
Macon
Perry
Cordele
Tifton
Valdosta
75
NE
SW
G1 G2 G3 G4 G5 G6 G7 G8 G9 G10 G11 G12 G13 G14 G15 G16 G17 G18 G19 G20 G21 G22 G23 G24 G25 G26 G27 G28 G29 G30 G31 G32 G33 G34 G35 G36 G37 G38 G39 G40 G41 G42 G43 G44 G45 G46 G47 G48 G49 G50 G51 G52 G53
Walker G1
Catoosa G2
Whitfield G3
Murray G4
Gilmer G5
Gordon G6
Pickens G7
Bartow G8
Cherokee G9
Paulding G10
Cobb G11
Douglas G12
Fulton G13
De Kalb G14
Clayton G15
Rockdale G16
Fayette G17
Henry G18
Newton G19
Spalding G20
Butts G21
Jasper G22
Pike G23
Lamar G24
Upson G25
Monroe G26
Jones G27
Bibb G28
Crawford G29
Peach G30
Twiggs G31
Macon G32
Houston G33
Bleckley G34
Sumter G35
Dooly G36
Pulaski G37
Dodge G38
Lee G39
Crisp G40
Wilcox G41
Turner G42
Ben Hill G43
Worth G44
Tift G45
Irwin G46
Colquitt G47
Cook G48
Berrien G49
Lanier G50
Brooks G51
Lowndes G52
Echols G53

INTERSTATE-75 RV PARK & CAMPGROUND SITES

State	I-75 Exit	Direction	Campground	Phone	# of Sites	Open	Rates	Distance in Miles	Driving Directions
MI	18	W	Camp Lord Willing	734-243-2052	288	all year	$16-20/family	1	1 miles West on Nadeau Rd; follow signs to campground
OH	179	W	Fire Lake	888-879-2267	100	4/15-10/15	$18-$20/2people	2½	1½ miles W on 6; ½ m S on 25; ½ m W on Kramer Road
OH	164	E	Pleasant View	419-299-3897	300	all year	$17-19/fam.	1	¾ m E on 613; ¼ m SE on 218
OH	161	E	Shady Lake	419-423-3490	139	all year	$17/fam.	2½	½ m E on 99; 1½ m N on CR 220; ½ m W on 101
OH	145	E	Twin Lake Park	419-477-5255	100	4/15-10/15	$17-25/fam.	3/4	¼ m S on 235; ½ m E on 34
OH	110	E	KOA Wapakonata	800-562-9872	76	2/25-1/3	$25/2p	1½	¾ m E to first intersection; ¾ m N on Cemetery Rd.
OH	82	E	Poor Farmer's	937-368-2449	540	all year	$14/fam.	6¾	6 m E on 36; ¾ m S on Lost Creek Shelley Rd.
OH	14	W	Quality Inn RV Park	513-771-5252	11	all year	$25/vehicle	¼	¼ mile west on Glendale-Milford Rd
OH	10	W	Woodland Trailer	513-931-8845	20	all year	$18/2p	4¼	4 m W on Galbraith; ¼ m S on Daly
KY	166	E	KOA Cincinnati - South	800-562-9151	108	all year	$25/2p	2¼	¼ m E on 491; 2 m S on 25
KY	159	W	Dry Ridge Camper's Village	859-824-5836	70	all year	$20/vehicle	1.2	50 yds W on 22; 1 m N on Service Rd.
KY	120	E	Kentucky Horse Park S/P	800-370-6416	260	all year	unknown	1	1 m E on 1973
KY	95	E	Fort Boonesborough S/P	859-527-3131	167	all year	unknown	5.9	4 9/10m E on 627; 1m S on 338
KY	76	W	Oh Kentucky Campground	859-986-1150	120	all year	$10-12/vehicle	1/4	¼ m W on Hwy 21
KY	76	W	Walnut Meadow Campground	859-986-6180	123	all year	$10-12/2p	1/2	½m W on Hwy 21
KY	62	E	KOA Renfro Valley	800-562-2475	110	all year	$19.50-$20.50/2	1½	1½ m N on Hwy 25
KY	62	E	Renfro Valley RV Park	800-765-7464	199	3/1-12/15	$19-21/vehicle	¼	¼ mile east on Highway 25
KY	38	E	Levi Jackson Wilderness Rd S/P	606-878-8000	188	all year	unknown	4.3	2 m E on 192; 2 3/10 m S on 25
KY	29	W	KOA Corbin	800-562-8132	90	all year	$15.50-22/2p	1/2	¼ m W on 770; ¼ m S (follow signs)
KY	11	W	Williamsburg Travel Trailer Park	800-426-3267	56	all year	$10/4p	1/4	¼ m W on Hwy 92
TN	134	W	Cove Lake S/P	423-566-9701	97	all year	unknown	1	east of I-75 on Hwy 25; park entrance on left
TN	128	E	Norris Dam State Park	865-426-7461	90	all year	unknown	7	see map on page 55; 7 miles east on US441
TN	122	E	Big Ridge S/P	615-992-5523	52	all year	unknown	12	12 E on Hwy 61
TN	122	E	Fox Inn Campground	865-494-9386	98	all year	$15-20/2p	3/5	3/5 m E on Hwy 61
TN	62	W	KOA Sweetwater Valley	800-562-9224	63	all year	$19-20.50/fam.	1	¾ m W on Oakland; follow signs S
TN	49	E	Athens I-75 Campground	423-745-9199	60	all year	$17-18/2p	3/4	¾ m E on Hwy 30
TN	20	W	KOA North Cleveland	800-562-9039	87	all year	$18-20/2p	1	½ m W on County Rd; follow signs ½ m
TN	1	W	Holiday Trav-L-Park	800-693-2877	171	all year	$20.50-22.50/2p	3/4	¼ m W on Hwy 41; ½ m S on Mack Smith Rd.

INTERSTATE-75 RV PARK & CAMPGROUND SITES

State	I-75 Exit	Direction	Campground	Phone	# of Sites	Open	Rates	Distance in Miles	Driving Directions
GA	350	W	KOA Chattanooga S KOA	800-562-4167	145	all year	$20.50-23.50/2p	1/4	¼m W on Hwy 2, entrance on right
GA	315	E	KOA Calhoun	800-562-7512	87	all year	$19.95-22.95/2p	1½	1½ m E on Hwy 156
GA	296	W	KOA Cartersville	800-562-2841	117	all year	$15-19/2p	1/4	¼ m W on Cassville Rd.
GA	283	E	Allatoona Landing	800-346-7305	140	all year	$18.75-24.50/4p	2	2 miles E on Allatoona Rd
GA	278	E	Holiday Marina Harbour & CG	707-974-2575	44	all year	$15-18/2p	2¼	¾m E on Glade Rd; 1m N on Tanyard Ck.; ½ m E on Groover's
GA	269	W	KOA Atlanta N (Kennesaw)	800-562-4194	230	all year	$20-28/2p	2 1/10	1½ m W on Barrett; ½ m N on Hwy 41; 1/10 m Battlefield Pkwy
GA	222	W	KOA Atlanta S (McDonough)	800-562-6073	145	all year	$25-27/2p	1/4	¼ m W on Frontage Rd.
GA	198	W	High Falls Campground	800-428-0132	124	all year	$14/family	1/10	1/10 m W on High Falls Rd; entrance on right
GA	186	E	KOA Forsyth	800-562-8614	110	all year	$19-21/2p	3/5	1/10 m E on Juliette Rd; ½ m N on County Rd.
GA	136	E	Boland's RV Park	912-987-3371	65	all year	$16.50/2p	1/3	¼ m E on Hwy 341; 1/10 m N on Perimeter Rd.
GA	136	W	Crossroads Travel Park	912-987-3141	64	all year	$17/2p	1/10	1/10 m W on Hwy 341; entrance on left
GA	135	W	Fair Harbor RV Park	912-988-8844	150	all year	$20/vehicle	1/4	¼ m W of exit 42; entrance on right
GA	97	W	KOA Cordele	800-562-0275	73	all year	$16-22.50/2p	1/4	¼ m W on Rockhouse Rd.
GA	92	W	Southern Gates RV	912-273-6464	46	all year	$18/family	1/4	¼m W on Deep Creek Rd; entrance on right
GA	84	W	Knight's RV Park	912-567-3334	81	all year	$8.95/2people	1/10	1/10m W on Amboy Rd; entrance on right
GA	60	W	Amy's South GA RV Park	912-386-8441	86	all year	$16.50/2p	1	1m W on South Central Ave.
GA	39	W	Reed Bingham S/P	912-896-3551	46	all year	unknown	6	6m W on Hwy 37
GA	18	W	River Park	912-244-8397	62	all year	$14/2p	1/10	1/10 m W on Hwy 133
GA	5	E	Eagles Roost Campground	912-559-5192	140	all year	$17/2p	3/5	100 ft E; ½ m S on Frontage Rd

We hope that these I-75 RV Park and Campground tables help you in your travels. We recommend that you purchase a current copy of ***Woodall's Campground Directory*** (available from most bookstores and amazon.com). This comprehensive directory covers all the key parks and campgrounds state by state, across North America.

In addition, if you are not already a member, consider joining the ***Good Sam Club.*** The benefits are numerous, and include discounts at various campgrounds and on propane purchases, special RV insurance, etc. Good Sam publishes the ***Trailer Life Campground and RV Park & Services Directory,*** another excellent source of parks and campgrounds. Phone 1-800-234-3450 for membership information and services.

Both of these directories include information about RV services and suppliers (parts) -- and tourist attractions along the way.

Northbound Route

From the Florida Border to Detroit

Insider Tip for Northbound Travelers
Northbound Photographs

Driving north with the sun over your shoulder makes the roadside scenery much more interesting and acceptable for mobile in-car photography. In particular, look closely at the rock cuts in north Tennessee and south Kentucky. Early morning sun angled across cuts on the west side of the interstate and late afternoon sun lighting rock cuts on the east will reveal all sorts of interesting things such as the vertical drill holes used for the dynamite charges when the road was being built.

If using an automatic camera from inside the car, don't forget to turn off the auto focusing feature (otherwise it will tend to focus on your car window glass) and set for as high a shutter speed as possible. If you don't have a high shutter speed, then try and "lock" your camera on the subject by panning as the car moves forward.

Never pull on to the soft shoulder for your photograph - an interstate shoulder is a very dangerous place to be and should only be used for emergency stops.

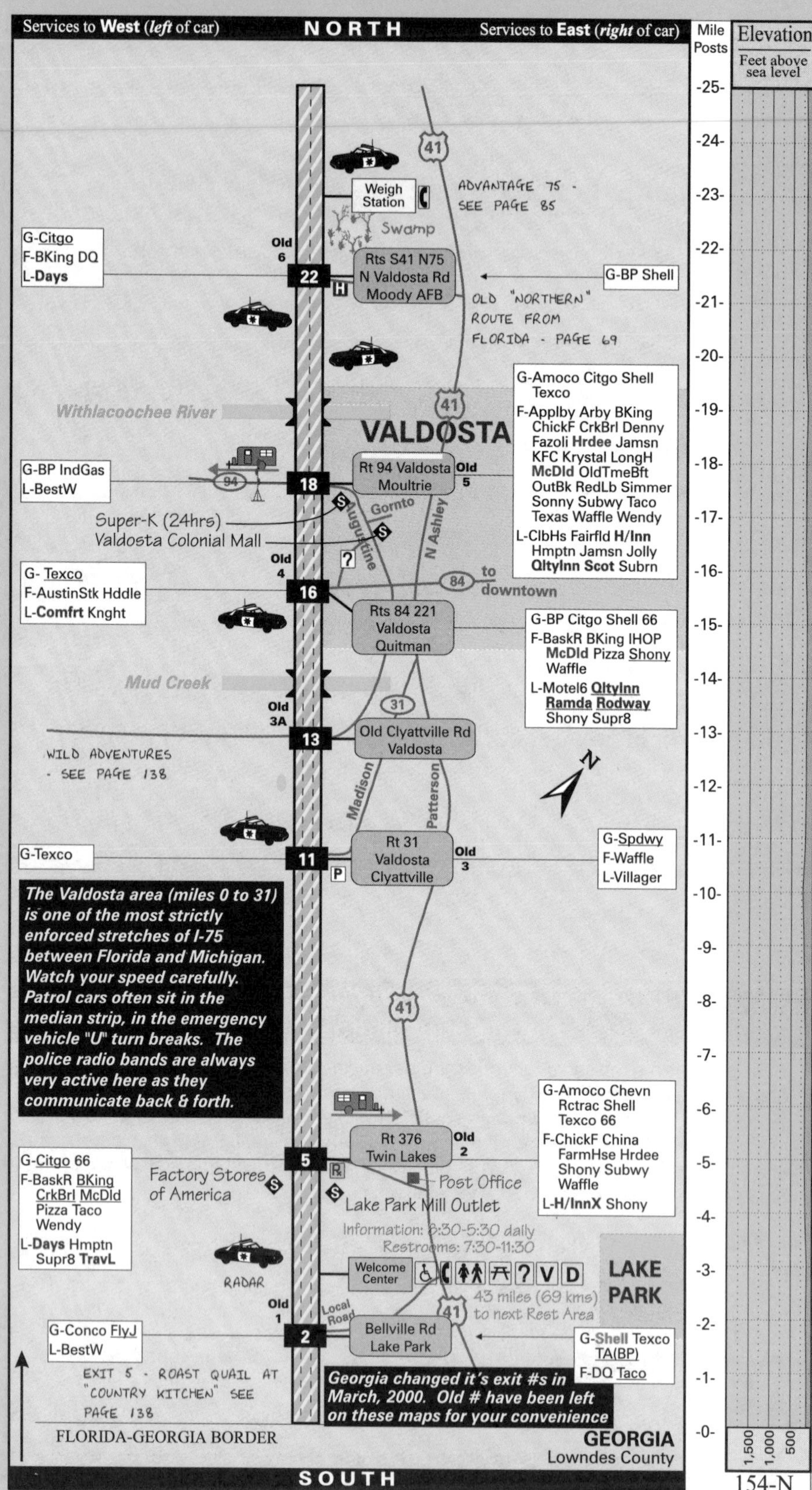

Services to West (left of car)
NORTH
Services to East (right of car)
Mile Posts
Elevation
Feet above sea level
Weigh Station
ADVANTAGE 75 - SEE PAGE 85
Swamp
G-Citgo
F-BKing DQ
L-Days
Old 6
22
Rts S41 N75
N Valdosta Rd
Moody AFB
G-BP Shell
OLD "NORTHERN" ROUTE FROM FLORIDA - PAGE 69
G-Amoco Citgo Shell Texco
F-Applby Arby BKing ChickF CrkBrl Denny Fazoli Hrdee Jamsn KFC Krystal LongH McDld OldTmeBft OutBk RedLb Simmer Sonny Subwy Taco Texas Waffle Wendy
L-ClbHs Fairfld H/Inn Hmptn Jamsn Jolly QltyInn Scot Subrn
Withlacoochee River
VALDOSTA
G-BP IndGas
L-BestW
18
Rt 94 Valdosta
Moultrie
Old 5
Super-K (24hrs)
Valdosta Colonial Mall
Gornto
Augustine
N Ashley
G- Texco
F-AustinStk Hddle
L-Comfrt Knght
Old 4
16
to downtown
Rts 84 221
Valdosta
Quitman
G-BP Citgo Shell 66
F-BaskR BKing IHOP McDld Pizza Shony Waffle
L-Motel6 QltyInn Ramda Rodway Shony Supr8
Mud Creek
Old 3A
13
Old Clyattville Rd
Valdosta
WILD ADVENTURES - SEE PAGE 138
Madison
Patterson
G-Texco
11
Rt 31
Valdosta
Clyattville
Old 3
G-Spdwy
F-Waffle
L-Villager
The Valdosta area (miles 0 to 31) is one of the most strictly enforced stretches of I-75 between Florida and Michigan. Watch your speed carefully. Patrol cars often sit in the median strip, in the emergency vehicle "U" turn breaks. The police radio bands are always very active here as they communicate back & forth.
G-Amoco Chevn Rctrac Shell Texco 66
F-ChickF China FarmHse Hrdee Shony Subwy Waffle
L-H/InnX Shony
G-Citgo 66
F-BaskR BKing CrkBrl McDld Pizza Taco Wendy
L-Days Hmptn Supr8 TravL
5
Rt 376
Twin Lakes
Old 2
Factory Stores of America
Post Office
Lake Park Mill Outlet
Information: 8:30-5:30 daily
Restrooms: 7:30-11:30
Welcome Center
RADAR
43 miles (69 kms) to next Rest Area
LAKE PARK
Old 1
Local Road
G-Conco FlyJ
L-BestW
2
Bellville Rd
Lake Park
G-Shell Texco TA(BP)
F-DQ Taco
EXIT 5 - ROAST QUAIL AT "COUNTRY KITCHEN" SEE PAGE 138
Georgia changed it's exit #s in March, 2000. Old # have been left on these maps for your convenience
FLORIDA-GEORGIA BORDER
GEORGIA
Lowndes County
SOUTH
-25- -24- -23- -22- -21- -20- -19- -18- -17- -16- -15- -14- -13- -12- -11- -10- -9- -8- -7- -6- -5- -4- -3- -2- -1- -0-
1,500 1,000 500

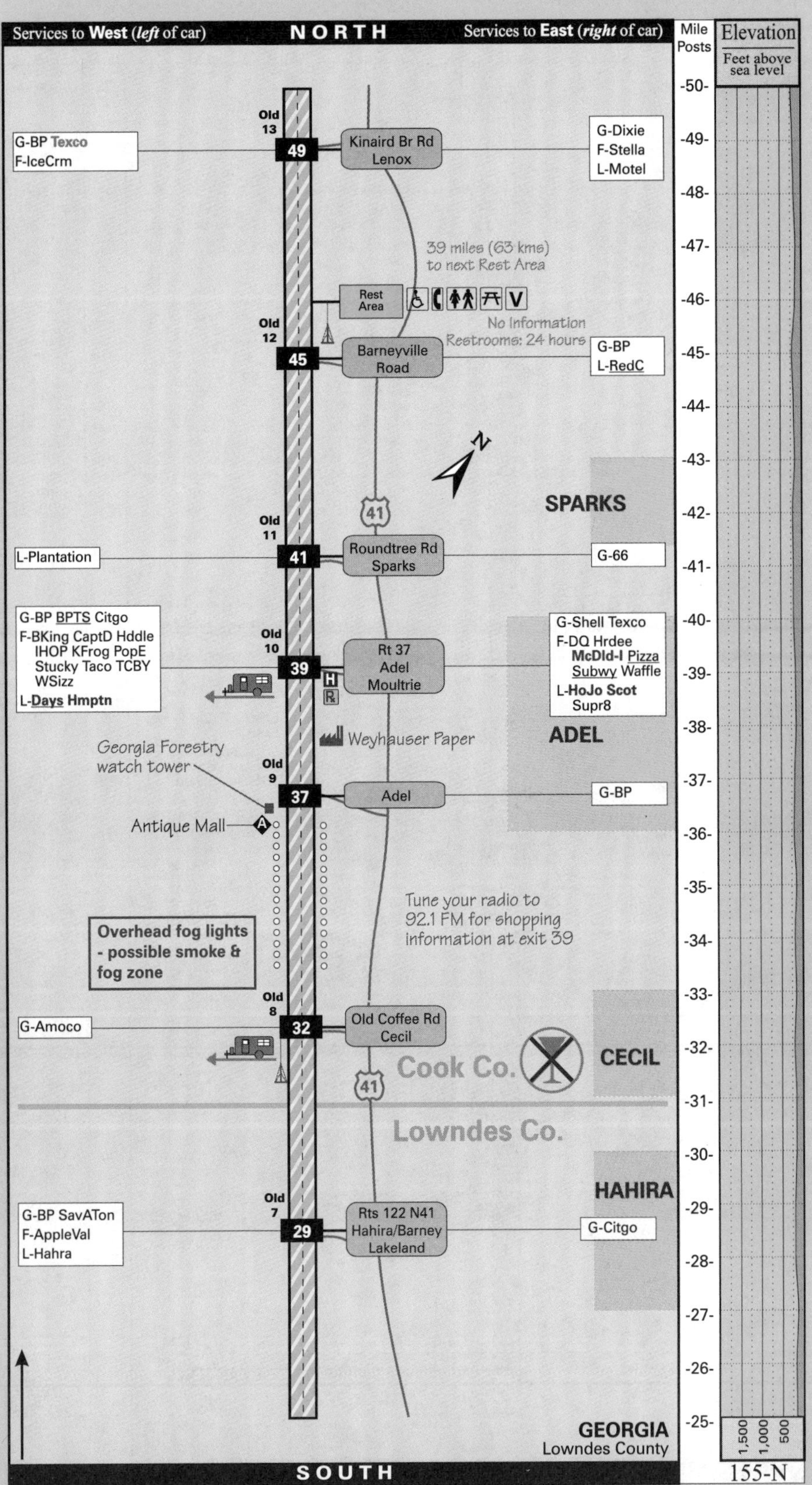

Services to West (left of car)
NORTH
Services to East (right of car)
Mile Posts
Elevation
Feet above sea level
Old 13
49
G-BP Texco
F-IceCrm
Kinaird Br Rd
Lenox
G-Dixie
F-Stella
L-Motel
39 miles (63 kms) to next Rest Area
Rest Area
V
No Information
Restrooms: 24 hours
Old 12
45
Barneyville Road
G-BP
L-RedC
N
41
SPARKS
Old 11
41
L-Plantation
Roundtree Rd
Sparks
G-66
G-BP BPTS Citgo
F-BKing CaptD Hddle IHOP KFrog PopE Stucky Taco TCBY WSizz
L-Days Hmptn
Old 10
39
H
Rt 37
Adel
Moultrie
G-Shell Texco
F-DQ Hrdee McDld-I Pizza Subwy Waffle
L-HoJo Scot Supr8
Weyhauser Paper
ADEL
Georgia Forestry watch tower
Old 9
37
Adel
G-BP
Antique Mall
A
Tune your radio to 92.1 FM for shopping information at exit 39
Overhead fog lights - possible smoke & fog zone
Old 8
32
G-Amoco
Old Coffee Rd
Cecil
Cook Co.
CECIL
41
Lowndes Co.
HAHIRA
Old 7
29
G-BP SavATon
F-AppleVal
L-Hahra
Rts 122 N41
Hahira/Barney
Lakeland
G-Citgo
-50- -49- -48- -47- -46- -45- -44- -43- -42- -41- -40- -39- -38- -37- -36- -35- -34- -33- -32- -31- -30- -29- -28- -27- -26- -25-
1,500 1,000 500
GEORGIA
Lowndes County
SOUTH

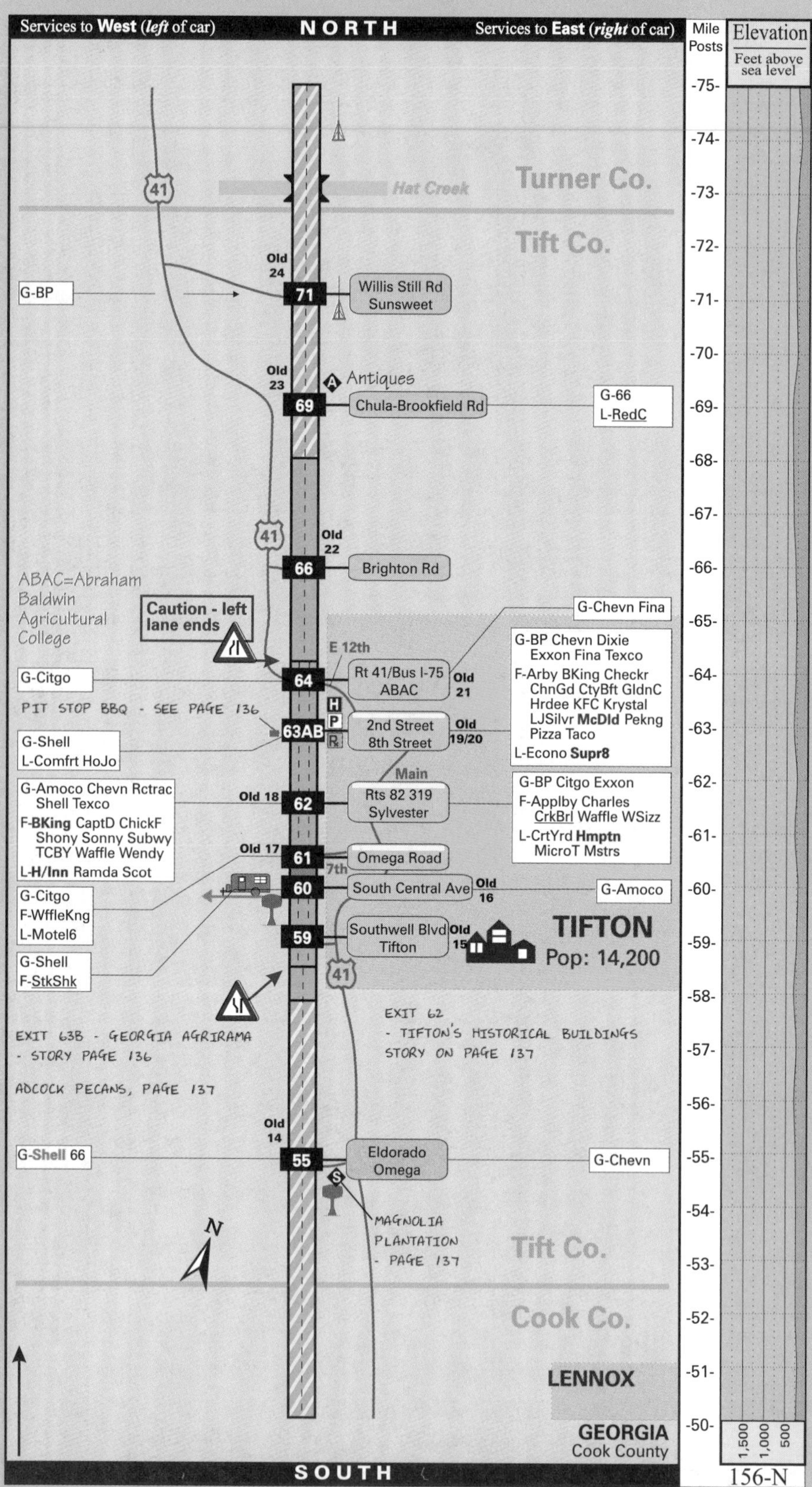
Services to West (left of car)
NORTH
Services to East (right of car)
Mile Posts
Elevation
Feet above sea level
Turner Co.
Hat Creek
Tift Co.
41
Old 24
G-BP
71
Willis Still Rd
Sunsweet
Old 23
Antiques
69
Chula-Brookfield Rd
G-66
L-RedC
41
Old 22
66
Brighton Rd
ABAC=Abraham Baldwin Agricultural College
Caution - left lane ends
G-Chevn Fina
E 12th
G-Citgo
64
Rt 41/Bus I-75
ABAC
Old 21
G-BP Chevn Dixie Exxon Fina Texco
F-Arby BKing Checkr ChnGd CtyBft GldnC Hrdee KFC Krystal LJSilvr McDld Pekng Pizza Taco
L-Econo Supr8
PIT STOP BBQ - SEE PAGE 136
G-Shell
L-Comfrt HoJo
63AB
2nd Street
8th Street
Old 19/20
Main
G-Amoco Chevn Rctrac Shell Texco
F-BKing CaptD ChickF Shony Sonny Subwy TCBY Waffle Wendy
L-H/Inn Ramda Scot
Old 18
62
Rts 82 319
Sylvester
G-BP Citgo Exxon
F-Applby Charles CrkBrl Waffle WSizz
L-CrtYrd Hmptn MicroT Mstrs
Old 17
61
Omega Road
7th
G-Citgo
F-WffleKng
L-Motel6
60
South Central Ave
Old 16
G-Amoco
59
Southwell Blvd
Tifton
Old 15
TIFTON
Pop: 14,200
G-Shell
F-StkShk
41
EXIT 63B - GEORGIA AGRIRAMA - STORY PAGE 136
ADCOCK PECANS, PAGE 137
EXIT 62 - TIFTON'S HISTORICAL BUILDINGS STORY ON PAGE 137
Old 14
G-Shell 66
55
Eldorado
Omega
G-Chevn
MAGNOLIA PLANTATION - PAGE 137
N
Tift Co.
Cook Co.
LENNOX
GEORGIA
Cook County
SOUTH
-75- -74- -73- -72- -71- -70- -69- -68- -67- -66- -65- -64- -63- -62- -61- -60- -59- -58- -57- -56- -55- -54- -53- -52- -51- -50-
1,500 1,000 500

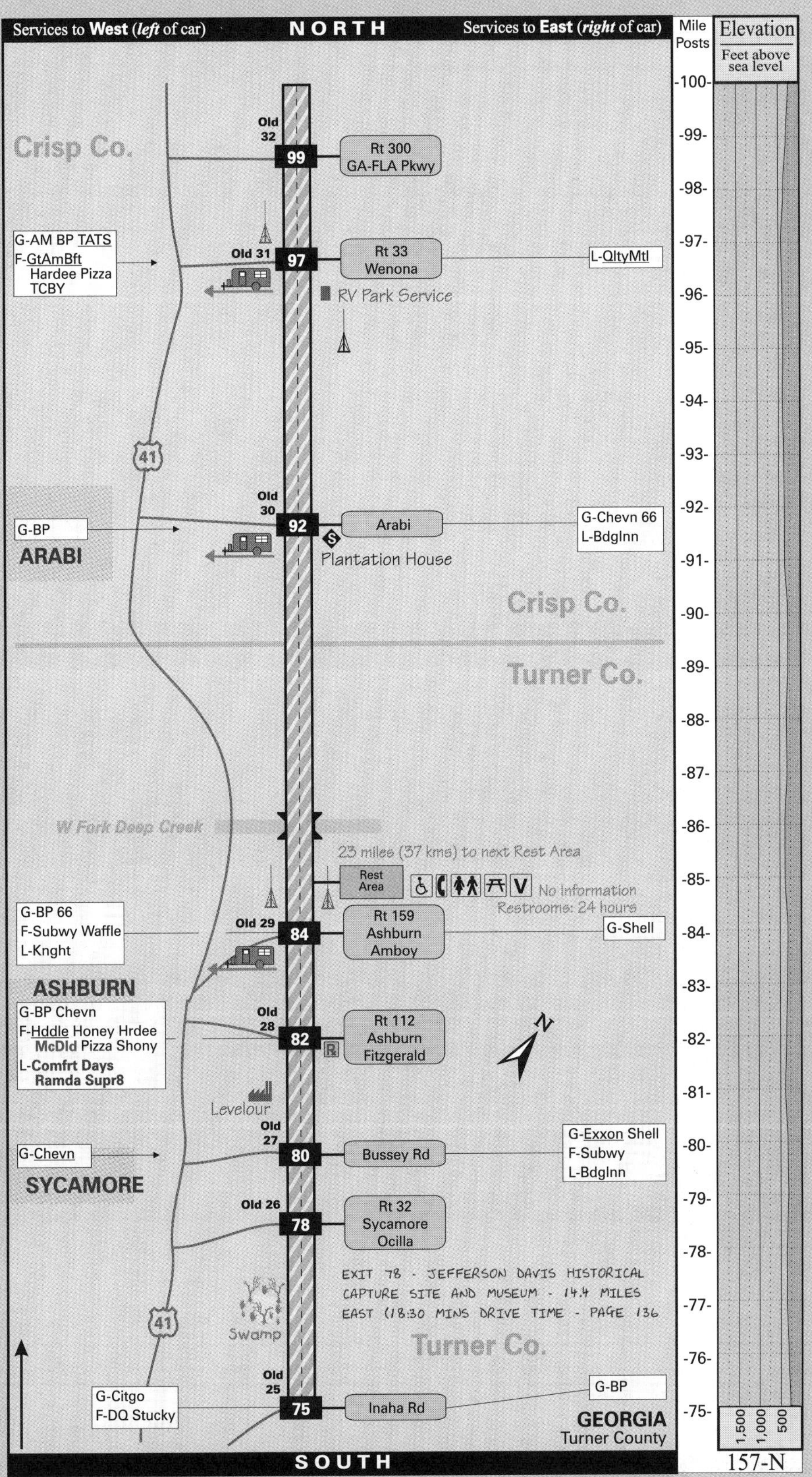
Services to West (left of car)
NORTH
Services to East (right of car)
Crisp Co.
Old 32
99
Rt 300
GA-FLA Pkwy
G-AM BP TATS
F-GtAmBft
Hardee Pizza
TCBY
Old 31
97
Rt 33
Wenona
L-QltyMtl
RV Park Service
41
Old 30
92
G-BP
ARABI
Arabi
G-Chevn 66
L-BdgInn
Plantation House
Crisp Co.
Turner Co.
W Fork Deep Creek
23 miles (37 kms) to next Rest Area
Rest Area
No Information
Restrooms: 24 hours
G-BP 66
F-Subwy Waffle
L-Knght
Old 29
84
Rt 159
Ashburn
Amboy
G-Shell
ASHBURN
G-BP Chevn
F-Hddle Honey Hrdee
McDld Pizza Shony
L-Comfrt Days
Ramda Supr8
Old 28
82
Rt 112
Ashburn
Fitzgerald
N
Levelour
Old 27
80
G-Chevn
SYCAMORE
Bussey Rd
G-Exxon Shell
F-Subwy
L-BdgInn
Old 26
78
Rt 32
Sycamore
Ocilla
EXIT 78 - JEFFERSON DAVIS HISTORICAL CAPTURE SITE AND MUSEUM - 14.4 MILES EAST (18:30 MINS DRIVE TIME - PAGE 136
41
Swamp
Turner Co.
Old 25
75
G-Citgo
F-DQ Stucky
Inaha Rd
G-BP
GEORGIA
Turner County
SOUTH
Mile Posts
-100-
-99-
-98-
-97-
-96-
-95-
-94-
-93-
-92-
-91-
-90-
-89-
-88-
-87-
-86-
-85-
-84-
-83-
-82-
-81-
-80-
-79-
-78-
-77-
-76-
-75-
Elevation
Feet above sea level
1,500
1,000
500

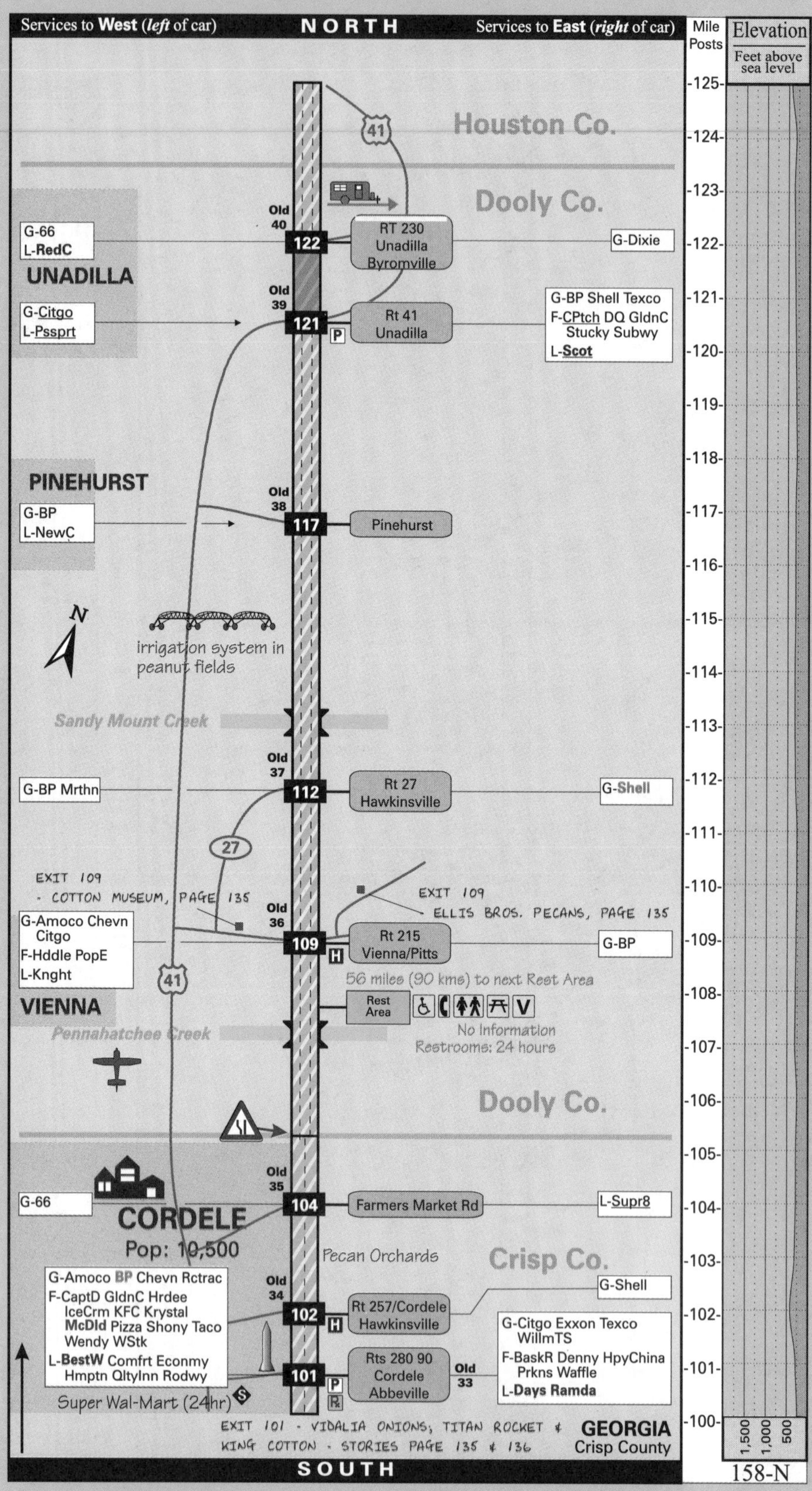

Services to West (left of car)
NORTH
Services to East (right of car)
Mile Posts
Elevation
Feet above sea level
Houston Co.
Dooly Co.
41
Old 40
122
RT 230 Unadilla Byromville
G-66
L-RedC
G-Dixie
UNADILLA
Old 39
121
Rt 41 Unadilla
G-Citgo
L-Pssprt
G-BP Shell Texco
F-CPtch DQ GldnC Stucky Subwy
L-Scot
PINEHURST
Old 38
117
Pinehurst
G-BP
L-NewC
irrigation system in peanut fields
N
Sandy Mount Creek
Old 37
112
Rt 27 Hawkinsville
G-BP Mrthn
G-Shell
27
EXIT 109 - COTTON MUSEUM, PAGE 135
EXIT 109 ELLIS BROS. PECANS, PAGE 135
Old 36
109
Rt 215 Vienna/Pitts
G-Amoco Chevn Citgo
F-Hddle PopE
L-Knght
G-BP
56 miles (90 kms) to next Rest Area
Rest Area
No Information
Restrooms: 24 hours
VIENNA
Pennahatchee Creek
Dooly Co.
Old 35
104
Farmers Market Rd
G-66
L-Supr8
CORDELE
Pop: 10,500
Pecan Orchards
Crisp Co.
Old 34
102
Rt 257/Cordele Hawkinsville
G-Shell
G-Amoco BP Chevn Rctrac
F-CaptD GldnC Hrdee IceCrm KFC Krystal McDld Pizza Shony Taco Wendy WStk
L-BestW Comfrt Econmy Hmptn QltyInn Rodwy
101
Rts 280 90 Cordele Abbeville
Old 33
G-Citgo Exxon Texco WillmTS
F-BaskR Denny HpyChina Prkns Waffle
L-Days Ramda
Super Wal-Mart (24hr)
EXIT 101 - VIDALIA ONIONS; TITAN ROCKET & KING COTTON - STORIES PAGE 135 & 136
GEORGIA
Crisp County
SOUTH
-125- -124- -123- -122- -121- -120- -119- -118- -117- -116- -115- -114- -113- -112- -111- -110- -109- -108- -107- -106- -105- -104- -103- -102- -101- -100-
1,500 1,000 500

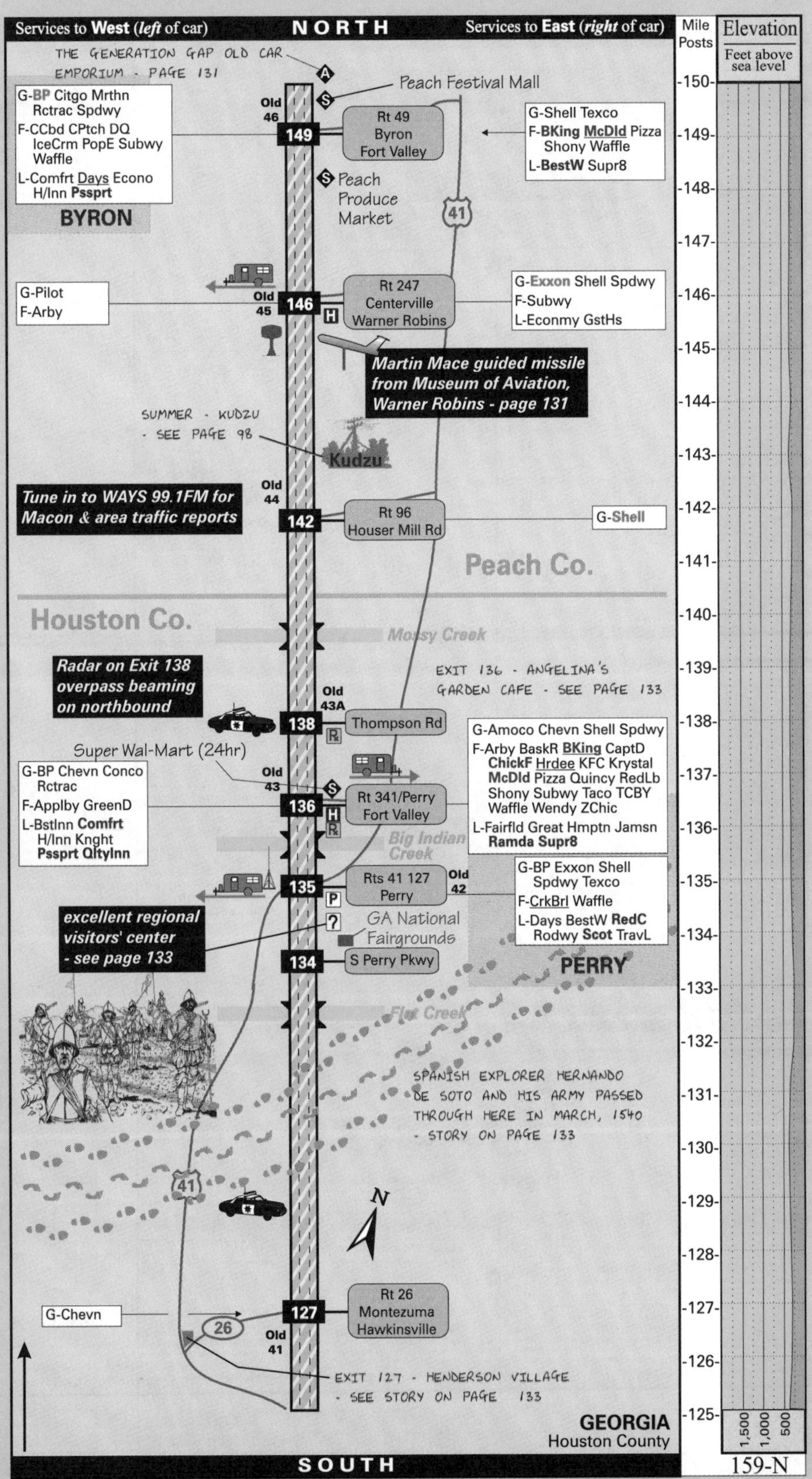

Services to West (left of car)
NORTH
Services to East (right of car)
Mile Posts
Elevation
Feet above sea level
THE GENERATION GAP OLD CAR EMPORIUM - PAGE 131
Peach Festival Mall
G-BP Citgo Mrthn Rctrac Spdwy
F-CCbd CPtch DQ IceCrm PopE Subwy Waffle
L-Comfrt Days Econo H/Inn Pssprt
BYRON
Old 46
149
Rt 49 Byron Fort Valley
G-Shell Texco
F-BKing McDld Pizza Shony Waffle
L-BestW Supr8
Peach Produce Market
41
G-Pilot
F-Arby
Old 45
146
Rt 247 Centerville Warner Robins
G-Exxon Shell Spdwy
F-Subwy
L-Econmy GstHs
Martin Mace guided missile from Museum of Aviation, Warner Robins - page 131
SUMMER - KUDZU - SEE PAGE 98
Kudzu
Tune in to WAYS 99.1FM for Macon & area traffic reports
Old 44
142
Rt 96 Houser Mill Rd
G-Shell
Peach Co.
Houston Co.
Mossy Creek
Radar on Exit 138 overpass beaming on northbound
EXIT 136 - ANGELINA'S GARDEN CAFE - SEE PAGE 133
Old 43A
138
Thompson Rd
Super Wal-Mart (24hr)
G-BP Chevn Conco Rctrac
F-Applby GreenD
L-BstInn Comfrt H/Inn Knght Pssprt QltyInn
Old 43
136
Rt 341/Perry Fort Valley
G-Amoco Chevn Shell Spdwy
F-Arby BaskR BKing CaptD ChickF Hrdee KFC Krystal McDld Pizza Quincy RedLb Shony Subwy Taco TCBY Waffle Wendy ZChic
L-Fairfld Great Hmptn Jamsn Ramda Supr8
Big Indian Creek
135
Rts 41 127 Perry
Old 42
G-BP Exxon Shell Spdwy Texco
F-CrkBrl Waffle
L-Days BestW RedC Rodwy Scot TravL
excellent regional visitors' center - see page 133
GA National Fairgrounds
134
S Perry Pkwy
PERRY
Flat Creek
SPANISH EXPLORER HERNANDO DE SOTO AND HIS ARMY PASSED THROUGH HERE IN MARCH, 1540 - STORY ON PAGE 133
41
N
G-Chevn
127
Rt 26 Montezuma Hawkinsville
26
Old 41
EXIT 127 - HENDERSON VILLAGE - SEE STORY ON PAGE 133
GEORGIA
Houston County
SOUTH
-150- -149- -148- -147- -146- -145- -144- -143- -142- -141- -140- -139- -138- -137- -136- -135- -134- -133- -132- -131- -130- -129- -128- -127- -126- -125-
1,500 1,000 500

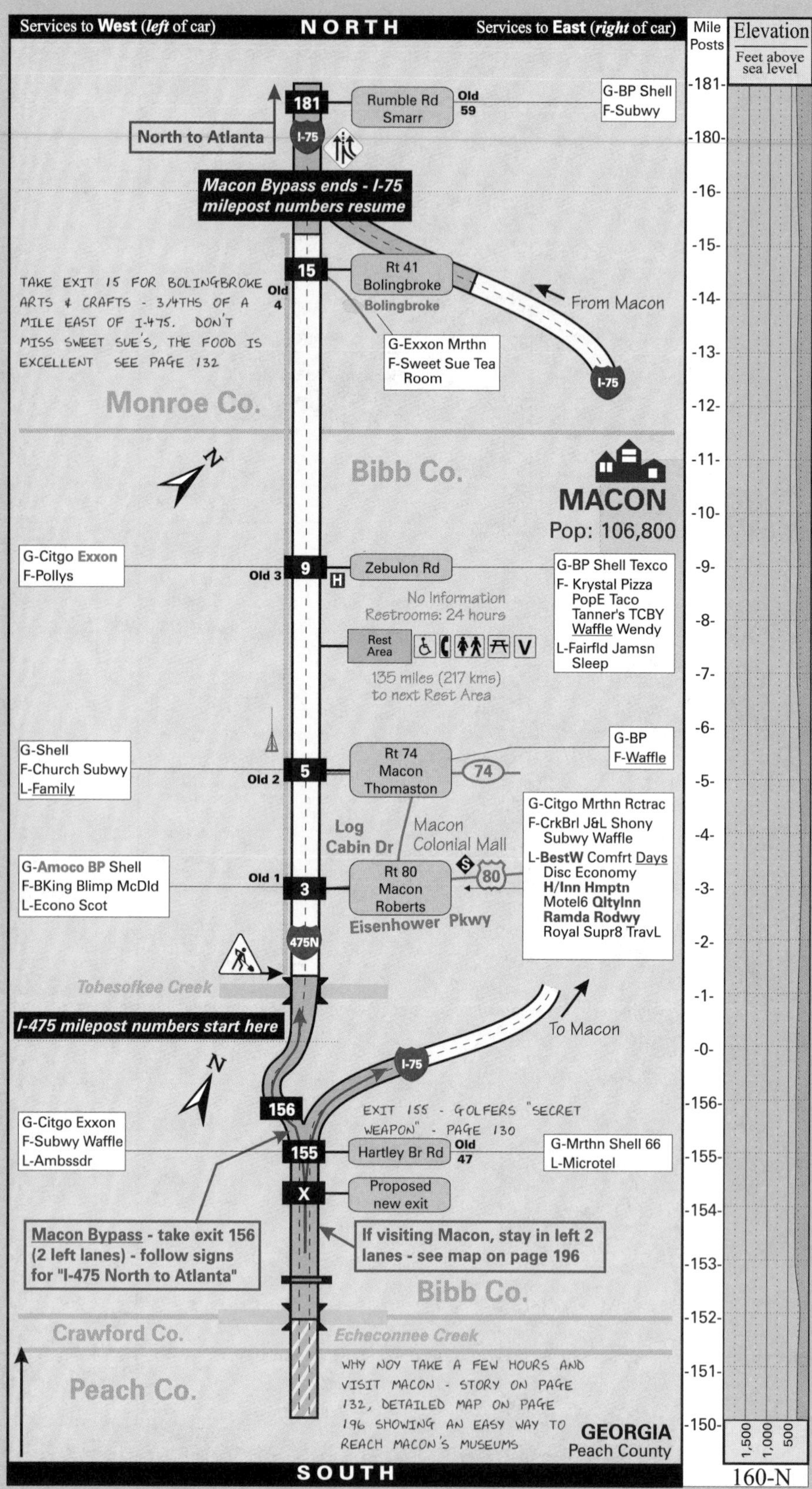

Services to West (left of car)
NORTH
Services to East (right of car)
Mile Posts
Elevation
Feet above sea level
181
Rumble Rd
Smarr
Old 59
G-BP Shell
F-Subwy
North to Atlanta
I-75
Macon Bypass ends - I-75 milepost numbers resume
15
Rt 41
Bolingbroke
Bolingbroke
Old 4
TAKE EXIT 15 FOR BOLINGBROKE ARTS & CRAFTS - 3/4THS OF A MILE EAST OF I-475. DON'T MISS SWEET SUE'S, THE FOOD IS EXCELLENT SEE PAGE 132
G-Exxon Mrthn
F-Sweet Sue Tea Room
From Macon
Monroe Co.
Bibb Co.
MACON
Pop: 106,800
G-Citgo Exxon
F-Pollys
Old 3
9
Zebulon Rd
G-BP Shell Texco
F- Krystal Pizza PopE Taco Tanner's TCBY Waffle Wendy
L-Fairfld Jamsn Sleep
No Information
Restrooms: 24 hours
Rest Area
135 miles (217 kms) to next Rest Area
G-Shell
F-Church Subwy
L-Family
Old 2
5
Rt 74
Macon
Thomaston
74
G-BP
F-Waffle
Log Cabin Dr
Macon Colonial Mall
G-Citgo Mrthn Rctrac
F-CrkBrl J&L Shony Subwy Waffle
L-BestW Comfrt Days Disc Economy H/Inn Hmptn Motel6 QltyInn Ramda Rodwy Royal Supr8 TravL
G-Amoco BP Shell
F-BKing Blimp McDld
L-Econo Scot
Old 1
3
Rt 80
Macon
Roberts
80
Eisenhower Pkwy
475N
Tobesofkee Creek
I-475 milepost numbers start here
To Macon
156
EXIT 155 - GOLFERS "SECRET WEAPON" - PAGE 130
G-Citgo Exxon
F-Subwy Waffle
L-Ambssdr
155
Hartley Br Rd
Old 47
G-Mrthn Shell 66
L-Microtel
X
Proposed new exit
Macon Bypass - take exit 156 (2 left lanes) - follow signs for "I-475 North to Atlanta"
If visiting Macon, stay in left 2 lanes - see map on page 196
Bibb Co.
Crawford Co.
Echeconnee Creek
Peach Co.
WHY NOY TAKE A FEW HOURS AND VISIT MACON - STORY ON PAGE 132, DETAILED MAP ON PAGE 196 SHOWING AN EASY WAY TO REACH MACON'S MUSEUMS
GEORGIA
Peach County
SOUTH
-181- -180- -16- -15- -14- -13- -12- -11- -10- -9- -8- -7- -6- -5- -4- -3- -2- -1- -0- -156- -155- -154- -153- -152- -151- -150-
1,500 1,000 500

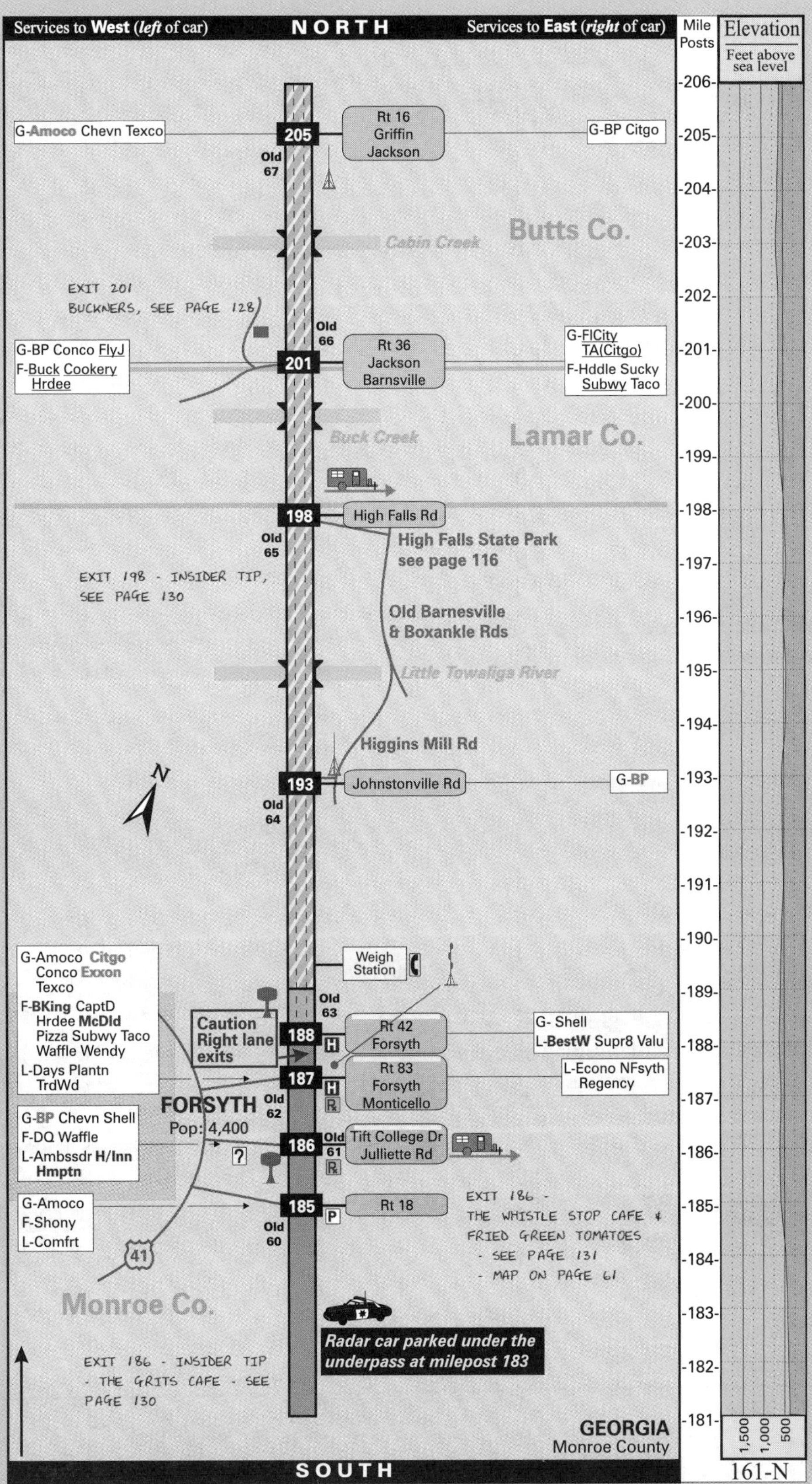

Services to West (left of car)
NORTH
Services to East (right of car)
Mile Posts
Elevation
Feet above sea level
G-Amoco Chevn Texco
205
Rt 16 Griffin Jackson
G-BP Citgo
Old 67
Cabin Creek
Butts Co.
EXIT 201 BUCKNERS, SEE PAGE 128
Old 66
G-BP Conco FlyJ
F-Buck Cookery Hrdee
201
Rt 36 Jackson Barnsville
G-FlCity TA(Citgo)
F-Hddle Sucky Subwy Taco
Buck Creek
Lamar Co.
198
High Falls Rd
Old 65
High Falls State Park see page 116
EXIT 198 - INSIDER TIP, SEE PAGE 130
Old Barnesville & Boxankle Rds
Little Towaliga River
Higgins Mill Rd
N
193
Johnstonville Rd
G-BP
Old 64
G-Amoco Citgo Conco Exxon Texco
F-BKing CaptD Hrdee McDld Pizza Subwy Taco Waffle Wendy
L-Days Plantn TrdWd
Weigh Station
Old 63
Caution Right lane exits
188
Rt 42 Forsyth
G- Shell
L-BestW Supr8 Valu
187
Rt 83 Forsyth Monticello
L-Econo NFsyth Regency
FORSYTH
Pop: 4,400
Old 62
G-BP Chevn Shell
F-DQ Waffle
L-Ambssdr H/Inn Hmptn
Old 61
186
Tift College Dr Julliette Rd
G-Amoco
F-Shony
L-Comfrt
185
Rt 18
Old 60
EXIT 186 - THE WHISTLE STOP CAFE & FRIED GREEN TOMATOES - SEE PAGE 131 - MAP ON PAGE 61
41
Monroe Co.
Radar car parked under the underpass at milepost 183
EXIT 186 - INSIDER TIP - THE GRITS CAFE - SEE PAGE 130
GEORGIA
Monroe County
SOUTH
-206- -205- -204- -203- -202- -201- -200- -199- -198- -197- -196- -195- -194- -193- -192- -191- -190- -189- -188- -187- -186- -185- -184- -183- -182- -181-
1,500 1,000 500

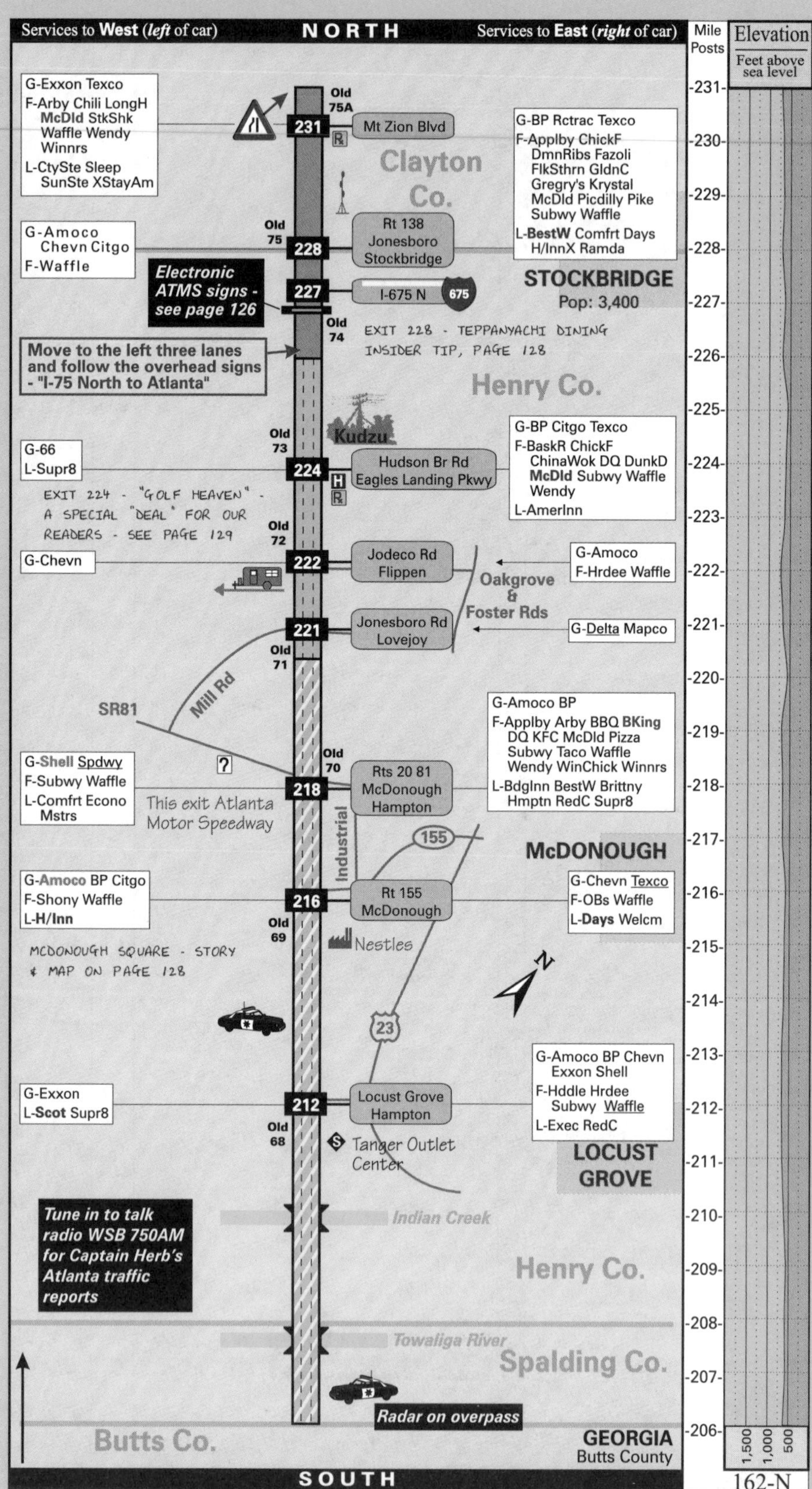

Services to West (left of car)
NORTH
Services to East (right of car)
Mile Posts
Elevation
Feet above sea level
G-Exxon Texco
F-Arby Chili LongH McDld StkShk Waffle Wendy Winnrs
L-CtySte Sleep SunSte XStayAm
Old 75A
231
Mt Zion Blvd
G-BP Rctrac Texco
F-Applby ChickF DmnRibs Fazoli FlkSthrn GldnC Gregry's Krystal McDld Picdilly Pike Subwy Waffle
L-BestW Comfrt Days H/InnX Ramda
Clayton Co.
G-Amoco Chevn Citgo
F-Waffle
Old 75
228
Rt 138 Jonesboro Stockbridge
Electronic ATMS signs - see page 126
227
I-675 N
675
STOCKBRIDGE
Pop: 3,400
Old 74
EXIT 228 - TEPPANYACHI DINING INSIDER TIP, PAGE 128
Move to the left three lanes and follow the overhead signs - "I-75 North to Atlanta"
Henry Co.
Kudzu
Old 73
G-66
L-Supr8
224
Hudson Br Rd Eagles Landing Pkwy
G-BP Citgo Texco
F-BaskR ChickF ChinaWok DQ DunkD McDld Subwy Waffle Wendy
L-AmerInn
EXIT 224 - "GOLF HEAVEN" - A SPECIAL "DEAL" FOR OUR READERS - SEE PAGE 129
Old 72
G-Chevn
222
Jodeco Rd Flippen
G-Amoco
F-Hrdee Waffle
Oakgrove & Foster Rds
221
Jonesboro Rd Lovejoy
G-Delta Mapco
Old 71
Mill Rd
SR81
G-Amoco BP
F-Applby Arby BBQ BKing DQ KFC McDld Pizza Subwy Taco Waffle Wendy WinChick Winnrs
L-BdgInn BestW Brittny Hmptn RedC Supr8
G-Shell Spdwy
F-Subwy Waffle
L-Comfrt Econo Mstrs
Old 70
218
Rts 20 81 McDonough Hampton
This exit Atlanta Motor Speedway
155
Industrial
McDONOUGH
G-Amoco BP Citgo
F-Shony Waffle
L-H/Inn
216
Rt 155 McDonough
G-Chevn Texco
F-OBs Waffle
L-Days Welcm
Old 69
Nestles
MCDONOUGH SQUARE - STORY & MAP ON PAGE 128
N
23
G-Amoco BP Chevn Exxon Shell
F-Hddle Hrdee Subwy Waffle
L-Exec RedC
G-Exxon
L-Scot Supr8
212
Locust Grove Hampton
Old 68
Tanger Outlet Center
LOCUST GROVE
Indian Creek
Tune in to talk radio WSB 750AM for Captain Herb's Atlanta traffic reports
Henry Co.
Towaliga River
Spalding Co.
Radar on overpass
Butts Co.
GEORGIA
Butts County
SOUTH
-231- -230- -229- -228- -227- -226- -225- -224- -223- -222- -221- -220- -219- -218- -217- -216- -215- -214- -213- -212- -211- -210- -209- -208- -207- -206-
1,500 1,000 500

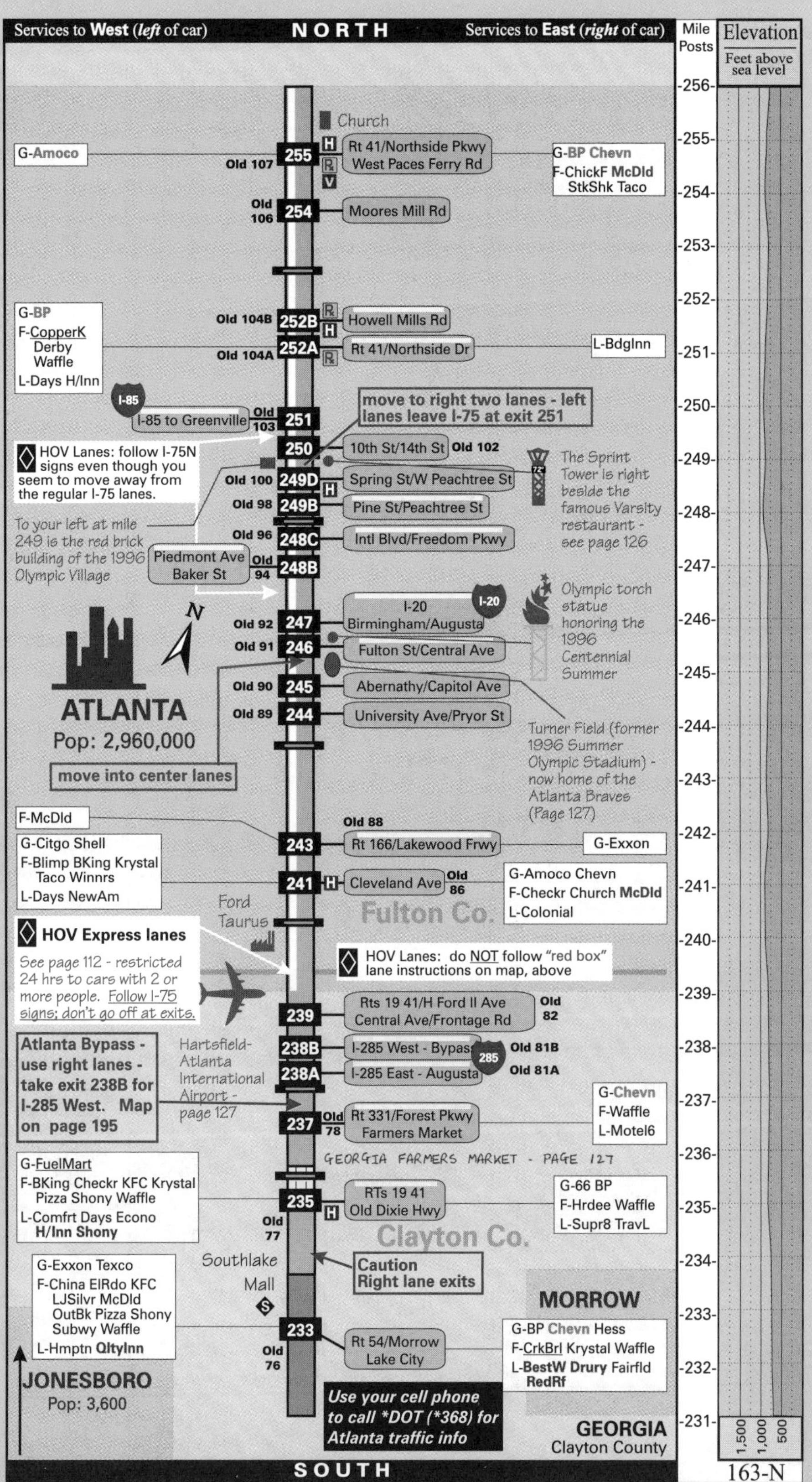

Services to West (left of car)
NORTH
Services to East (right of car)
Mile Posts
Elevation
Feet above sea level
Church
G-Amoco
255 Old 107
Rt 41/Northside Pkwy West Paces Ferry Rd
G-BP Chevn F-ChickF McDld StkShk Taco
254 Old 106
Moores Mill Rd
G-BP F-CopperK Derby Waffle L-Days H/Inn
252B Old 104B
Howell Mills Rd
252A Old 104A
Rt 41/Northside Dr
L-BdgInn
I-85
I-85 to Greenville
251 Old 103
move to right two lanes - left lanes leave I-75 at exit 251
HOV Lanes: follow I-75N signs even though you seem to move away from the regular I-75 lanes.
250
10th St/14th St Old 102
The Sprint Tower is right beside the famous Varsity restaurant - see page 126
249D Old 100
Spring St/W Peachtree St
249B Old 98
Pine St/Peachtree St
To your left at mile 249 is the red brick building of the 1996 Olympic Village
248C Old 96
Intl Blvd/Freedom Pkwy
Piedmont Ave Baker St
248B Old 94
247 Old 92
I-20 Birmingham/Augusta
I-20
Olympic torch statue honoring the 1996 Centennial Summer
N
ATLANTA
Pop: 2,960,000
246 Old 91
Fulton St/Central Ave
245 Old 90
Abernathy/Capitol Ave
244 Old 89
University Ave/Pryor St
Turner Field (former 1996 Summer Olympic Stadium) - now home of the Atlanta Braves (Page 127)
move into center lanes
F-McDld
243 Old 88
Rt 166/Lakewood Frwy
G-Exxon
G-Citgo Shell F-Blimp BKing Krystal Taco Winnrs L-Days NewAm
241 Old 86
Cleveland Ave
G-Amoco Chevn F-Checkr Church McDld L-Colonial
Ford Taurus
Fulton Co.
HOV Express lanes
See page 112 - restricted 24 hrs to cars with 2 or more people. Follow I-75 signs; don't go off at exits.
HOV Lanes: do NOT follow "red box" lane instructions on map, above
239 Old 82
Rts 19 41/H Ford II Ave Central Ave/Frontage Rd
Atlanta Bypass - use right lanes - take exit 238B for I-285 West. Map on page 195
Hartsfield-Atlanta International Airport - page 127
238B Old 81B
I-285 West - Bypass
285
238A Old 81A
I-285 East - Augusta
237 Old 78
Rt 331/Forest Pkwy Farmers Market
G-Chevn F-Waffle L-Motel6
GEORGIA FARMERS MARKET - PAGE 127
G-FuelMart F-BKing Checkr KFC Krystal Pizza Shony Waffle L-Comfrt Days Econo H/Inn Shony
235 Old 77
RTs 19 41 Old Dixie Hwy
G-66 BP F-Hrdee Waffle L-Supr8 TravL
Clayton Co.
Southlake Mall
Caution Right lane exits
MORROW
G-Exxon Texco F-China ElRdo KFC LJSilvr McDld OutBk Pizza Shony Subwy Waffle L-Hmptn QltyInn
233 Old 76
Rt 54/Morrow Lake City
G-BP Chevn Hess F-CrkBrl Krystal Waffle L-BestW Drury Fairfld RedRf
JONESBORO
Pop: 3,600
Use your cell phone to call *DOT (*368) for Atlanta traffic info
GEORGIA
Clayton County
SOUTH
-256- -255- -254- -253- -252- -251- -250- -249- -248- -247- -246- -245- -244- -243- -242- -241- -240- -239- -238- -237- -236- -235- -234- -233- -232- -231-
1,500 1,000 500

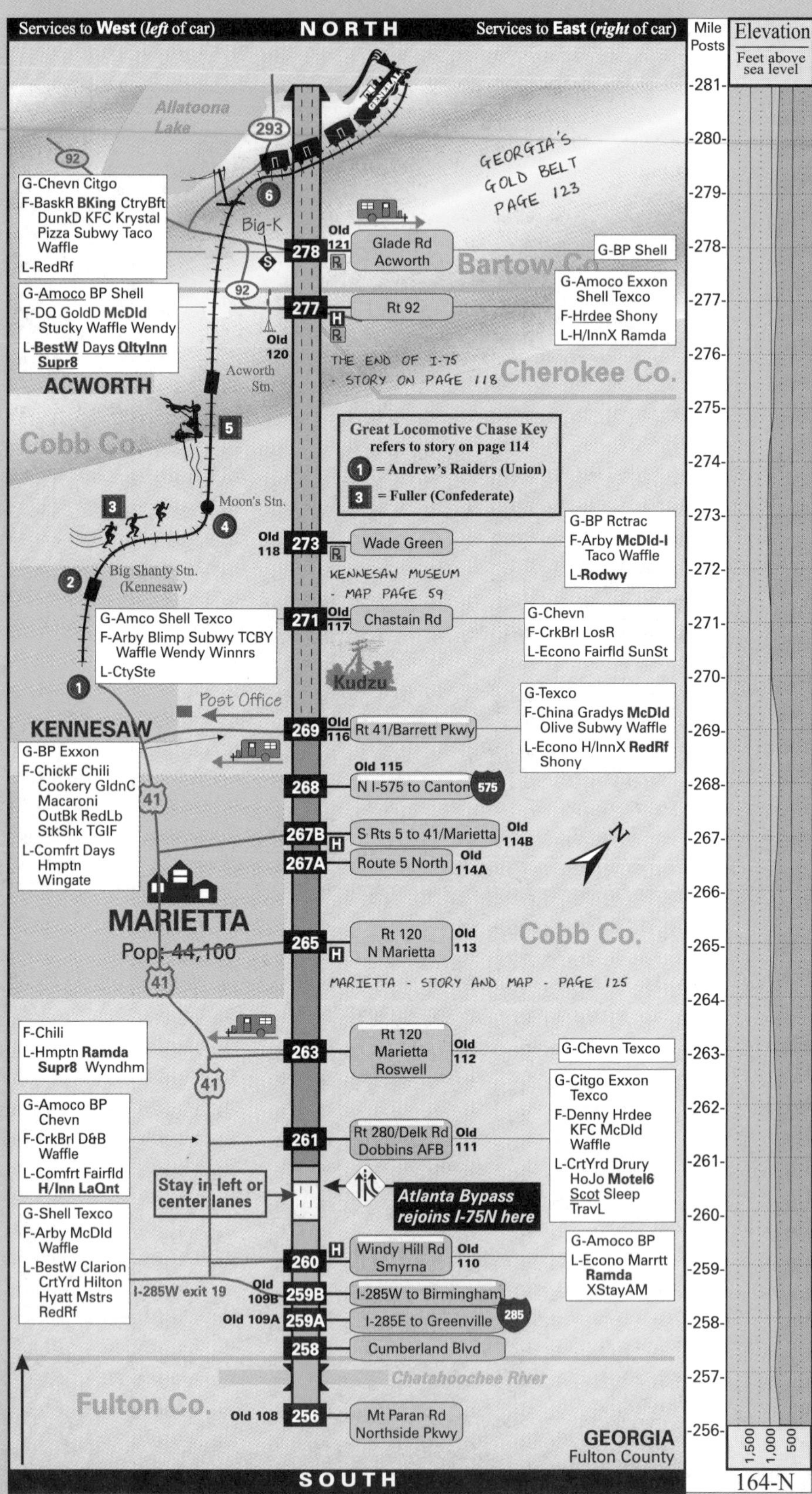

Services to West (left of car)
NORTH
Services to East (right of car)
Mile Posts
Elevation
Feet above sea level
Allatoona Lake
293
92
GENERAL
GEORGIA'S GOLD BELT PAGE 123
G-Chevn Citgo
F-BaskR BKing CtryBft DunkD KFC Krystal Pizza Subwy Taco Waffle
L-RedRf
6
Big-K
Old 121
278
Glade Rd Acworth
G-BP Shell
Bartow Co.
G-Amoco BP Shell
F-DQ GoldD McDld Stucky Waffle Wendy
L-BestW Days QltyInn Supr8
92
277
Rt 92
Old 120
G-Amoco Exxon Shell Texco
F-Hrdee Shony
L-H/InnX Ramda
ACWORTH
Acworth Stn.
THE END OF I-75 - STORY ON PAGE 118
Cherokee Co.
5
Cobb Co.
Great Locomotive Chase Key
refers to story on page 114
1 = Andrew's Raiders (Union)
3 = Fuller (Confederate)
3
Moon's Stn.
4
Old 118
273
Wade Green
G-BP Rctrac
F-Arby McDld-I Taco Waffle
L-Rodwy
2
Big Shanty Stn. (Kennesaw)
KENNESAW MUSEUM - MAP PAGE 59
G-Amco Shell Texco
F-Arby Blimp Subwy TCBY Waffle Wendy Winnrs
L-CtySte
271
Old 117
Chastain Rd
G-Chevn
F-CrkBrl LosR
L-Econo Fairfld SunSt
1
Kudzu
Post Office
KENNESAW
269
Old 116
Rt 41/Barrett Pkwy
G-Texco
F-China Gradys McDld Olive Subwy Waffle
L-Econo H/InnX RedRf Shony
G-BP Exxon
F-ChickF Chili Cookery GldnC Macaroni OutBk RedLb StkShk TGIF
L-Comfrt Days Hmptn Wingate
41
Old 115
268
N I-575 to Canton
575
267B
S Rts 5 to 41/Marietta
Old 114B
267A
Route 5 North
Old 114A
N
MARIETTA
Pop: 44,100
265
Rt 120 N Marietta
Old 113
Cobb Co.
41
MARIETTA - STORY AND MAP - PAGE 125
F-Chili
L-Hmptn Ramda Supr8 Wyndhm
263
Rt 120 Marietta Roswell
Old 112
G-Chevn Texco
41
G-Amoco BP Chevn
F-CrkBrl D&B Waffle
L-Comfrt Fairfld H/Inn LaQnt
261
Rt 280/Delk Rd Dobbins AFB
Old 111
G-Citgo Exxon Texco
F-Denny Hrdee KFC McDld Waffle
L-CrtYrd Drury HoJo Motel6 Scot Sleep TravL
Stay in left or center lanes
Atlanta Bypass rejoins I-75N here
G-Shell Texco
F-Arby McDld Waffle
L-BestW Clarion CrtYrd Hilton Hyatt Mstrs RedRf
260
Windy Hill Rd Smyrna
Old 110
G-Amoco BP
L-Econo Marrtt Ramda XStayAM
I-285W exit 19
Old 109B
259B
I-285W to Birmingham
Old 109A
259A
I-285E to Greenville
285
258
Cumberland Blvd
Chatahoochee River
Fulton Co.
Old 108
256
Mt Paran Rd Northside Pkwy
GEORGIA
Fulton County
SOUTH
-281- -280- -279- -278- -277- -276- -275- -274- -273- -272- -271- -270- -269- -268- -267- -266- -265- -264- -263- -262- -261- -260- -259- -258- -257- -256-
1,500 1,000 500
164-N

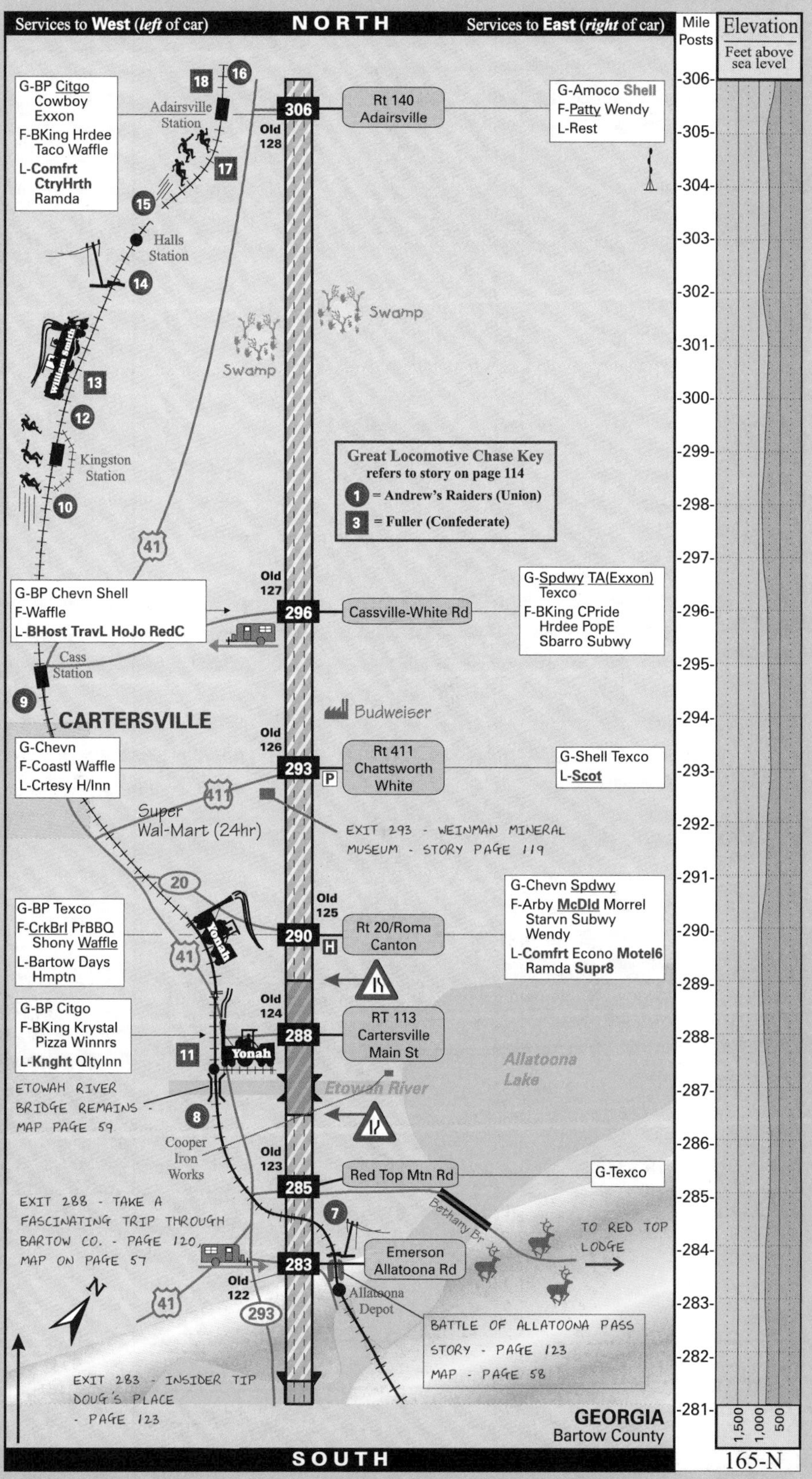
Services to West (left of car)
NORTH
Services to East (right of car)
Mile Posts
Elevation
Feet above sea level
G-BP Citgo Cowboy Exxon
F-BKing Hrdee Taco Waffle
L-Comfrt CtryHrth Ramda
Adairsville Station
306
Old 128
Rt 140 Adairsville
G-Amoco Shell
F-Patty Wendy
L-Rest
Halls Station
Swamp
Swamp
William Smith
Kingston Station
Great Locomotive Chase Key
refers to story on page 114
1 = Andrew's Raiders (Union)
3 = Fuller (Confederate)
41
G-BP Chevn Shell
F-Waffle
L-BHost TravL HoJo RedC
Old 127
296
Cassville-White Rd
G-Spdwy TA(Exxon) Texco
F-BKing CPride Hrdee PopE Sbarro Subwy
Cass Station
CARTERSVILLE
Budweiser
G-Chevn
F-Coastl Waffle
L-Crtesy H/Inn
Old 126
293
Rt 411 Chattsworth White
G-Shell Texco
L-Scot
411
Super Wal-Mart (24hr)
EXIT 293 - WEINMAN MINERAL MUSEUM - STORY PAGE 119
20
G-BP Texco
F-CrkBrl PrBBQ Shony Waffle
L-Bartow Days Hmptn
Yonah
Old 125
290
Rt 20/Roma Canton
G-Chevn Spdwy
F-Arby McDld Morrel Starvn Subwy Wendy
L-Comfrt Econo Motel6 Ramda Supr8
G-BP Citgo
F-BKing Krystal Pizza Winnrs
L-Knght QltyInn
Old 124
288
RT 113 Cartersville Main St
Yonah
Allatoona Lake
ETOWAH RIVER BRIDGE REMAINS - MAP PAGE 59
Etowah River
Cooper Iron Works
Old 123
285
Red Top Mtn Rd
G-Texco
EXIT 288 - TAKE A FASCINATING TRIP THROUGH BARTOW CO. - PAGE 120, MAP ON PAGE 57
Bethany Br
TO RED TOP LODGE
283
Emerson Allatoona Rd
Old 122
293
Allatoona Depot
BATTLE OF ALLATOONA PASS STORY - PAGE 123 MAP - PAGE 58
EXIT 283 - INSIDER TIP DOUG'S PLACE - PAGE 123
GEORGIA
Bartow County
SOUTH
-306- -305- -304- -303- -302- -301- -300- -299- -298- -297- -296- -295- -294- -293- -292- -291- -290- -289- -288- -287- -286- -285- -284- -283- -282- -281-
1,500 1,000 500

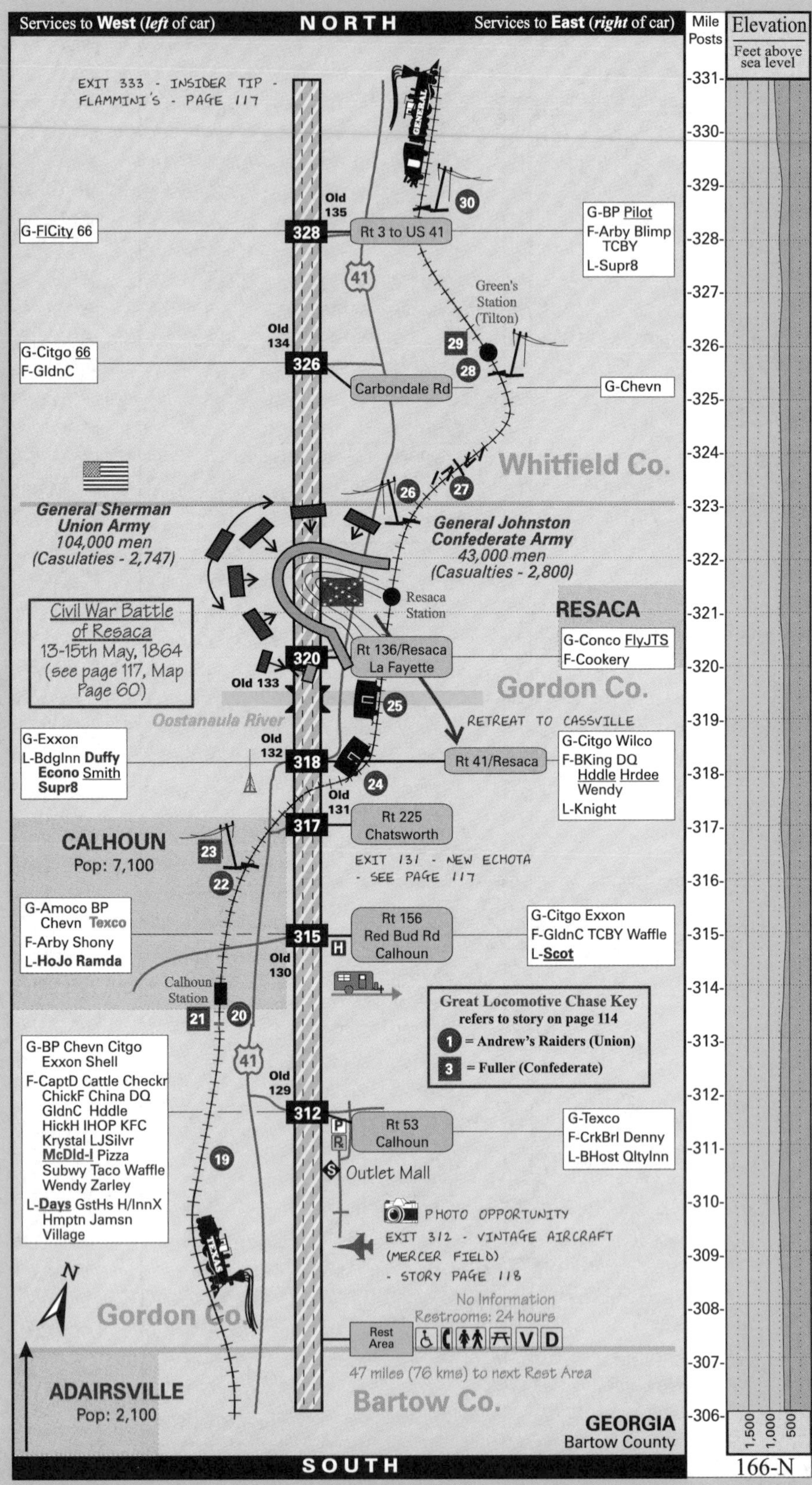

Services to West (left of car)
NORTH
Services to East (right of car)
Mile Posts
Elevation
Feet above sea level
EXIT 333 - INSIDER TIP - FLAMMINI'S - PAGE 117
Old 135
328
Rt 3 to US 41
G-FlCity 66
G-BP Pilot
F-Arby Blimp TCBY
L-Supr8
41
Green's Station (Tilton)
Old 134
326
Carbondale Rd
G-Citgo 66
F-GldnC
G-Chevn
Whitfield Co.
General Sherman
Union Army
104,000 men
(Casualties - 2,747)
General Johnston
Confederate Army
43,000 men
(Casualties - 2,800)
Resaca Station
RESACA
Civil War Battle of Resaca
13-15th May, 1864
(see page 117, Map Page 60)
320
Old 133
Rt 136/Resaca La Fayette
G-Conco FlyJTS
F-Cookery
Gordon Co.
Oostanaula River
RETREAT TO CASSVILLE
Old 132
318
Rt 41/Resaca
G-Exxon
L-BdgInn Duffy Econo Smith Supr8
G-Citgo Wilco
F-BKing DQ Hddle Hrdee Wendy
L-Knight
Old 131
317
Rt 225 Chatsworth
CALHOUN
Pop: 7,100
EXIT 131 - NEW ECHOTA - SEE PAGE 117
315
Rt 156 Red Bud Rd Calhoun
Old 130
G-Amoco BP Chevn Texco
F-Arby Shony
L-HoJo Ramda
G-Citgo Exxon
F-GldnC TCBY Waffle
L-Scot
Calhoun Station
Great Locomotive Chase Key
refers to story on page 114
1 = Andrew's Raiders (Union)
3 = Fuller (Confederate)
41
Old 129
312
Rt 53 Calhoun
G-BP Chevn Citgo Exxon Shell
F-CaptD Cattle Checkr ChickF China DQ GldnC Hddle HickH IHOP KFC Krystal LJSilvr McDld-I Pizza Subwy Taco Waffle Wendy Zarley
L-Days GstHs H/InnX Hmptn Jamsn Village
G-Texco
F-CrkBrl Denny
L-BHost QltyInn
Outlet Mall
PHOTO OPPORTUNITY
EXIT 312 - VINTAGE AIRCRAFT (MERCER FIELD) - STORY PAGE 118
N
Gordon Co.
No Information
Restrooms: 24 hours
Rest Area
47 miles (76 kms) to next Rest Area
ADAIRSVILLE
Pop: 2,100
Bartow Co.
GEORGIA
Bartow County
SOUTH
-331- -330- -329- -328- -327- -326- -325- -324- -323- -322- -321- -320- -319- -318- -317- -316- -315- -314- -313- -312- -311- -310- -309- -308- -307- -306-
1,500 1,000 500

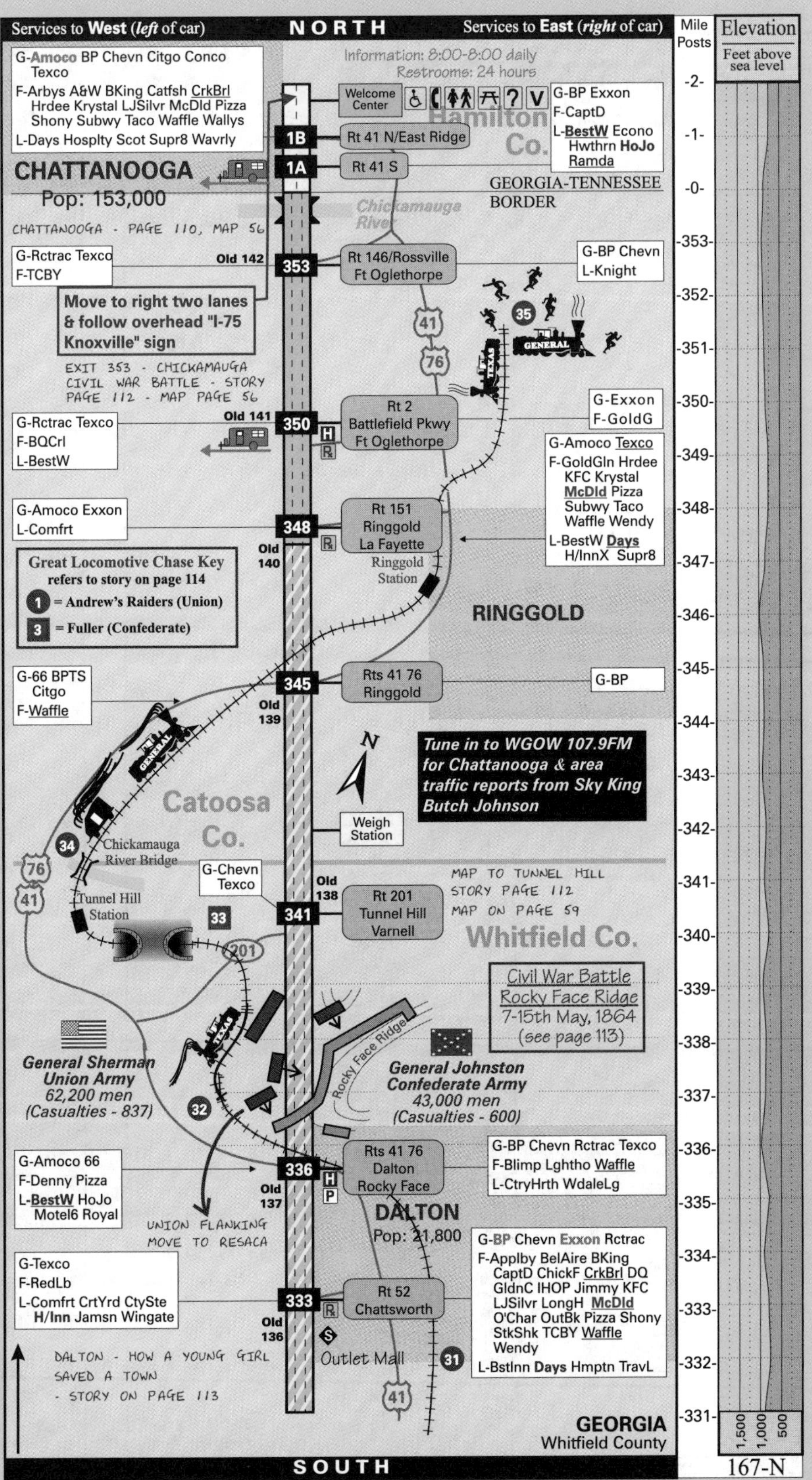

Services to West (left of car)
NORTH
Services to East (right of car)
Mile Posts
Elevation
Feet above sea level
G-Amoco BP Chevn Citgo Conco Texco
F-Arbys A&W BKing Catfsh CrkBrl Hrdee Krystal LJSilvr McDld Pizza Shony Subwy Taco Waffle Wallys
L-Days Hosplty Scot Supr8 Wavrly
Information: 8:00-8:00 daily
Restrooms: 24 hours
Welcome Center
G-BP Exxon
F-CaptD
L-BestW Econo Hwthrn HoJo Ramda
Hamilton Co.
1B
Rt 41 N/East Ridge
1A
Rt 41 S
CHATTANOOGA
Pop: 153,000
GEORGIA-TENNESSEE BORDER
Chickamauga River
CHATTANOOGA - PAGE 110, MAP 56
G-Rctrac Texco
F-TCBY
Old 142
353
Rt 146/Rossville Ft Oglethorpe
G-BP Chevn
L-Knight
Move to right two lanes & follow overhead "I-75 Knoxville" sign
41
76
35
GENERAL
EXIT 353 - CHICKAMAUGA CIVIL WAR BATTLE - STORY PAGE 112 - MAP PAGE 56
G-Rctrac Texco
F-BQCrl
L-BestW
Old 141
350
Rt 2 Battlefield Pkwy Ft Oglethorpe
G-Exxon
F-GoldG
G-Amoco Texco
F-GoldGln Hrdee KFC Krystal McDld Pizza Subwy Taco Waffle Wendy
L-BestW Days H/InnX Supr8
G-Amoco Exxon
L-Comfrt
348
Old 140
Rt 151 Ringgold La Fayette
Ringgold Station
Great Locomotive Chase Key refers to story on page 114
1 = Andrew's Raiders (Union)
3 = Fuller (Confederate)
RINGGOLD
G-66 BPTS Citgo
F-Waffle
345
Old 139
Rts 41 76 Ringgold
G-BP
GENERAL
N
Tune in to WGOW 107.9FM for Chattanooga & area traffic reports from Sky King Butch Johnson
Catoosa Co.
Weigh Station
34
Chickamauga River Bridge
76
41
Tunnel Hill Station
G-Chevn Texco
33
Old 138
341
Rt 201 Tunnel Hill Varnell
MAP TO TUNNEL HILL STORY PAGE 112 MAP ON PAGE 59
Whitfield Co.
201
Civil War Battle Rocky Face Ridge 7-15th May, 1864 (see page 113)
Rocky Face Ridge
TEXAS
General Sherman Union Army 62,200 men (Casualties - 837)
General Johnston Confederate Army 43,000 men (Casualties - 600)
32
G-Amoco 66
F-Denny Pizza
L-BestW HoJo Motel6 Royal
336
Old 137
Rts 41 76 Dalton Rocky Face
G-BP Chevn Rctrac Texco
F-Blimp Lghtho Waffle
L-CtryHrth WdaleLg
UNION FLANKING MOVE TO RESACA
DALTON
Pop: 21,800
G-Texco
F-RedLb
L-Comfrt CrtYrd CtySte H/Inn Jamsn Wingate
333
Old 136
Rt 52 Chattsworth
G-BP Chevn Exxon Rctrac
F-Applby BelAire BKing CaptD ChickF CrkBrl DQ GldnC IHOP Jimmy KFC LJSilvr LongH McDld O'Char OutBk Pizza Shony StkShk TCBY Waffle Wendy
L-BstInn Days Hmptn TravL
Outlet Mall
31
41
DALTON - HOW A YOUNG GIRL SAVED A TOWN - STORY ON PAGE 113
GEORGIA
Whitfield County
SOUTH
-2-
-1-
-0-
-353-
-352-
-351-
-350-
-349-
-348-
-347-
-346-
-345-
-344-
-343-
-342-
-341-
-340-
-339-
-338-
-337-
-336-
-335-
-334-
-333-
-332-
-331-
1,500
1,000
500

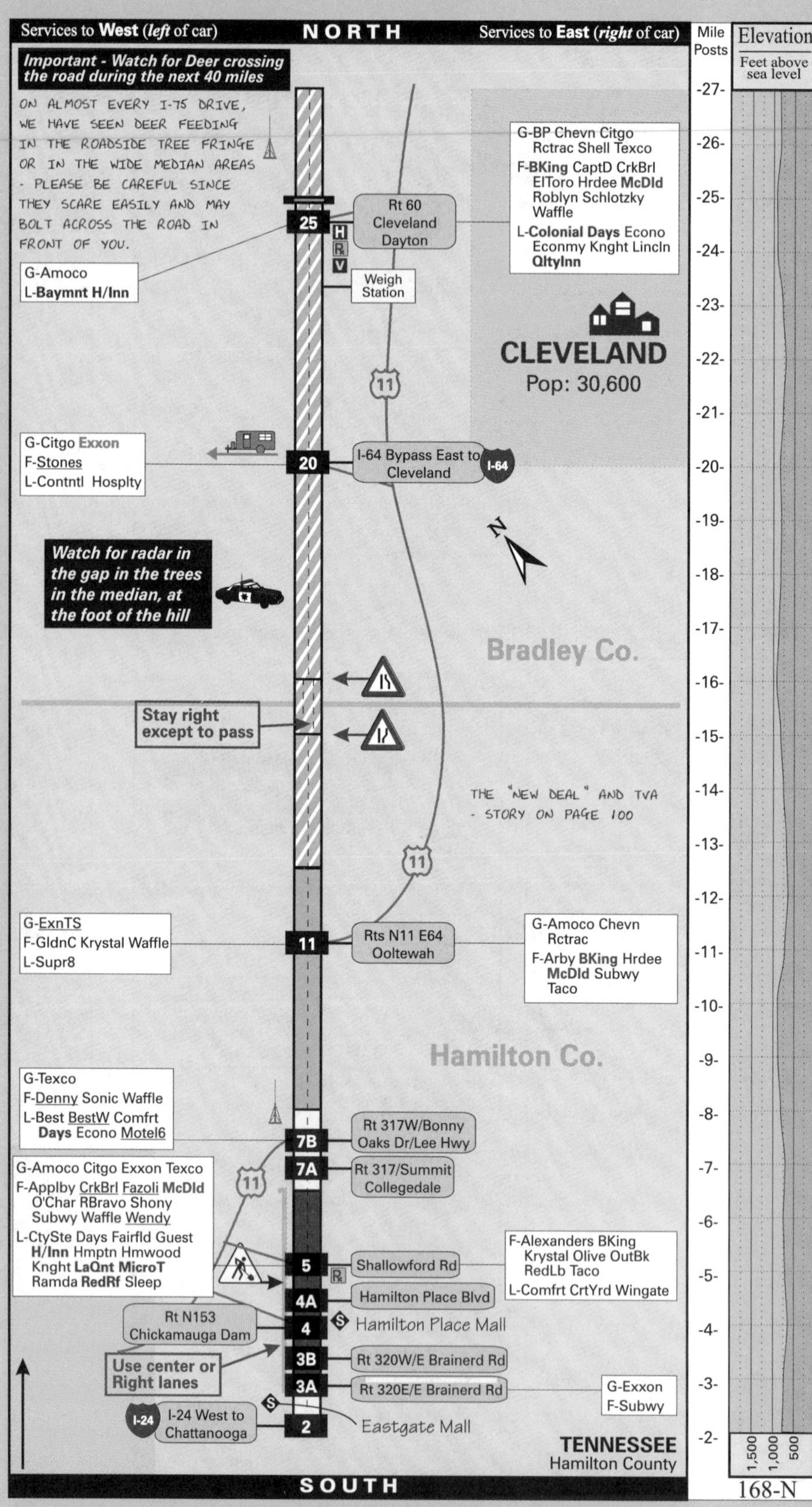

Services to West (left of car)
NORTH
Services to East (right of car)
Mile Posts
Elevation
Feet above sea level
Important - Watch for Deer crossing the road during the next 40 miles
ON ALMOST EVERY I-75 DRIVE, WE HAVE SEEN DEER FEEDING IN THE ROADSIDE TREE FRINGE OR IN THE WIDE MEDIAN AREAS - PLEASE BE CAREFUL SINCE THEY SCARE EASILY AND MAY BOLT ACROSS THE ROAD IN FRONT OF YOU.
25
Rt 60 Cleveland Dayton
G-BP Chevn Citgo Rctrac Shell Texco
F-BKing CaptD CrkBrl ElToro Hrdee McDld Roblyn Schlotzky Waffle
L-Colonial Days Econo Econmy Knght Lincln QltyInn
G-Amoco
L-Baymnt H/Inn
Weigh Station
CLEVELAND
Pop: 30,600
11
G-Citgo Exxon
F-Stones
L-Contntl Hosplty
20
I-64 Bypass East to Cleveland
I-64
Watch for radar in the gap in the trees in the median, at the foot of the hill
Bradley Co.
Stay right except to pass
THE "NEW DEAL" AND TVA - STORY ON PAGE 100
G-ExnTS
F-GldnC Krystal Waffle
L-Supr8
11
Rts N11 E64 Ooltewah
G-Amoco Chevn Rctrac
F-Arby BKing Hrdee McDld Subwy Taco
Hamilton Co.
G-Texco
F-Denny Sonic Waffle
L-Best BestW Comfrt Days Econo Motel6
7B
Rt 317W/Bonny Oaks Dr/Lee Hwy
7A
Rt 317/Summit Collegedale
G-Amoco Citgo Exxon Texco
F-Applby CrkBrl Fazoli McDld O'Char RBravo Shony Subwy Waffle Wendy
L-CtySte Days Fairfld Guest H/Inn Hmptn Hmwood Knght LaQnt MicroT Ramda RedRf Sleep
5
Shallowford Rd
F-Alexanders BKing Krystal Olive OutBk RedLb Taco
L-Comfrt CrtYrd Wingate
4A
Hamilton Place Blvd
4
Rt N153 Chickamauga Dam
Hamilton Place Mall
3B
Rt 320W/E Brainerd Rd
Use center or Right lanes
3A
Rt 320E/E Brainerd Rd
G-Exxon
F-Subwy
2
I-24
I-24 West to Chattanooga
Eastgate Mall
TENNESSEE
Hamilton County
SOUTH
-27- -26- -25- -24- -23- -22- -21- -20- -19- -18- -17- -16- -15- -14- -13- -12- -11- -10- -9- -8- -7- -6- -5- -4- -3- -2-
1,500 1,000 500

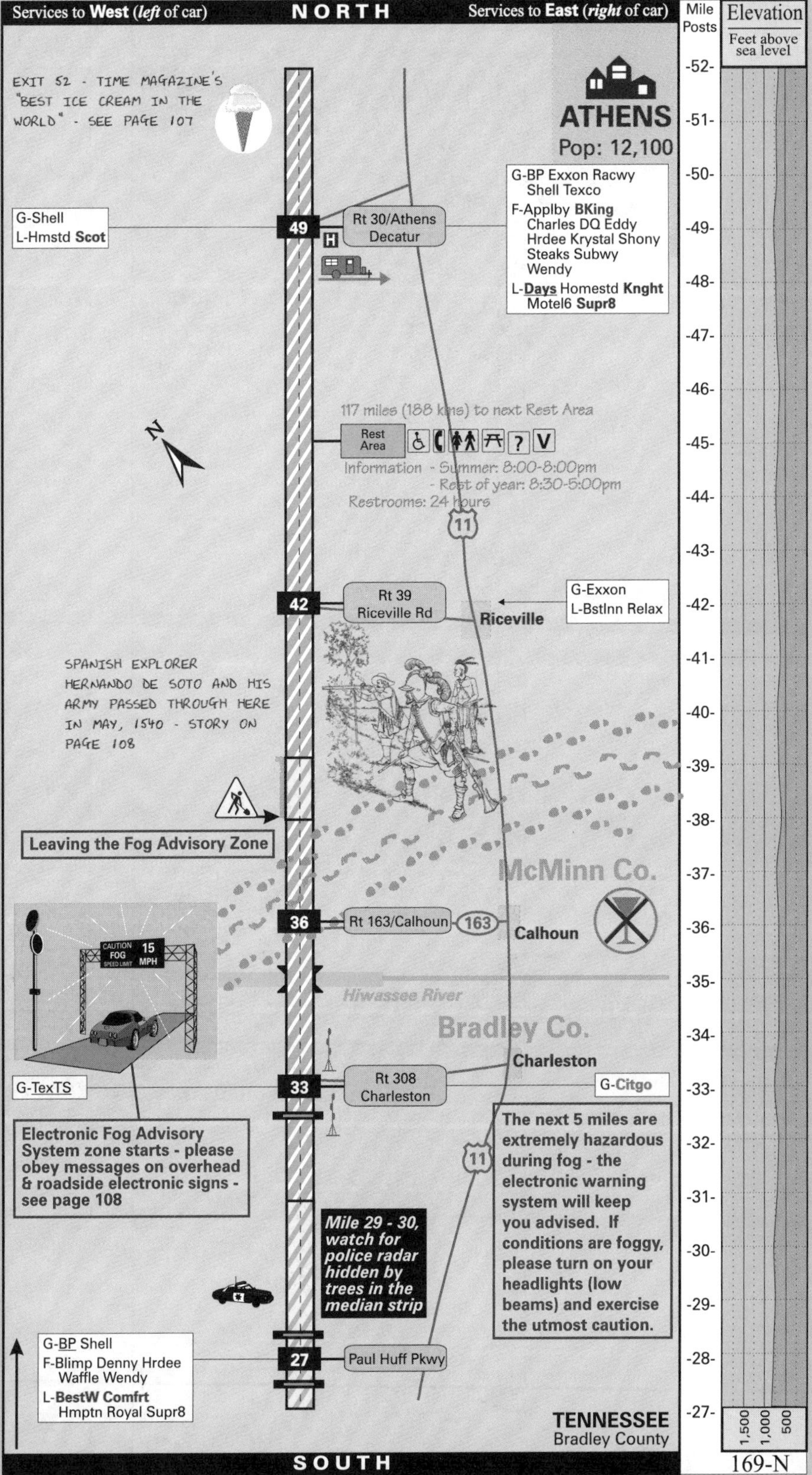
Services to West (left of car)
NORTH
Services to East (right of car)
Mile Posts
Elevation
Feet above sea level
EXIT 52 - TIME MAGAZINE'S "BEST ICE CREAM IN THE WORLD" - SEE PAGE 107
ATHENS
Pop: 12,100
G-BP Exxon Racwy Shell Texco
F-Applby BKing Charles DQ Eddy Hrdee Krystal Shony Steaks Subwy Wendy
L-Days Homestd Knght Motel6 Supr8
G-Shell
L-Hmstd Scot
49
Rt 30/Athens Decatur
H
117 miles (188 kms) to next Rest Area
Rest Area
?
V
Information - Summer: 8:00-8:00pm
- Rest of year: 8:30-5:00pm
Restrooms: 24 hours
11
42
Rt 39 Riceville Rd
Riceville
G-Exxon
L-BstInn Relax
SPANISH EXPLORER HERNANDO DE SOTO AND HIS ARMY PASSED THROUGH HERE IN MAY, 1540 - STORY ON PAGE 108
Leaving the Fog Advisory Zone
McMinn Co.
36
Rt 163/Calhoun
163
Calhoun
CAUTION FOG SPEED LIMIT 15 MPH
Hiwassee River
Bradley Co.
Charleston
G-TexTS
33
Rt 308 Charleston
G-Citgo
Electronic Fog Advisory System zone starts - please obey messages on overhead & roadside electronic signs - see page 108
The next 5 miles are extremely hazardous during fog - the electronic warning system will keep you advised. If conditions are foggy, please turn on your headlights (low beams) and exercise the utmost caution.
11
Mile 29 - 30, watch for police radar hidden by trees in the median strip
G-BP Shell
F-Blimp Denny Hrdee Waffle Wendy
L-BestW Comfrt Hmptn Royal Supr8
27
Paul Huff Pkwy
TENNESSEE
Bradley County
SOUTH
-52- -51- -50- -49- -48- -47- -46- -45- -44- -43- -42- -41- -40- -39- -38- -37- -36- -35- -34- -33- -32- -31- -30- -29- -28- -27-
1,500 1,000 500

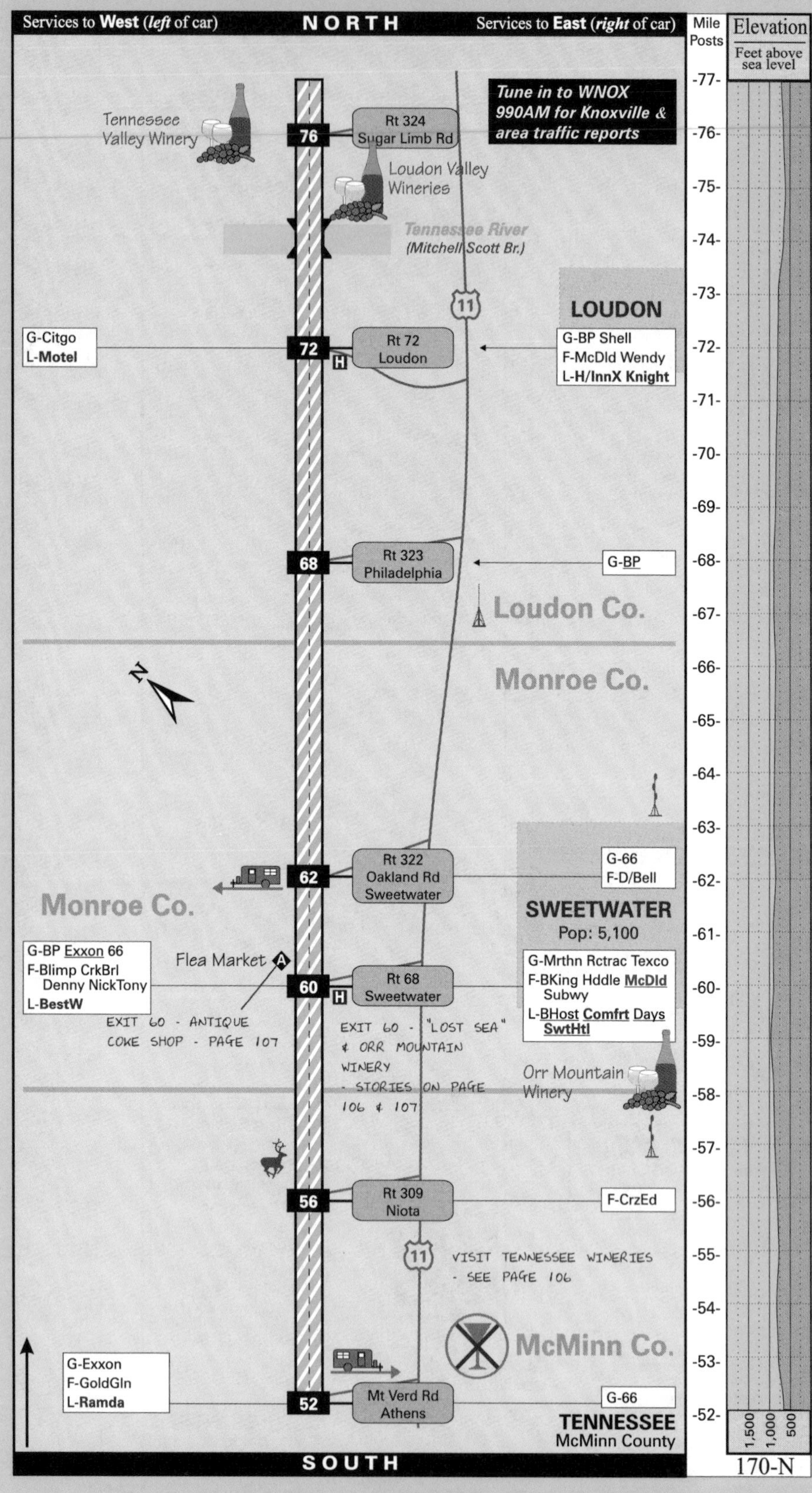
Services to West (left of car)
NORTH
Services to East (right of car)
Mile Posts
Elevation
Feet above sea level
Tune in to WNOX 990AM for Knoxville & area traffic reports
Tennessee Valley Winery
76
Rt 324 Sugar Limb Rd
Loudon Valley Wineries
Tennessee River (Mitchell Scott Br.)
LOUDON
G-Citgo
L-Motel
72
Rt 72 Loudon
G-BP Shell
F-McDld Wendy
L-H/InnX Knight
68
Rt 323 Philadelphia
G-BP
Loudon Co.
Monroe Co.
62
Rt 322 Oakland Rd Sweetwater
G-66
F-D/Bell
Monroe Co.
SWEETWATER
Pop: 5,100
G-BP Exxon 66
F-Blimp CrkBrl Denny NickTony
L-BestW
Flea Market
60
Rt 68 Sweetwater
G-Mrthn Rctrac Texco
F-BKing Hddle McDld Subwy
L-BHost Comfrt Days SwtHtl
EXIT 60 - ANTIQUE COKE SHOP - PAGE 107
EXIT 60 - "LOST SEA" & ORR MOUNTAIN WINERY - STORIES ON PAGE 106 & 107
Orr Mountain Winery
56
Rt 309 Niota
F-CrzEd
11
VISIT TENNESSEE WINERIES - SEE PAGE 106
McMinn Co.
G-Exxon
F-GoldGln
L-Ramda
52
Mt Verd Rd Athens
G-66
TENNESSEE
McMinn County
SOUTH
-77- -76- -75- -74- -73- -72- -71- -70- -69- -68- -67- -66- -65- -64- -63- -62- -61- -60- -59- -58- -57- -56- -55- -54- -53- -52-
1,500 1,000 500

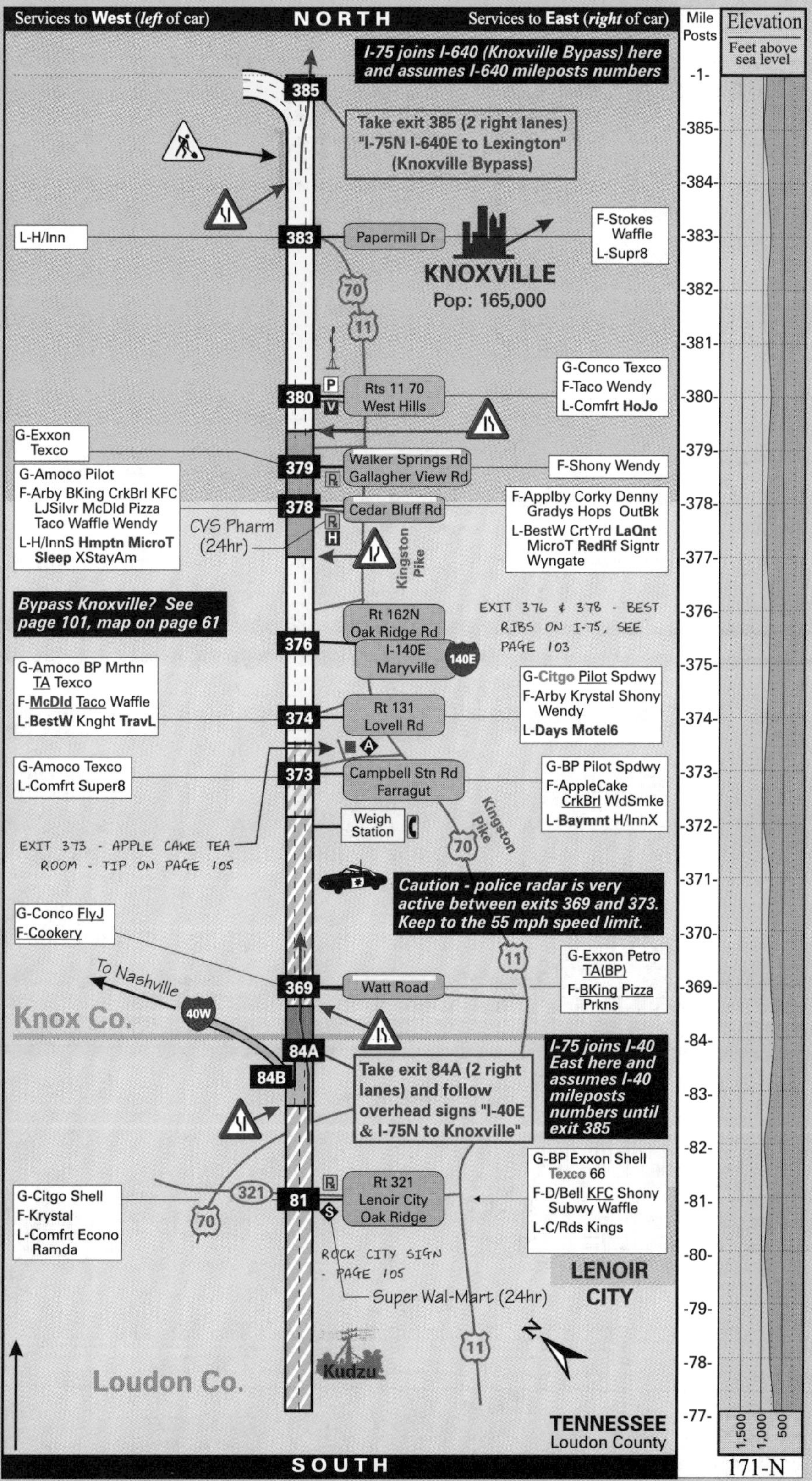

Services to West (left of car)
NORTH
Services to East (right of car)
I-75 joins I-640 (Knoxville Bypass) here and assumes I-640 mileposts numbers
385
Take exit 385 (2 right lanes) "I-75N I-640E to Lexington" (Knoxville Bypass)
L-H/Inn
383
Papermill Dr
F-Stokes Waffle
L-Supr8
KNOXVILLE
Pop: 165,000
70
11
G-Conco Texco
F-Taco Wendy
L-Comfrt HoJo
380
Rts 11 70 West Hills
G-Exxon Texco
379
Walker Springs Rd Gallagher View Rd
F-Shony Wendy
G-Amoco Pilot
F-Arby BKing CrkBrl KFC LJSilvr McDld Pizza Taco Waffle Wendy
L-H/InnS Hmptn MicroT Sleep XStayAm
378
Cedar Bluff Rd
CVS Pharm (24hr)
F-Applby Corky Denny Gradys Hops OutBk
L-BestW CrtYrd LaQnt MicroT RedRf Signtr Wyngate
Kingston Pike
Bypass Knoxville? See page 101, map on page 61
Rt 162N Oak Ridge Rd
EXIT 376 & 378 - BEST RIBS ON I-75, SEE PAGE 103
376
I-140E Maryville
140E
G-Amoco BP Mrthn TA Texco
F-McDld Taco Waffle
L-BestW Knght TravL
374
Rt 131 Lovell Rd
G-Citgo Pilot Spdwy
F-Arby Krystal Shony Wendy
L-Days Motel6
G-Amoco Texco
L-Comfrt Super8
373
Campbell Stn Rd Farragut
G-BP Pilot Spdwy
F-AppleCake CrkBrl WdSmke
L-Baymnt H/InnX
Weigh Station
Kingston Pike
EXIT 373 - APPLE CAKE TEA ROOM - TIP ON PAGE 105
Caution - police radar is very active between exits 369 and 373. Keep to the 55 mph speed limit.
G-Conco FlyJ
F-Cookery
To Nashville
369
Watt Road
G-Exxon Petro TA(BP)
F-BKing Pizza Prkns
40W
Knox Co.
84A
84B
Take exit 84A (2 right lanes) and follow overhead signs "I-40E & I-75N to Knoxville"
I-75 joins I-40 East here and assumes I-40 mileposts numbers until exit 385
321
81
Rt 321 Lenoir City Oak Ridge
G-BP Exxon Shell Texco 66
F-D/Bell KFC Shony Subwy Waffle
L-C/Rds Kings
G-Citgo Shell
F-Krystal
L-Comfrt Econo Ramda
ROCK CITY SIGN - PAGE 105
Super Wal-Mart (24hr)
LENOIR CITY
Kudzu
Loudon Co.
TENNESSEE
Loudon County
SOUTH
Mile Posts
Elevation
Feet above sea level
-1-
-385-
-384-
-383-
-382-
-381-
-380-
-379-
-378-
-377-
-376-
-375-
-374-
-373-
-372-
-371-
-370-
-369-
-84-
-83-
-82-
-81-
-80-
-79-
-78-
-77-
1,500
1,000
500

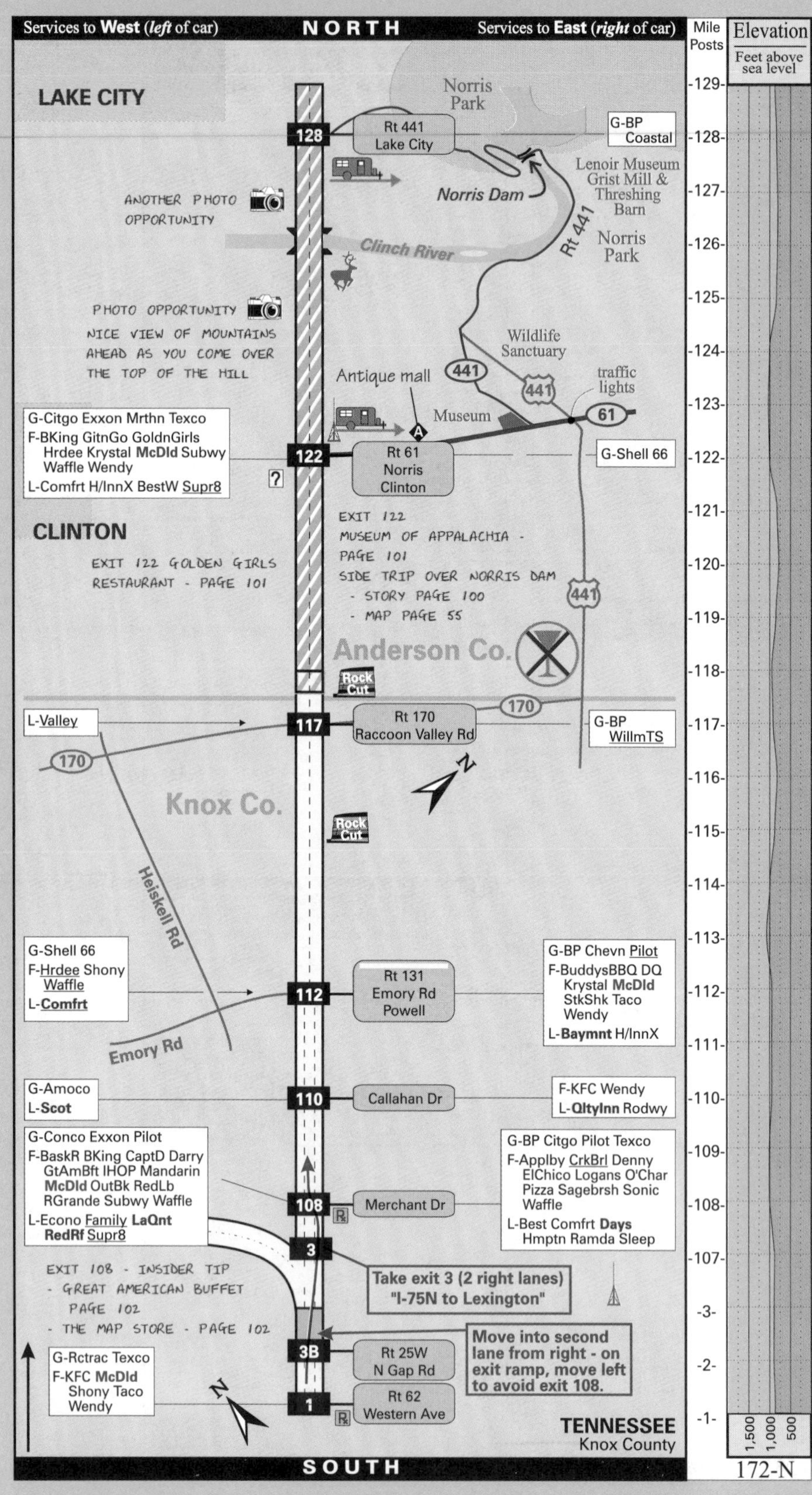

Services to West (left of car)
NORTH
Services to East (right of car)
Mile Posts
Elevation
Feet above sea level
LAKE CITY
Norris Park
128
Rt 441 Lake City
G-BP Coastal
Norris Dam
Lenoir Museum Grist Mill & Threshing Barn
ANOTHER PHOTO OPPORTUNITY
Clinch River
Rt 441
Norris Park
PHOTO OPPORTUNITY
NICE VIEW OF MOUNTAINS AHEAD AS YOU COME OVER THE TOP OF THE HILL
Wildlife Sanctuary
441
traffic lights
Antique mall
61
Museum
G-Citgo Exxon Mrthn Texco
F-BKing GitnGo GoldnGirls Hrdee Krystal McDld Subwy Waffle Wendy
L-Comfrt H/InnX BestW Supr8
122
Rt 61 Norris Clinton
G-Shell 66
CLINTON
EXIT 122 MUSEUM OF APPALACHIA - PAGE 101
SIDE TRIP OVER NORRIS DAM - STORY PAGE 100 - MAP PAGE 55
EXIT 122 GOLDEN GIRLS RESTAURANT - PAGE 101
Anderson Co.
Rock Cut
L-Valley
117
Rt 170 Raccoon Valley Rd
170
G-BP WillmTS
Knox Co.
Heiskell Rd
G-Shell 66
F-Hrdee Shony Waffle
L-Comfrt
112
Rt 131 Emory Rd Powell
G-BP Chevn Pilot
F-BuddysBBQ DQ Krystal McDld StkShk Taco Wendy
L-Baymnt H/InnX
Emory Rd
G-Amoco
L-Scot
110
Callahan Dr
F-KFC Wendy
L-QltyInn Rodwy
G-Conco Exxon Pilot
F-BaskR BKing CaptD Darry GtAmBft IHOP Mandarin McDld OutBk RedLb RGrande Subwy Waffle
L-Econo Family LaQnt RedRf Supr8
108
Merchant Dr
G-BP Citgo Pilot Texco
F-Applby CrkBrl Denny ElChico Logans O'Char Pizza Sagebrsh Sonic Waffle
L-Best Comfrt Days Hmptn Ramda Sleep
3
Take exit 3 (2 right lanes) "I-75N to Lexington"
EXIT 108 - INSIDER TIP - GREAT AMERICAN BUFFET PAGE 102 - THE MAP STORE - PAGE 102
3B
Rt 25W N Gap Rd
Move into second lane from right - on exit ramp, move left to avoid exit 108.
G-Rctrac Texco
F-KFC McDld Shony Taco Wendy
1
Rt 62 Western Ave
TENNESSEE Knox County
SOUTH
-129- -128- -127- -126- -125- -124- -123- -122- -121- -120- -119- -118- -117- -116- -115- -114- -113- -112- -111- -110- -109- -108- -107- -3- -2- -1-
1,500 1,000 500

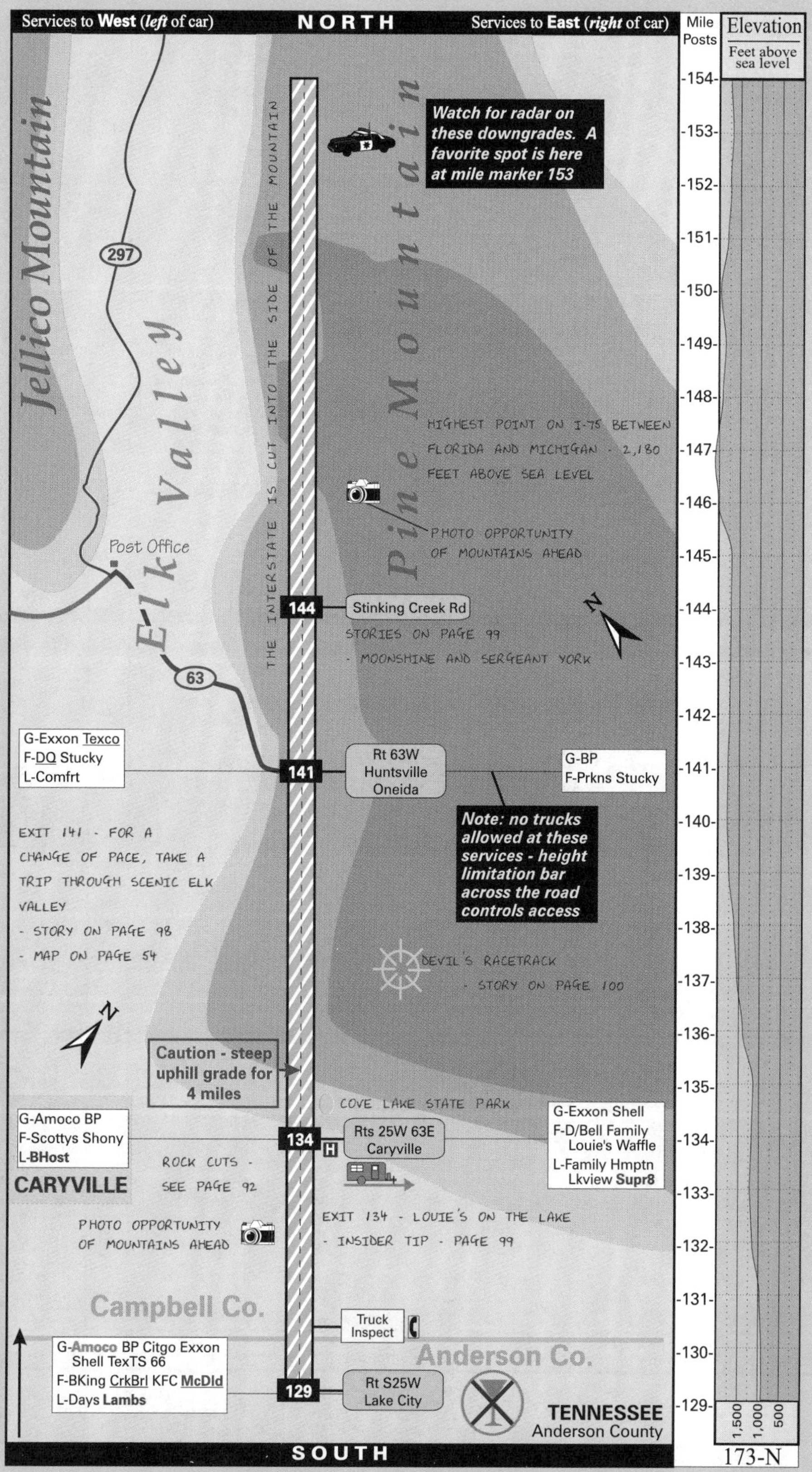

Services to West (left of car)
NORTH
Services to East (right of car)
Mile Posts
Elevation
Feet above sea level
Jellico Mountain
Elk Valley
Pine Mountain
297
63
Post Office
THE INTERSTATE IS CUT INTO THE SIDE OF THE MOUNTAIN
Watch for radar on these downgrades. A favorite spot is here at mile marker 153
HIGHEST POINT ON I-75 BETWEEN FLORIDA AND MICHIGAN - 2,180 FEET ABOVE SEA LEVEL
PHOTO OPPORTUNITY OF MOUNTAINS AHEAD
144
Stinking Creek Rd
STORIES ON PAGE 99
- MOONSHINE AND SERGEANT YORK
G-Exxon Texco
F-DQ Stucky
L-Comfrt
141
Rt 63W Huntsville Oneida
G-BP
F-Prkns Stucky
Note: no trucks allowed at these services - height limitation bar across the road controls access
EXIT 141 - FOR A CHANGE OF PACE, TAKE A TRIP THROUGH SCENIC ELK VALLEY
- STORY ON PAGE 98
- MAP ON PAGE 54
DEVIL'S RACETRACK
- STORY ON PAGE 100
Caution - steep uphill grade for 4 miles
COVE LAKE STATE PARK
G-Amoco BP
F-Scottys Shony
L-BHost
CARYVILLE
134
Rts 25W 63E Caryville
G-Exxon Shell
F-D/Bell Family Louie's Waffle
L-Family Hmptn Lkview Supr8
ROCK CUTS - SEE PAGE 92
EXIT 134 - LOUIE'S ON THE LAKE
- INSIDER TIP - PAGE 99
PHOTO OPPORTUNITY OF MOUNTAINS AHEAD
Campbell Co.
Truck Inspect
Anderson Co.
G-Amoco BP Citgo Exxon Shell TexTS 66
F-BKing CrkBrl KFC McDld
L-Days Lambs
129
Rt S25W Lake City
TENNESSEE
Anderson County
SOUTH
-154-
-153-
-152-
-151-
-150-
-149-
-148-
-147-
-146-
-145-
-144-
-143-
-142-
-141-
-140-
-139-
-138-
-137-
-136-
-135-
-134-
-133-
-132-
-131-
-130-
-129-
1,500
1,000
500

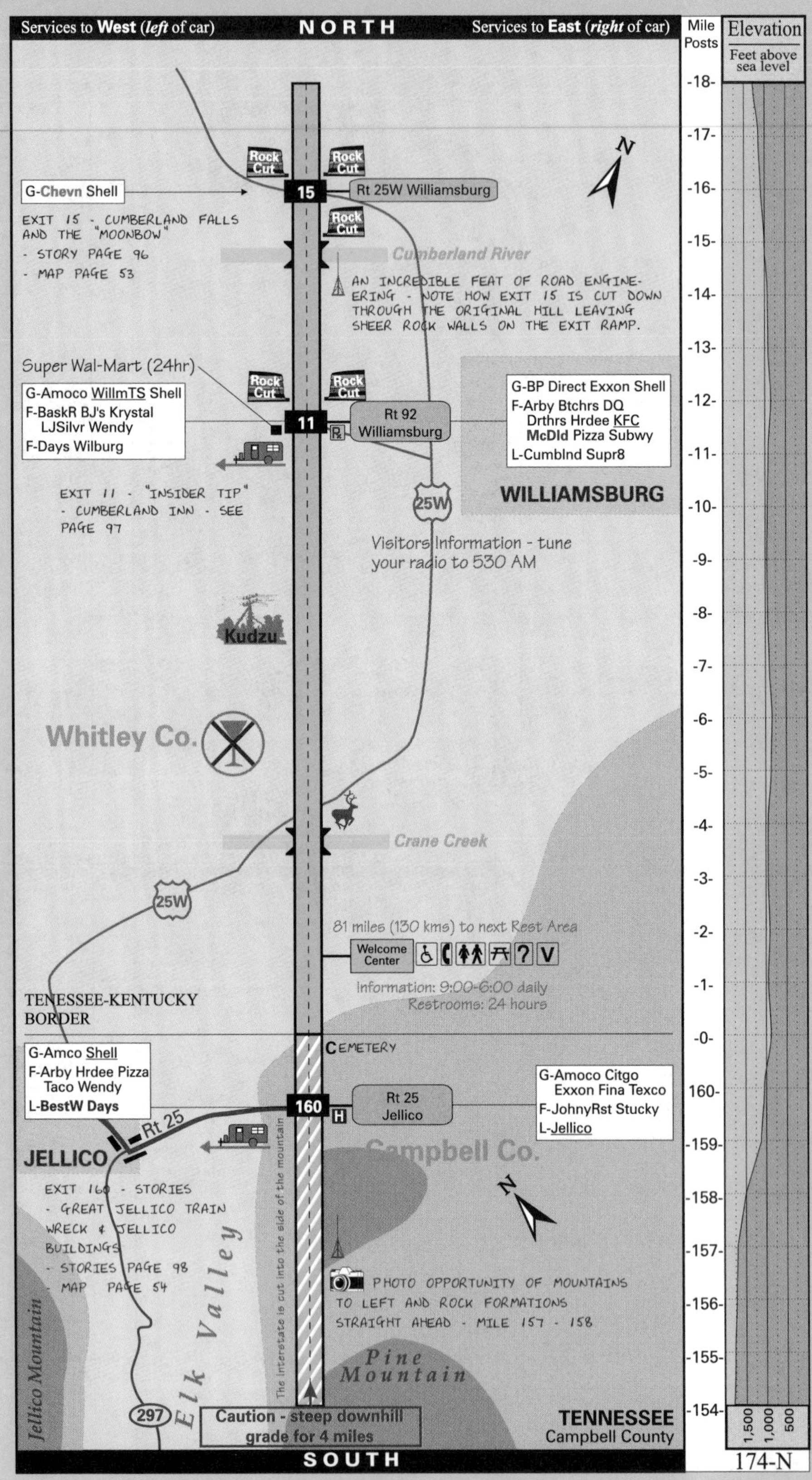

Services to West (left of car)
NORTH
Services to East (right of car)
Mile Posts
Elevation
Feet above sea level
-18-
-17-
-16-
-15-
-14-
-13-
-12-
-11-
-10-
-9-
-8-
-7-
-6-
-5-
-4-
-3-
-2-
-1-
-0-
160-
-159-
-158-
-157-
-156-
-155-
-154-
Rock Cut
G-Chevn Shell
15
Rt 25W Williamsburg
EXIT 15 - CUMBERLAND FALLS AND THE "MOONBOW"
- STORY PAGE 96
- MAP PAGE 53
Cumberland River
AN INCREDIBLE FEAT OF ROAD ENGINEERING - NOTE HOW EXIT 15 IS CUT DOWN THROUGH THE ORIGINAL HILL LEAVING SHEER ROCK WALLS ON THE EXIT RAMP.
Super Wal-Mart (24hr)
G-Amoco WillmTS Shell
F-BaskR BJ's Krystal LJSilvr Wendy
F-Days Wilburg
11
Rt 92 Williamsburg
G-BP Direct Exxon Shell
F-Arby Btchrs DQ Drthrs Hrdee KFC McDld Pizza Subwy
L-Cumblnd Supr8
WILLIAMSBURG
25W
EXIT 11 - "INSIDER TIP" - CUMBERLAND INN - SEE PAGE 97
Visitors Information - tune your radio to 530 AM
Kudzu
Whitley Co.
Crane Creek
25W
81 miles (130 kms) to next Rest Area
Welcome Center
Information: 9:00-6:00 daily
Restrooms: 24 hours
TENESSEE-KENTUCKY BORDER
CEMETERY
G-Amco Shell
F-Arby Hrdee Pizza Taco Wendy
L-BestW Days
160
Rt 25 Jellico
G-Amoco Citgo Exxon Fina Texco
F-JohnyRst Stucky
L-Jellico
Rt 25
JELLICO
Campbell Co.
EXIT 160 - STORIES
- GREAT JELLICO TRAIN WRECK & JELLICO BUILDINGS
- STORIES PAGE 98
- MAP PAGE 54
The interstate is cut into the side of the mountain
PHOTO OPPORTUNITY OF MOUNTAINS TO LEFT AND ROCK FORMATIONS STRAIGHT AHEAD - MILE 157 - 158
Elk Valley
Pine Mountain
Jellico Mountain
297
Caution - steep downhill grade for 4 miles
TENNESSEE
Campbell County
1,500
1,000
500
SOUTH

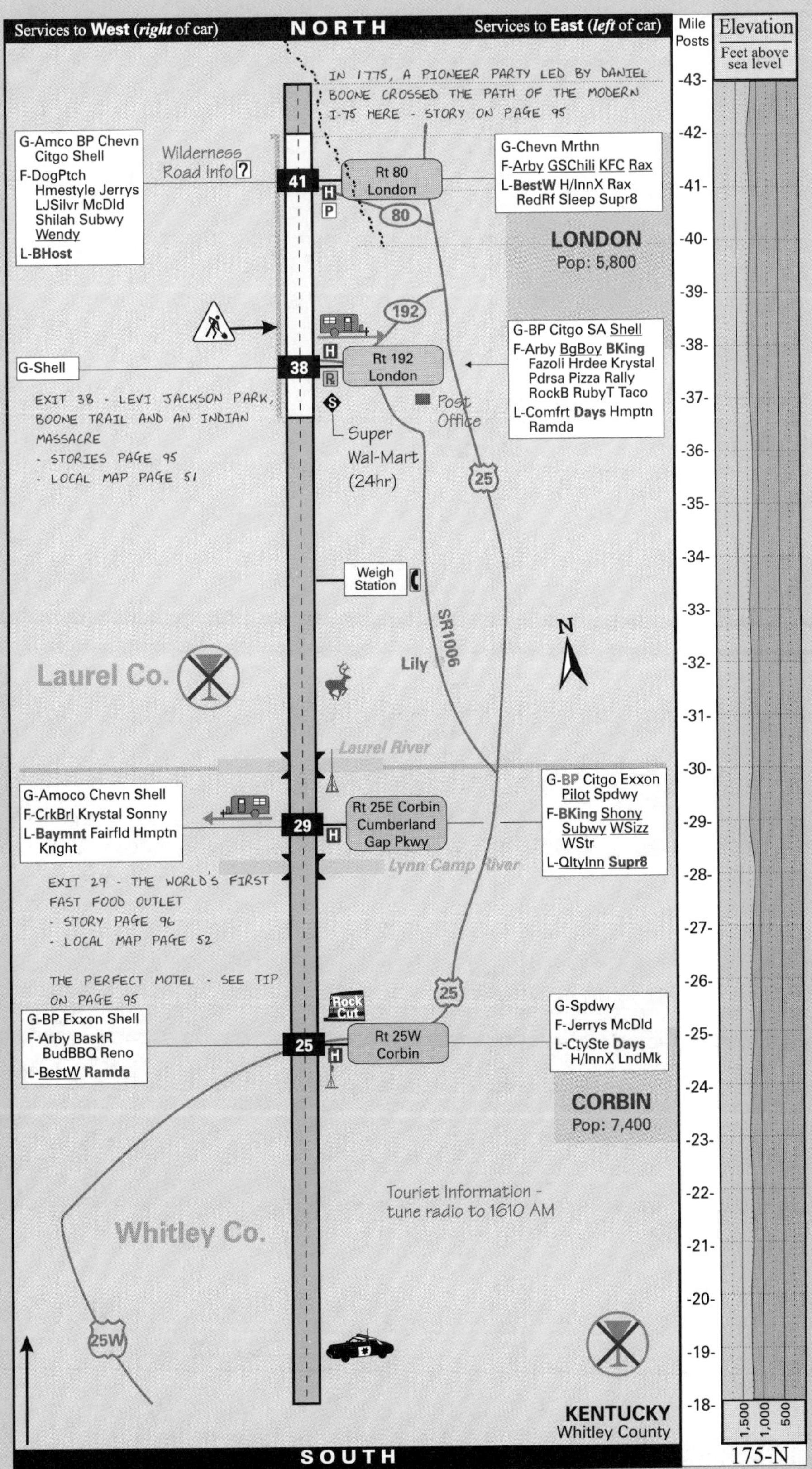

Services to West (right of car)
NORTH
Services to East (left of car)
IN 1775, A PIONEER PARTY LED BY DANIEL BOONE CROSSED THE PATH OF THE MODERN I-75 HERE - STORY ON PAGE 95
G-Amco BP Chevn Citgo Shell
F-DogPtch Hmestyle Jerrys LJSilvr McDld Shilah Subwy Wendy
L-BHost
Wilderness Road Info
41
Rt 80 London
80
G-Chevn Mrthn
F-Arby GSChili KFC Rax
L-BestW H/InnX Rax RedRf Sleep Supr8
LONDON
Pop: 5,800
192
G-Shell
38
Rt 192 London
G-BP Citgo SA Shell
F-Arby BgBoy BKing Fazoli Hrdee Krystal Pdrsa Pizza Rally RockB RubyT Taco
L-Comfrt Days Hmptn Ramda
EXIT 38 - LEVI JACKSON PARK, BOONE TRAIL AND AN INDIAN MASSACRE
- STORIES PAGE 95
- LOCAL MAP PAGE 51
Post Office
Super Wal-Mart (24hr)
25
Weigh Station
SR1006
N
Lily
Laurel Co.
Laurel River
G-Amoco Chevn Shell
F-CrkBrl Krystal Sonny
L-Baymnt Fairfld Hmptn Knght
29
Rt 25E Corbin Cumberland Gap Pkwy
G-BP Citgo Exxon Pilot Spdwy
F-BKing Shony Subwy WSizz WStr
L-QltyInn Supr8
Lynn Camp River
EXIT 29 - THE WORLD'S FIRST FAST FOOD OUTLET
- STORY PAGE 96
- LOCAL MAP PAGE 52
THE PERFECT MOTEL - SEE TIP ON PAGE 95
25
Rock Cut
G-BP Exxon Shell
F-Arby BaskR BudBBQ Reno
L-BestW Ramda
25
Rt 25W Corbin
G-Spdwy
F-Jerrys McDld
L-CtySte Days H/InnX LndMk
CORBIN
Pop: 7,400
Tourist Information - tune radio to 1610 AM
Whitley Co.
25W
KENTUCKY
Whitley County
SOUTH
Mile Posts
-43- -42- -41- -40- -39- -38- -37- -36- -35- -34- -33- -32- -31- -30- -29- -28- -27- -26- -25- -24- -23- -22- -21- -20- -19- -18-
Elevation
Feet above sea level
1,500
1,000
500

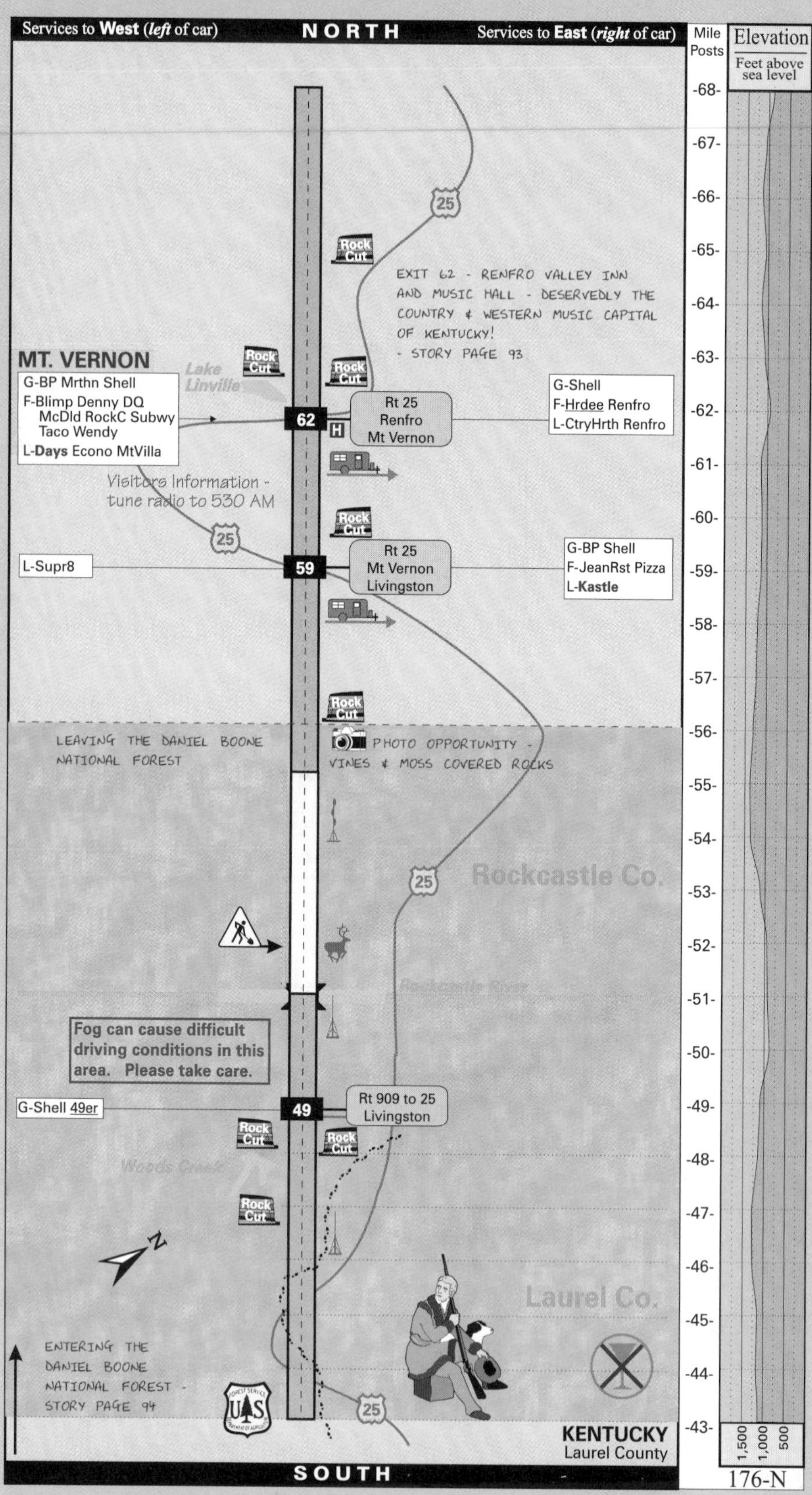

Services to West (left of car)
NORTH
Services to East (right of car)
Mile Posts
Elevation
Feet above sea level
EXIT 62 - RENFRO VALLEY INN AND MUSIC HALL - DESERVEDLY THE COUNTRY & WESTERN MUSIC CAPITAL OF KENTUCKY!
- STORY PAGE 93
MT. VERNON
G-BP Mrthn Shell
F-Blimp Denny DQ McDld RockC Subwy Taco Wendy
L-Days Econo MtVilla
Lake Linville
62
Rt 25 Renfro Mt Vernon
G-Shell
F-Hrdee Renfro
L-CtryHrth Renfro
Visitors Information - tune radio to 530 AM
L-Supr8
59
Rt 25 Mt Vernon Livingston
G-BP Shell
F-JeanRst Pizza
L-Kastle
LEAVING THE DANIEL BOONE NATIONAL FOREST
PHOTO OPPORTUNITY - VINES & MOSS COVERED ROCKS
Rockcastle Co.
Rockcastle River
Fog can cause difficult driving conditions in this area. Please take care.
G-Shell 49er
49
Rt 909 to 25 Livingston
Woods Creek
Laurel Co.
ENTERING THE DANIEL BOONE NATIONAL FOREST - STORY PAGE 94
KENTUCKY
Laurel County
SOUTH
-68- -67- -66- -65- -64- -63- -62- -61- -60- -59- -58- -57- -56- -55- -54- -53- -52- -51- -50- -49- -48- -47- -46- -45- -44- -43-
1,500 1,000 500

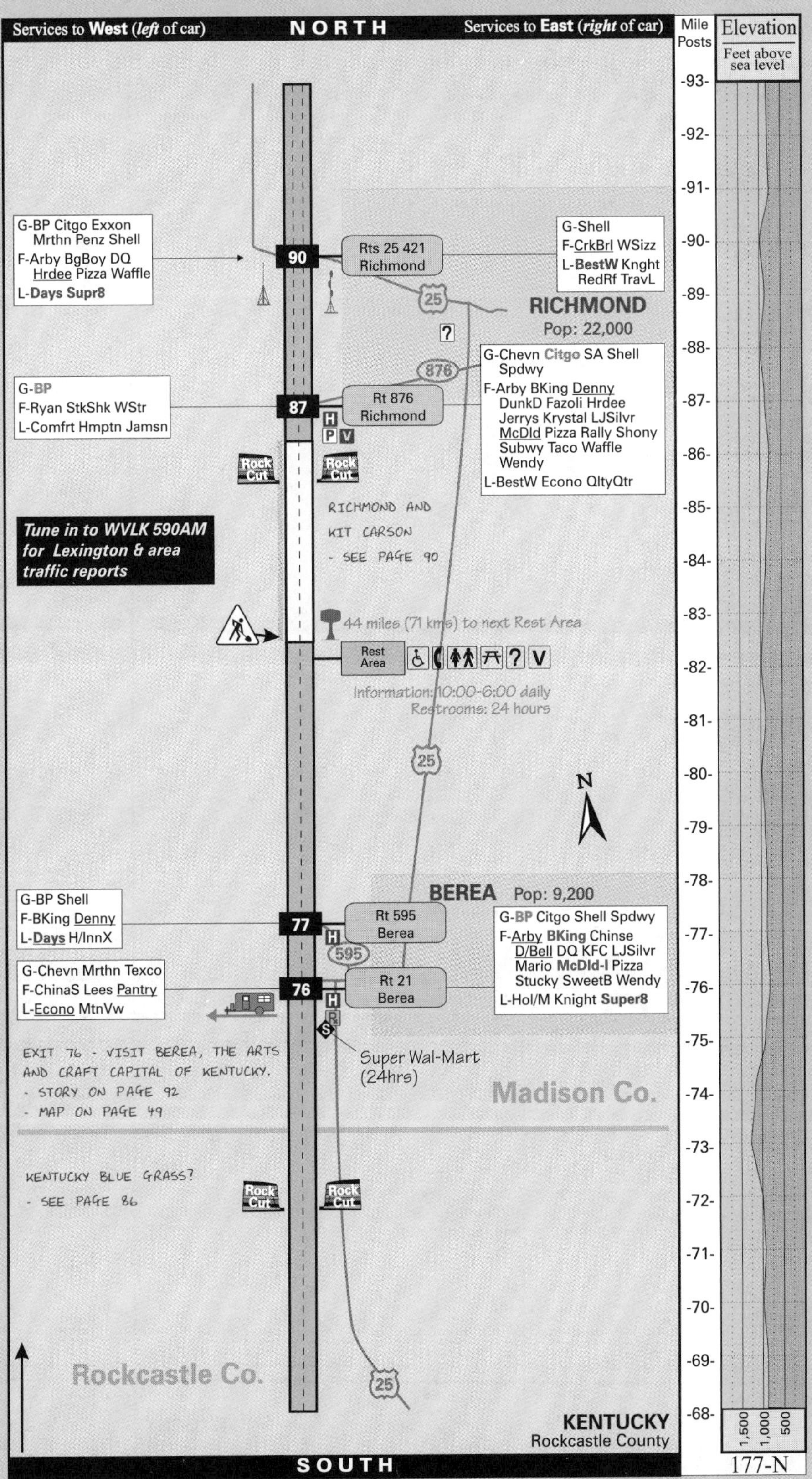

Services to West (left of car)
NORTH
Services to East (right of car)
Mile Posts
Elevation
Feet above sea level
G-BP Citgo Exxon Mrthn Penz Shell
F-Arby BgBoy DQ Hrdee Pizza Waffle
L-Days Supr8
90
Rts 25 421 Richmond
G-Shell
F-CrkBrl WSizz
L-BestW Knght RedRf TravL
25
RICHMOND
Pop: 22,000
876
G-Chevn Citgo SA Shell Spdwy
F-Arby BKing Denny DunkD Fazoli Hrdee Jerrys Krystal LJSilvr McDld Pizza Rally Shony Subwy Taco Waffle Wendy
L-BestW Econo QltyQtr
G-BP
F-Ryan StkShk WStr
L-Comfrt Hmptn Jamsn
87
Rt 876 Richmond
Rock Cut
Rock Cut
RICHMOND AND KIT CARSON - SEE PAGE 90
Tune in to WVLK 590AM for Lexington & area traffic reports
44 miles (71 kms) to next Rest Area
Rest Area
Information: 10:00-6:00 daily
Restrooms: 24 hours
25
N
BEREA Pop: 9,200
G-BP Shell
F-BKing Denny
L-Days H/InnX
77
Rt 595 Berea
595
G-BP Citgo Shell Spdwy
F-Arby BKing Chinse D/Bell DQ KFC LJSilvr Mario McDld-I Pizza Stucky SweetB Wendy
L-Hol/M Knight Super8
G-Chevn Mrthn Texco
F-ChinaS Lees Pantry
L-Econo MtnVw
76
Rt 21 Berea
Super Wal-Mart (24hrs)
EXIT 76 - VISIT BEREA, THE ARTS AND CRAFT CAPITAL OF KENTUCKY.
- STORY ON PAGE 92
- MAP ON PAGE 49
Madison Co.
KENTUCKY BLUE GRASS?
- SEE PAGE 86
Rock Cut
Rock Cut
Rockcastle Co.
25
KENTUCKY
Rockcastle County
SOUTH
-93-
-92-
-91-
-90-
-89-
-88-
-87-
-86-
-85-
-84-
-83-
-82-
-81-
-80-
-79-
-78-
-77-
-76-
-75-
-74-
-73-
-72-
-71-
-70-
-69-
-68-
1,500
1,000
500

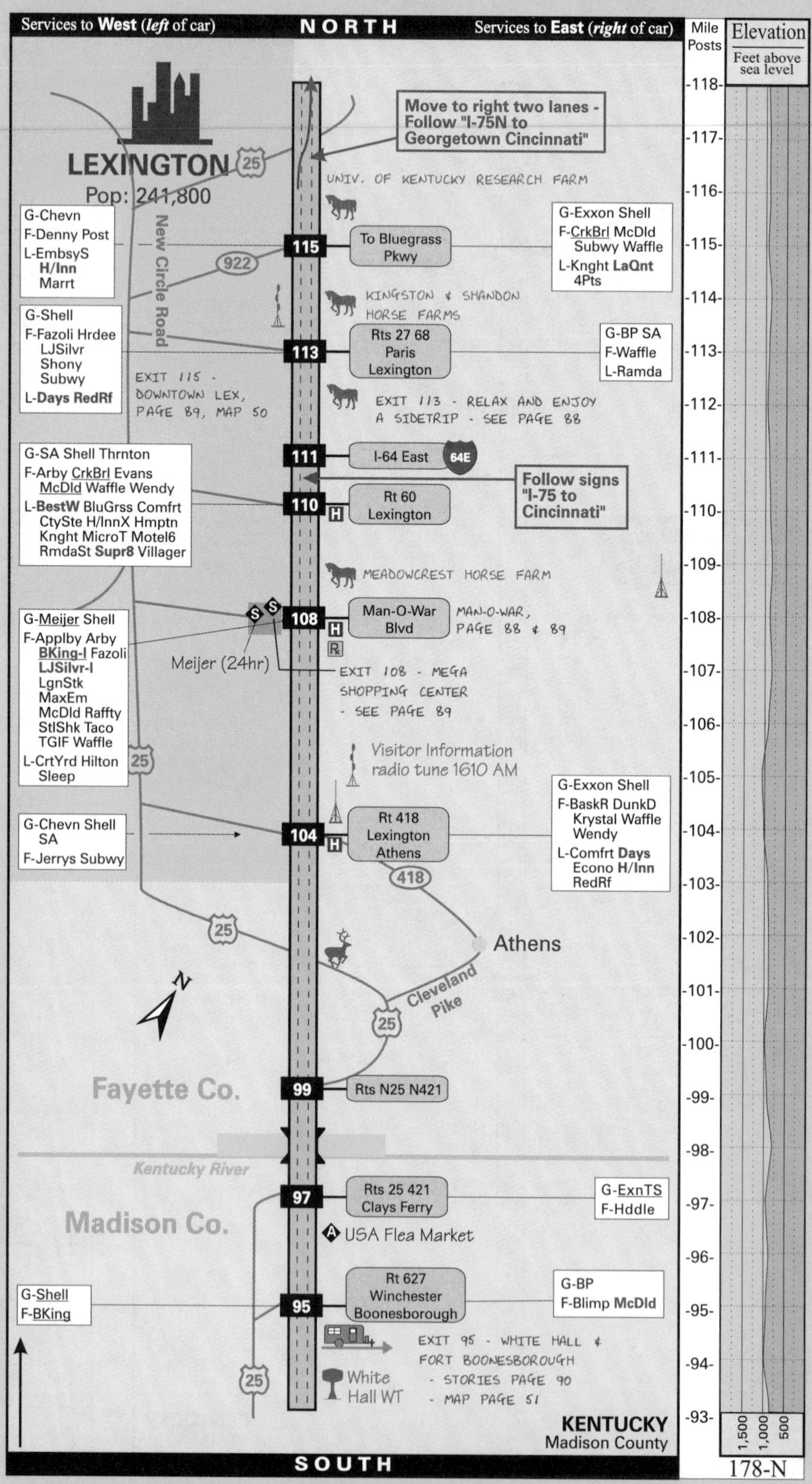

Services to West (left of car)
NORTH
Services to East (right of car)
Mile Posts
Elevation
Feet above sea level
LEXINGTON
Pop: 241,800
Move to right two lanes - Follow "I-75N to Georgetown Cincinnati"
UNIV. OF KENTUCKY RESEARCH FARM
G-Chevn
F-Denny Post
L-EmbsyS H/Inn Marrt
115
To Bluegrass Pkwy
G-Exxon Shell
F-CrkBrl McDld Subwy Waffle
L-Knght LaQnt 4Pts
New Circle Road
922
KINGSTON & SHANDON HORSE FARMS
G-Shell
F-Fazoli Hrdee LJSilvr Shony Subwy
L-Days RedRf
113
Rts 27 68 Paris Lexington
G-BP SA
F-Waffle
L-Ramda
EXIT 115 - DOWNTOWN LEX, PAGE 89, MAP 50
EXIT 113 - RELAX AND ENJOY A SIDETRIP - SEE PAGE 88
G-SA Shell Thrnton
F-Arby CrkBrl Evans McDld Waffle Wendy
L-BestW BluGrss Comfrt CtySte H/InnX Hmptn Knght MicroT Motel6 RmdaSt Supr8 Villager
111
I-64 East
64E
Follow signs "I-75 to Cincinnati"
110
Rt 60 Lexington
MEADOWCREST HORSE FARM
G-Meijer Shell
F-Applby Arby BKing-I Fazoli LJSilvr-I LgnStk MaxEm McDld Raffty StlShk Taco TGIF Waffle
L-CrtYrd Hilton Sleep
108
Man-O-War Blvd
MAN-O-WAR, PAGE 88 & 89
Meijer (24hr)
EXIT 108 - MEGA SHOPPING CENTER - SEE PAGE 89
Visitor Information radio tune 1610 AM
G-Chevn Shell SA
F-Jerrys Subwy
104
Rt 418 Lexington Athens
418
G-Exxon Shell
F-BaskR DunkD Krystal Waffle Wendy
L-Comfrt Days Econo H/Inn RedRf
Athens
Cleveland Pike
25
Fayette Co.
99
Rts N25 N421
Kentucky River
97
Rts 25 421 Clays Ferry
G-ExnTS
F-Hddle
Madison Co.
USA Flea Market
G-Shell
F-BKing
95
Rt 627 Winchester Boonesborough
G-BP
F-Blimp McDld
EXIT 95 - WHITE HALL & FORT BOONESBOROUGH - STORIES PAGE 90 - MAP PAGE 51
White Hall WT
KENTUCKY
Madison County
SOUTH
-118- -117- -116- -115- -114- -113- -112- -111- -110- -109- -108- -107- -106- -105- -104- -103- -102- -101- -100- -99- -98- -97- -96- -95- -94- -93-
1,500 1,000 500

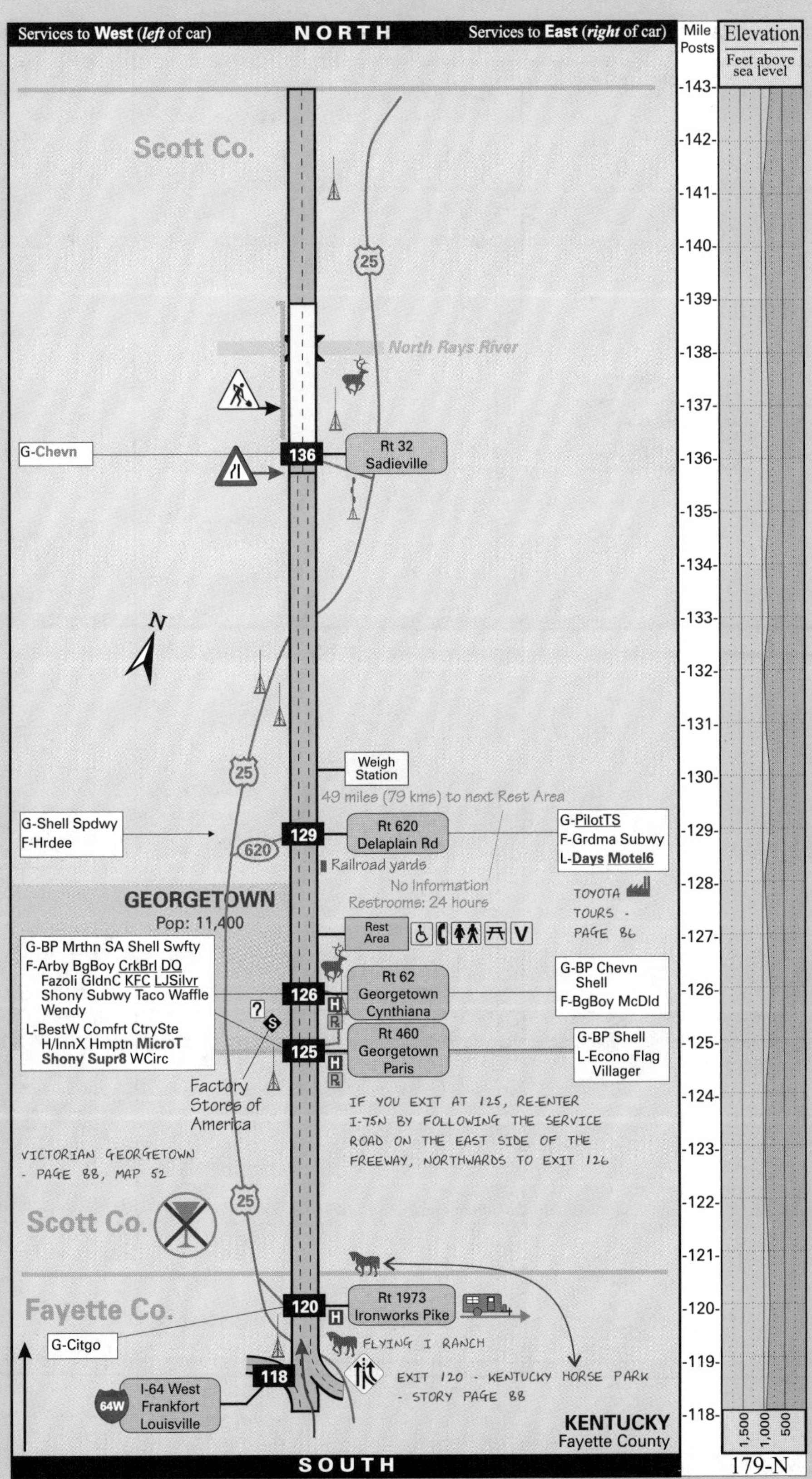

Services to West (left of car)
NORTH
Services to East (right of car)
Mile Posts
Elevation
Feet above sea level
Scott Co.
25
North Rays River
G-Chevn
136
Rt 32
Sadieville
Weigh Station
49 miles (79 kms) to next Rest Area
G-Shell Spdwy
F-Hrdee
129
620
Rt 620
Delaplain Rd
G-PilotTS
F-Grdma Subwy
L-Days Motel6
Railroad yards
No Information
Restrooms: 24 hours
GEORGETOWN
Pop: 11,400
TOYOTA TOURS - PAGE 86
Rest Area
V
G-BP Mrthn SA Shell Swfty
F-Arby BgBoy CrkBrl DQ Fazoli GldnC KFC LJSilvr Shony Subwy Taco Waffle Wendy
L-BestW Comfrt CtrySte H/InnX Hmptn MicroT Shony Supr8 WCirc
126
Rt 62
Georgetown
Cynthiana
G-BP Chevn Shell
F-BgBoy McDld
125
Rt 460
Georgetown
Paris
G-BP Shell
L-Econo Flag Villager
Factory Stores of America
IF YOU EXIT AT 125, RE-ENTER I-75N BY FOLLOWING THE SERVICE ROAD ON THE EAST SIDE OF THE FREEWAY, NORTHWARDS TO EXIT 126
VICTORIAN GEORGETOWN - PAGE 88, MAP 52
Scott Co.
Fayette Co.
120
Rt 1973
Ironworks Pike
G-Citgo
FLYING I RANCH
118
64W
I-64 West
Frankfort
Louisville
EXIT 120 - KENTUCKY HORSE PARK - STORY PAGE 88
KENTUCKY
Fayette County
SOUTH
-143- -142- -141- -140- -139- -138- -137- -136- -135- -134- -133- -132- -131- -130- -129- -128- -127- -126- -125- -124- -123- -122- -121- -120- -119- -118-
1,500
1,000
500

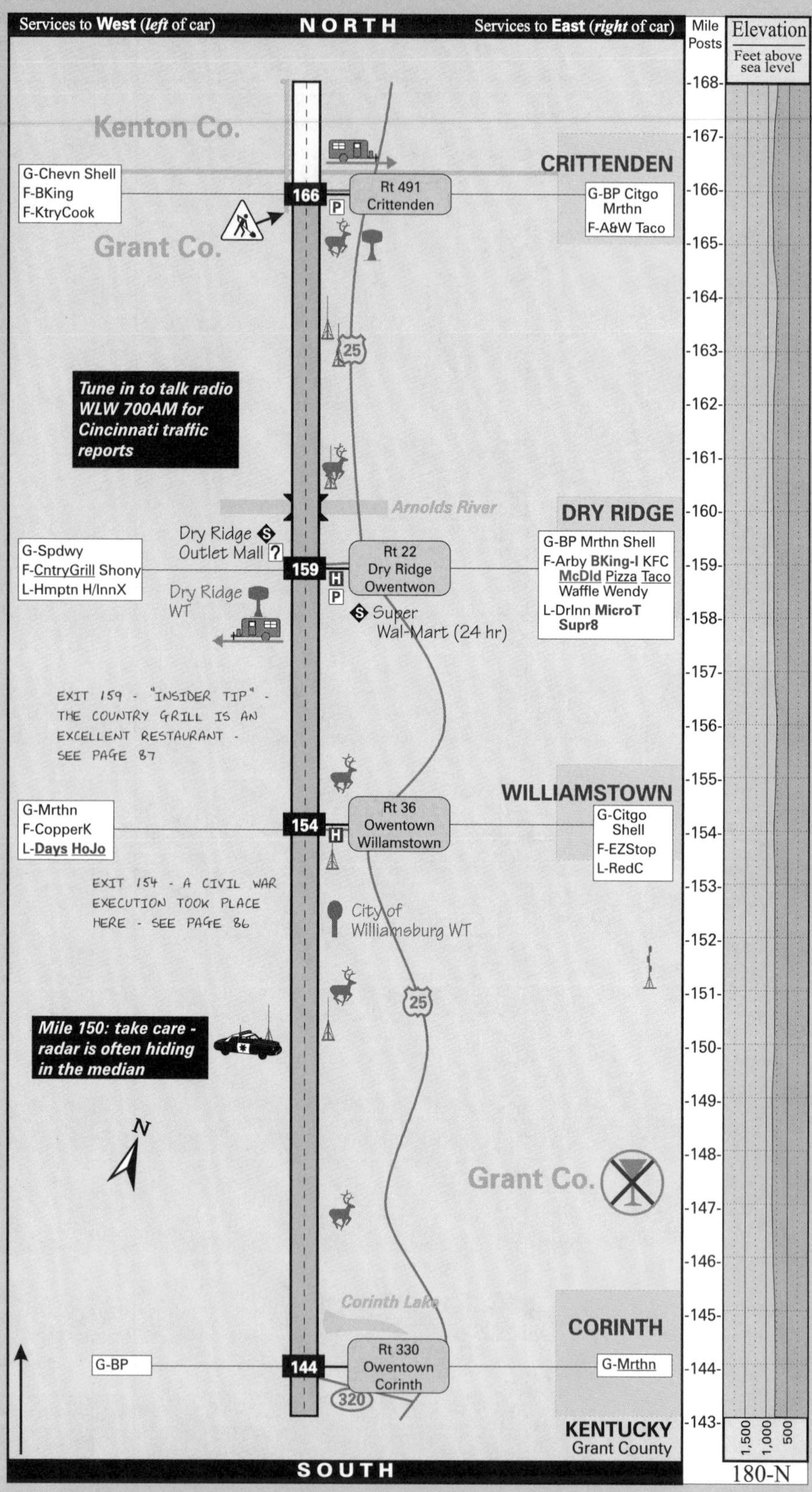

Services to West (left of car)
NORTH
Services to East (right of car)
Mile Posts
Elevation
Feet above sea level
Kenton Co.
CRITTENDEN
G-Chevn Shell
F-BKing
F-KtryCook
166
Rt 491 Crittenden
G-BP Citgo Mrthn
F-A&W Taco
Grant Co.
25
Tune in to talk radio WLW 700AM for Cincinnati traffic reports
Arnolds River
DRY RIDGE
Dry Ridge Outlet Mall
G-Spdwy
F-CntryGrill Shony
L-Hmptn H/InnX
159
Rt 22 Dry Ridge Owentwon
G-BP Mrthn Shell
F-Arby BKing-I KFC McDld Pizza Taco Waffle Wendy
L-DrInn MicroT Supr8
Dry Ridge WT
Super Wal-Mart (24 hr)
EXIT 159 - "INSIDER TIP" - THE COUNTRY GRILL IS AN EXCELLENT RESTAURANT - SEE PAGE 87
WILLIAMSTOWN
G-Mrthn
F-CopperK
L-Days HoJo
154
Rt 36 Owentown Willamstown
G-Citgo Shell
F-EZStop
L-RedC
EXIT 154 - A CIVIL WAR EXECUTION TOOK PLACE HERE - SEE PAGE 86
City of Williamsburg WT
25
Mile 150: take care - radar is often hiding in the median
N
Grant Co.
Corinth Lake
CORINTH
G-BP
144
Rt 330 Owentown Corinth
G-Mrthn
320
KENTUCKY
Grant County
SOUTH
-168- -167- -166- -165- -164- -163- -162- -161- -160- -159- -158- -157- -156- -155- -154- -153- -152- -151- -150- -149- -148- -147- -146- -145- -144- -143-
1,500 1,000 500

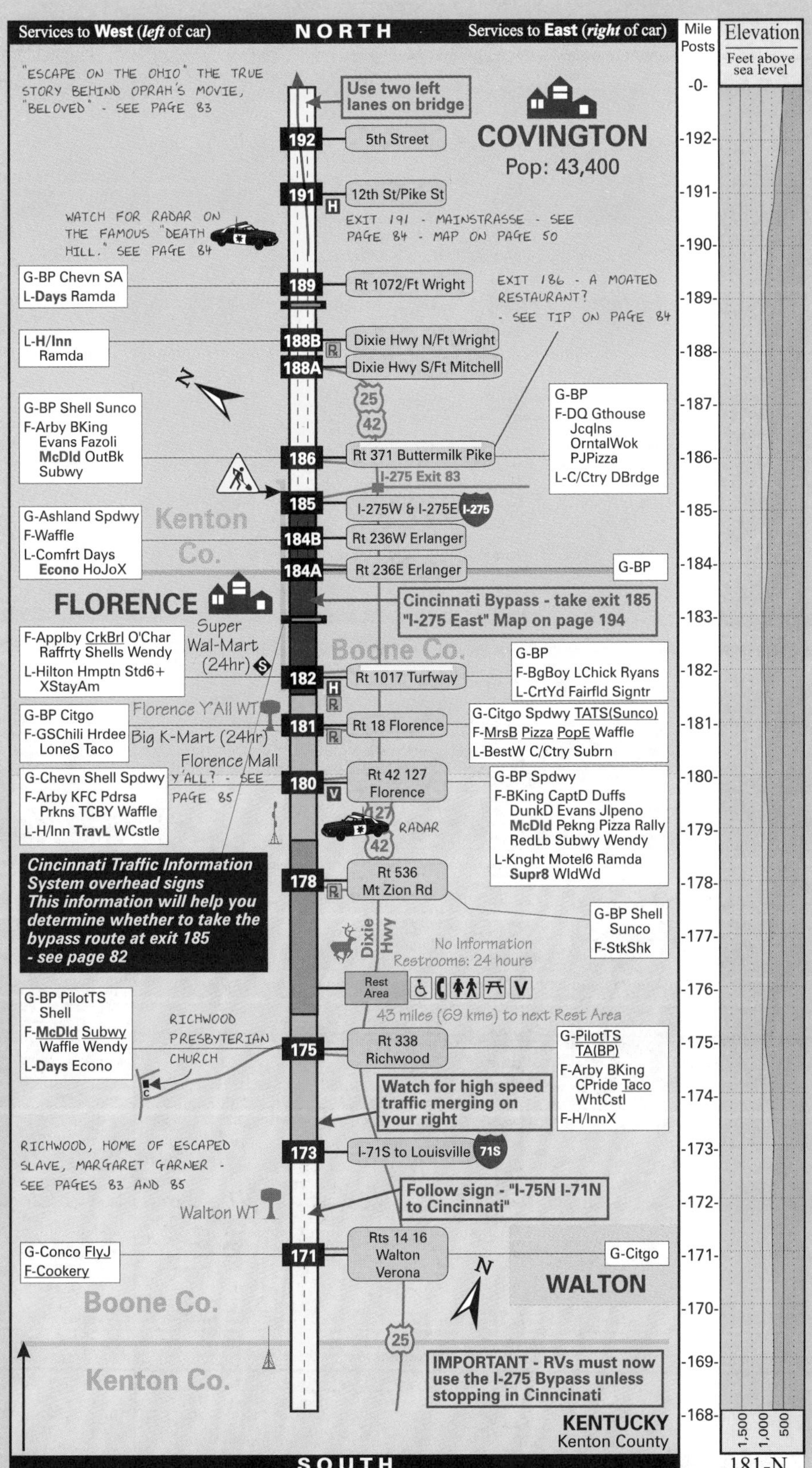
Services to West (left of car)
NORTH
Services to East (right of car)
Mile Posts
Elevation
Feet above sea level
"ESCAPE ON THE OHIO" THE TRUE STORY BEHIND OPRAH'S MOVIE, "BELOVED" - SEE PAGE 83
Use two left lanes on bridge
COVINGTON
Pop: 43,400
192 5th Street
191 12th St/Pike St
WATCH FOR RADAR ON THE FAMOUS "DEATH HILL." SEE PAGE 84
EXIT 191 - MAINSTRASSE - SEE PAGE 84 - MAP ON PAGE 50
G-BP Chevn SA
L-Days Ramda
189 Rt 1072/Ft Wright
EXIT 186 - A MOATED RESTAURANT? - SEE TIP ON PAGE 84
L-H/Inn Ramda
188B Dixie Hwy N/Ft Wright
188A Dixie Hwy S/Ft Mitchell
G-BP Shell Sunco
F-Arby BKing Evans Fazoli McDld OutBk Subwy
186 Rt 371 Buttermilk Pike
G-BP
F-DQ Gthouse Jcqlns OrntalWok PJPizza
L-C/Ctry DBrdge
I-275 Exit 83
185 I-275W & I-275E
G-Ashland Spdwy
F-Waffle
L-Comfrt Days Econo HoJoX
Kenton Co.
184B Rt 236W Erlanger
184A Rt 236E Erlanger
G-BP
FLORENCE
Cincinnati Bypass - take exit 185 "I-275 East" Map on page 194
F-Applby CrkBrl O'Char Raffrty Shells Wendy
L-Hilton Hmptn Std6+ XStayAm
Super Wal-Mart (24hr)
Boone Co.
182 Rt 1017 Turfway
G-BP
F-BgBoy LChick Ryans
L-CrtYd Fairfld Signtr
G-BP Citgo
F-GSChili Hrdee LoneS Taco
Florence Y'All WT
Big K-Mart (24hr)
181 Rt 18 Florence
G-Citgo Spdwy TATS(Sunco)
F-MrsB Pizza PopE Waffle
L-BestW C/Ctry Subrn
Florence Mall
G-Chevn Shell Spdwy
F-Arby KFC Pdrsa Prkns TCBY Waffle
L-H/Inn TravL WCstle
Y'ALL? - SEE PAGE 85
180 Rt 42 127 Florence
G-BP Spdwy
F-BKing CaptD Duffs DunkD Evans Jlpeno McDld Pekng Pizza Rally RedLb Subwy Wendy
L-Knght Motel6 Ramda Supr8 WldWd
RADAR
Cincinnati Traffic Information System overhead signs
This information will help you determine whether to take the bypass route at exit 185
- see page 82
178 Rt 536 Mt Zion Rd
G-BP Shell Sunco
F-StkShk
Dixie Hwy
No Information
Restrooms: 24 hours
Rest Area
43 miles (69 kms) to next Rest Area
G-BP PilotTS Shell
F-McDld Subwy Waffle Wendy
L-Days Econo
RICHWOOD PRESBYTERIAN CHURCH
175 Rt 338 Richwood
G-PilotTS TA(BP)
F-Arby BKing CPride Taco WhtCstl
F-H/InnX
Watch for high speed traffic merging on your right
RICHWOOD, HOME OF ESCAPED SLAVE, MARGARET GARNER - SEE PAGES 83 AND 85
173 I-71S to Louisville
Follow sign - "I-75N I-71N to Cincinnati"
Walton WT
G-Conco FlyJ
F-Cookery
171 Rts 14 16 Walton Verona
G-Citgo
WALTON
Boone Co.
Kenton Co.
IMPORTANT - RVs must now use the I-275 Bypass unless stopping in Cincinnati
KENTUCKY
Kenton County
SOUTH
-0- -192- -191- -190- -189- -188- -187- -186- -185- -184- -183- -182- -181- -180- -179- -178- -177- -176- -175- -174- -173- -172- -171- -170- -169- -168-
1,500 1,000 500

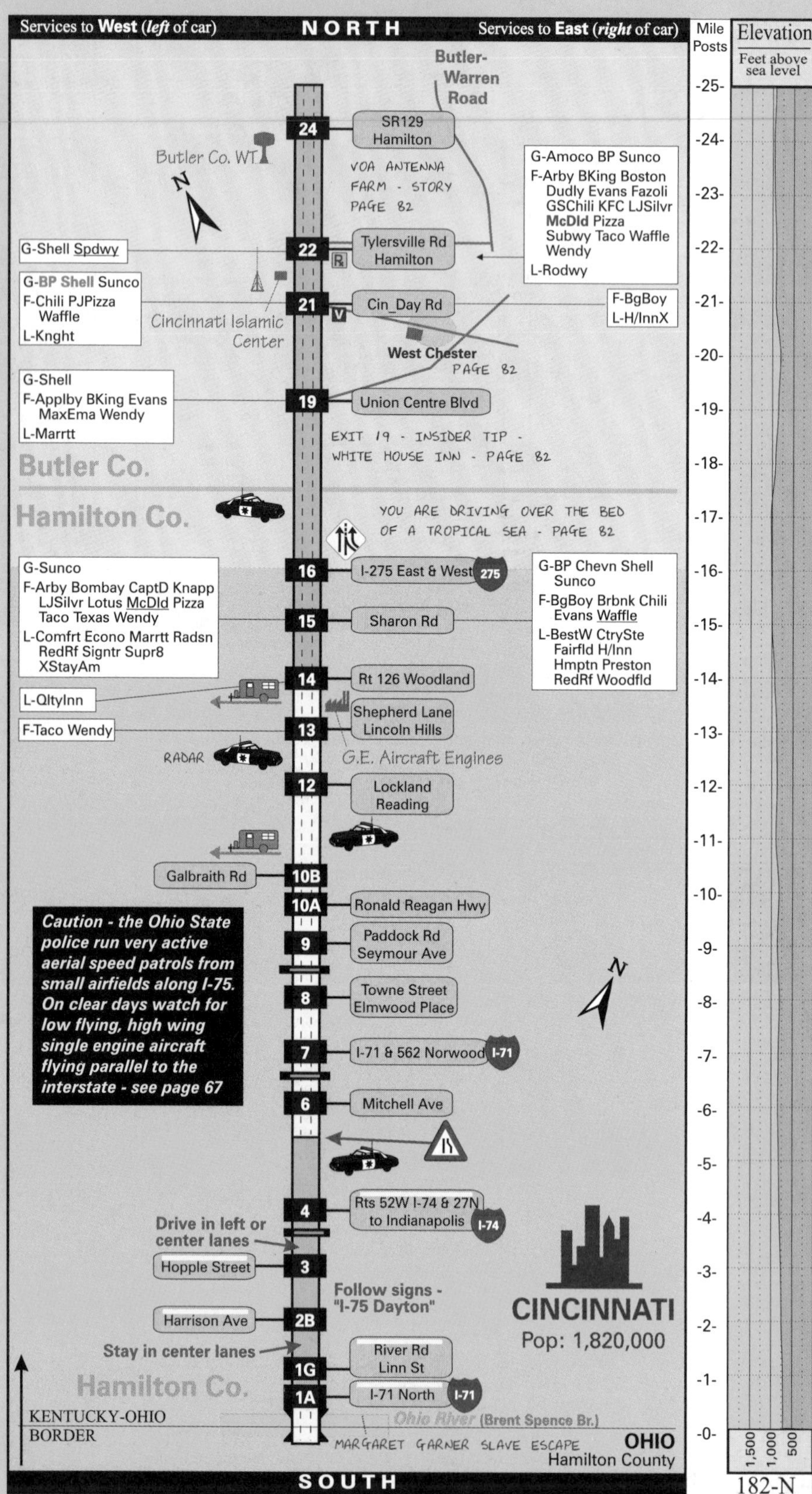

Services to West (left of car)
NORTH
Services to East (right of car)
Mile Posts
Elevation
Feet above sea level
Butler-Warren Road
24
SR129 Hamilton
Butler Co. WT
VOA ANTENNA FARM - STORY PAGE 82
G-Amoco BP Sunco
F-Arby BKing Boston Dudly Evans Fazoli GSChili KFC LJSilvr McDld Pizza Subwy Taco Waffle Wendy
L-Rodwy
G-Shell Spdwy
22
Tylersville Rd Hamilton
G-BP Shell Sunco
F-Chili PJPizza Waffle
L-Knght
21
Cin_Day Rd
F-BgBoy
L-H/InnX
Cincinnati Islamic Center
West Chester
PAGE 82
G-Shell
F-Applby BKing Evans MaxEma Wendy
L-Marrtt
19
Union Centre Blvd
EXIT 19 - INSIDER TIP - WHITE HOUSE INN - PAGE 82
Butler Co.
Hamilton Co.
YOU ARE DRIVING OVER THE BED OF A TROPICAL SEA - PAGE 82
G-Sunco
F-Arby Bombay CaptD Knapp LJSilvr Lotus McDld Pizza Taco Texas Wendy
L-Comfrt Econo Marrtt Radsn RedRf Signtr Supr8 XStayAm
16
I-275 East & West
275
G-BP Chevn Shell Sunco
F-BgBoy Brbnk Chili Evans Waffle
L-BestW CtrySte Fairfld H/Inn Hmptn Preston RedRf Woodfld
15
Sharon Rd
L-QltyInn
14
Rt 126 Woodland
F-Taco Wendy
13
Shepherd Lane Lincoln Hills
RADAR
G.E. Aircraft Engines
12
Lockland Reading
Galbraith Rd
10B
10A
Ronald Reagan Hwy
Caution - the Ohio State police run very active aerial speed patrols from small airfields along I-75. On clear days watch for low flying, high wing single engine aircraft flying parallel to the interstate - see page 67
9
Paddock Rd Seymour Ave
8
Towne Street Elmwood Place
N
7
I-71 & 562 Norwood
I-71
6
Mitchell Ave
4
Rts 52W I-74 & 27N to Indianapolis
I-74
Drive in left or center lanes
3
Hopple Street
Follow signs - "I-75 Dayton"
CINCINNATI
Pop: 1,820,000
Harrison Ave
2B
Stay in center lanes
River Rd Linn St
1G
Hamilton Co.
1A
I-71 North
I-71
KENTUCKY-OHIO BORDER
Ohio River (Brent Spence Br.)
MARGARET GARNER SLAVE ESCAPE
OHIO
Hamilton County
SOUTH
-25- -24- -23- -22- -21- -20- -19- -18- -17- -16- -15- -14- -13- -12- -11- -10- -9- -8- -7- -6- -5- -4- -3- -2- -1- -0-
1,500
1,000
500

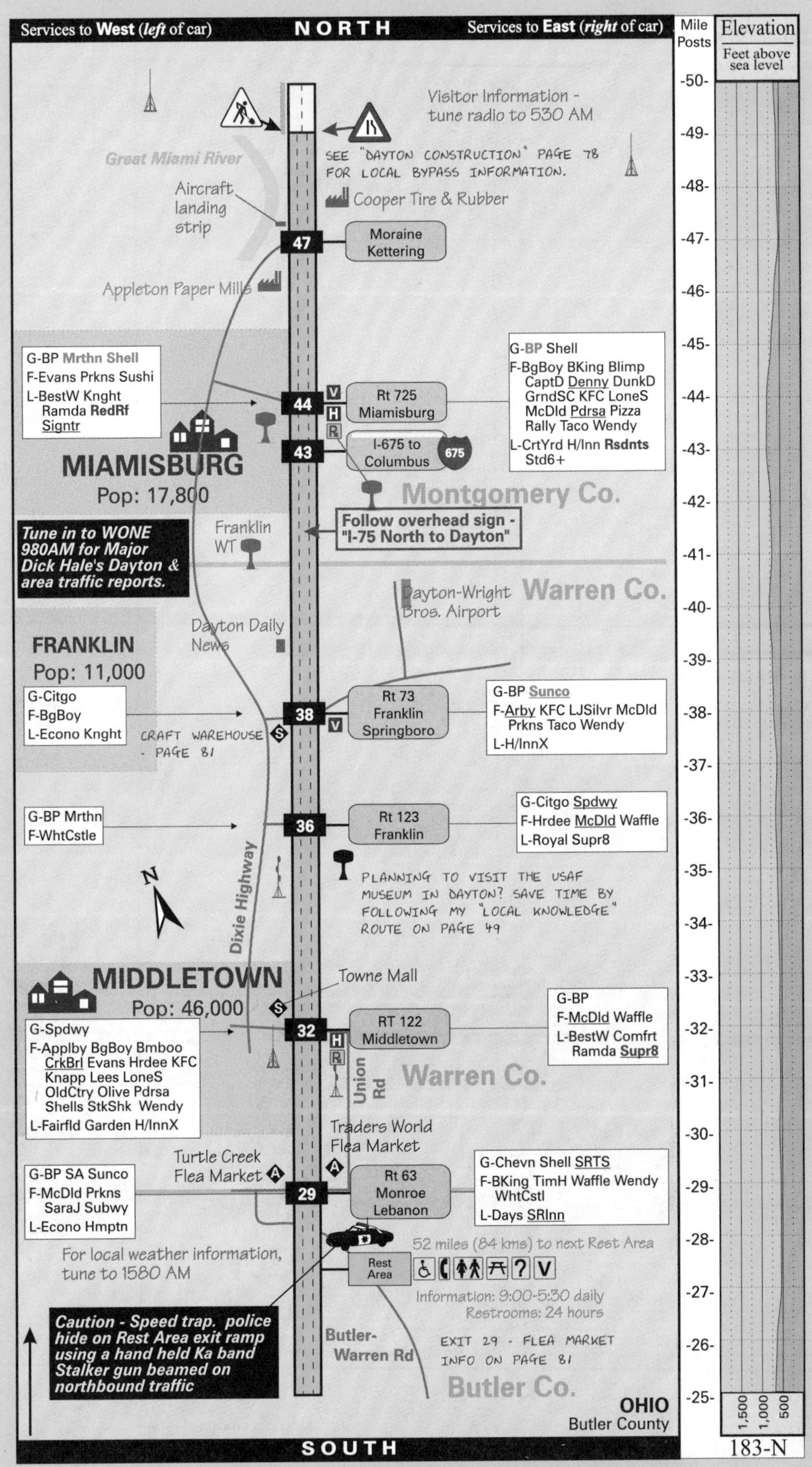

Services to West (left of car)
NORTH
Services to East (right of car)
Mile Posts
Elevation
Feet above sea level
Visitor Information - tune radio to 530 AM
SEE "DAYTON CONSTRUCTION" PAGE 78 FOR LOCAL BYPASS INFORMATION.
Great Miami River
Aircraft landing strip
Cooper Tire & Rubber
47
Moraine Kettering
Appleton Paper Mills
G-BP Mrthn Shell
F-Evans Prkns Sushi
L-BestW Knght Ramda RedRf Signtr
44
Rt 725 Miamisburg
G-BP Shell
F-BgBoy BKing Blimp CaptD Denny DunkD GrndSC KFC LoneS McDld Pdrsa Pizza Rally Taco Wendy
L-CrtYrd H/Inn Rsdnts Std6+
43
I-675 to Columbus
675
MIAMISBURG
Pop: 17,800
Montgomery Co.
Tune in to WONE 980AM for Major Dick Hale's Dayton & area traffic reports.
Franklin WT
Follow overhead sign - "I-75 North to Dayton"
Dayton-Wright Bros. Airport
Warren Co.
FRANKLIN
Pop: 11,000
Dayton Daily News
G-Citgo
F-BgBoy
L-Econo Knght
38
Rt 73 Franklin Springboro
G-BP Sunco
F-Arby KFC LJSilvr McDld Prkns Taco Wendy
L-H/InnX
CRAFT WAREHOUSE - PAGE 81
G-BP Mrthn
F-WhtCstle
36
Rt 123 Franklin
G-Citgo Spdwy
F-Hrdee McDld Waffle
L-Royal Supr8
PLANNING TO VISIT THE USAF MUSEUM IN DAYTON? SAVE TIME BY FOLLOWING MY "LOCAL KNOWLEDGE" ROUTE ON PAGE 49
Dixie Highway
N
MIDDLETOWN
Pop: 46,000
Towne Mall
G-Spdwy
F-Applby BgBoy Bmboo CrkBrl Evans Hrdee KFC Knapp Lees LoneS OldCtry Olive Pdrsa Shells StkShk Wendy
L-Fairfld Garden H/InnX
32
RT 122 Middletown
G-BP
F-McDld Waffle
L-BestW Comfrt Ramda Supr8
Union Rd
Warren Co.
Traders World Flea Market
Turtle Creek Flea Market
G-BP SA Sunco
F-McDld Prkns SaraJ Subwy
L-Econo Hmptn
29
Rt 63 Monroe Lebanon
G-Chevn Shell SRTS
F-BKing TimH Waffle Wendy WhtCstl
L-Days SRInn
52 miles (84 kms) to next Rest Area
Rest Area
For local weather information, tune to 1580 AM
Information: 9:00-5:30 daily
Restrooms: 24 hours
Caution - Speed trap. police hide on Rest Area exit ramp using a hand held Ka band Stalker gun beamed on northbound traffic
Butler-Warren Rd
EXIT 29 - FLEA MARKET INFO ON PAGE 81
Butler Co.
OHIO
Butler County
SOUTH
-50- -49- -48- -47- -46- -45- -44- -43- -42- -41- -40- -39- -38- -37- -36- -35- -34- -33- -32- -31- -30- -29- -28- -27- -26- -25-
1,500 1,000 500

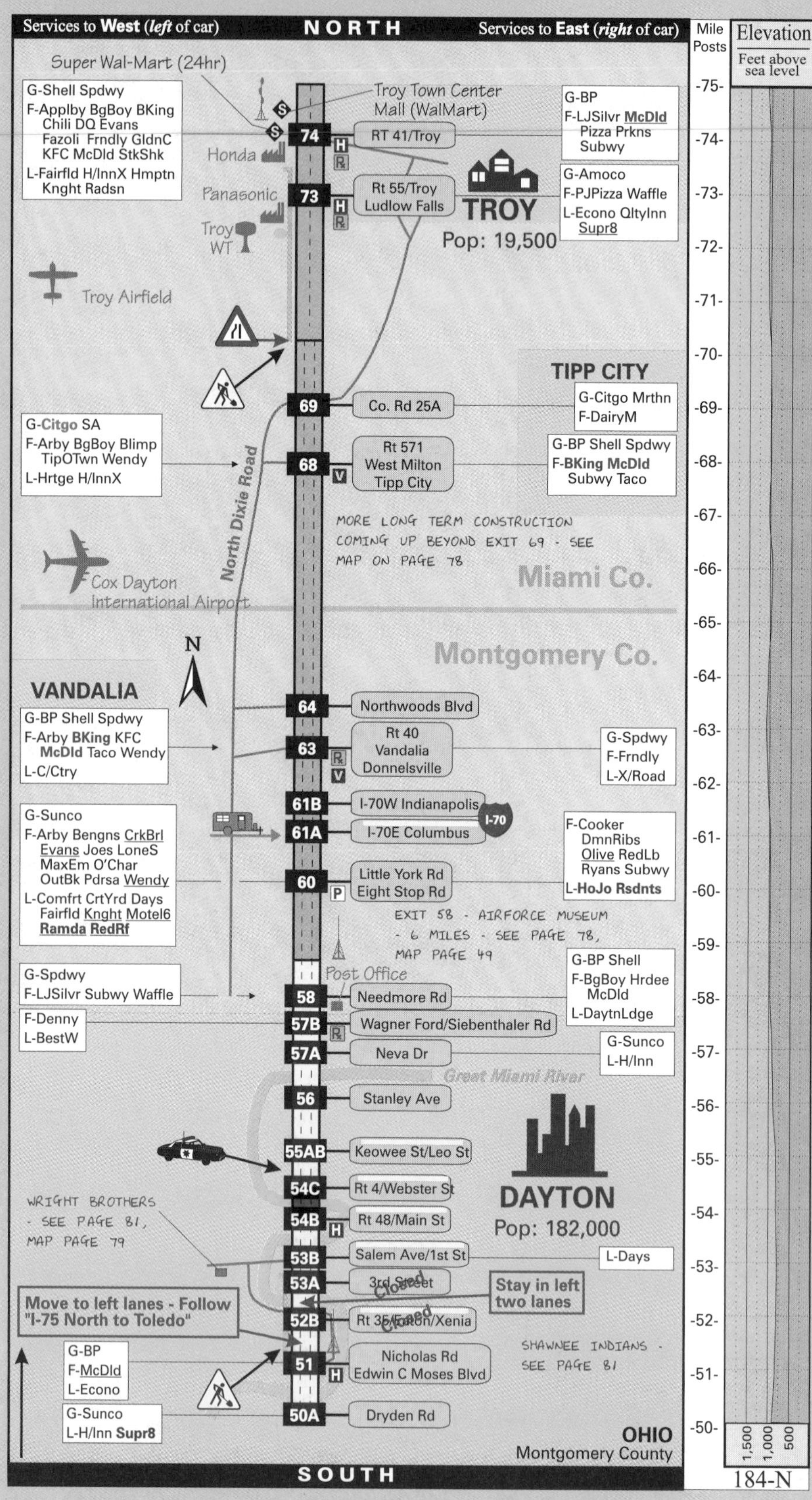
Services to West (left of car)
NORTH
Services to East (right of car)
Mile Posts
Elevation
Feet above sea level
Super Wal-Mart (24hr)
G-Shell Spdwy
F-Applby BgBoy BKing Chili DQ Evans Fazoli Frndly GldnC KFC McDld StkShk
L-Fairfld H/InnX Hmptn Knght Radsn
Troy Town Center Mall (WalMart)
74
RT 41/Troy
G-BP
F-LJSilvr McDld Pizza Prkns Subwy
Honda
Panasonic
73
Rt 55/Troy Ludlow Falls
TROY
Pop: 19,500
G-Amoco
F-PJPizza Waffle
L-Econo QltyInn Supr8
Troy WT
Troy Airfield
TIPP CITY
69
Co. Rd 25A
G-Citgo Mrthn
F-DairyM
G-Citgo SA
F-Arby BgBoy Blimp TipOTwn Wendy
L-Hrtge H/InnX
68
Rt 571 West Milton Tipp City
G-BP Shell Spdwy
F-BKing McDld Subwy Taco
North Dixie Road
MORE LONG TERM CONSTRUCTION COMING UP BEYOND EXIT 69 - SEE MAP ON PAGE 78
Cox Dayton International Airport
Miami Co.
Montgomery Co.
N
VANDALIA
64
Northwoods Blvd
G-BP Shell Spdwy
F-Arby BKing KFC McDld Taco Wendy
L-C/Ctry
63
Rt 40 Vandalia Donnelsville
G-Spdwy
F-Frndly
L-X/Road
61B
I-70W Indianapolis
I-70
61A
I-70E Columbus
G-Sunco
F-Arby Bengns CrkBrl Evans Joes LoneS MaxEm O'Char OutBk Pdrsa Wendy
L-Comfrt CrtYrd Days Fairfld Knght Motel6 Ramda RedRf
60
Little York Rd Eight Stop Rd
F-Cooker DmnRibs Olive RedLb Ryans Subwy
L-HoJo Rsdnts
EXIT 58 - AIRFORCE MUSEUM - 6 MILES - SEE PAGE 78, MAP PAGE 49
Post Office
G-Spdwy
F-LJSilvr Subwy Waffle
58
Needmore Rd
G-BP Shell
F-BgBoy Hrdee McDld
L-DaytnLdge
F-Denny
L-BestW
57B
Wagner Ford/Siebenthaler Rd
57A
Neva Dr
G-Sunco
L-H/Inn
Great Miami River
56
Stanley Ave
55AB
Keowee St/Leo St
DAYTON
Pop: 182,000
54C
Rt 4/Webster St
WRIGHT BROTHERS - SEE PAGE 81, MAP PAGE 79
54B
Rt 48/Main St
53B
Salem Ave/1st St
L-Days
53A
3rd Street
Closed
Stay in left two lanes
Move to left lanes - Follow "I-75 North to Toledo"
52B
Rt 35/Dayton/Xenia
Closed
SHAWNEE INDIANS - SEE PAGE 81
G-BP
F-McDld
L-Econo
51
Nicholas Rd Edwin C Moses Blvd
G-Sunco
L-H/Inn Supr8
50A
Dryden Rd
OHIO
Montgomery County
SOUTH
-75- -74- -73- -72- -71- -70- -69- -68- -67- -66- -65- -64- -63- -62- -61- -60- -59- -58- -57- -56- -55- -54- -53- -52- -51- -50-
1,500 1,000 500
184-N

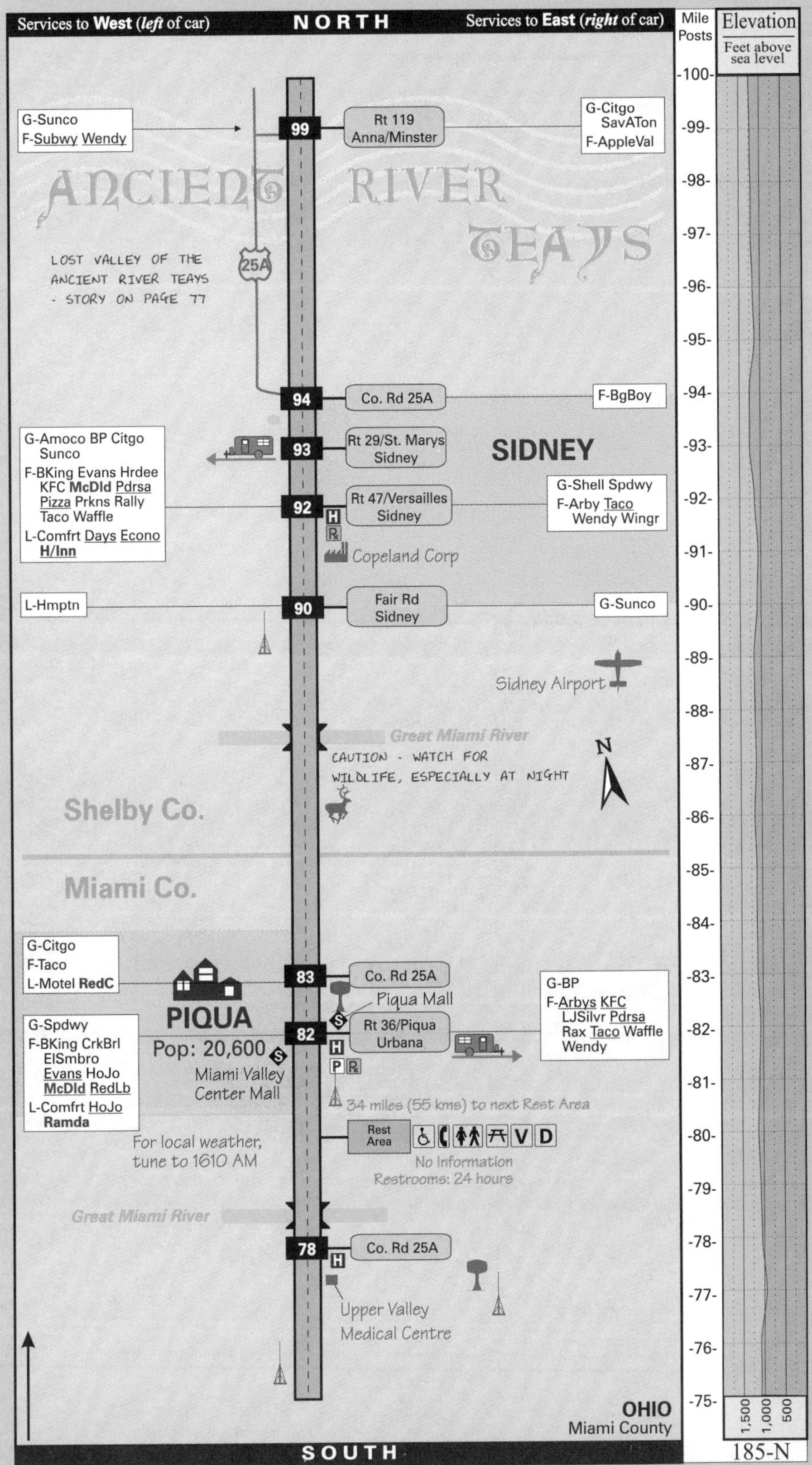

Services to West (left of car)
NORTH
Services to East (right of car)
Mile Posts
Elevation
Feet above sea level
G-Sunco
F-Subwy Wendy
99
Rt 119 Anna/Minster
G-Citgo SavATon
F-AppleVal
ANCIENT RIVER TEAYS
LOST VALLEY OF THE ANCIENT RIVER TEAYS - STORY ON PAGE 77
25A
94
Co. Rd 25A
F-BgBoy
G-Amoco BP Citgo Sunco
F-BKing Evans Hrdee KFC McDld Pdrsa Pizza Prkns Rally Taco Waffle
L-Comfrt Days Econo H/Inn
93
Rt 29/St. Marys Sidney
SIDNEY
92
Rt 47/Versailles Sidney
G-Shell Spdwy
F-Arby Taco Wendy Wingr
Copeland Corp
L-Hmptn
90
Fair Rd Sidney
G-Sunco
Sidney Airport
Great Miami River
CAUTION - WATCH FOR WILDLIFE, ESPECIALLY AT NIGHT
N
Shelby Co.
Miami Co.
G-Citgo
F-Taco
L-Motel RedC
83
Co. Rd 25A
Piqua Mall
G-BP
F-Arbys KFC LJSilvr Pdrsa Rax Taco Waffle Wendy
PIQUA
Pop: 20,600
G-Spdwy
F-BKing CrkBrl ElSmbro Evans HoJo McDld RedLb
L-Comfrt HoJo Ramda
82
Rt 36/Piqua Urbana
Miami Valley Center Mall
34 miles (55 kms) to next Rest Area
Rest Area
No information
Restrooms: 24 hours
For local weather, tune to 1610 AM
Great Miami River
78
Co. Rd 25A
Upper Valley Medical Centre
-100- -99- -98- -97- -96- -95- -94- -93- -92- -91- -90- -89- -88- -87- -86- -85- -84- -83- -82- -81- -80- -79- -78- -77- -76- -75-
1,500 1,000 500
OHIO
Miami County
SOUTH

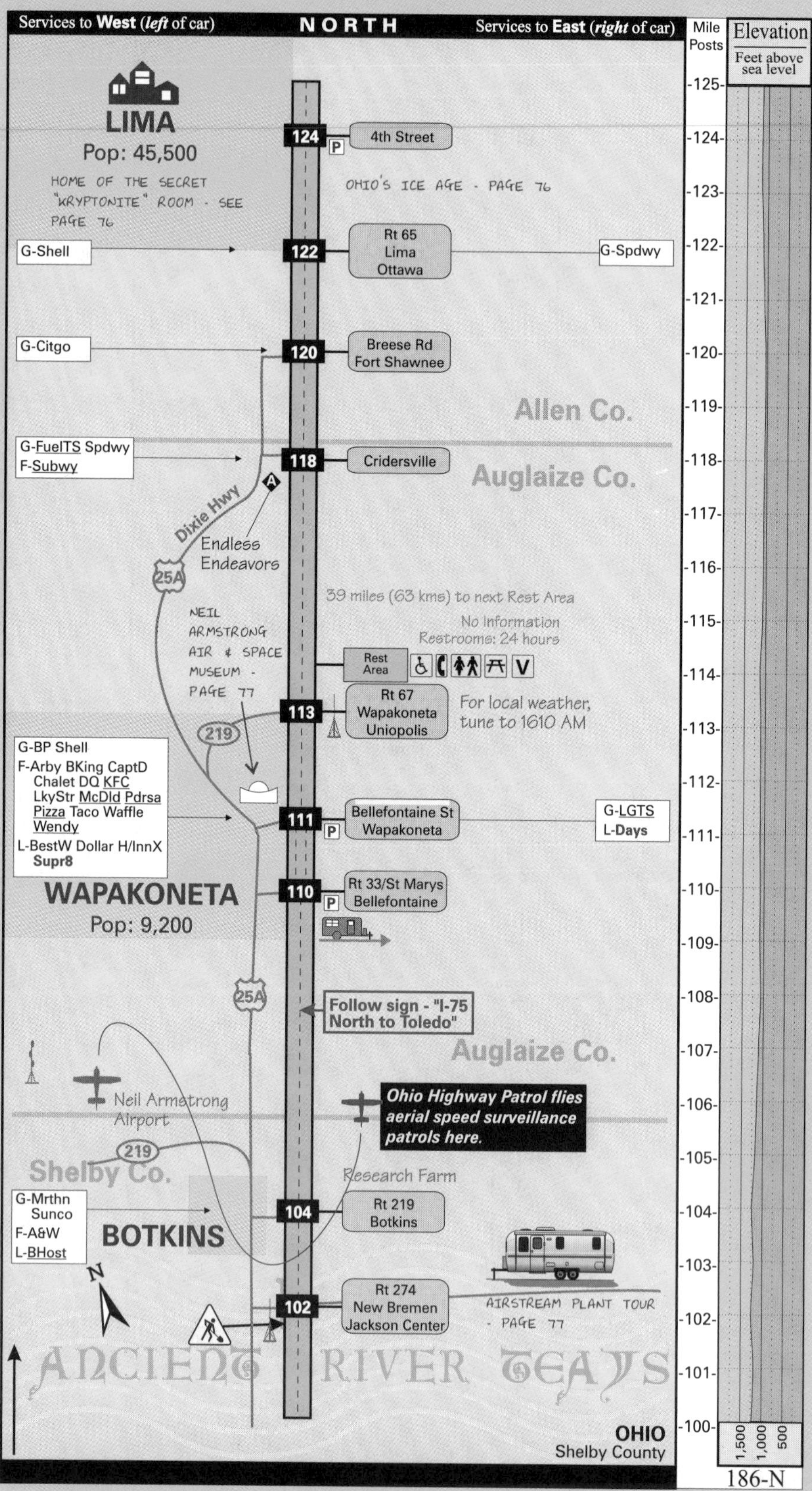

Services to West (left of car)
NOHTH
Services to East (right of car)
Mile Posts
Elevation
Feet above sea level
LIMA
Pop: 45,500
HOME OF THE SECRET "KRYPTONITE" ROOM - SEE PAGE 76
124
P
4th Street
OHIO'S ICE AGE - PAGE 76
G-Shell
122
Rt 65
Lima
Ottawa
G-Spdwy
G-Citgo
120
Breese Rd
Fort Shawnee
Allen Co.
G-FuelTS Spdwy
F-Subwy
118
Cridersville
Auglaize Co.
A
Dixie Hwy
Endless
Endeavors
25A
39 miles (63 kms) to next Rest Area
No Information
Restrooms: 24 hours
NEIL ARMSTRONG AIR & SPACE MUSEUM - PAGE 77
Rest Area
V
113
Rt 67
Wapakoneta
Uniopolis
For local weather, tune to 1610 AM
219
G-BP Shell
F-Arby BKing CaptD Chalet DQ KFC LkyStr McDld Pdrsa Pizza Taco Waffle Wendy
L-BestW Dollar H/InnX Supr8
111
P
Bellefontaine St
Wapakoneta
G-LGTS
L-Days
WAPAKONETA
Pop: 9,200
110
P
Rt 33/St Marys
Bellefontaine
25A
Follow sign - "I-75 North to Toledo"
Auglaize Co.
Neil Armstrong Airport
Ohio Highway Patrol flies aerial speed surveillance patrols here.
219
Shelby Co.
Research Farm
G-Mrthn Sunco
F-A&W
L-BHost
104
Rt 219
Botkins
BOTKINS
N
102
Rt 274
New Bremen
Jackson Center
AIRSTREAM PLANT TOUR - PAGE 77
ANCIENT RIVER TEAYS
OHIO
Shelby County
-125-
-124-
-123-
-122-
-121-
-120-
-119-
-118-
-117-
-116-
-115-
-114-
-113-
-112-
-111-
-110-
-109-
-108-
-107-
-106-
-105-
-104-
-103-
-102-
-101-
-100-
1,500
1,000
500
186-N

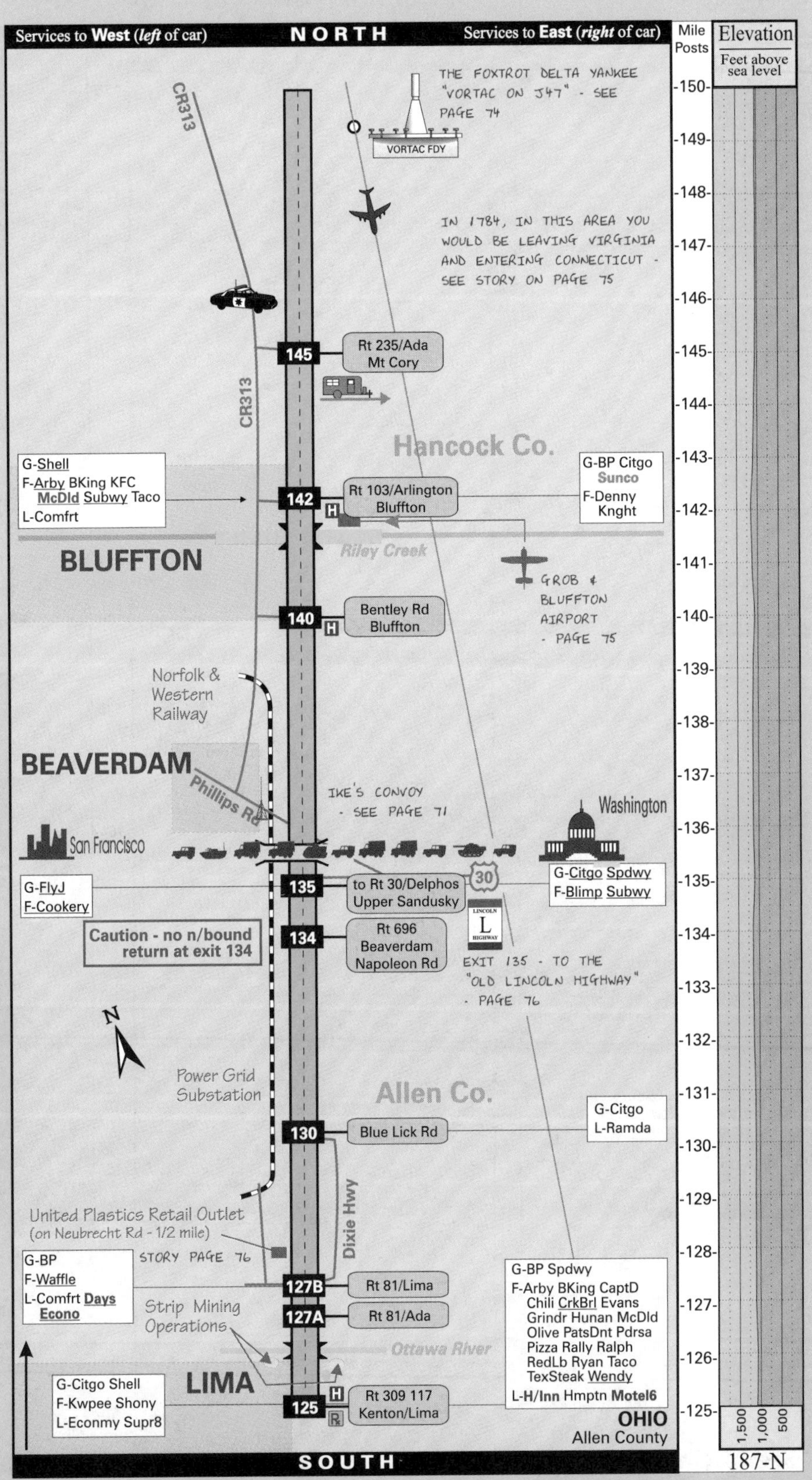

Services to West (left of car)
NORTH
Services to East (right of car)
Mile Posts
Elevation
Feet above sea level
CR313
THE FOXTROT DELTA YANKEE "VORTAC ON J47" - SEE PAGE 74
VORTAC FDY
IN 1784, IN THIS AREA YOU WOULD BE LEAVING VIRGINIA AND ENTERING CONNECTICUT - SEE STORY ON PAGE 75
145
Rt 235/Ada Mt Cory
CR313
Hancock Co.
G-Shell
F-Arby BKing KFC McDld Subwy Taco
L-Comfrt
142
Rt 103/Arlington Bluffton
G-BP Citgo Sunco
F-Denny Knght
BLUFFTON
Riley Creek
GROB & BLUFFTON AIRPORT - PAGE 75
140
Bentley Rd Bluffton
Norfolk & Western Railway
BEAVERDAM
Phillips Rd
IKE'S CONVOY - SEE PAGE 71
Washington
San Francisco
G-FlyJ
F-Cookery
135
to Rt 30/Delphos Upper Sandusky
30
G-Citgo Spdwy
F-Blimp Subwy
Caution - no n/bound return at exit 134
134
Rt 696 Beaverdam Napoleon Rd
LINCOLN L HIGHWAY
EXIT 135 - TO THE "OLD LINCOLN HIGHWAY" - PAGE 76
N
Power Grid Substation
Allen Co.
130
Blue Lick Rd
G-Citgo
L-Ramda
Dixie Hwy
United Plastics Retail Outlet
(on Neubrecht Rd - 1/2 mile)
STORY PAGE 76
G-BP
F-Waffle
L-Comfrt Days Econo
127B
Rt 81/Lima
127A
Rt 81/Ada
Strip Mining Operations
Ottawa River
G-BP Spdwy
F-Arby BKing CaptD Chili CrkBrl Evans Grindr Hunan McDld Olive PatsDnt Pdrsa Pizza Rally Ralph RedLb Ryan Taco TexSteak Wendy
L-H/Inn Hmptn Motel6
LIMA
G-Citgo Shell
F-Kwpee Shony
L-Econmy Supr8
125
Rt 309 117 Kenton/Lima
OHIO
Allen County
SOUTH
-150-
-149-
-148-
-147-
-146-
-145-
-144-
-143-
-142-
-141-
-140-
-139-
-138-
-137-
-136-
-135-
-134-
-133-
-132-
-131-
-130-
-129-
-128-
-127-
-126-
-125-
1,500
1,000
500
187-N

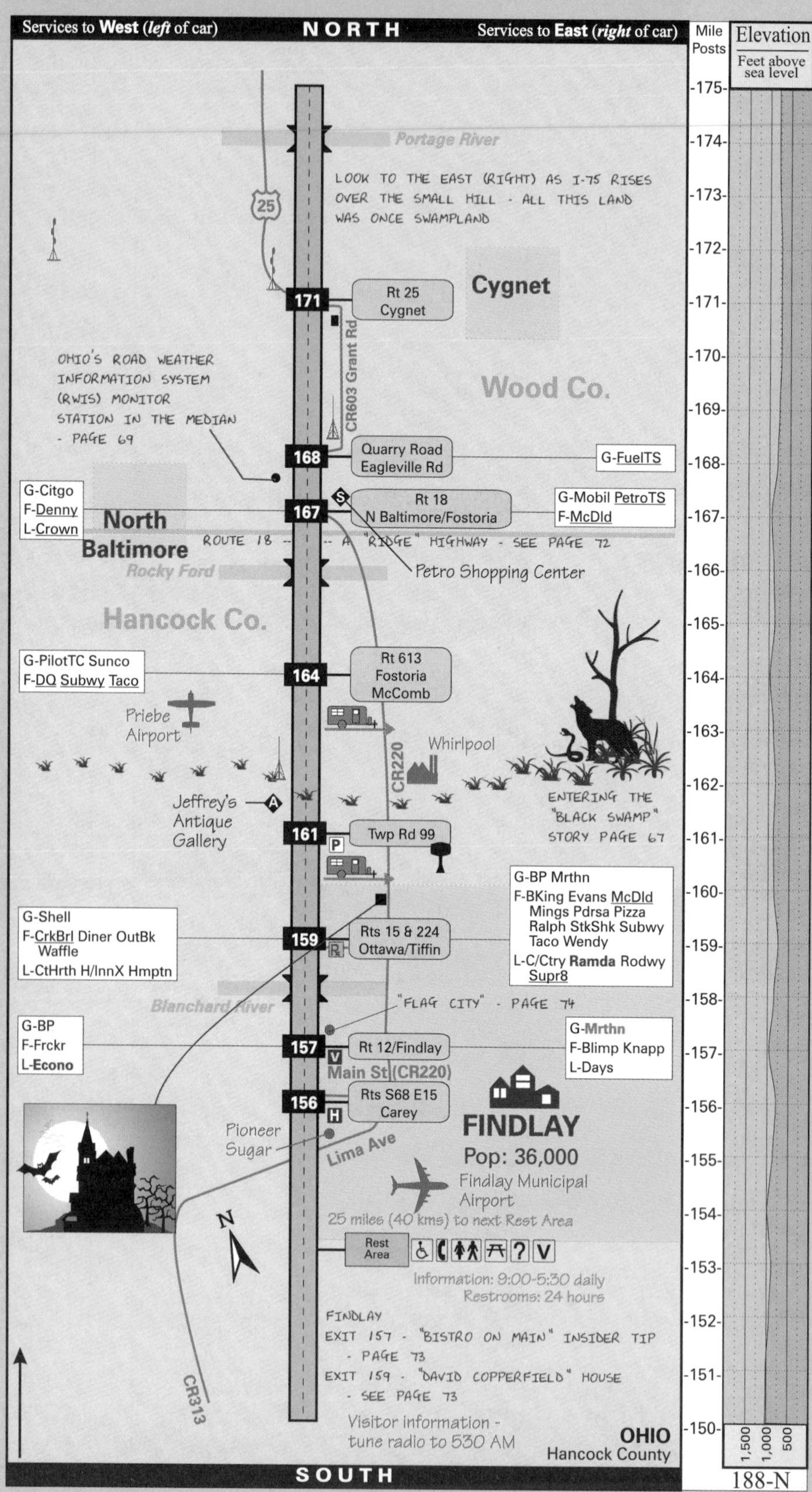

Services to West (left of car)
NORTH
Services to East (right of car)
Mile Posts
Elevation
Feet above sea level
Portage River
LOOK TO THE EAST (RIGHT) AS I-75 RISES OVER THE SMALL HILL - ALL THIS LAND WAS ONCE SWAMPLAND
25
171
Rt 25 Cygnet
Cygnet
CR603 Grant Rd
OHIO'S ROAD WEATHER INFORMATION SYSTEM (RWIS) MONITOR STATION IN THE MEDIAN - PAGE 69
Wood Co.
168
Quarry Road Eagleville Rd
G-FuelTS
G-Citgo
F-Denny
L-Crown
167
Rt 18 N Baltimore/Fostoria
G-Mobil PetroTS
F-McDld
North Baltimore
ROUTE 18 -- A "RIDGE" HIGHWAY - SEE PAGE 72
Petro Shopping Center
Rocky Ford
Hancock Co.
G-PilotTC Sunco
F-DQ Subwy Taco
164
Rt 613 Fostoria McComb
Priebe Airport
Whirlpool
CR220
Jeffrey's Antique Gallery
ENTERING THE "BLACK SWAMP" STORY PAGE 67
161
Twp Rd 99
G-BP Mrthn
F-BKing Evans McDld Mings Pdrsa Pizza Ralph StkShk Subwy Taco Wendy
L-C/Ctry Ramda Rodwy Supr8
G-Shell
F-CrkBrl Diner OutBk Waffle
L-CtHrth H/InnX Hmptn
159
Rts 15 & 224 Ottawa/Tiffin
Blanchard River
"FLAG CITY" - PAGE 74
G-BP
F-Frckr
L-Econo
157
Rt 12/Findlay
G-Mrthn
F-Blimp Knapp
L-Days
Main St (CR220)
156
Rts S68 E15 Carey
Pioneer Sugar
Lima Ave
FINDLAY
Pop: 36,000
Findlay Municipal Airport
25 miles (40 kms) to next Rest Area
N
Rest Area
Information: 9:00-5:30 daily
Restrooms: 24 hours
FINDLAY
EXIT 157 - "BISTRO ON MAIN" INSIDER TIP - PAGE 73
EXIT 159 - "DAVID COPPERFIELD" HOUSE - SEE PAGE 73
CR313
Visitor information - tune radio to 530 AM
OHIO
Hancock County
SOUTH
-175- -174- -173- -172- -171- -170- -169- -168- -167- -166- -165- -164- -163- -162- -161- -160- -159- -158- -157- -156- -155- -154- -153- -152- -151- -150-
1,500 1,000 500

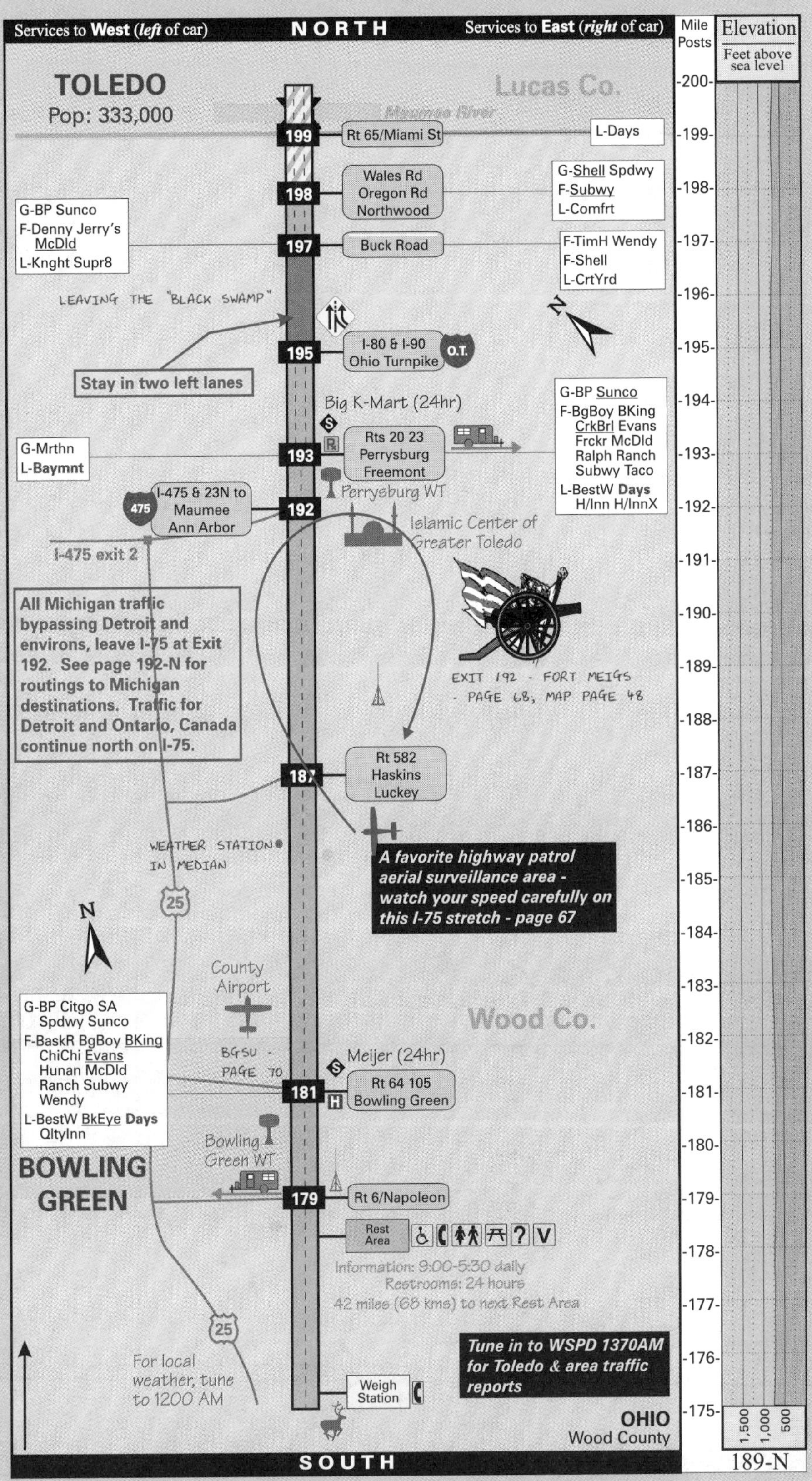

Services to West (left of car)
NORTH
Services to East (right of car)
Mile Posts
Elevation
Feet above sea level
TOLEDO
Pop: 333,000
Lucas Co.
Maumee River
199
Rt 65/Miami St
L-Days
198
Wales Rd
Oregon Rd
Northwood
G-Shell Spdwy
F-Subwy
L-Comfrt
G-BP Sunco
F-Denny Jerry's McDld
L-Knght Supr8
197
Buck Road
F-TimH Wendy
F-Shell
L-CrtYrd
LEAVING THE "BLACK SWAMP"
195
I-80 & I-90
Ohio Turnpike
O.T.
Stay in two left lanes
Big K-Mart (24hr)
G-BP Sunco
F-BgBoy BKing
CrkBrl Evans
Frckr McDld
Ralph Ranch
Subwy Taco
L-BestW Days
H/Inn H/InnX
G-Mrthn
L-Baymnt
193
Rts 20 23
Perrysburg
Freemont
Perrysburg WT
475
I-475 & 23N to
Maumee
Ann Arbor
192
Islamic Center of Greater Toledo
I-475 exit 2
All Michigan traffic bypassing Detroit and environs, leave I-75 at Exit 192. See page 192-N for routings to Michigan destinations. Traffic for Detroit and Ontario, Canada continue north on I-75.
EXIT 192 - FORT MEIGS - PAGE 68; MAP PAGE 48
187
Rt 582
Haskins
Luckey
WEATHER STATION IN MEDIAN
A favorite highway patrol aerial surveillance area - watch your speed carefully on this I-75 stretch - page 67
25
N
County Airport
Wood Co.
G-BP Citgo SA
Spdwy Sunco
F-BaskR BgBoy BKing
ChiChi Evans
Hunan McDld
Ranch Subwy
Wendy
L-BestW BkEye Days
QltyInn
BGSU - PAGE 70
Meijer (24hr)
181
Rt 64 105
Bowling Green
Bowling Green WT
BOWLING GREEN
179
Rt 6/Napoleon
Rest Area
Information: 9:00-5:30 daily
Restrooms: 24 hours
42 miles (68 kms) to next Rest Area
25
Tune in to WSPD 1370AM for Toledo & area traffic reports
For local weather, tune to 1200 AM
Weigh Station
OHIO
Wood County
SOUTH
-200- -199- -198- -197- -196- -195- -194- -193- -192- -191- -190- -189- -188- -187- -186- -185- -184- -183- -182- -181- -180- -179- -178- -177- -176- -175-
1,500
1,000
500

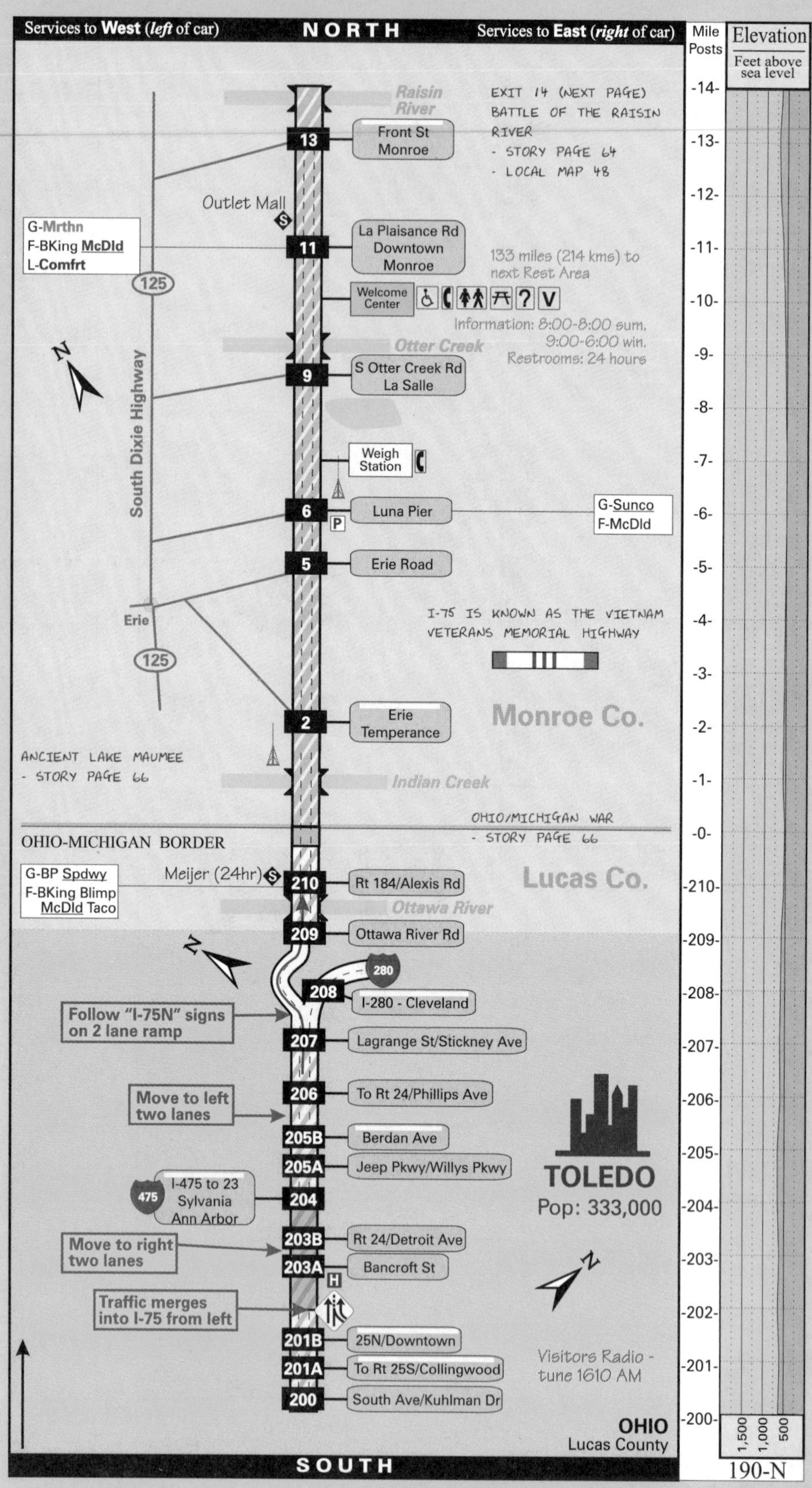

Services to West (left of car)
NORTH
Services to East (right of car)
Mile Posts
Elevation
Feet above sea level
Raisin River
EXIT 14 (NEXT PAGE)
BATTLE OF THE RAISIN RIVER
- STORY PAGE 64
- LOCAL MAP 48
13
Front St Monroe
Outlet Mall
G-Mrthn
F-BKing McDld
L-Comfrt
11
La Plaisance Rd Downtown Monroe
133 miles (214 kms) to next Rest Area
125
Welcome Center
Information: 8:00-8:00 sum. 9:00-6:00 win.
Restrooms: 24 hours
Otter Creek
9
S Otter Creek Rd La Salle
South Dixie Highway
Weigh Station
6
Luna Pier
G-Sunco
F-McDld
5
Erie Road
Erie
I-75 IS KNOWN AS THE VIETNAM VETERANS MEMORIAL HIGHWAY
125
2
Erie Temperance
Monroe Co.
ANCIENT LAKE MAUMEE
- STORY PAGE 66
Indian Creek
OHIO/MICHIGAN WAR
- STORY PAGE 66
OHIO-MICHIGAN BORDER
G-BP Spdwy
F-BKing Blimp McDld Taco
Meijer (24hr)
210
Rt 184/Alexis Rd
Lucas Co.
Ottawa River
209
Ottawa River Rd
280
208
I-280 - Cleveland
Follow "I-75N" signs on 2 lane ramp
207
Lagrange St/Stickney Ave
Move to left two lanes
206
To Rt 24/Phillips Ave
205B
Berdan Ave
205A
Jeep Pkwy/Willys Pkwy
475
I-475 to 23 Sylvania Ann Arbor
204
TOLEDO
Pop: 333,000
Move to right two lanes
203B
Rt 24/Detroit Ave
203A
Bancroft St
Traffic merges into I-75 from left
201B
25N/Downtown
201A
To Rt 25S/Collingwood
Visitors Radio - tune 1610 AM
200
South Ave/Kuhlman Dr
OHIO
Lucas County
SOUTH
-14- -13- -12- -11- -10- -9- -8- -7- -6- -5- -4- -3- -2- -1- -0- -210- -209- -208- -207- -206- -205- -204- -203- -202- -201- -200-
1,500 1,000 500

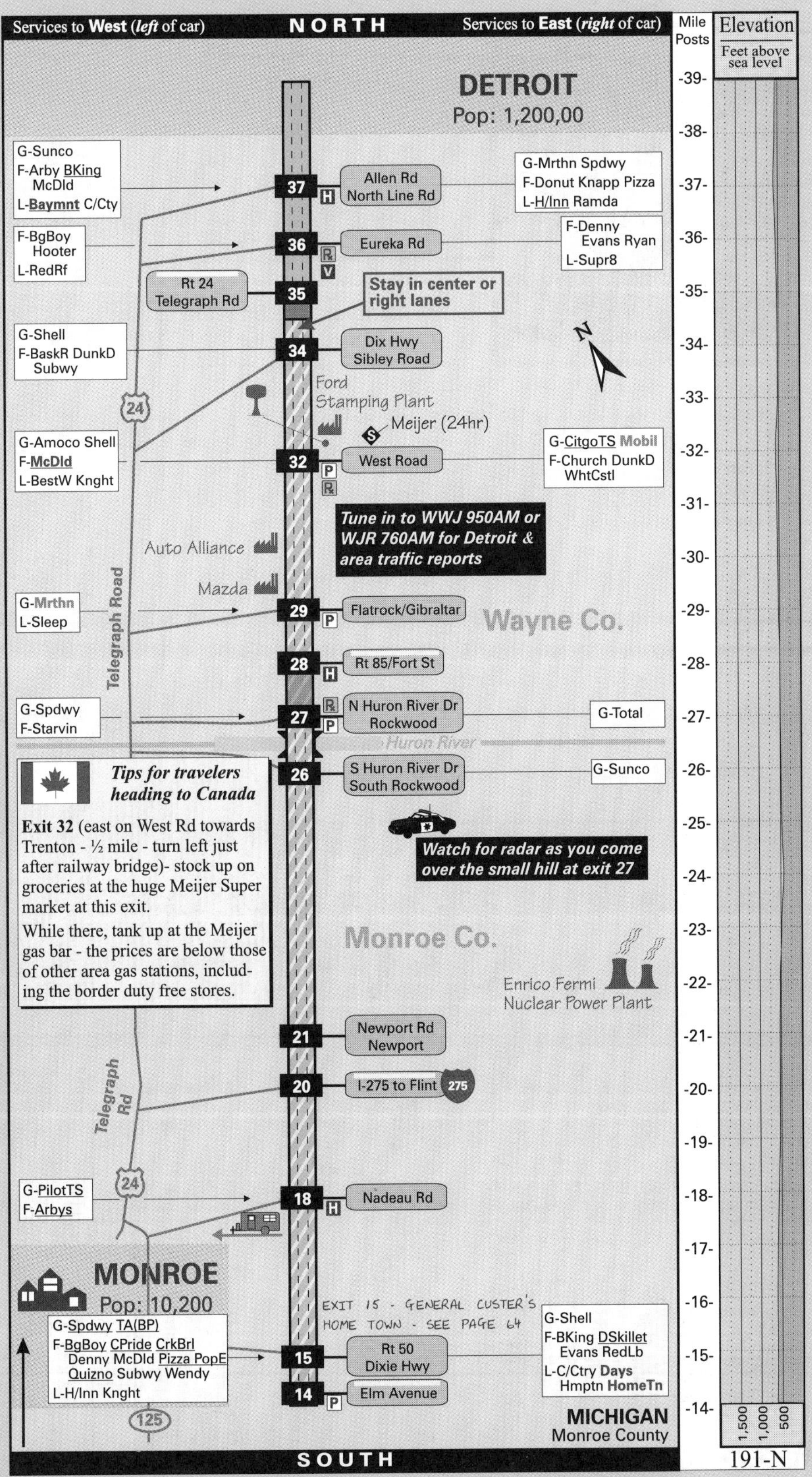

Tips for travelers heading to Canada

Exit 32 (east on West Rd towards Trenton - ½ mile - turn left just after railway bridge)- stock up on groceries at the huge Meijer Super market at this exit.

While there, tank up at the Meijer gas bar - the prices are below those of other area gas stations, including the border duty free stores.

THANKS FOR LETTING ME RIDE WITH YOU ON YOUR JOURNEY NORTH. HAVE A SAFE TRIP, NO MATTER WHERE YOUR FINAL DESTINATION LIES.

Dave

Here is a handy guide to some ***Michigan*** & ***Ontario*** (Canada) Destinations . . .

Ann Arbor - Toledo(I-475) > MI Border(US23) > Ann Arbor = 52 miles

Lansing - Toledo(I-475) > MI Border(US23) > Brighton(I-96) > Lansing = 115 miles

Flint - Toledo(I-475) > MI Border(US 23) > Ann Arbor(US23) > Flint = 106 miles

Grand Rapids - Toledo(I-475) > MI Border(US23) > Brighton(I-96) > Grand Rapids = 179 miles

Saginaw - Toledo(I-475) > MI Border(US 23) > Ann Arbor(US23) > Flint(I-75) = 138 miles

London, ON - Windsor(Hwy401) > London = 190 Kms (118 miles)

Hamilton, ON - Windsor(Hwy401) > Exit235(Hwy403) > Brantford(Hwy2) > Jnctn(Hwy403) > Hamilton = 309 Kms (192 miles)

Kitchener, ON - Windsor(Hwy401) > = 286 Kms (178 miles)

Toronto, ON - Windsor(Hwy401) > Toronto = 350 Kms (217 miles)

Ottawa, ON - Windsor(Hwy401) > Prescott(Hwy16) > Ottawa = 800 Kms (497 miles)

DETROIT
Pop: 1,200,000

NORTH

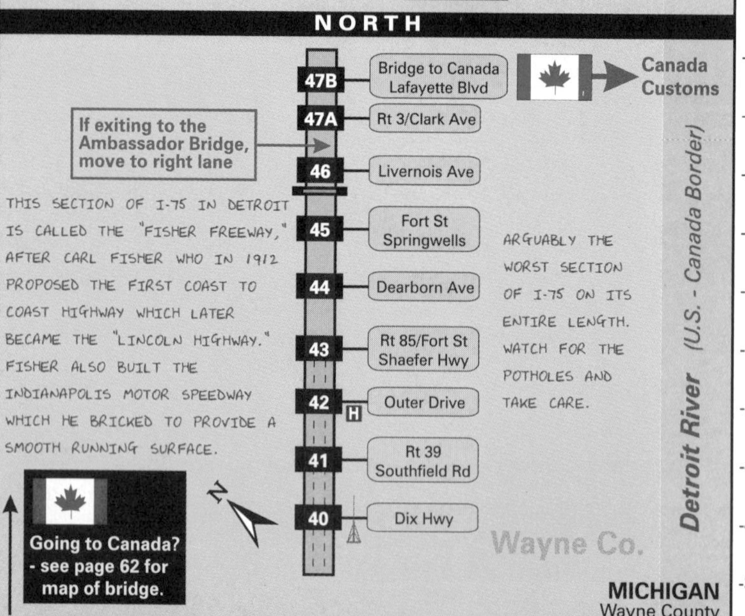

THIS SECTION OF I-75 IN DETROIT IS CALLED THE "FISHER FREEWAY," AFTER CARL FISHER WHO IN 1912 PROPOSED THE FIRST COAST TO COAST HIGHWAY WHICH LATER BECAME THE "LINCOLN HIGHWAY." FISHER ALSO BUILT THE INDIANAPOLIS MOTOR SPEEDWAY WHICH HE BRICKED TO PROVIDE A SMOOTH RUNNING SURFACE.

ARGUABLY THE WORST SECTION OF I-75 ON ITS ENTIRE LENGTH. WATCH FOR THE POTHOLES AND TAKE CARE.

Going to Canada? - see page 62 for map of bridge.

MICHIGAN
Wayne County

SOUTH

Mile Posts: -48- -47- -46- -45- -44- -43- -42- -41- -40- -39-

Elevation — Feet above sea level: 1,500 1,000 500

Beating the Rush Hour Blues

Nobody likes rush hour traffic and each year it seems to get worse no matter where you are. Fortunately, I-75 cities have some of the best traffic reporters in the Nation - on the ground and in the air - to speed you through the interstate cities. We have assembled the *best-of-the-best*, as our **I-75 Traffic Reporter Team** to help you on your drive through their areas.

Cincinnati and Atlanta (thanks, Herb) bypass maps are on the following pages. A special thanks to Dayton's Dick Hale for providing my readers with special Troy and Dayton bypass information (see page 78 & 79).

Detroit - morning rush hours are 7:00-9:00; afternoon, 4:00-6:30. For best traffic information, tune in the team of ***John Bailey*** (on the ground) and ***Tracy Gary*** (in the air) on **WWJ 950AM.**

Toledo - morning rush hours are 7:30-9:00; afternoon, 4:30-6:00. **WSPD-1370AM's** ***Lyn Cassidy*** will keep you moving with her reports every 10 mins.

Dayton - morning rush hours are 7:30-9:00; afternoon, 4:30-6:00. Join ***Major Dick Hale - "The Dixter"*** on **WONE 980AM's** *"Airwatch Traffic."*

Cincinnati - morning rush hours are 5:30-9:00; afternoon, 3:30-6:30. Helicopter traffic reports from **WLW 700AM**'s ***John Phillips*** and ***Dave Armbruster*** every 10 minutes in rush time & "top-of-the-hour" at other times.

Lexington - On **WVLK 590AM,** our morning rush hour (7:00-9:00) guy is ***John Wesley Brett***; afternoons (4:30-5:30) are handled by ***Scott Wilson***.

Knoxville - morning rush hours are 7:00-9:00; afternoon, 4:30-6:00. Listen to ***Dave Foulk*** on **WNOX 990AM's** morning traffic and ***Ed Rupp*** in the afternoon.

Chattanooga - morning rush hours are 7:00-9:00; afternoon, 4:30-6:30 . . . but they shouldn't bother your too much unless morning I-24 traffic backs up onto I-75. Stay tuned to **WOGT 107.9FM's** ***Sky King Butch Johnson*** to check this out. Butch also has a great website at *www.chattairtraffic.com.*

Atlanta - morning rush hours are 7:00-9:00; afternoon, 4:30(2:00 on Fri.)-6:30. **WSB 750AM's** ***Captain Herb Emory*** is in the air in the WSB chopper - on the job - every 6 minutes - all over the city and bypass routes.

Macon - You're on the I-475 Macon Bypass so you should be OK . . . **WAYS 99.1FM's** ***Mike Wade*** at the Traffic Center will keep an eye on thing for you, though.

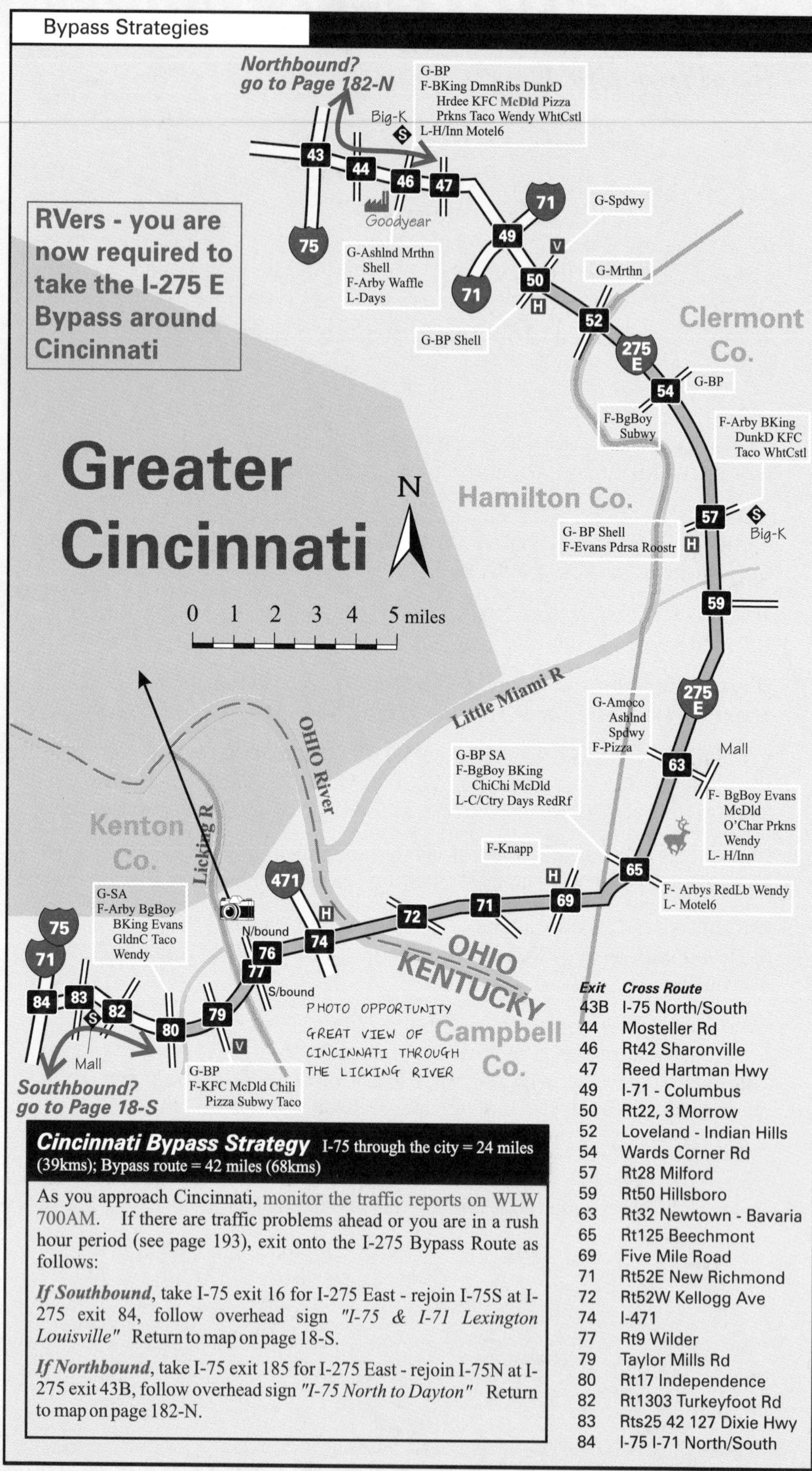

Cincinnati Bypass Strategy I-75 through the city = 24 miles (39kms); Bypass route = 42 miles (68kms)

As you approach Cincinnati, monitor the traffic reports on WLW 700AM. If there are traffic problems ahead or you are in a rush hour period (see page 193), exit onto the I-275 Bypass Route as follows:

If Southbound, take I-75 exit 16 for I-275 East - rejoin I-75S at I-275 exit 84, follow overhead sign *"I-75 & I-71 Lexington Louisville"* Return to map on page 18-S.

If Northbound, take I-75 exit 185 for I-275 East - rejoin I-75N at I-275 exit 43B, follow overhead sign *"I-75 North to Dayton"* Return to map on page 182-N.

Exit	*Cross Route*
43B	I-75 North/South
44	Mosteller Rd
46	Rt42 Sharonville
47	Reed Hartman Hwy
49	I-71 - Columbus
50	Rt22, 3 Morrow
52	Loveland - Indian Hills
54	Wards Corner Rd
57	Rt28 Milford
59	Rt50 Hillsboro
63	Rt32 Newtown - Bavaria
65	Rt125 Beechmont
69	Five Mile Road
71	Rt52E New Richmond
72	Rt52W Kellogg Ave
74	I-471
77	Rt9 Wilder
79	Taylor Mills Rd
80	Rt17 Independence
82	Rt1303 Turkeyfoot Rd
83	Rts25 42 127 Dixie Hwy
84	I-75 I-71 North/South

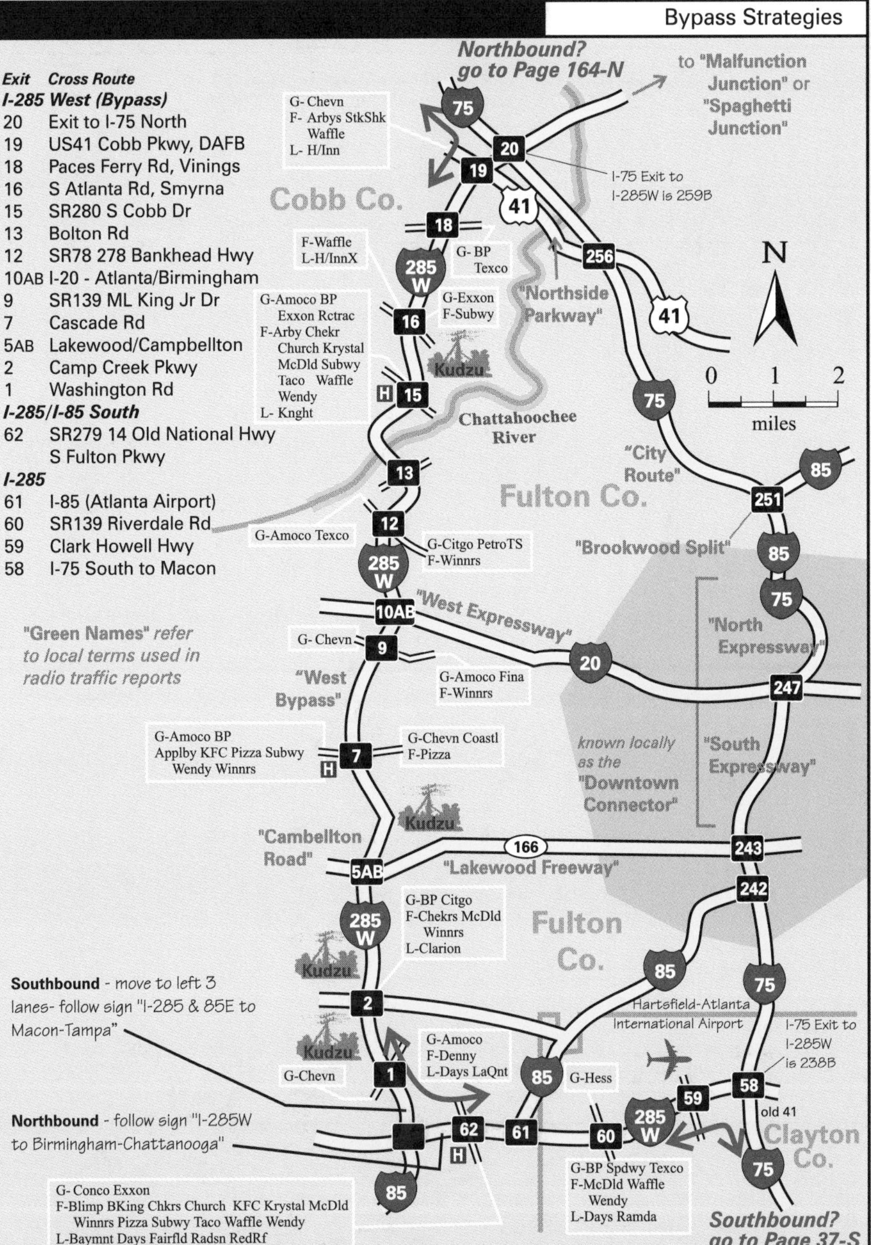

Atlanta Bypass Strategy

I-75 through the city = **20** miles (32kms); Bypass route = 25 miles (40kms)

As you approach Atlanta, **monitor the traffic reports on WSB 750AM**. If there are traffic problems ahead or you are in a rush hour period (see page 193), exit onto the I-285 Bypass Route as follows:

If Southbound - move to two right lanes after exit 260 - leave I-75 at exit 259 & follow overhead sign *"I-75 Macon Tampa"* - on ramp, stay right until after split for I-75 North then move ***left quickly*** because ramp becomes single lane. Rejoin I-75 South at I-285 exit 58 (return to map on page 37-S).

If Northbound - leave I-75N at exit 238B, for I-285W. At I-285W, exit 19, move to two right lanes - take exit 20 and follow overhead sign *"I-75 to Marietta/Chattanooga"* - on ramp, move to the left two lanes and - ***slow down***, very tight left corner coming up. Rejoin I-75N (return to map on page 164-N).

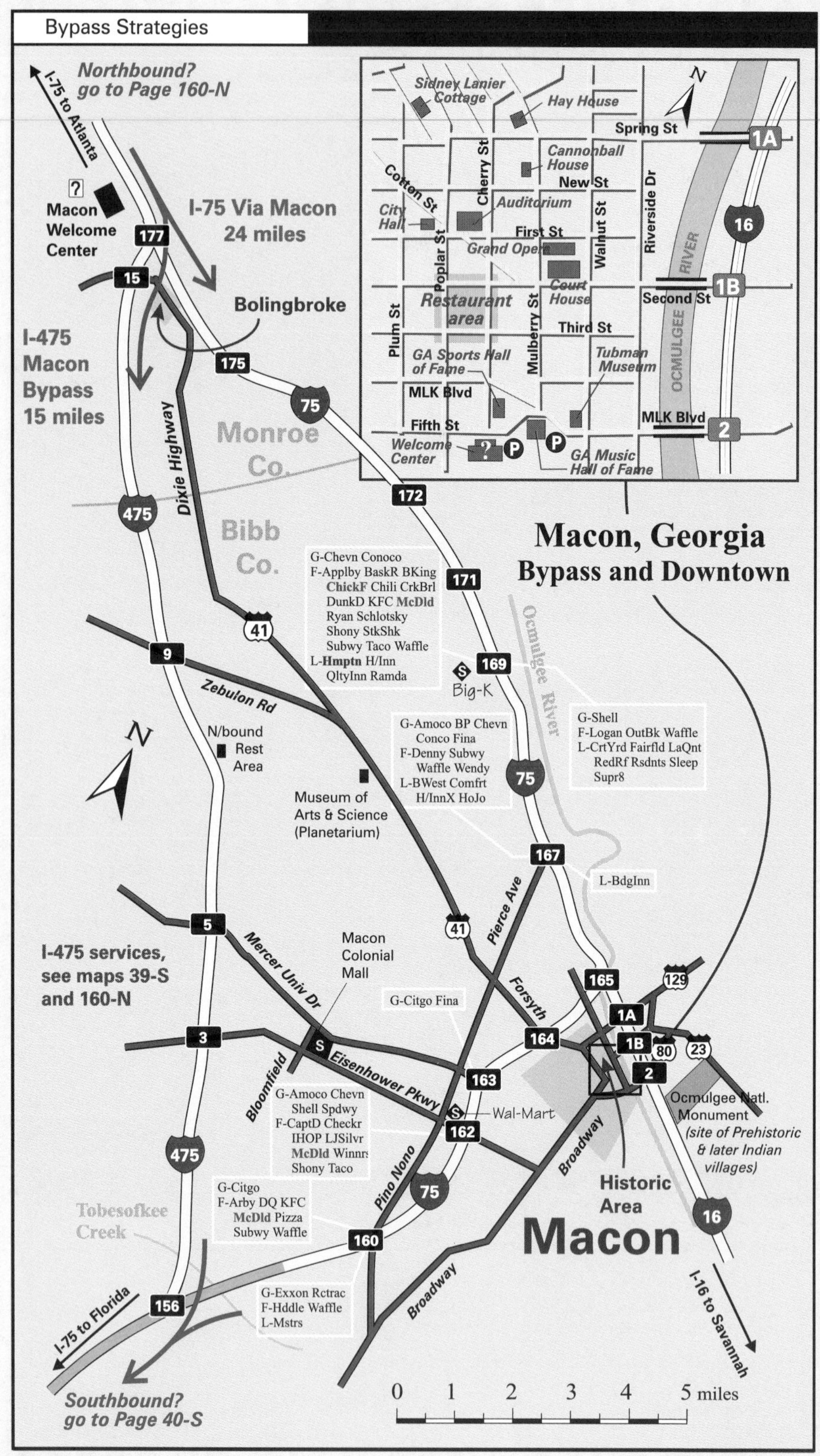

Northbound? go to Page 160-N
I-75 to Atlanta
Macon Welcome Center
I-75 Via Macon 24 miles
Bolingbroke
I-475 Macon Bypass 15 miles
Dixie Highway
Monroe Co.
Bibb Co.
Zebulon Rd
N/bound Rest Area
Museum of Arts & Science (Planetarium)
I-475 services, see maps 39-S and 160-N
Mercer Univ Dr
Macon Colonial Mall
Bloomfield
Eisenhower Pkwy
Pierce Ave
Forsyth
Pino Nono
Broadway
Wal-Mart
Big-K
Ocmulgee River
Tobesofkee Creek
G-Chevn Conoco
F-Applby BaskR BKing ChickF Chili CrkBrl DunkD KFC McDld Ryan Schlotsky Shony StkShk Subwy Taco Waffle
L-Hmptn H/Inn QltyInn Ramda
G-Amoco BP Chevn Conco Fina
F-Denny Subwy Waffle Wendy
L-BWest Comfrt H/InnX HoJo
G-Shell
F-Logan OutBk Waffle
L-CrtYrd Fairfld LaQnt RedRf Rsdnts Sleep Supr8
L-BdgInn
G-Citgo Fina
G-Amoco Chevn Shell Spdwy
F-CaptD Checkr IHOP LJSilvr McDld Winnrs Shony Taco
G-Citgo
F-Arby DQ KFC McDld Pizza Subwy Waffle
G-Exxon Rctrac
F-Hddle Waffle
L-Mstrs
Ocmulgee Natl. Monument (site of Prehistoric & later Indian villages)
Historic Area
Macon
I-16 to Savannah
I-75 to Florida
Southbound? go to Page 40-S
0 1 2 3 4 5 miles
Sidney Lanier Cottage
Hay House
Spring St
Cannonball House
Cotton St
Cherry St
New St
City Hall
Auditorium
First St
Grand Opera
Poplar St
Walnut St
Riverside Dr
Court House
Restaurant area
Second St
Plum St
Mulberry St
Third St
GA Sports Hall of Fame
Tubman Museum
Ocmulgee River
MLK Blvd
Fifth St
Welcome Center
GA Music Hall of Fame

Macon, Georgia
Bypass and Downtown

A word about this year's listings.

Many of our readers now have home computers with access to the Internet, and use them to obtain travel information. If you don't have these resources available to you, visit your local public library and ask a librarian to help you. Most libraries now have Internet access available for their patrons . . . and staff to help you if you're unfamiliar with computers.

In the listings below, I have included Internet website addresses where applicable. Purchasers of this book can also obtain the most recent I-75 information such as gas prices, construction, etc., by visiting our website at - **www.i75online.com**.

Allatoona Pass, by William Scaife
pub: Etowah Valley Historical Society (ISBN: 0-9619508-8-9). A very well researched book detailing the horrendous Civil War battle at Allatoona Pass in Georgia.

American Association of Retired Persons (AARP), - (www.aarp.org).
Box 199, Long Beach CA 90801. Every eligible person should belong to this organization; the annual membership is so low and the benefits broad.

American Automobile Association (AAA) - (www.aaa.com).
Check phone book for number of your local club. Emergency road number: **1-800-AAA-HELP**, (in Canada: 1-800-CAA-HELP). I would not consider traveling by car without this membership. I have had to use emergency services on several occasion and always found AAA to be responsive and solved my problems easily. Great peace of mind!

Armored Cav, by Tom Clancy,
pub: Berkley Books, NY Available at most bookstores (ISBN: 0-425-15836-5). An excellent book, jammed with facts for those who enjoy military subjects. The source of information about Lima's Kryptonite room and the Abrams M1A2 Battle Tank.

Battlefield Atlas of the Civil War,
pub: NAPCA, 8 W Madison St, Baltimore MD 21201 (phone: 301-659-0220)

Canadian Association of Retired Persons (CARP) - (www.fifty-plus.net).
27 Queen Street, Suite 1304, Toronto ON M5C 2M8

Canadian Automobile Association (CAA) - (www.caa.ca).
Check phone book for number of your local club. Emergency road number: **1-800-CAA-HELP**, (in the USA: 1-800-AAA-HELP)

Canadian Snowbird Association, - (www.snowbirds.org)
180 Lesmill Road, North York ON M3B 2T5 (phone: 1-800-265-3200). If you are Canadian, and spend your winters in the South, you should consider becoming a member of this organization. Low annual membership fees, many discounts and benefits, this 100,000+ members organization is the "voice" of the Canadian "snowbirds."

City Behind A Fence, Oak Ridge TN 1942-1946
Indispensable source for anybody interested in the development of the atomic bomb, and the role played by Oak Ridges during the war years. Available through the Univ. of TN Press - ISBN: 0-87049-303-4

Civil War Battlefield Guide,
pub: by Houghton Mifflin (ISBN: 0-395-52282-X)

Consumer Reports Travel Buying Guide,
101 Truman Ave., Yonkers NY 10703 Available at most bookstores. Issued annually, this guide provides an insight into various aspects of the tourist industry.

Delorme Mapping Company, - (www.delorme.com).
Box 298, Freeport, MN 04032; phone: 1-800-227-1656. Available at many truck stops and bookstores. Delorme issues an excellent set of large scale map guides, state by state.

All I-75 states have been covered; We wouldn't travel to Florida without our Delorme large scale guide (Atlas and Gazetteer) in our car.

Georgia, North - Planning to spend any time in Georgia north of Atlanta? Visit this excellent website at ***www.ngeorgia.com***. It's one of the best source of information for this area.

Long Hunter, The, (Life of Daniel Boone), by L. Elliott
May be out of print (ISBN: 0-88349-066-8), but try your local library. One of the best accounts we have read of Daniel Boone, and his travels.

MA - Market America Motel Discount Coupon Books
Box 7069, Gadsden AL 35906 (phone: 256-547-4321). Send away for your coupon books before you travel. MA charge $2 per book, to cover postage and handling ($3 to Canada).

PassPorter Walt Disney World 2000, by Jennifer Watson & Dave Marx
pub:PassPorter Travel Press (ISBN: 0-9668994-1-5). This excellent book is highly recommend to those planning a visit to WDW. Winner of four major awards, it is a WDW travel guide, planner, organizer . . . and unusual journal and keepsake, providing a wonderful memento of your visit.

State Travel Information - how to get official travel information for each I-75 state.
Michigan: 1-888-78-GREAT (784-7328); website - ***www.michigan.org***
Ohio: 1-800-BUCKEYE (282-5393); website - ***www.ohiotourism.com***
Kentucky: 1-800-225-TRIP (225-8747); website - ***www.tourky.com***
Tennessee: 1-800-GO2-TENN (462-8366); website - ***www.gotennessee.com***
Georgia: 1-800-VISIT-GA (847-4842); website - ***www.georgia.org***
Florida: 1-888-7FLA USA (735-2872); website - ***www.flausa.com***

Traveler Discount Guide Hotel Coupons - (formerly - EIG) -(www.roomsaver.com).
4205 NW 6th Street, Gainesville FL 32609; phone: 1-800-332-3948. Send for your free coupon books before you travel. EIG charges $3 s&h for the first book, plus $1 for each additional. Add $5 for guides mailed to Canada. You can also print your coupons before you travel, from EIG's website.

Traveling With Your Pet (The AAA Petbook)
Contains many pet travel tips and 466 pages listing "pet friendly" motels. An excellent resource book for people traveling with pets - available from any AAA (or CAA) office.

Trailer Life (Good Sam) RV Park & Services Directory, - (www.goodsamclub.com).
Box 11097, Des Moines IA 50336 phone: 1-800-234-3450. One of the two essential campground and RV services guides to have aboard your RV (see also, "Woodall's")

Unofficial Guide to Walt Disney World, by Bob Sehlinger
pub: Prentice Hall. Order through most bookstores (ISBN 0-02-863-727-5). Don't consider a visit to WDW without this book. Far superior to any of the other guides ("official" and "unofficial") because it is *objective*. Many money and time saving tips.

Valentine Research, - (www.valentine1.com).
10280 Alliance Road, Cincinnati OH 45242 (order: 1-800-331-3030). Annual tests conducted by major car magazines, consistently rate the Valentine One radar detector with laser warning as the best detection equipment available, by far.

War of 1812 (ISBNs: 0-14-010855-6, 0-14-020888-2).
"The Invasion of Canada" and *"Flames Across the Border"* by Pierre Berton (Penguin) are excellent, very readable books about the War of 1812. Well researched; great detail.

Woodall's Campground Directory, - (www.woodalls.com).
13976 West Polo Trail Dr., Lake Forest, IL 60045 (order: 1-800-323-9076). Available at RV dealers, most large bookstores or at Woodall's website, this is one of the two essential campground and RV services guides to have aboard your RV (the other is "Trailer Life" - see above).

Abbreviations used our maps

Space limitations in the maps necessitate the use of abbreviations for many of the fuel stations, restaurants and motels listed. For your convenience, the abbreviations used are listed on the next two pages.

GAS & DIESEL

49er . . . . . 49er Gas Co
66 . . . . Phillips 66
Chevn . . Chevron USA
Conco . . . . Conoco
FlCity . . . . Fuel City
IndGas . . . . any independent gas stn
Meijer . Meijer Gas Bar
Mrthn . . . Marathon Oil
Omga . . . . Omega
Penz . . . . Pennzoil
Pilot . . . . Pilot
Racwy . . . . . . Raceway
Rctrac . . . . . . Racetrac
SA . . . . SuperAmerica
Spdwy . . . . Speedway
Sunco . . . . Sunoco
Swfty . . . . . Swifty Gas
Texco . . . . Texaco
Thrntn . . . . . Thorntons

TRUCK STOPS (TS)

BPTS . . . . BP TS
DltaTS . . . . . . Delta TS
ExnTS . . . . . Exxon TS
FlyJ . . . . . . Flying J TS
FuelTS . . Fuel Mart TS
LGTS . . . . L & G TS
PilotTS . . . . . . Pilot TS
SRTS . . . . Stoney Ridge TS
TA(brand) . . . . TravelCenters of America
TexTS . . . . . Texaco TS
WillmTS . . . . . Williams

FOOD

Applby . . . . Appleby's
Arby . . . . Arbys
BaskR . Baskin-Robbins
Bengn . . . . . Bennigans
BgBoy . . . . Big Boy Family Restaurant
BKing . . . . Burger King
Blimp . . . . Blimpies
Bombay . . . . . Bombay Bicycle Club
Boston . Boston Market
Brangus . . Steak House
Brchrs . . . . . Butcher's
BrewH . . . Brew House
Buckr . . . . . . Buckner's Family Rest
Burbnk . Burbanks BBQ
C/Kit . Country Kitchen
CaptD . . . . Captain D's
CBkn . . . . Country Bumpkin
CCbd . . . . Country Cupboard
Charles . . . . . Sea Food
Checkr . . . . . Checkers
ChiChi . . . . . . Chi Chi's
ChickF . . . . Chick-Fil-A
ChinaHt . . . . China Hut
ChkW . . . . Chuck Wagon BBQ
ChnGd . . China Garden
Church . . . . . . Chicken
CntryGrill . . . . Country Grill
CopperK . . . . . Copper Kettle
Corky . . . . Corky's Ribs
CPride . . Country Pride
CPtch . . . Cotton Patch Restaurant
CrkBrl . . Cracker Barrel
CrzEd . . . . . . Crazy Eds Restaurant
CtryBft . Country Buffet
D/Bell . . . . . Dinner Bell
Denny . . . . . . Denny's
Diner . . Denny's Diner
DmnRibs . . . . Damons
Donut . . . . Donut Shop
DQ . . . . . . Dairy Queen
Drthrs . . . . . . Druther's
Dudly . . . . . . Dudley's
Duffs . . . . . Duff's Rest
DunkD . . . . Dunkin Doughnut
Dutch . . . Dutch Pantry Restaurant
Evans . . . . . Bob Evans
Family . . . . Family Rest
Fazoli . . . . Fazzoli's
FlkSthrn Folk Southern
Frckr . . . Fricker's Rest
Frndly . . . . Friendly Restaurant
GldnC . . Golden Corral
GldnGln Golden Gallon
Goodflw . Goodfellows
Grdma . . . . Grandma's Kitchen
Grindr . . . WJ Grinders
GrndSC . . Grindestone Charlies
GtAmBft . . . . Great American Buffet
Gthouse . . . Gatehouse
Hddle . . Huddle House
HickH . . Hickory House
HoJo . . . . Howard Johnson
Honey . . . . Honey Bun
Hooter . . . . . . Hooters
Hrdee . . Hardee's Rest
IceCrm . . . . Ice Cream Churn
IHOP . . . . International House Of Pancakes
J&L . . J&L Famous Pits
Jcqlns . . . . . Jacqelines
Jerry's . . . Jerry's Rest
KFC . . . Kentucky Fried Chicken
KFrog . . . . . . King Frog Restaurant
Knapp . . . Bob Knapp's Restaurant
Krystal . . . Krystal Rest
LChick . . Lee's Country Chicken
Lees . . Lees Restaurant
Lghtho . . . . Lighthouse
LJSilvr . . . . Long John Silver
LkyStr . . . . Lucky Steer Restaurant
LgnStk . . . Logan Steak
LoneS . . . . . Lone Star Steaks
LongH . . . . . Longhorn Steaks
LosR . . . . . . Los Reyes
Louie's . . . . Louie's on the Lake
MaxEma Max&Emma's
McDld . . . . McDonalds
McDld-I . . . McDonalds . . with Inside Playarea
Morrel . . . . . . Morrel's Restaurant
O'Char . . . . O'Charlies
OldCtry . . Old Country Buffet
Olive . . . . Olive Garden
OutBk . . . . Outback Steakhouse
Pantry . . . . Pantry Rest
PatsDnt . . . Pats Donuts
PatTS . . . . . . Patty's TS Restaurant
Pdrsa . . . . . Ponderosa Steakhouse
Pekng . . Peking House
Petes . . . . Pestio Petes
Picdilly . . . . . . Picadilly
Pizza . . . . Pizza Hut
PJPizza . . . Papa Jones Pizza
PopE . . . . Popeye's
Prkns . . . . Perkin's Family Restaurant
Quincy . . . . . Quincy's Steak House
Raffty . . . . . . Rafferty's
Rally . . . . Rally Drive-In
Ralph . . . . Ralphies
Rax . . Rax Restaurants
RedLb . . . Red Lobster
RibS . . . . Ribeye Steakhouse
RockB . . . . Rock-A-Billy
RockC . . . . . Rockcastle Steak
Ryan . . . . Ryan's Family Steakhouse
SaraJ . . . . . . Sara Jane
Schlotzky . Schlotzky's Deli
Shony . . . . . Shoney's
Sonic . . . . 50's Drive In
Sonny . . Sonny's BBQ
Starvn . Starvin' Marvin
StkH . . . . Steak House
StkShk . Steak & Shake
Stones . . . . Stone's TS Restaurant
Stucky . . . . . Stuckey's
Subwy . . . . . . Subway
Taco . . . . Taco Bell
TCBY . . The Country's Best Yogurt
TexSteak . . West Texas Steakhouse
TGIF . . . . . TGI Friday's
TimH . . . . . Tim Horton
Waffle . . . Waffle House
Wallys . . . Wally's Rest
Wendy . . . . . . Wendy's
WhtCstl . . White Castle
Wilson . . . . . . Wilson's BBQ Pit
Wingr . . . . Wingers
Winnrs . Winner's Rest
WSizz . Western Sizzlin' Steakhouse
WStk . Western Stk Ho
WStr . . . Western Steer Steakhouse

NOTE: Fast food restaurants with childrens' play areas are printed in red on the maps.

An "-I" after the name indicates that the play area is indoors.

LODGING

Ambssdr . Ambassador
AmInn . . American Inn
Baymnt . Baymont Inns & Suites
BdgInn. . Budget Inn of America
BestW . . Best Western
BgSav. . . . Big Savings Motel
BHost . . . Budget Host
BkEye . . . . . . Buckeye Budget Motor Hotel
BluGrs . . . . . Bluegrass
Brittny . Brittany Motor Inn
BstInn. . . . . . . Best Inn
C/Ctry . . Cross Country Inn
C/Rds . . . Cross Roads
ClubHs. ClubHouse Inn
Colonial . . Colonial Inn
Comfrt . . . Comfort Inn
Contntl . . . Continental Inn
Crown. . . . . Crown Inn
Crtesy . . . . . . Courtesy
CrtYrd . . . . . Courtyard by Marriot
CstlGt . . . . Castle Gate
CtryHrth . . . . . Country Hearth
CtySte. . . Country Inns & Suites
Cumberlnd . . Cumberland Inn
Days . . . . Days Inn
DBrdge. . . Drawbridge Inn
DRInn . . Dry Ridge Inn
Duffy . . . Duffy's Motel
Econmy . . . . Economy Motel
Econo. . . Econo Lodge
EmbsyS . . . . Embassy Suites
Exec. . . . Executive Inn
Fairfld . . . . Fairfield Inn
Family . . Family Inns of America
Flag . . . . Flag Inn
FShip . . Friendship Inn
GstHse . . Guest House Inn
Guest . . . . . . Guest Inn
H/Inn . . . . . Holiday Inn
H/InnS Holiday Inn Select
H/InnX. . . . Holiday Inn Express
Hahra . . . . . Hahira Inn
Hwthrn . . . Hawthorne Suites
Hilton. . . Hilton Hotels
Hmptn . . Hampton Inn
Hmstd . . . . Homestead
HmWood . Homewood
HoJo. . . . . Howard Johnson
Hol/M . . Holiday Motel
Holly . . . . Holly Lodge
HomeTn . . Hometown
Hosplty. . . . Hospitality Inn
Hrtge . . Heritage Motel
Jamsn. . . Jameson Inn
Jellico . . . . . Jellico Inn
Jolly. . . . . Jolly Inn
Kings. . . . . . Kings Inn
Knght . . . . Knights Inn/Court
LaQnt . . . La Quinta Inn
Lkview . . Lakeview Inn
Marrtt . . Marriot Hotels
MicroT . . Microtel Inns
Motel. . . . . any unidentified motel
Motel6 . . . . Motel6
Motor . . . . . Motor Inn
Mstrs . . . . Masters Inn
MtnVw . . . . . Mountain View Motel
NewAm . . . . New American Inn
NewC. . . . . New Colony Inn
NFsyth . . New Forsyth Inn
Pssprt . . . Passport Inn
QltyInn. . . . Quality Inn
QltyMtl. . Quality Motel
QltyQtr. . . . . . . Quality Quarter Inn
Radsn . . . Radisson Inn
Ramda . . . Ramada Inn
RedC . . Red Carpet Inn
RedRf . . . Red Roof Inn
Regency . Regency Inn
Relax . . . . . . Relax Inn
Renfro . . Renfro Valley Motel
Rest. . . . . Rest Inn
RmdaSt . . . . . Ramada Suites
Rodwy . . Rodeway Inn
Rsdnts . . Residents Inn
Scot . . . . . Scottish Inn
Shertn. . . . . . Sheraton Hotels
Shony . . Shoney's Inn
Signtr. . . Signature Inn
Sleep. . . . . . Sleep Inn
SRInn. . . Stoney Ridge Inn
Std6+ . . . Studio6 Plus
Subrn . . . . . Suburban Motel
Supr8 . . . . Super 8 Motels
SwtHtl . . . Sweetwater Hotel
TravInn . . . . Travel Inn
TravL . . . . . Travelodge
TrdWd . . . Trade Winds Motel
Valley . . . . . . Valley Inn
Wavrly . . . . . . Waverly Motel
WCstle . . White Castle
WdaleLg . . Willowdale Lodge
Welcm . . Welcome Inn
WGate . . Westgate Inn
Wilburg . Williamsburg Motel
Wilsn . . . . . Wilson Inn
Wingate . . Wingate Inn
WldWd . . . . Wildwood Inn
Woodfld Woodfield
WPark . . West Park Inn
Wyndm. . . . Wyndham
XstayAm . . . Extended Stay America

A Word to our Readers . . .

Please note that we have not listed gas, food or lodging in the downtown areas of Detroit, Toledo, Dayton, Cincinnati and Atlanta. We feel that access to such facilities (and easy return to the Interstate) is often difficult for those not familiar with streets in the area.

Furthermore, downtown facilities tend to be higher priced, catering more to the business traveler than vacationer - travel bargains will generally be found elsewhere. This Guide has been written with the long distance interstate traveler in mind, and accordingly we recommend staying or eating at facilities outside these areas.

Unless a facility is specifically mentioned in the "Insider Tips," ***inclusion in the Guide does not constitute a recommendation on the part of the publisher or author.*** We are however, interested in receiving your comments about facilities and other useful travel tips.

Finally - every effort has been made to ensure the accuracy of the Guide's listings. Prior to printing this edition, two personal survey trips were made along the I-75, cross-checking information and ensuring that services were where they were supposed to be. The most recent survey was completed just a month prior to publication. We have included all major road construction projects encountered on this trip, although many may be completed before you head south.

DATE		MILEAGE			FUEL	DAILY EXPENSE RECORD						OVERNIGHT STOP			
(M/D)	DAY	START	STOP	DIFF	(Gals)	B/FAST	LUNCH	DINNER	GAS	MISC	TOTAL	STATE	EXIT#	LOCATION	MOTEL
A	B	C	D	E	F	G	H	I	J	K	L	M	N	O	P

- Enter the **Date** (month/day), and the **Day** of the week (e.g.. Mon, Tues, etc.) in columns A & B.
- At the beginning of the first day, record your car's odometer reading in **Mileage Start** (column C). After finishing with the car each evening, record the odometer reading in **Mileage Stop** (column D). Post the same number in column C for the next day.

  To calculate the number of miles driven during the day, deduct column C from column D, and enter the result in **Difference** (column E).
- To calculate your daily **Miles per Gallon**, make sure you fill up your tank before you start your journey (do not enter these gallons on the chart).

  Keep a note of the number of fuel gallons purchased during each day.

  Each morning before you start, fill up your car and add these gallons to the fuel purchased during the previous day's run. Record this total for the previous day in column F.

  Divide the total number of miles driven during the previous day (column E) by the total number of gallons used (column F). The result will be your Miles per Gallon for the previous day.
- **Daily expenses** can be recorded in columns G to K, and totaled for the day in column L. Post your motel costs and sundry expenses in column L.
- Record details of your **Overnight Stops** in columns M to P.

DATE		MILEAGE			FUEL	DAILY EXPENSE RECORD						OVERNIGHT STOP			
(M/D)	DAY	START	STOP	DIFF	(Gals)	B/FAST	LUNCH	DINNER	GAS	MISC	TOTAL	STATE	EXIT#	LOCATION	MOTEL
A	B	C	D	E	F	G	H	I	J	K	L	M	N	O	P

- Enter the **Date** (month/day), and the **Day** of the week (e.g.. Mon, Tues, etc.) in columns A & B.
- At the beginning of the first day, record your car's odometer reading in **Mileage Start** (column C). After finishing with the car each evening, record the odometer reading in **Mileage Stop** (column D). Post the same number in column C for the next day.

  To calculate the number of miles driven during the day, deduct column C from column D, and enter the result in **Difference** (column E).
- To calculate your daily **Miles per Gallon**, make sure you fill up your tank before you start your journey (do not enter these gallons on the chart).

  Keep a note of the number of fuel gallons purchased during each day.

  Each morning before you start, fill up your car and add these gallons to the fuel purchased during the previous day's run. Record this total for the previous day in column F.

  Divide the total number of miles driven during the previous day (column E) by the total number of gallons used (column F). The result will be your Miles per Gallon for the previous day.
- **Daily expenses** can be recorded in columns G to K, and totaled for the day in column L. Post your motel costs and sundry expenses in column L.
- Record details of your **Overnight Stops** in columns M to P.

Help me write our 10th Anniversary edition of . . .
. . . "Along Interstate-75"

Please help me continue to make this ***your*** book. Each year, I receive many interesting letters from our readers. Before going to press, we review *every* suggestion and try and incorporate as many of them as possible into next year's edition. This way, I am able to make sure that the guide continues to meet *your needs*.

Please use the space below to record your recommendations or changes to the book's information. Use the other side for your comments and other suggestions. Tell me what you like about the guide, or what you don't like — we are constantly trying to improve it for you. To be considered for the 2002 guide though, we must have your submission by May 31, 2001. — Dave

---

To: *Dave Hunter, c/o Mile Oak Publishing Inc.,*
Suite 81, 20 Mineola Road East,
Mississauga ON Canada L5G 4N9

From:

☐ ✔ **Please add my name to your mailing list.**
We do not give our mailing list to other; we only send one mailing per year, which includes our pre-publication discount offer.

Name: ____________ Phone: ____________

Address: ____________

____

City: ____________ State/Prov: ____________ Zip/PC ____________

My recommendation or change in information:

(If recommending a facility, please include as much information as possible:)

State: ______ Exit #: ______ Facility Name: ____________

East or West of Interstate: ______ Owner/Mngr's Name: ____________

Their Phone #: ____________ Gas ☐ Food ☐ Lodging ☐ Other ☐

Recommendation or Information to be changed:

____

____

____

____

____

____

Please use the other side for your comments or suggestions:

My comments and suggestions for next year's edition:

Offer expires September 30, 2001

Florida's I-75 Map
and our Annual Newsletter
with tips and hints for Florida visitors

☐ Check (✔) box to left; fill in your name & address in the space below, and mail or fax this form to Mile Oak Publishing (see address and fax number below) - we will send you a free copy of Dave Hunter's black & white panel strip-map of the ***Interstate-75 to Tampa, Florida and his Florida Newsletter . . .*** . . . all mailed within 48 hours of receipt of this form.

Name: ....

Address: ....

....

City: .... State/Prov.: ....

ZIP/Postal Code: .... Phone: ....

BOOK ORDER FORM

Need another copy of *Along Interstate-75*?
. . . use this handy Mail Order Form or visit our website at
www.i75online.com

Please send me ____ copies of *Along Interstate-75, 9th edition* to my address shown above. I enclose my check for $ __________ (see below for prices).

Please make your check payable to *Mile Oak Publishing Inc.* We mail within 24 hrs of receiving your order.

Orders shipped to US addresses: # of books x $19.95 + shipping ($3 first book/$1.25 each addnl). Amount payable in US funds.

Orders shipped to Canadian Addresses: # of books x $24.95 + shipping ($5 first book/$1.50 each additional). Add 7% GST calculated on cost of total order. Amount payable in Canadian funds.

Along I-75 may also be ordered through BCH Company at **1-800-431-1579** (all major cards)

Please feel free to photocopy if you need extra copies of this form.

How to contact us:

By mail: **Mile Oak Publishing Inc.,**
Suite 81, 20 Mineola Road East,
Mississauga, ON Canada L5G 4N9

Phone: **905-274-4356**; Fax: **905-274-8656**; Email: **mile_oak@compuserve.com**